SECURITIES AND CAPITAL MARKETS LAW IN CHINA

SECURITIES AND CAPITAL MARKETS LAW IN CHINA

Robin Hui Huang

Professor, Faculty of Law
Chinese University of Hong Kong

OXFORD
UNIVERSITY PRESS

Great Clarendon Street, Oxford, OX2 6DP,
United Kingdom

Oxford University Press is a department of the University of Oxford.
It furthers the University's objective of excellence in research, scholarship,
and education by publishing worldwide. Oxford is a registered trade mark of
Oxford University Press in the UK and in certain other countries

© Robin Hui Huang 2014

The moral rights of the author have been asserted

First Edition published in 2014

Impression: 1

All rights reserved. No part of this publication may be reproduced, stored in
a retrieval system, or transmitted, in any form or by any means, without the
prior permission in writing of Oxford University Press, or as expressly permitted
by law, by licence or under terms agreed with the appropriate reprographics
rights organization. Enquiries concerning reproduction outside the scope of the
above should be sent to the Rights Department, Oxford University Press, at the
address above

You must not circulate this work in any other form
and you must impose this same condition on any acquirer

Crown copyright material is reproduced under Class Licence
Number C01P0000148 with the permission of OPSI
and the Queen's Printer for Scotland

Published in the United States of America by Oxford University Press
198 Madison Avenue, New York, NY 10016, United States of America

British Library Cataloguing in Publication Data
Data available

Library of Congress Control Number: 2014942231

ISBN 978–0–19–968794–7

Printed and bound by
CPI Group (UK) Ltd, Croydon, CR0 4YY

Links to third party websites are provided by Oxford in good faith and
for information only. Oxford disclaims any responsibility for the materials
contained in any third party website referenced in this work.

To my wife and son

FOREWORD

According to statistics published by the World Federation of Stock Exchanges, the market capitalization of the Shanghai Securities Exchange as at the end of March 2014 was US $2,376.03 billion, placing it seventh in the world ranking of stock markets. At the same point in time the Shenzhen Securities Exchange had a market capitalization of US $1,429.45 billion, ranking it twelfth. With securities markets of such size, one would have expected an expansive literature on securities regulation in China. While the field is expanding, such an expansive literature does not yet exist in China. The reasons are many.

Securities markets (in the sense of traded stock and bond markets) only began in 1990 in China, and so they have a history of only about 24 years. The Securities Law was not passed until late in 1998, coming into effect on 1 July 1999. Prior to that, the securities markets were regulated by a raft of various national and municipal regulations. The regulator, the China Securities Regulatory Commission (CSRC), was not founded until 1992 and so has even less history than the securities markets. Thus from the beginning, the regulatory system has been involved with catching up with the many issues which the markets have created—as markets are always prone to create—from time to time. Despite this, the markets have grown and prospered.

The securities markets are not the only means by which capital may be raised by the real economy. In the past ten years, a bond market with issuers from both the private and public sectors has been promoted by both the securities and banking industries. Banks and trust companies provide capital to the real economy and there is a growing private equity and venture capital sector in the country. Thus, the term 'capital markets' has acquired currency, indicating markets for raising capital taking place either within or outside the two main securities exchanges.

A distinguishing feature of emerging markets is that they are not burdened by legacy systems. Today, the PRC capital markets (be they in the securities or the banking sector) are among the most highly automated in the world. But the introduction of the latest innovations in technology has itself brought problems.

In the credit sector, where the banks should predominate, we now have the phenomenon of such internet-driven vehicles as Ali Pay and the proliferation of peer-to-peer credit systems, also driven by the internet. The regulation of Ali Pay as a payments system has not prevented it from paying interest on balances in payment accounts, thereby transforming the system into a deposit-taking institution without the regulatory safeguards of banks. Fortunately, there is some regulatory hold on Ali Pay to ensure that it is not engaged in large-scale maturity transformation (namely, taking short-term deposits and making long-term investments). The People's Bank, the regulator of payment systems, has reassured the public that the risks associated with Ali Pay are being properly managed. Let us hope that will continue. Peer-to-peer lending platforms, conducted on the internet, are unregulated. They are filling the void left by a lack of credit to small and medium enterprises offered by banks and the general lack of capital-raising opportunities in the capital markets for these entities. It is said that there are over 500 peer-to-peer internet platforms and the largest is lending at five times the size of the Lending Club (soon to be listed on the US markets, and said by the financial press to be raising over US $500 million in its IPO).

Advanced technology has also more than once been responsible for mishaps in the stock markets. The most spectacular of the recent failures of computer systems happened to Ever Bright Securities one morning in 2013, when within seconds its computers generated buy orders for more than RMB 23 billion (far exceeding the capital of the firm), sending the Shanghai Composite Index from a 1 per cent loss to over 5 per cent gain within those few seconds. According to media reports, 7.3 billion of these orders were executed by the trading system in the Shanghai Securities Exchange. Realizing their mistake, the management of Ever Bright Securities took remedial action, including selling ETFs and contracts in the futures market. The systems of internal controls and risk management in the firm were clearly deficient. The CSRC took quick action and penalized the firm as well as the senior management. The aftermath of this incident continues to be a matter of heated debate in China as to where the fault lay and what remedial actions are needed on a market-wide basis. A court action, undertaken by the senior executives of Ever Bright against the CSRC for unlawful penalties, is pending in the PRC courts.

The proliferation of wealth management products on the one hand dis-intermediates the banks, but on the other pours enormous risks into the markets. These products are short-term in nature and are issued either by trust companies or corporates (some not listed). The short prospectuses accompanying these issues go nowhere near to identifying the risks involved. The label 'shadow banking' has been placed on this phenomenon. Regulation obviously needs to be developed to deal with this.

Episodes such as the Ever Bright incident and the proliferation of technology-based finance and 'shadow banking' illustrate that the capital markets in China are in a developmental stage, and accordingly, there is a great need for rational debate and thought both within the markets and within the government. Such debate and thought should be informed by the best in research and publications.

Professor Robin Huang has filled this need by producing this book, which is one of the most comprehensive I have come across in the English language with regard to regulation of the securities markets in China.

Foreword

Recent research from many sources has confirmed that the private sector has outstripped the state sector in the real economy. In particular, the private sector has been a more powerful creator of new employment. This means that the capital markets have to adapt to ensure that the private sector does receive its fair share of capital and that the regulatory system is competition-neutral, ensuring that the most efficient intermediation takes place.

The capital markets in China still have a long way to go in terms of further development. Despite their size in global terms, the combined market capitalization of the Shanghai and Shenzhen Securities Markets is less than 50 per cent of national gross domestic product. Comparing this to, say, the US securities markets, which are over 120 per cent of US GDP, shows that the PRC securities markets are underdeveloped and financing to the real economy is being provided by other sources, including the banking sector and the largely unregulated shadow banking and internet financing.

Professor Huang starts his book with an overview of the financial system and points to the need for a holistic approach to development and regulation of the Chinese capital markets. This holistic approach requires a deep understanding of all the sectors of the financial system. The overview in the first chapter of Professor Huang's book is therefore the perfect prism through which the reader may view the detailed workings of the regulation of the securities markets, which are masterfully laid out in the rest of the book.

The Chinese securities markets are clearly something which global investors will continue to be interested in, and Professor Huang's book will not only inform them and their advisers but also offer another platform for further research and thought. Professor Huang is to be congratulated for this fine effort.

Anthony Neoh, SC
Chief Advisor to the China Securities Regulatory Commission (1999–2004)
Chairman of the Hong Kong Securities and Futures Commission (1995–1998)
Hong Kong
July 2014

PREFACE

The strong growth of the Chinese economy is changing the landscape of world economic order for the next phase of world history. Now, as the world's second largest economy, China has a greater need than ever before to develop efficient securities and capital markets if it wants to enjoy continued economic success. Hence, there has been rapidly increasing interest in Chinese laws concerning the securities and capital markets. As an emerging as well as transitional economy, China has established a securities regulatory regime which differs from its western counterparts in some significant ways and exhibits many intriguing Chinese characteristics. Without a doubt, the topic of Chinese securities and capital markets law is of both academic and practical significance.

Notwithstanding the significance of the topic, there are surprisingly few existing English-language books in this area. This is probably due to the complexity of the subject matter, the fast pace at which the underlying markets are developing in China, and the inherent difficulty in accessing relevant Chinese materials. This book thus represents an effort to fill the gap.

This book seeks to achieve several goals. The first is to present a contextualized and practical account of Chinese securities and capital markets law, giving readers nuanced understandings of what the law is and why it is the way that it is. It contains useful details that can be easily found as needed, yet more information is provided than just recitation of statutes and rules. Second, it tries to go beyond 'law in books' to examine 'law in action', paying attention to the enforcement of the law as well as the legal and market institutions affecting the operation of the law. Third, it takes a comparative approach, so as to allow readers to better understand and evaluate the merits and demerits of Chinese law. Finally, conscious that this book is intended for an international audience, it covers some topics of particular relevance to foreign investors, such as foreign investment access and cross-border mergers and acquisitions in China.

This book is composed of 12 chapters, divided into four parts. Part 1 introduces the central themes of the book and states the objectives of the study. This includes an overview of the securities and capital markets in China, a contextual discussion of the market development and its characteristics, and a critical analysis of the regulatory framework and possible reform routes.

Part 2 is dedicated to the regulation of securities offerings and listings. Specifically, it first looks at the legal regime for securities offerings in China. This is followed by a discussion of issues concerning the listing of securities. The final chapter of this part examines what legal consequences would follow as a result of defective information disclosure for relevant parties involved in the process.

Having examined how securities are offered and listed, Part 3 turns to the regulation of trading in securities. It starts with an overview of the securities enforcement structure, comprising the government regulator and self-regulatory bodies such as stock exchanges. Then it examines various forms of market misconduct, including, but not limited to, market manipulation and insider trading. It also provides a legal analysis of securities investment funds in China.

Part 4 is focused on mergers and acquisitions in China. To begin with, it discusses domestic takeovers, namely takeovers of Chinese listed companies by Chinese nationals. As noted earlier, this book is intended for an international audience, and thus it is important to cover the legal regime for foreign mergers and acquisitions in China, which has become an increasingly attractive vehicle for foreign investment in China. The rules specific to foreign mergers and acquisitions operate as a supplement to relevant domestic laws in that they set out additional government approval requirements. Together, the three chapters in this part provide relatively complete coverage of legal issues that foreigners may face in carrying out mergers and acquisitions in China.

ACKNOWLEDGEMENTS

There are so many people I would like to thank for their encouragement and support to me. This book project was supported by the Australian Research Council Discovery Grant Project on 'Regulatory Responses to the Global Financial Crisis' and the Hong Kong Research Grants Council Theme-based Research Grant Scheme Project on 'Enhancing Hong Kong's Future as a Leading International Financial Centre', as well as by Direct Grant projects at the Faculty of Law, Chinese University of Hong Kong.

This book draws on my many years of teaching and writing in the area of securities and capital markets law. I am grateful for the support and good counsel of my former colleagues in the faculty of law of the University of New South Wales and my current colleagues in the faculty of law of the Chinese University of Hong Kong. Earlier drafts of some of the chapters in the book were first developed and tested in classrooms at the institutions with which I have been proudly associated, and portions of this book spring from articles I published previously.

I should also thank my editors at Oxford University Press for editing the manuscript intelligently and efficiently and in the process making it better. I owe a special debt of gratitude to the six anonymous reviewers who provided extensive comments on my proposal for this book, which proved invaluable in outlining and writing the text.

Finally, I thank my family members, who have been generous with their moral support during the development of this project. At least they will now have a better idea of what I have been doing for all these years.

Robin Hui Huang
Hong Kong
August 2014

CONTENTS

Table of Cases	xix
Table of Legislation	xxiii
List of Abbreviations	xxix

PART I: INTRODUCTION

1. China's Financial Markets

1.1. Introduction	1.01
1.2. Evolution of China's Financial Markets	1.07
1.3. Overview of Financial Markets in China	1.15
1.4. Characteristics of China's Financial Markets	1.45
1.5. China and Global Financial Markets	1.62

2. Financial Regulatory Framework

2.1. Introduction	2.01
2.2. The Current Financial Regulatory Structure	2.03
2.3. Characteristics and Problems	2.39
2.4. The Future of China's Financial Regulatory Framework	2.60
2.5. Conclusion	2.85

PART II: REGULATION OF SECURITIES OFFERINGS AND LISTINGS

3. Securities Offerings

3.1. Regulatory Model: Disclosure-based vs Merits-review	3.01
3.2. Disclosure and Market Efficiency	3.14
3.3. Regulatory Structure: Public Offerings vs Private Placement	3.23
3.4. China Securities Regulatory Commission (CSRC) Approval Regime	3.31
3.5. Securities Offerings by Listed Companies	3.48

4. **Securities Listings**
   - 4.1. Overview ... 4.01
   - 4.2. Criteria for Initial Public Offering (IPO) ... 4.10
   - 4.3. The Procedure ... 4.76
   - 4.4. Information Disclosure Requirements ... 4.88
   - 4.5. Sponsorship ... 4.107
   - 4.6. Pricing and Underwriting ... 4.142

5. **Post-listing Issues**
   - 5.1. Introduction ... 5.01
   - 5.2. Information Disclosure ... 5.04
   - 5.3. Corporate Governance of Listed Companies ... 5.19
   - 5.4. Listing Suspension and Delisting ... 5.74

6. **Liability for Misrepresentation**
   - 6.1. Overview ... 6.01
   - 6.2. Substantive Rules of Civil Litigation ... 6.13
   - 6.3. Procedural Rules of Civil Litigation ... 6.39
   - 6.4. Comments ... 6.78

PART III: REGULATION OF TRADING IN SECURITIES

7. **Market Misconduct (Other Than Insider Trading)**
   - 7.1. Introduction ... 7.01
   - 7.2. Types of Misconduct ... 7.02
   - 7.3. Market Manipulation ... 7.13

8. **Insider Trading**
   - 8.1. Introduction ... 8.01
   - 8.2. Background ... 8.05
   - 8.3. What Constitutes Insider Trading in China? ... 8.10
   - 8.4. How Is the Law Enforced? ... 8.43
   - 8.5. Conclusion ... 8.76

9. **Securities Investment Fund**
   - 9.1. Introduction ... 9.01
   - 9.2. Organizational Structure of the SIF ... 9.07
   - 9.3. Publicly Offered Fund ... 9.55

9.4. Non-publicly Offered Fund	9.88
9.5. Fund Services Institutions	9.98
9.6. Fund Association	9.115

PART IV: MERGERS AND ACQUISITIONS

10. Takeovers of Listed Companies (1)

10.1. Introduction	10.01
10.2. Shareholding Structure in Listed Companies	10.21
10.3. China's Takeover Law and Activities	10.39
10.4. The Guiding Principles for Takeover Regulation	10.47
10.5. The Mandatory Bid Rule	10.61
10.6. Tender Offer Rules	10.77
10.7. Compulsory Buyout	10.89
10.8. Indirect Takeovers and Management Buyouts	10.92
10.9. Disclosure of Substantial Shareholdings	10.95
10.10. Financial Consultants	10.101
10.11. Continuous Supervision	10.110
10.12. Comments	10.114

11. Takeovers of Listed Companies (2)

11.1. Introduction	11.01
11.2. Takeover Defences Under Chinese Law	11.04
11.3. Takeover Defences in Practice	11.19
11.4. Analysis and Implications	11.43
11.5. A New Regime for Takeover Defences	11.56

12. The Regulation of Foreign M&A

12.1. Introduction	12.01
12.2. Legal Framework for Foreign M&A in China	12.07
12.3. The 2006 Foreign M&A Regulation: Overview	12.14
12.4. The 2006 Foreign M&A Regulation: Basic Rules	12.26
12.5. Regulation of Special Purpose Vehicles	12.61
12.6. National Security Review	12.70
12.7. Summary	12.100

Index	347

TABLE OF CASES

CHINA

Changjiang Konggu 8.59
Chen Jianliang (2007) No 15 (Administrative Penalty Decision by the CSRC, 2007,
    No 15, promulgated by the China Securities Regulatory Commission, 28 April 2007)
    (Zhongguo Zhengjianhui Xingzheng Chufa Juedingshu) 8.72
Chen Ningfeng v Chen Jianliang 8.72, 8.74
Chen Zhuling v Datang Telecommunications Technology Ltd Co (Securities
    Misrepresentation Compensation Dispute case), (2009) First Hearing Civil
    Judgement by the First Intermediate People's Court of Beijing City, No 8216 ... 6.30–6.31
Chen Zuling v Pan Haishen (2009) Yi Zhong Min Chu Zi No 8217 (Civil Judgment,
    The First Intermediate Court of Beijing, 2009) 8.73
Cheng Wenshui and Liu Yanze 7.46

Deng Jun & Qu Li (2008) No 46 (The Administrative Penalty Decision of the CSRC,
    2008, No 46, promulgated by the China Securities Regulatory Commission,
    November 10, 2008) (Zhongguo Zhengjianhui Xingzheng Chufa Juedingshu) 8.31
Dongfang Electronics 6.68

Guangdong Meiya 6.53

Huang Guangyu 8.60, 8.65, 8.74

Kuang Yong 8.23–8.24

Lihua Chen et al v Daqing Lianyi Ltd Co and Shenyin Wanguo Securities Ltd Co,
    Second Hearing Civil Judgement, The High People's Court of Helongjiang
    Province, 21 December 2004 .... 6.42–6.45
Liu Zhongmin v Bohai Group 6.08

NanGan Gufen and Chengshang Group 10.46

Pan Haishen (2008) No. 12 (The Administrative Penalty Decision of the CSRC, 2008,
    No 12, promulgated by the China Securities Regulatory Commission,
    16 March 2008) (Zhongguo Zhengjianhui Xingzheng Chufa Juedingshu) 8.21

Qu Xiang (2008) No 49 (The Administrative Penalty Decision of the CSRC, 2008,
    No 49, promulgated by the China Securities Regulatory Commission,
    20 November 2008) (Zhongguo Zhengjianhui Xingzheng Chufa Juedingshu) 8.60

Sanlian Shangshe v Guomei Dianqi High Court of Shandong Province, Minshi
    Caiding Shu [Civil Order] (2009) Lu Shang Chu Zi Di 2-1 Hao [Commercial case
    report, First instance, No 2-1] 11.41
Shenshen Fang 8.59

Shenzhen Baoan (1993) (Decision of the China Securities Regulatory Commission on the Punishment of the Shanghai Subsidiary Company of Shenzhen Baoan Group Company, the Baoan Huayang Health Care Production Company, and the Shenzhen Ronggang Baoling Electrical Lighting Company for Breaching the Securities Regulations, 4 Zhongguo Zhengquan Jiandu Guanli Weiyuanhui Gonggao (China Securities Regulatory Commission Official Bulletin) (25 October 1993) 10.45
ST Jiuzhou 6.40
Su Wanfu v Nantong Technology Investment Group Ltd Co (Securities Misrepresentation Compensation Dispute case), (2006) First Hearing Civil Judgment by the Intermediate People's Court of Nanjing City, No 250; appealed as (2007) Second Hearing Civil Judgment by the High People's Court of Jiangsu Province, No 112 .... 6.33, 6.38

Tang Jian (2008) No 22 (The Administrative Penalty Decision of the CSRC, 2008, No 22, promulgated by the China Securities Regulatory Commission, 8 April 2008)(Zhongguo Zhengjianhui Xingzheng Chufa Juedingshu) 8.38–8.40, 9.25–9.26

Wang Jianzhong) (2008) No 42 (CSRC Administrative Sanction Decision, 2008, No 42). 7.34–7.36, 7.47
Wang Jianzhong and Beijing Shoufang Ltd 7.47

Yin Guangxia 6.36
Yue Meidi 10.93

Zhou Jianming (2007) No 35 (CSRC Administrative Sanction Decision, 2007 No 35). 7.33–7.34

AUSTRALIA

Donald v Australian Securities and Investments Commission (2001) 38 ACSR 10; [2001] AATA 366 .... 7.63

Fame Decorator Agencies Pty Ltd v Jeffries Industries Ltd (1998) 28 ACSR 58 .... 7.59

UNITED KINGDOM

R v de Berenger (1814) 3 Maule & S 67; 105 ER 536 .... 7.14–7.16
R v Takeover Panel, ex p Datafin PLC [1987] 1 All ER 564 .... 11.62

UNITED STATES

Accord Stotland v GAF Corp, No 6876, 1983 Del Ch LEXIS 477 (Del Ch Sept 1, 1983) 11.58

Chiarella v United States 445 U.S. 222 (1980) 8.35, 8.37

Dirks v SEC, 463 U.S. 646 (1983) 8.24, 8.35, 8.37

Ernst & Ernst v Hochfelder 425 US 185 .... 7.68

Greenfield v Heublein, Inc, 742 F.2d 751, 756 (3d Cir 1984) 5.14

Johnson v Trueblood, 629 F.2d 287 (3d Cir 1980) 11.58

Moran v Household Int'l, Inc, 500 A.2d 1346, 1357 (Del 1985) 11.72

Table of Cases

Paramount Communications, Inc v QVC Network Inc 637 A.2d 34 (Del 1994) . . . 11.60, 11.73
Paramount Communications, Inc v Time, Inc 571 A.2d 1140 (Del 1989). 11.60
Parter v Marshall Field & Co, 646 F.2d 271 (7th Cir 1981). 11.58

Revlon Inc v MacAndrews & Forbes Holdings, Inc 506 A.2d 173 (Del 1985) 11.59–11.60
Rubinstein v Collins, 20 F.3d 160, 170 (5th Cir 1994) 5.14

SEC v Texas Gulf Sulphur 401 F.2d 833 (2d Cir. 1968), cert denied,
    394 U.S. 976 (1969) 8.35
State Teachers Retirement Board v Fluor Corp, 654 F.2d 843, 850 (2d Cir 1981) 5.14

United States v Martha Stewart and Peter Bacanovic, 305 F. Supp. 2d 368
    (S.D.N.Y. 2004). 8.41
United States v O'Hagan 521 U.S. 642 (1997). 8.35, 8.37
Unitrin, Inc v American General Corp 651 A.2d 1361 (Del 1995) 11.73
Unocal Corp v Mesa Petroleum Co 493 A.2d 946 (Del. 1985) 11.58, 11.60, 11.72–11.73

TABLE OF LEGISLATION

CHINA

Laws

The Constitution of the People's Republic of China, promulgated by the National People's Congress in 1982, amended in 1988, 1993, 1999 and 2004, (ZhongHua Renmin Gongheguo Xianfa)............ 10.27, 10.28, 10.32

Law of the PRC on Banking Regulation and Supervision, promulgated by the Standing Committee of the National People's Congress in 2003, amended in 2006 (Zhonghua Renmin Gongheguo Yinhangye Jiandu Guanli Fa)..................... 2.12

Civil Procedure Law of the People's Republic of China, passed by the National People's Congress on 9 April 1991, amended on 28 October 2007 and on 31 August 2012 (Zhonghua Renmin Gongheguo Minshi Susongfa) 6.60–6.61

Law of the PRC on Civil Servants, issued by the Standing Committee of the National People's Congress on 27 April 2005, effective 1 Jan 2006 (Zhonghua Renmin Gongheguo Gongwuyuan Fa) 2.54

Law of the PRC on Commercial Banks, adopted at the 13th session of the Standing Committee of the 8th National People's Congress of the PRC on 10 May 1995, amended on 27 December 2003 (Zhonghua Renmin Gongheguo Shangye Yinhang Fa).................... 2.12

Company Law of the People's Republic of China, promulgated by the Standing Commission of the National People's Congress, 29 December 1993, effective 1 July 1994, amended in 1999, 2004, 2005 and 2013 (Zhonghua Renming Gongheguo Gongsi Fa)............. 10.41, 11.05, 11.12–11.15, 11.27

Criminal Law of the PRC, promulgated by the National People's Congress in 1997, amended many times (Zhonghua Renming Gongheguo Xing Fa) 3.26, 7.40, 8.22, 8.44, 8.45

Criminal Procedural Law of the PRC, promulgated by the National People's Congress on 1 July 1979, amended in 1996 and 2012 (Zhonghua Renmin Gongheguo Xingshi Susong Fa)............... 6.46

General Principles of the Civil Law of the PRC, promulgated by the National People's Congress 12 April 1986, effective 1 January 1987, amended in 2009 (Zhonghua Renmin Gongheguo Minfa Tongze) 6.50

Law of the PRC on Insurance, adopted at the 14th session of the Standing Committee of the 8th National People's Congress of the People's Republic of China on 30 June 1995, amended 28 October 2002 and 28 February 2009 (Zhonghua Renmin Gongheguo Baoxian Fa)......... 2.19, 2.20, 2.21, 2.56

Law of the PRC on the People's Bank of China, adopted at the 3rd session of the Standing Committee of the 8th National People's Congress of the PRC on 18 March 1995, amended on 27 December 2003 (Zhonghua Renmin Gongheguo Zhongguo Renmin Yinhang Fa)........ 2.06, 2.07, 2.39, 2.40

Securities Investment Fund Law of the PRC, promulgated by the Standing Committee of the National People's Congress on 28 October 2003, amended 28 December 2012

(Zhonghua Renming Gongheguo
Zhengquan Touzi Jijin Fa) ... 9.04–9.05,
9.29, 9.48, 9.75,
9.108, 9.113–9.114
Law of the PRC on Securities,
promulgated by the 6th session of
the Standing Committee of the 9th
National People's Congress of the
PRC on 29 December 1998 and
effective from 1 July 1999, amended
in 2004, 2005, and 2013
(Zhonghua Renming Gongheguo
Zhengquanfa) 2.22, 2.25,
3.06, 4.03, 6.07,
6.11–6.12, 7.10,
8.05, 8.69, 9.05,
9.113, 11.05, 11.06
Trust Law of the PRC, promulgated by
the Standing Committee of the
National People's Congress on
28 April 2001, effective from
1 October 2001 (Zhonghua Renmin
Gongheguo Xintuo Fa) 9.05

Regulations and Rules

Measures of Charging Litigation
Fees, Promulgated by the State
Council on 29 December 2006,
effective from 1 April 2007 (Susong
Feiyong Jiaona Banfa) 6.76
Provisional Regulations for the
Administration of Stock Issuance
and Transaction, promulgated by the
State Council Securities Commission
on 22 April 1993 (Gupiao Faxing Yu
Jiaoyi Guanli Zanxing Tiaoli) 10.39
Notice of the General Office of the State
Council on the Establishment of the
Security Review System for Mergers
and Acquisitions of Domestic
Enterprises by Foreign Investors
(issued by the State Council on 3
February 2011, effective 3 March 2011
(Guowuyuan Bangongting guanyu
Jianli Waiguo Touzizhe Bingou
Jingnei Qiye Anquan Shencha
Zhidu de Tongzhi) 12.73, 12.80
Notice on the Suspension of Transfer of
State Shares and Legal Person Shares
of Listed Companies to Foreign
Investors, promulgated by the State
Council in September 1995 (Zanting
jiang Shangshi Gongsi Guojiagu he
Farengu Zhuanrang Geiyu Waishang
de Tongzhi).................. 12.12
Several Opinions of the State Council on
Encouraging and Guiding the
Healthy Development of Private
Investment, issued by the State
Council, 12 May 2010 (Guowuyuan
guanyu Guli he Yindao Minjian
Touzi Jiankang Fazhan de
Ruogan Yijian) 12.73
Opinions of the State Council on
Encouraging and Supporting the
Development of Non-Public
Ownership Economy, promulgated
by the State Council on 25 February
2007 (Guowuyuan Guanyu Guli
Zhichi he Yindao Getisiyindeng
Feiguoyouzhi Jingji Fazhan de
Ruogan Yijian) 10.114
Measures for the Administration of
Initial Public Offering and Listing of
Stock, promulgated by the CSRC in
2006 (Shouci Gongkai Faxing Gupiao
bing Shangshi Guanli Banfa) 4.15
Measures for the Administration of Initial
Public Offerings and Listing on the
Second Board Market, promulgated
by the CSRC in 2009 (Shouci
Gongkai Faxing Gupiao bing zai
Chuangyeban Shangshi Guanli
Zanxing Banfa)................. 4.15
Measures for the Administration of
Securities Exchanges, promulgated
by the China Securities Regulatory
Commission on 10 December 1997,
amended on 12 December 2001
(Zhengquan Jiaoyisuo
Guanli Banfa) 2.45
Measures for the Administration of
Securities Offering and
Underwriting, promulgated by the
CSRC in 2006, amended in 2010,
2012 (Zhengquan Faxing yu
Chengxiao Guanli Banfa) 4.142
Administrative Measures for the
Disclosure of Information of Listed
Companies, issued by the CSRC in
2007 (Shangshi Gongsi Xinxi Pilu
Guanli Banfa) 5.10
Provisional Measures on Investing in
Tradable Shares on China's Stock
Market by Qualified Foreign
Institutional Investors, promulgated
by the CSRC in November 2002,
revised in 2006 (Hege Jingwai Jigou
Touzizhe Jingnei Zhengquan Touzi
Guanli Zanxing Banfa).......... 10.34

Table of Legislation

Measures of the China Securities Regulatory Commission for the Issuance Examination Committee, promulgated by the CSRC in 2006, amended in 2009 (Zhongguo Zhengquan Jiandu Guanli Weiyuanhui Faxing Shenhe Weiyuanhui Banfa) 3.33

Administrative Measures for the Material Asset Reorganizations of Listed Companies, issued by the CSRC on 16 April 2008, effective 18 May 2008, and amended in 2011 (Shangshi Gongsi Zhongda Zichan Chongzu Guanli Banfa) 5.39

Measures for Regulating Information Disclosure of the Changes in Shareholdings of Listed Companies, promulgated by the China Securities Regulatory Commission on 28 September 2002, effective 1 December 2002, repealed 1 September 2006 (Shangshi Gongsi Gudong Chigu Biandong Xinxi Pilu Guanli Banfa) 10.40, 10.95, 11.06

Measures for Regulating Takeovers of Listed Companies, promulgated by CSRC on 31 July 2006 and effective from 1 September 2006, amended in 2008 and 2012 (Shangshi Gongsi Shougou Guanli Banfa) . . . 10.40, 10.42, 10.48, 10.61, 10.72–10.73, 10.77, 10.93–10.94, 10.114, 11.05–11.11

Decision on the Revision of Article 63 of the 2006 Takeover Measure, promulgated by the CSRC on 27 August 2008 (Guanyu Xiugai Shangshi Gongsi Shougou Guanli Banfa Di 63 Tiao de Guiding) 10.75

Measures for Regulating Takeovers of Listed Companies, promulgated by the China Securities Regulatory Commission on 28 September 2002, effective 1 December 2002, repealed 1 September 2006 (Shangshi Gongsi Shougou Guanli Banfa) 10.40, 10.77, 10.81, 10.83–10.84, 11.06

Administrative Measures for Securities Offerings by Listed Companies, promulgated by the CSRC in 2006, amended later (Shangshi Gongsi Zhengquan Faxing Guanli Banfa) 3.51, 3.59–3.60

Measures on the Shareholding Structure Reform of Listed Companies, promulgated by the CSRC on 4 September 2005 (Shangshi Gongsi Guquan Fenzhi Gaige Guanli Banfa) 10.37, 10.120

Administrative Measures for the Sponsorship Business of the Issuance and Listing of Securities, promulgated by the CSRC in 2008, amended in 2009 (Zhengquan Faxing Shangshi Baojian Yewu Guanli Banfa) 4.111

Implementation Plan for the System of Different Routes for the Approval of Mergers and Acquisitions, issued by the CSRC on 13 September 2013 (Binggou Chongzu Shenhe Fendao Zhi Shishi FangAn) 10.109

No 13 of the Rule for Preparing Information Disclosure Documents by Companies Conducting Public Offerings of Securities—Special Rules for the Content and Format of Quarterly Reports, issued by the CSRC in 2003, revised in 2007, 2008 (Gongkai Faxing Zhengquan de Gongsi Xinxi Pilu Bianbao Guize Di 13 Hao—Jidu Baogao Neirong yu Geshi Tebie Guiding) 5.07

Rules on Administrating the Shares Held by Directors, Supervisors and Senior Management in Their Company and Changes to Their Shareholdings, promulgated by the China Securities Regulatory Commission, 5 April 2007 (Shangshi Gongsi Dongshi, Jianshi he Gaoji Guanli Renyuan Suochi Bengongsi Gufen jiqi Biandong Guanli Guize) 8.06

Notice on Regulating the Information Disclosure Issue of Listed Companies and the Behaviour of Relevant Parties Concerned, promulgated by the China Securities Regulatory Commission, 29 January 2008 (Guanyu Guifan Shangshi Gongsi Xinxi Pilu ji Xiangguan Gefang Xingwei de Tongzhi) 8.06

Notice of the CSRC Regarding the Printing and Distribution of the '(Provisional) Guide for the Recognition and Confirmation of Manipulative Behaviour in the Securities Markets' and the '(Provisional) Guide for the

Recognition and Confirmation of Insider Trading Behaviour in the Securities Markets', promulgated by the China Securities Regulatory Commission (Zhongguo Zhengquan Jiandu Guanli Weiyuanhui Guanyu 'Zhenquan Shichang Caozong Xingwei Rending Zhiyin (Shixing)' ji 'Zhengquan Shichang Neimu Jiaoyi Xingwei Rending Zhiyin (Shixing)' de Tongzhi) 8.13

Notice of the CSRC on the Rigorous Implementation of IPO Listing Standards in Approving Backdoor Listings, issued by the CSRC in November 2013 (Zhongguo Zhengquan Jiandu Guanli Weiyuanhui Guanyu zai Jieke Shangshi Shenhe zhong Yange Zhixing Shouci Gongkai Faxing Gupiao Shangshi Biaozhun de Tongzhi).................10.20

Fourth Opinion on the Application of the Law Governing Securities and Futures, promulgated by the CSRC on 19 May 2009 (Zhengquan Qihuo Falu Shiyong Yijian No 4)........10.65

Guidelines for the Articles of Association of Listed Companies, promulgated by CSRC on 16 March 2006, amended 9 October 2008 (Shangshi Gongsi Zhangcheng Zhiyin 5.71, 11.05, 11.16–11.18

Guidance Opinion on the Establishment of an Independent Director System in Listed Companies, issued by the CSRC in August 2001 (Guanyu zai Shangshi Gongsi Jianli Duli Dongshi Zhidu de Zhidao Yijian) 5.22

Opinion on Preventing and Combating Insider Trading in the Capital Markets in accordance with the Law, promulgated by the China Securities Regulatory Commission, the Ministry of Public Security, the Ministry of Supervision, the State-owned Assets Supervision and Administration Commission, and the National Bureau of Corruption Prevention, 16 November 2010 (Guanyu Yifa Daji he Fangkong Ziben Shichang Neimu Jiaoyi de Yijian)...........8.09

Provisional Guidance on Identification of Market Manipulation on Securities Markets, issued by the CSRC on 27 March 2007 (Zhengquan Shichang Caozong Xingwei Rending Zhiyin (Shixing)).....................7.22

Administrative Measures for the Strategic Investment in Listed Companies by Foreign Investors, promulgated in December 2005 (Waiguo Touzizhe dui Shangshi Gongsi Zhanlue Touzi Guanli Banfa)..................12.13

Interim Provisions on the Utilization of Foreign Investment to Restructure State-owned Enterprises, promulgated in January 2003 (Liyong Waizi Gaizu Guoyou Qiye Zanxing Guiding) 12.13

Provisions of the Ministry of Commerce on the Implementation of the Security Review System for Mergers and Acquisitions of Domestic Enterprises by Foreign Investors (issued by the Ministry of Commerce on 25 August 2011, effective 1 September 2011) (Shangwubu Shishi Waiguo Touzizhe Binggou Jingnei Qiye Anquan Shencha Zhidu de Guiding) 12.80

Provisions on M&A of Domestic Enterprises by Foreign Investors, issued by the Ministry of Commerce on 22 June 2009 (Shangwubu Guangyu Waiguo Touzizhe Binggou Jingnei Qiye de Guiding) ... 12.08, 12.13

Provisions on the M&A of Domestic Enterprises by Foreign Investors, promulgated in August 2006 by Minister of Commerce, State-owned Assets Supervision and Administration Commission, State Administration of Taxation, State Administration for Industry and Commerce, China Securities Regulatory Commission, State Administration of Foreign Exchange (Guanyu Waiguo Touzizhe Binggou Jingnei Qiye de Guiding)..................12.08

Notice on Relevant Issues Regarding the Transfer to Foreign Investors of State Shares and Legal Person Shares of Listed Companies, promulgated by the Ministry of Finance, the CSRC, the State Economic and Trade Commission in November 2002 (Guanyu xiang Waishang

Zhuanrang Shangshi Gongsi Guoyougu he Farengu Youguan Wenti de Tongzhi) 12.13

Several Opinions on the Issues regarding Foreign Investment in Listed Companies, promulgated by the MOFTEC and CSRC in November 2001 (Guanyu Shangshi Gongsi Sheji Waishang Touzi Youguan Wenti de Ruogan Yijian) 12.13

Provisional Measures for the Administration of Lawyers' Service Charges, promulgated by the Ministry of Justice on 3 March 1007, repealed (Lvshi Fuwu Shoufei Guanli Zanxing Banfa) 6.72

Measures for the Administration of Lawyers' Service Charges, promulgated by the National Development and Reform Commission and the Ministry of Justice on 13 April 2006, effective 1 December 2006 (Lvshi Fuwu Shoufei Guanli Banfa) 6.72, 6.74

Tentative Rules on Foreign Acquisitions of State-owned Enterprises, promulgated by the State Economic and Trade Commission in August 1999 (Waishang Shougou Guoyou Qiye de Zanxing Guiding) 12.13

Judicial Interpretations of the Supreme Peoples' Court

Rules on the Jurisdiction and Acceptance of Cases Relating to the Regulatory Function of Stock Exchanges, issued by the Supreme People's Court in 2005 (Guanyu dui yu Zhengquan Jiaoyisuo Jianguan Zhineng Xiangguan de Susong Anjian Guanxia yu Shouli Wenti de Guiding). 2.26, 2.36

Minutes of the Symposium Held by the Supreme Court on Various Issues Associated with Conducting Judicial Review of the Evidence in Securities Administrative Penalty Cases, issued by the Supreme Court on 13 July 2011 (Zuigao Renmin Fayuan Guanyu Shenli Zhengquan Xingzheng Chufa Anjian Zhengju Ruogan Wenti de Zuotanhui Jiyao) 8.27

Notice of the Supreme People's Procuratorate and the Ministry of Public Security on Issuing the Provisions (II) of the Supreme People's Procuratorate and the Ministry of Public Security on the Standards for Filing Criminal Cases under the Jurisdiction of the Public Security Organs for Investigation and Prosecution, issued on 05 July 2010 by the Ministry of Public Security and the Supreme People's Procuratorate (Zuigao Renmin Jianchayuan, GongAnBu Guanyu Yinfa 'Zuigao Renmin Jianchayuan, GongAnBu Guanyu GongAn Jiguan Guanxia de Xingshi Anjian LiAn Zuisu Biaozhun de Guiding (2) de Tongzhi) 7.42

Notice of the Supreme People's Court on Relevant Issues of Filing of Civil Tort Dispute Cases Arising from Misrepresentation on the Securities Market (15 January 2002) (Zuigao Renmin Fayuan Guanyu Shouli Zhengquan Shichang Yin Xujiachengshu Yinfa de Minshi Qinquan Jiufen Anjian Youguan Wenti de Tongzhi) 6.10, 6.60, 6.63

Notice of the Supreme People's Court on Temporary Refusal of Filings of Securities-related Civil Compensation Cases (21 September 2001) (Zuigao Renmin Fayuan Guanyu she Zhengquan Minshi Peichang Anjian Zan Buyu Shouli de Tongzhi) 6.10

Provisions of the Supreme People's Court Concerning the Acceptance and Trial of Civil Compensation Securities Suits Involving Misrepresentation, effective from 1 February 2003 (Zuigao Renmin Fayuan Guanyu Shenli Zhengquan Shichang Yin Xujia Chenshu Yinfa De Minshi Peichang Anjian De Ruogan Guiding) 6.10, 6.11, 6.12, 6.16, 6.19, 6.37, 6.78–6.79

Judicial Interpretation on Several Issues concerning the Application of Insider Trading Law in Criminal Cases, promulgated on 29 March 2012, effective 1 June 2012) (Zuigao Renmin Fayuan and Zuigao Renmin Jianchayuan Guanyu Banli Neimu Jiaoyi and

Xielu Neimu Xinxi Xingshi Anjian Juti Yingyong Falv Ruogan Wenti de Jieshi) 8.05
Opinion of the Supreme People's Court on the Several Questions Concerning the Application of the 'Civil Procedure Law of the PRC', issued on 14 July 1992, amended in December 2008 (Zuigao Renmin Fayuan Guanyu Shiyong 'Zhonghua Renmin Gongheguo Minshi Susong Fa' Ruogan Wenti de Yijian).........6.61

Stock Exchanges Listing Rules

Shanghai Stock Exchange Shares Listing Rules (2012 edition) (Shanghai Zhengquan Jiaoyisuo Gupiao Shangshi Guize) 4.70, 5.12, 5.13, 5.68, 5.70, 5.72, 5.73
Shanghai Stock Exchange, Share Listing Rules, promulgated 1998, amended 2000, 2001, 2002, 2004, and 2006 (Shanghai Zhengquan Jiaoyisuo Gupiao Shangshi Guize).........10.41
Shenzhen Stock Exchange Shares Listing Rules (2012 edition) (Shenzhen Zhengquan Jiaoyisuo Gupiao Shangshi Guize) 4.73
Shenzhen Stock Exchange Second Board Shares Listing Rules (2012 edition) (Shenzhen Zhengquan Jiaoyisuo Chuangyeban Gupiao Shangshi Guize).......................4.74

AUSTRALIA

Australian Securities and Investment Commission Act 2001 ....2.64
Corporations Act 2001 ...10.64, 10.67, 10.76, 10.86, 10.90, 10.92, 10.98, 10.125, 10.126, 10.130,
Foreign Acquisitions and Takeovers Act 1975 ....12.98

EUROPEAN UNION

Market Abuse Directive 7.70

UNITED KINGDOM

Statutes

Financial Services and Markets Act 2000............. 7.69, 7.70, 7.71

Subordinate legislation

Financial Services and Markets Act 2001 (Market Abuse) Regulations 2005 (SI 381/2005) 7.70

Panel on Takeovers and Mergers

The Takeover Code (2006)..... 11.61–11.63, 11.75–11.81

UNITED STATES

17 C.F.R. § 240.13d–1(e)(2)(ii) (2004).....................10.97
17 C.F.R. § 240.13d–2(a)............10.97
17 C.F.R. § 240.13d–3 (2004)........10.92
17 C.F.R. §249.308 (2000) 5.14
Defense Production Act 1950..........12.97
Exon-Florio amendment 1988 (50 U.S.C. App §2170) 12.97
Dodd-Frank Wall Street Reform and Consumer Protection Act H.R. 4173....... 2.62, 2.75–2.77, 2.80
Foreign Investment and National Security Act of 2007 ....12.97
Investment Company Act of 1940 (US), 15 U.S.C 9.08
Securities Act 1933..................6.27
Securities Exchange Act 1934..........7.67, 7.68, 8.07, 10.97
Williams Act Pub L No 90-4393, 82 Stat 454 (1 968), codified as amended at 15 U.S.C. (2000).................10.58, 10.91

LIST OF ABBREVIATIONS

ABC	Agricultural Bank of China
APRA	Australian Prudential Regulatory Authority
ASIC	Australian Securities and Investment Commission
BOC	Bank of China
CBOC	Construction Bank of China
CBRC	China Banking Regulatory Commission
CFIUS	Committee on Foreign Investment in the United States
CFTC	Commodity Futures Trading Commission
CIRC	China Insurance Regulatory Commission
CJV	Contractual joint venture enterprises
CNY	Chinese yuan
CSIPFC	China Securities Investor Protection Fund Company
CSRC	China Securities Regulatory Commission
EJV	Equity joint venture enterprises
FATA	Foreign Acquisitions and Takeovers Act 1975
FDI	Foreign direct investment
FIE	Foreign-invested enterprises
FIRB	Foreign Investment Review Board
GDP	Gross domestic product
GEM	Growth Enterprise Market
GFC	Global financial crisis
ICBC	Industrial and Commercial Bank of China
IEC	Issuance Examination Committee of the China Securities Regulatory Commission
IPO	Initial public offerings
M&A	Mergers and Acquisitions
MOFCOM	Ministry of Commerce
MOFTEC	Ministry of Foreign Trade and Economic Cooperation
NDRC	National Development and Reform Commission
NPL	Non-performing loans
OTC	Over-the-counter market
PBC	People's Bank of China
PICC	People's Insurance Company of China
PRC	People's Republic of China
QFII	Qualified Foreign Institutional Investors
RETM	Regional Equity Trading Markets
RMB	renminbi
SAC	Securities Association of China
SAFE	State Administration of Foreign Exchange of the People's Republic of China
SAIC	State Administration for Industry and Commerce

List of Abbreviations

SASAC	State Owned Asset Supervision and Administration Commission
SCSC	State Council Securities Commission
SEC	US Securities and Exchange Commission
SFCHK	Securities and Futures Commission of Hong Kong
SME	Small-and-Medium Enterprise
SOE	State-owned enterprises
SPC	Supreme People's Court
SPV	Special purpose vehicle
SRO	Self-regulatory organization
TBM	Third Board Markets
VIE	Variable interest entity
WFOE	Wholly foreign-owned enterprises
WTO	World Trade Organization

Part I

INTRODUCTION

1

CHINA'S FINANCIAL MARKETS

1.1. Introduction	1.01	1.4. Characteristics of China's Financial Markets	1.45
1.2. Evolution of China's Financial Markets	1.07	1.4.1. Unbalanced market structure	1.45
1.2.1. Before 1978: no financial regulation in the true sense	1.07	1.4.2. State ownership of financial institutions	1.48
1.2.2. 1978–1992: centralized and single regulator	1.09	1.4.3. Share ownership patterns in listed companies	1.50
1.2.3. 1992–present: multiple sector-based regulators	1.13	1.4.4. Policy market	1.54
		1.4.5. The gaming nature of the markets	1.58
1.3. Overview of Financial Markets in China	1.15	1.5. China and Global Financial Markets	1.62
1.3.1. Banking	1.16	1.5.1. The global financial crisis of 2008: implications for China	1.62
1.3.2. Securities market	1.25	1.5.2. Shanghai: toward a new global financial centre	1.70
1.3.3. Insurance market	1.43		

1.1. Introduction

The term 'financial markets' (or capital markets) does not have a legally defined meaning in the People's Republic of China (China). It is sometimes said to be the market where financial products are traded. But what are financial products? Again, there is no clear definition and they are referred to as products that are traded in financial markets. In this way, we can be faced with the problem of circularity in defining financial markets. **1.01**

Given the ever-developing nature of financial markets, it may be neither necessary nor feasible to hammer out a definition. Rather, the term 'financial markets' can be better understood by reference to its economic function of effecting transfers between capital providers or investors, namely people with surplus capital, and capital users, namely people seeking capital for productive purposes. The capital transfer can be effected either directly between capital providers and users, or indirectly through intermediaries such as banks. **1.02**

1.03 Depending on the character of the financial intermediation employed or the type of the financial product issued, a financial market includes a range of different submarkets. Money markets and securities markets are, for instance, among the principal submarkets. The term 'money markets' is sometimes used to refer to the institutional networks which bring together lenders and borrowers of short-term funds. Classic examples of products traded in the money markets are commercial paper, promissory notes, and certificates of deposits. In contrast, securities markets concentrate on long-term debt and equity instruments, such as shares and debentures, with the stock exchanges as their principle form.

1.04 The focus of this book is on the law governing securities markets in China, but the discussion will be placed, where appropriate, in the broader context of Chinese financial markets. This is important, as the tide of financial modernization and innovation has made the traditional boundaries of financial sectors such as banking, insurance, and securities increasingly blurred.

1.05 Securities markets can be classified into a primary market and secondary market, according to the different functions. The primary market serves the function of transferring capital from investors to fund users by way of issuance of securities by companies. This is a process of capital formation and securities issuance. The secondary market then provides the trading forum for securities issued in the primary market. The principal example of this is the stock exchanges where the securities are quoted and traded through a centralized system.

1.06 While the secondary market does not contribute directly to capital formation, it provides important support. First, it provides liquidity by enabling investors to convert securities they hold into cash, ideally at minimum cost and with speed and ease. For investors, the availability of liquidity is often a very important consideration. Second, the secondary market has the function of price discovery and thus helps to establish the cost of capital for the issuance of securities in the primary market. When determining the issue price, one usually looks at important indicators in the secondary market—most notably the ratio of share market price to after-tax earnings per share (the P/E figure). This is the financial figure most commonly used to judge the profitability of a listed company. A high P/E figure means that the share price is high and thus the company can raise funds cheaply.

1.2. Evolution of China's Financial Markets

1.2.1. Before 1978: no financial regulation in the true sense

1.07 After the founding of the People's Republic of China (PRC) in 1949, the Communist Party of China gradually steered the nation toward a centrally planned economy modelled on that operating in the Soviet Union. Under the so-called 'Socialist Transformation' policy, private businesses were turned over to collective ownership and eventually state ownership. Thereafter, as the economy was centrally planned and composed overwhelmingly of state-owned enterprises (SOE), there was little need for the existence of financial markets to fund businesses and allocate resources.

Hence, the financial markets established before the 'Socialist Transformation' policy were dismantled during this time. First, all stock exchanges ceased to operate in 1952, putting an end to the securities market. Second, the People's Insurance Company of China (PICC) was shut down in 1959, quickly followed by the closure of the insurance market altogether.[1] Finally, in the banking sector, the People's Bank of China (PBC) became the only bank operating in China both as the central bank and as a commercial bank. Although the PBC provided the traditional service of saving and lending, it functioned essentially as an instrument of the government rather than a real commercial bank, as understood in western economies. The PBC was used primarily as a conduit through which state money was channelled to fund SOEs under orders from the government. In short, there was no financial regulation in the true sense of the term.

1.2.2. 1978–1992: centralized and single regulator

In 1978, the economic reform policy was introduced by the Third Plenary Session of the 11th National People's Congress, marking an important watershed in the development of China's financial markets and indeed the general economy. First, the banking system was reformed to keep up with the transition to a market-oriented economy. As a starting point, the 'Big Four' state-owned banks were established or re-opened to provide specialized services, including the Agricultural Bank of China (ABC) in January 1979 for the agricultural sector, the Bank of China (BOC) in March 1979 for foreign exchange businesses, the Construction Bank of China (CBOC) in May 1983 for big construction projects, and the Industrial and Commercial Bank of China (ICBC) in January 1984 to take over the commercial activities of the PBC.

In order to increase market competition in the banking sector, permission was given for more commercial banks—most of which are jointly owned by the state and private investors—to be set up at the national and local levels. Examples include the Communication Bank in 1987. In 1994, three policy banks—the China Development Bank, the Agricultural Development Bank of China, and the Export-import Bank of China—were created to free the 'Big Four' banks from the provision of policy loans, enabling them to function as real commercial banks.

The other parts of the financial system also underwent significant reforms and developed rapidly. The securities market was brought back to life in the early 1980s, culminating in the establishment of Shanghai Stock Exchange and Shenzhen

---

[1] Linbo Fan, 'The Insurance Market System' in Joseph J. Norton et al (eds), *Financial Regulation in the Greater China Area: Mainland China, Taiwan and Hong Kong SAR* (London: Kluwer Law International, 2000), 158.

Stock Exchange in 1990 and 1991 respectively. Likewise, the insurance market was revived with the reopening of the PICC in 1980 and the formation of more insurance companies thereafter.

1.12 As a consequence of the reform, the PBC took on a dual role in financial regulation. It performed the major functions of the central bank while at the same time supervising and regulating the whole financial system, including banking, securities, and insurance. Thus, this effectively rendered the PBC the single financial regulator at that time.

1.2.3. 1992–present: multiple sector-based regulators

1.13 With the rapid development of the financial markets since the early 1990s, China has been moving steadily toward a sector-based regulatory model with separate regulators for banking, securities and insurance.[2] First, in October 1992, responsibility for securities regulation was spun off from the PBC to the State Council Securities Commission (SCSC) and the China Securities Regulatory Commission (CSRC). These two securities regulators were merged and the surviving CSRC was vested with the exclusive authority to regulate the securities market in April 1998. Second, in keeping with the booming insurance market, the China Insurance Regulatory Commission (CIRC) was established in November 1998. Finally, in April 2003, the China Banking Regulatory Commission (CBRC) was set up to take over the function of direct banking regulation from the PBC.

1.14 Together with the PBC as the central bank, the above three highly specialized and mutually independent regulatory commissions make up China's financial regulatory framework, collectively referred to as *Yihang Sanhui* (one bank, three commissions). Different regulatory commissions are responsible for the administration and supervision of different financial sectors, namely banking, securities, and insurance. This sector-based regulatory model corresponds to the segmentation of financial services and markets in China, a policy commonly known as *Fenye Jingying, Fenye Jianguan* (separate operation, separate regulation). As shall be discussed later, the adoption of this regulatory regime has been heavily influenced by overseas experience, particularly that of the US.

1.3. Overview of Financial Markets in China

1.15 As China's current financial markets and regulation are essentially structured along the traditional lines of banking, securities, and insurance, the three sectors will be discussed in turn.

---

[2] For fuller discussion of the development of China's financial reform after its WTO accession, see eg James Barth et al (eds), *Financial Restructuring and Reform in Post-WTO China* (London: Kluwer, 2006).

1.3.1. Banking

1.3.1.1. Chinese banks

1.16 Apart from the central bank,[3] there are several different types of institutions in China's banking system, including *guoyou shangye yinhang*, other commercial banks, policy banks, and non-bank financial institutions. All commercial banks take the legal form of a company, being either a limited liability company or a joint-stock limited company.[4] As shall be explained, this complex banking system is attributable to a host of historical, political, and cultural factors.

1.17 The first category comprises the state-owned commercial banks (*guoyou shangye yinhang*), chiefly the so-called 'Big Four', including the Bank of China, the ICBC, the CBOC, and the ABC. As noted before, these banks were previously specialized banks, but are all now developing into comprehensive commercial banks. Due to their historical background and strong foundation, they are very large, with huge client bases, and together command the lion's share of the market in terms of public savings, deposits, and loans.[5]

1.18 In order to meet the challenge brought about by China's accession to the World Trading Organization (WTO), reforms have been carried out to improve the quality of the 'Big Four' banks and eventually secure their listing on the stock market. On 27 October 2005, the CBOC made the breakthrough, becoming the first of the 'Big Four' banks to be listed in HK. This was followed by the Bank of China, which was listed in HK on 1 June 2006 and dual-listed in Shanghai soon after on 5 July 2006. A couple of months later, the ICBC was dual-listed in HK and Shanghai simultaneously on 16 October 2006. In July 2010, the ABC was finally dual-listed in Shanghai and HK, in what was then the world's largest initial public offering by value.

1.19 Second, there are three state-owned policy banks, including the China Development Bank, the Agricultural Development Bank of China, and the Export-import Bank of China. As discussed earlier, these three banks were established in 1994 to take over the provision of policy loans from the 'Big Four' banks. They specialize in different areas and operate independently of each other: the China Development Bank is charged with financing key construction projects of the state; the Agricultural Development Bank of China handles policy loans in the agricultural sector; and the Export-import Bank of China provides policy financial support for the import and export of capital goods such as mechanical and electrical products

---

[3] For more discussion of the central bank in China, see Chapter 2.
[4] Zhonghua Renmin Gongheguo Shangye Yinhang Fa [Law of the PRC on Commercial Banks] (adopted at the 13th session of the Standing Committee of the 8th National People's Congress of the PRC on 10 May 1995, amended on 27 December 2003), art 2.
[5] Yang Li et al (eds), *2006 Annual Report on China's Financial Development [Zhongguo Jinrong Fazhan Baogao 2006]* (Beijing: Social Sciences Academic Press, 2006), 76–9.

and complete sets of equipment. In recent years policy banks, particularly the China Development Bank, have tried to engage in commercial banking business.

1.20 Third, about a dozen so-called joint-stock commercial banks (*gufenzhi shangye yinhang*) have been established since the 1980s, such as the Merchant Bank, the Minsheng Bank, the Pudong Development Bank, and the Shenzhen Development Bank (now renamed PingAn Bank). A common feature of these banks is that they are small or medium-sized and relatively efficient. Originally they conducted business on a regional basis; they have since been gradually branching out nationwide to rival the large state-owned banks.

1.21 Further, there is a residual group of banking or non-banking financial institutions engaged in deposit-taking and lending business. This includes, among others, urban commercial banks, rural commercial banks, urban credit unions, and rural credit unions. Urban/rural commercial banks transformed from urban/rural credit unions, respectively. As part of the overall financial reform programme, urban credit unions sprang up like mushrooms from the beginning of the 1980s, and totalled more than 5,000 by the 1990s. Credit unions were, however, found to have many problems in relation to risk management, and thus since the mid-1990s, the central government has implemented the policy of transforming credit unions into commercial banks. There are now more than 100 urban commercial banks nationwide. In general, urban commercial banks are small in size and are positioned to serve the local economy, particularly small and medium-sized businesses. Hence, commercial banks in more economically developed regions, such as Shanghai Bank, have grown more rapidly.

1.22 Finally, it is worth noting the recent establishment of the Postal Savings Bank of China. As early as 1986, the postal office was allowed to engage in deposit-taking business, and in 2004 its scope of business expanded to full-scale banking services. In March 2007, the postal banking business was spun off to establish the Postal Savings Bank of China. This bank takes advantage of the nationwide network of the post office and claims to serve the agricultural sector, small and medium-sized enterprises, and individual clients. It has recently experienced rapid growth and, as of the end of 2011, was ranked the sixth largest commercial bank in China, after the 'Big Four' and the Bank of Communications.

1.3.1.2. Foreign banks

1.23 An increasing number of foreign banks have entered the Chinese market, particularly after China's WTO accession in 2001. The presence of foreign banks in China takes several different forms. The first form is the so-called foreign-invested legal person bank (*waizi faren yinhang*), which is incorporated as an independent legal person under the Chinese law. Second, foreign banks can set up China branches (*waiguo yinhang fenhang*), which are not independent legal persons in China. The final form is the representative office of foreign banks. The representative office cannot engage in substantive business in China, and is set up by foreign banks usually as the first step of their China adventure to gather relevant information on whether, and how, they should proceed further. As of the end of 2011 there were 39 foreign-invested legal person banks, 93 foreign bank branches, and 207 foreign bank representative offices, with the foreign banks coming from a total of 47 countries and regions.[6]

As per its WTO commitment, China has gradually removed previous restrictions on various issues, such as geographical location, client type, and business scope, for foreign banks to operate in China. Now, foreign banks are given national treatment: foreign-invested legal person banks are treated in the same way as Chinese banks with respect to business scope and regulatory standard; as foreign bank branches are not independent legal persons, they are still subject to some business restrictions, but the restrictions have been much reduced. In order to better perform its regulatory duty and protect the interests of depositors, the CBRC has encouraged foreign banks to transform their China branches into foreign-invested legal person banks. Compared to foreign bank branches, foreign-invested legal person banks are much larger in terms of value of assets and deposits. As of the end of 2011, foreign-invested legal person banks accounted for 87.66 per cent of all foreign bank assets in China and 95.56 per cent of deposits taken by foreign banks. 1.24

1.3.2. Securities market

1.3.2.1. Stock exchanges

As a major initiative of China's economic reform since the late 1970s, the securities market has been given much development priority by the Chinese leadership and thus has experienced rapid growth.[7] There are currently two national stock exchanges in Shanghai and Shenzhen, which were established in 1990 and 1991 respectively. By the end of 2012, the two exchanges were handling an aggregate of 2,494 listed companies, with a total market capitalization of 23.04 trillion yuan (CNY) (roughly USD 3.78 trillion), which accounted for about 44.36 per cent of China's gross domestic product (GDP) in 2012 and overall the Chinese stock market was ranked the second largest stock market in the world.[8] 1.25

The current relationship between the two stock exchanges in Shanghai and Shenzhen is more complementary than competitive, as a result of the governmental planning and control. Essentially, the CSRC decides in which markets the stock exchanges may operate, and what financial products can be traded 1.26

---

[6] From the official website of the CBRC, http://www.cbrc.gov.cn.
[7] For a fuller account of the development of China's securities market, see Hui Huang, *International Securities Markets: Insider Trading Law in China* (London: Kluwer Law International, 2006), Ch 2.
[8] CSRC, *2012 Annual Report*, 16, available at the official website of the CSRC, http://www.csrc.gov.cn.

there. The Shanghai Stock Exchange operates a Main Board market (*zhu ban*), while the Shenzhen Stock Exchange, in addition to its Main Board, established a Small-and-Medium Enterprise Board (*zhong xiao ban*, SME Board) in 2004 and a Growth Enterprise Market (*chuang ye ban*, GEM) in 2009.[9] In general, companies listed on the Main Board are larger, in terms of market capitalization, than their counterparts on the SME Board and the GEM.[10] In September 2000, the Shenzhen Stock Exchange stopped listing companies on its Main Board and concentrated on the development of the SME Board and the GEM.[11]

1.27 It is important to note that the equity structure of the Chinese stock market differs greatly from those in western nations. There are, depending on the criteria used, several different types of shares in China. Apart from the dichotomy of common and preferred shares, which is familiar to westerners, there are other special classifications, and these seem to be peculiar to China. This has resulted in the distinctive feature of market segmentation, which is essentially a historical product of China's progressive economic reform, with both economic and political reasons behind it.[12]

1.28 First, depending on the nationality of eligible traders and the currencies in which the shares are traded, there are traditionally two broad types of shares in the market: A-shares and B-shares. A-shares are basically limited to domestic investors, with both the principal and dividends denominated in the local currency, namely the CNY. In contrast, B-shares are generally designed for foreigners, including investors from Taiwan, Hong Kong, and Macau. While B-shares carry a face value denominated in CNY, they are traded in foreign currency on the basis of exchange rates at the time of transactions. No companies can issue B-shares unless they meet certain requirements prescribed by the government. So far, only about 100 companies have been approved to issue B-shares. In terms of market capitalization, B-shares account for a fairly small proportion, both in individual companies and as a whole, and thus their impact on the market is quite limited. A point to note is that, due to market segmentation, although B-shares carry the same voting and other relevant rights as A-shares, the prices of A-shares and B-shares for the same listed company are always different, sometimes by a significant degree.

1.29 Second, and more importantly, A-shares have been further sub-divided into three subsets in light of the strictly defined groups of shareholders in China: state shares (*guojia gu*); legal person shares (*faren gu*); and public individual shares (*shehui geren gu*). Only public individual shares may be freely traded on the stock exchange (they are therefore called tradable shares); state shares and legal person shares are subject

---

[9] The GEM is also called the ChiNext or the Second Board.
[10] For more discussion of the listing criteria of those submarkets, see Chapter 4.
[11] For this reason, the Main Board and SME Board of the Shenzhen Stock Exchange are sometimes collectively referred to as the Main Board of the Shenzhen Stock Exchange.
[12] For a detailed discussion of this, see Hui Huang, *International Securities Markets: Insider Trading Law in China* (London: Kluwer Law International, 2006), Ch 2.

to severe trading restrictions (and are therefore collectively called non-tradable shares). In general, non-tradable shares account for about two thirds of the shares in most listed companies.

As the economic reform proceeds, the government has been making great efforts to gradually solve the problem of market segmentation, with a view to bringing the market more in line with international norms. 1.30

The A-share/B-share distinction has become blurred over time. The severance of the A and B-share markets is largely due to the incomplete convertibility of renminbi (RMB) and China's restrictive foreign currency policy. For example, precluding domestic investors from taking up B-shares is regarded as a measure to preserve the nation's foreign currency reserve. As the RMB is moving toward convertibility and internationalization, the separation between A-shares and B-shares has started to disappear. On the one hand, since February 2001, B-shares have been made available for domestic investors to purchase with foreign currency; on the other, the A-share market is gradually being opened up to foreigners. For instance, since November 2002, large financial institutions that count as Qualified Foreign Institutional Investors (QFII) have been able to purchase a quota of tradable shares in the A-share market.[13] It is speculated that A-shares and B-shares markets will be merged in future, and thus the distinction between A-shares and B-shares will become history. 1.31

Compared with the smooth way in which the A-share/B-share distinction has been reduced, the tradable/non-tradable shares segregation has proven a much harder problem to address. Non-tradable shares were created by the government in the early 1990s to prevent uncontrolled sales of SOEs to the private sector, but the system artificially distorted the functioning of the market, becoming a serious impediment to its further development. For instance, in the face of a high percentage of non-tradable state shares in listed companies, hostile takeovers are practically impossible.[14] Since 2000, several unsuccessful experiments have been attempted to reform the non-tradable shares to make them freely tradable on the stock exchanges. 1.32

In April 2005, the CSRC issued a new plan for shareholding structure reform entitled *Guquan Fenzhi Gaige*. Unlike its predecessors, this plan adopts a market-based process rather than a government-imposed approach, and thus has proven to be a great success. Two points need to be noted about this reform. First, the reform takes a gradualist approach, and there is a legal limit on the percentage of non-tradable shares which can be made freely tradable on a yearly basis. The legal limit is just a minimum requirement, and the individual company can prescribe a more stringent 1.33

---

[13] There are other ways in which foreign investors may acquire A-shares in China. For more discussion, see Chapter 12.
[14] For more analysis of takeovers in China, see Chapter 10.

Introduction

limit. This means that it will take some time, maybe a considerable period of time in some cases, for the reform to be complete. The purpose of this is to spread the impact of the reform on the market over time. Second, under the reform, the holder of previously non-tradable shares—notably the state—is given the right, and not obligation, to sell the shares freely on the stock exchange. The state policy is to sell most state shares into private hands, retaining only a tiny core that the state deems crucial for national defence, energy security, and so on. Hence in foreseeable future, with all non-tradable shares becoming freely tradable, the Chinese stock market will assume a radically different landscape, which will have far-reaching implications for corporate governance as well as securities regulation.

1.34 Finally, some Chinese companies are cross-listed on overseas exchanges, and their shares listed there are named after the location of the exchanges. For instance, H-shares are shares listed on the Hong Kong Stock Exchange while N-shares are listed on the New York Stock Exchange. The trading of these shares is mainly subject to the laws of listing locations rather than Chinese laws. Additionally, the overseas market capitalization of such shares usually represents a very small fraction of the total market capitalization of individual companies. Therefore, these shares have very little impact on the Chinese stock market. Notwithstanding their diminished relevance to this discussion, they are noted here for the sake of completing the picture of China's stock market.

1.35 Apart from shares, there are other financial products traded on the stock exchanges, including bonds, securities investment funds, and warrants. In comparison with the equity markets operated by the two stock exchanges, their bond markets are much less developed. There are a variety of publicly traded bonds, including treasury bonds, local government bonds, enterprise bonds, corporate bonds, convertible bonds, and equity warrant bonds.

1.3.2.2. Futures exchanges

1.36 In addition to the two stock exchanges in Shanghai and Shenzhen, there are several futures exchanges in China. Futures products can be divided into commodity futures and financial futures. The three exchanges for trading commodity futures include the Shanghai Futures Exchange, whose trading products are mainly industrial materials such as metals, rubber, and fuel; the Zhenzhou Commodity Exchange, which specializes in the trading of agricultural products such as wheat, cotton, sugar, and rice; and the Dalian Commodity Exchange, where trading items are from the agricultural and industrial sectors, such as yellow bean, corn, palm oil, and coke. In 2011, the volume of commodities traded in the above three exchanges accounted for 38.03 per cent of the global volume of commodities trading.

1.37 Compared with its commodity futures counterpart, China's financial futures market is less developed. The China Financial Futures Exchange is currently the only place where financial futures are traded. It was established in 2006 in Shanghai, with five shareholders: the two stock exchanges and the three commodity futures exchanges. It was 2010 before it offered its first product, namely Shanghai-Shenzhen 300 Index Futures, but it has since released several other products.

1.3.2.3. Off-exchange markets

1.38 After the two national stock exchanges in Shanghai and Shenzhen were established in the early 1990s, all securities trading was required to be conducted on the exchanges. This in effect precluded the development of off-exchange markets. The 2005 Securities Law has changed the situation, providing that legally issued securities shall be traded on the stock exchanges or other places approved by the State Council.

1.39 As an effort by the Chinese government to build a multilayered capital market, the off-exchange markets cater for companies that are not listed in the two stock exchanges in Shanghai and Shenzhen. This is important, simply because the two stock exchanges in Shanghai and Shenzhen cannot meet the needs of the rapidly growing economy in China: as of the end of 2012, there were more than 100,000 joint-stock companies, but less than 2,500 of them had been listed in the two stock exchanges. In practice, the off-exchange markets can be broadly grouped into the following several categories.

1.40 The first category is the so-called 'Third Board Markets' (TBM, *san ban shi chang*), which can be further divided into two subgroups, the Old TBM and the New TBM. The Old TBM provides a trading place primarily for companies that are delisted from the two stock exchanges. In contrast, the New TBM is designed for companies that are high-tech growth enterprises and whose shares are being traded publicly for the first time. It is thus similar to the GEM of Shenzhen Stock Exchange, with the major difference being that its listing criteria are lower than those of the GEM. In 2006, companies in the Beijing Zhongguancun Science and Technology Park were the first to be listed on the New TBM. In August 2012, the State Council allowed the New TBM to expand to other three high-tech parks, including Shanghai Zhangjiang, Wuhan Donhu, and Tianjin Binhai. As of the end of 2012, there were 56 companies listed on the Old TBM and 200 companies on the New TBM. On 16 January 2013 a new trading platform, operated by the National Small and Medium-sized Enterprise Equity Transfer System Limited, was formally unveiled, marking a new era of the development of the TBM.

1.41 The second category is the so-called 'Regional Equity Trading Markets' (RETM, *quyu guquan jiaoyi shichang*). Unlike the TBM, which is approved by the State Council and accommodates companies nationwide, the RETM is set up by the local governments mainly to serve local companies which are not listed on the two stock exchanges in Shanghai and Shenzhen. The RETM consists of three different types of institutions: (1) the Local Property Trading Institution (*difang chanquan jiaoyi jigou*), which trades many types of property, including equity interests; (2) the

Introduction

Local Equity Trading Institution (*difang guquan jiaoyi jigou*), which specializes in the trading of equity interests; and (3) the Local Equity Custodian Institution (*difang guquan tuoguan jigou*), which is empowered to do equity transfer registration and thus can perform the function of effecting equity transfer.

1.42 The third category is the over-the-counter market (OTC). In late 2012, seven securities firms were allowed to operate OTC markets as a pilot project. The OTC markets are currently designed for the issuance and trading of private equity products.

1.3.3. Insurance market

1.43 As noted earlier, commercial insurance activity resumed in China in 1980 when the PICC was re-opened for business. In recent years, with the rapid progress of social security reform, the insurance market in China has been growing by leaps and bounds. As at the end of 2009 there were more than 130 insurance companies, in comparison with 52 in 2002; their overall business volume hit a record high of 1.1 trillion CNY, almost quadruple the figure of 2002, and their overall assets were worth 4.1 trillion CNY, representing a nearly five-fold increase from 2002. In terms of market capitalization, the China Life Insurance has become the largest listed insurance company in the world. Consistent with its WTO commitments, China has expedited the opening up of its insurance market, with up to 47 foreign insurance companies having entered the Chinese insurance market by the end of 2009.[15]

1.44 Several general observations can be made about the Chinese insurance market. First, as shown above, the market has grown very rapidly, with an average 24 per cent annual increase in insurance policy income for the first decade of the new millennium. Second, the market is highly concentrated, so as to form an effective oligopoly. At the end of 2009, up to 96 per cent of market share was collectively in the hands of the five largest insurance companies, including the PICC, China Life Insurance, China PingAn Insurance, New China Life Insurance Company, and China Pacific Insurance. Third, as China's social–economic reform deepens, the growth potential for the insurance market is huge. The depth of China's insurance market—as measured by the ratio of insurance policy income to GDP—was just 3 per cent in 2011, compared to the average figure of 5 per cent worldwide, and even 12 per cent in developed economies. The figure of insurance density in China was about CNY1062/person (roughly USD171) in 2011, while even in 2007 the figure was USD4,087 in the US and USD7,114 in the UK.[16] The CIRC aims to increase insurance depth and density to 5 per cent and CNY2100 during the period of the 12th Five-Year Plan.

---

[15] From the website of the CIRC, http://www.circ.gov.cn.
[16] Caifang Jiang, *Minzhu Diqu Baoxian Qiye Jinzheng Zhanlue Yanjiu [Research on Competition Strategies of Insurance Companies in Ethic Minority Regions]* (2009, Central South University), 6.

1.4. Characteristics of China's Financial Markets

1.4.1. Unbalanced market structure

China's transition toward a market-based economy has proven, 30 years on, to be a huge success, and the financial markets have developed significantly to support that transition. The chief tasks of any financial system are to attract savings and channel them as efficiently as possible to productive investments. China's financial system already does an outstanding job of effecting transfers between those with surplus resources for investment and those seeking funds for productive enterprise. However, since the financial system itself is in transition, there are still obstacles to its overall efficiency in allocating resources. Of particular relevance here is the unbalanced structure of the Chinese financial system in terms of the component markets.

1.45

The development has not been even among financial submarkets, with the banking sector having a highly dominant position. As a matter of tradition and culture, Chinese people save a lot by international standards, and most of their financial assets are held in bank deposits or in cash. In China, banks intermediate almost 75 per cent of the economy's capital; this figure is typically less than 20 per cent in developed countries.[17] This means that China depends too heavily upon the banking system for capital allocation, leading to the underdevelopment of other financing methods through securities markets such as bond and equity markets.

1.46

China's pattern of financial development can be explained by reference to political economy theories. To start with, political preferences before the era of economy reform clearly created path dependencies in shaping the current situation. As discussed earlier, during the era of the centrally planned economy, capital and products markets were virtually non-existent; at the early stage of economic reform, state-owned banks were the first batch of financial institutions to be set up to provide subsidized lending to capital-intensive infrastructure projects and manufacturing industries. Further, according to financial economists, debt finance is well suited to manufacturing where there are hard assets to pledge as collateral, whereas equity finance is more appropriate for high-growth sectors where assets are less tangible.[18] It is thus unsurprising to see the dominance of the banking market in China, a country which has developed a role for itself as the world's factory.

1.47

1.4.2. State ownership of financial institutions

The state owns or controls major Chinese financial institutions, resulting in a high level of concentration in the provision of financial services. For instance, the Big

1.48

---

[17] Diana Farrell et al, 'How Financial System Reform could Benefit China' (2006) (special edition) *The McKinsey Quarterly*, 46–47.
[18] Franklin Allen et al, 'Does Economic Structure Determine Financial Structure?' working paper, Wharton School, University of Pennsylvania, December 2006.

Introduction

Four state-owned commercial banks form the mainstay of China's banking system, accounting for 52.2 per cent of the total banking assets at the end of June 2008.[19] The remaining banks are relatively small, with joint-stock commercial banks and foreign banks representing only 14 per cent and 2.3 per cent respectively. The situation is even worse for the insurance industry, where just the two largest state-owned insurance companies, namely the PICC and China Life Insurance, together command a market share of 70 per cent.[20] The state-owned financial institutions effectively enjoy a collective monopoly in the financial services and markets.

1.49 State-owned financial institutions traditionally favour SOEs and provide limited financing to private enterprises in China. In response to the global financial crisis, in late 2008 China launched a massive 4 trillion CNY (US $586 billion) stimulus package, but much of this has been directed toward the sort of infrastructure projects that are dominated by large SOE.[21] Of more than 7 trillion CNY loaned out in the first half of 2009 by Chinese banks, only an estimated 10 per cent has gone to smaller firms. This represents inefficiency in the financial system, as private enterprises—domestic, foreign-owned, and joint ventures—are the engine of growth in China's economy, together contributing about 60 per cent of all GDP output, 68 per cent of China's exports, and half of national tax revenues.[22] In other words, China's small and medium-sized private firms do more for the national economy than large state-owned firms, but get less help from the financial system dominated by state-owned institutions. In practice, due to very limited access to banking loans, smaller firms have to resort to informal financing from friends and family, or to black-market lending schemes for which interest rates can be far higher than official bank rates. Empirical data show that smaller firms rely on informal or even illegal channels for more than one third of their financing needs.[23]

1.4.3. Share ownership patterns in listed companies

1.4.3.1. Individual participation in stock markets

1.50 The Chinese securities market has a very high proportion of individual investors. As of the end of 2011, there were about 0.203 billion trading accounts for shares and close-ended funds in China, of which 99.51 per cent were individual investors.[24]

---

[19] From the website of the CBRC, http://www.cbrc.gov.cn.
[20] From the website of the CIRC, http://www.circ.gov.cn.
[21] Yang Li (ed), *Zhongguo Jinrong Fazhan Baogao 2008–2009 [Report on China's Financial Development in the Year of 2008–2009]* (Beijing: Social Sciences Literature Press, 2009), 299–300.
[22] Li (ed), *Report 2008–2009*, 299–300.
[23] Jianjun Li et al, *Zhongguo Dixia Jinrong Guimo yu Hongguan Jingji Yingxiang Yanjiu [Research on the Macro-economic Impact of Underground Financing Scale in China]* (Beijing: China Finance Press, 2005), 76–81.
[24] CSRC, *2011 Annual Report of the CSRC* (2011), 19, available at the official website of the CSRC, http://www.csrc.gov.cn. Note, however, that the real number of individual shareholders in China should be smaller than that suggested by the number of trading accounts, because of the phenomenon of multiple accounts being used by investors.

Table 1 Holdings of the largest shareholders in Chinese listed companies

Largest shareholding	2002	2008
Above 50 per cent	40 per cent	20.8 per cent
Between 20 per cent and 50 per cent	52.6 per cent	64.9 per cent
Below 20 per cent	7.4 per cent	14.3 per cent

Sources: Lin Lefeng, *Zhongguo Shangshi Gongsi Guquan Jizhongdu Yanjiu [Research on the Level of Shareholding Concentration in Chinese Listed Companies]* (Beijing: Economic Management Press, 2005), 151; Deng Hui, 'Woguo Shanghai Gongsi Guquan Jizhong Moshi xia de Guquan Zhiheng Wenti' [Checks and Balances on the Controlling Shareholders under the Concentrated Ownership Structure of Chinese Listed Companies] (2008) 6 *Zhongguo Faxue [China Law Science]*, 145, 146.

According to a recent survey conducted by the Securities Association of China (SAC) and the China Securities Investor Protection Fund Company (CSIPFC),[25] most of these individual investors are middle-aged individuals or senior citizens, with an average age of 40 years. The majority of them (70 per cent) are on a low or middle income, and 35.2 per cent have an annual income below RMB 24,000 (US $3,582). Moreover, many Chinese individual investors may lack basic financial or investment knowledge, as about 45 per cent of them have no higher education.

1.4.3.2. Distribution of share ownership in listed companies

State ownership is very high in China's listed companies as a whole, generally representing two thirds of all shares of listed companies, as most listed companies have been transformed from SOE.

1.51

Since the late 1990s, the CSRC has been encouraging the growth of institutional investors as a strategic measure for the healthy development of China's capital markets. There are several different types of institutional investors, including securities investment funds, social security funds, annuities, insurance funds, securities firm funds, and qualified foreign institutional investors. There is evidence of a significant increase in institutional share ownership in China in recent years. As of the end of 2011, institutional investors altogether held about 73.45 per cent of tradable A-shares. However, since tradable A-shares account for only about one third of all Chinese shares, the figure for institutional holdings in total Chinese equities reduces to 24.48 per cent.[26] This is significantly lower than the proportion of equities held by their counterparts in the US and the UK, estimated at 52 per cent and 60 per cent respectively, as early as 1994.

1.52

---

[25] The Securities Association of China and the China Securities Investor Protection Fund Company, *Zhongguo Zhengquan Shichang Touzizhe Wenjuan Diaocha Fenxi Baogao [An Analytical Report on the Survey of Investors in China's Securities Markets]* (July 2007), 4.

[26] From the official website of the CSRC, http://www.csrc.gov.cn.

Introduction

1.53 At the level of the individual company, the share ownership structure has been found as follows:

As shown in the table 1, the percentage of companies whose largest shareholders have absolute control (more than 50 per cent shareholding) reduced from 40 per cent in 2002 to 20.8 per cent in 2008; the percentage with respect to relative controlling shareholders increased from 52.6 per cent to 64.9 per cent during the same period. The changes were the interim result of the shareholding structure reform launched by the CSRC in 2005. This suggests a transition from an absolute controlling shareholder model to a relative controlling shareholder model, but the overall level of ownership concentration in most Chinese listed companies remains high.

1.4.4. Policy market

1.54 The Chinese stock market was established by the government under its economic reform policy with the primary function of raising funds for financially distressed SOE. Ever since then, the government has painstakingly looked after the market in a paternalistic fashion. Hence, the Chinese stock market is the direct result of government policies, rather than a natural product of economic development as is the case in western countries. In practice, the government often directly intervenes in the market with administrative measures and policies. This role played by the government makes the market vulnerable to policies, which has led to its being called a 'policy market' (*Zhengce Shi*).

1.55 Indeed, market fluctuations in China are mostly caused by government policies. It is not uncommon that share prices have nothing to do with relevant corporate performance but are fairly sensitive to government policies. One study examining the major ups and downs of the market between 1991 and 1997 found that these movements were due not to economic factors but to material government policies.[27]

1.56 There is an interesting and peculiar method through which the government controls the development of the market in China. In the official government newspaper, the *People's Daily* (Renmin Ribao), the government often uses its editorials to exert an influence on the stock market. For instance, in response to the overheated market in 1996, the *People's Daily* published an editorial which bitterly criticized the mania of trading shares and pointed out that the market was full of irregularities and was too speculative.[28] As a result, the stock market slumped dramatically on three consecutive days. Likewise, after two years of a bear market, the *People's Daily* published another editorial to stimulate the market in 1999.[29]

---

[27] Liang Yang, *Neimu Jiaoyi Lun [Insider Trading]* (Beijing: Law Press, 2001).
[28] Editorial, 'Properly Viewing the Current Stock Market', *Renmin Ribao [People's Daily]* 15 December 1996, at 1.
[29] Editorial, 'Improving Confidence and Quickening Development', *Renmin Ribao [People's Daily]* 15 June 1999, at 1.

Not surprisingly, compared to the rule of law, government policies change more frequently and are much less predictable. In order to meet the needs of the rapidly growing market, the government has to change its policies correspondingly. One commentator has found at least 13 noticeable cases of the government directly interfering with the market before 2000, seven of which rescued and stimulated the market and the rest of which chilled and slowed it.[30] To a large degree, this situation remains today.

1.57

1.4.5. The gaming nature of the markets

The Chinese securities market, as an emerging market in a transitional economy, has one distinctive feature: that of being highly speculative. In 2001 Mr Wu Jinglian, a well-respected economist, compared the Chinese securities market to a casino, prompting hot debate on the way in which the Chinese securities market is run and regulated.[31] The gaming nature of the securities markets can be attributed to a host of cultural, social, economic, and political factors.

1.58

Compared to its more mature overseas counterparts, China's securities market has historically had a much higher P/E figure. The P/E figure in most developed stock markets is around 15–20, whereas in China it is about 45–55.[32] Such a high P/E means that share prices are generally far too high, departing considerably from the fundamentals of listed companies. Put differently, the intrinsic values of shares and share market prices have been disconnected and the pricing function of the market is ineffective. As the high P/E figure suggests, the market becomes flooded with speculative activities, which need to be expelled.

1.59

The high P/E figure's chilling effect on long-term investments is exacerbated by the fact that most listed companies in China do not distribute cash dividends, or if they do, they distribute them in a very low proportion to their already poor profits. Indeed, at present, most Chinese listed companies choose to give bonus shares (*Songgu*) instead of cash dividends to their shareholders. Thus, it is hard for investors to receive a return on their investments in the form of dividends, which leads them to trade shares in order to realize their gains.

1.60

As a consequence, the rate at which shares change hands on the Chinese stock market is significantly higher than that in its overseas counterparts. The high rate

1.61

---

[30] Zhiling Li, *Jiedu Zhongguo Gushi [Understand China's Stock Market]* (Shanghai: Sanlian Publishing House, 2002), 3.
[31] Tai Feng, 'It is Not Harsh to Describe the Market as a Casino', *Zhongguo Jingji Shibao [China Economic Times]* 15 February 2001, at 3; Jianjin Zhang, 'A Meaningful Debate on the Stock Market', *Jianghuai Chenbao [Jianghuai Morning]* 18 February 2001, at 3.
[32] In comparison, the P/E figure between China and overseas markets should not be taken at face value for a number of reasons, including the difference of sampling for calculation and the high proportion of non-tradable shares on China's market.

reflects the fact that Chinese investors enter the market in speculative mood and trade shares with a high frequency.

1.5. China and Global Financial Markets

1.5.1. The global financial crisis of 2008: implications for China

1.62 In China, the effects of the global financial crisis (GFC) have been severe, though certainly not quite as severe as in major overseas markets such as the US. The Chinese securities market was hard-hit during the GFC. The Shanghai Stock Exchange Composite Index slid from its peak of 6124 on 16 October 2007 all the way down to 1664 on 28 October 2008, representing a drop of 73 per cent in just one year.[33] This had the usual effect of forcing the CSRC to suspend the application of initial public offerings altogether for about ten months from September 2008, in a bid to prevent further market decline and panic.

1.63 Chinese financial firms were also reported to have suffered from the financial crisis. For instance, at the time that US investment bank Lehman Brothers filed for bankruptcy, the ICBC held a total of USD151.8 million in bonds of or related to Lehman; the Bank of China was reported to have extended USD50 million in credit to Lehman; and China Merchants Bank held USD70 million worth of bonds issued by Lehman. Moreover, significant losses have arisen from overseas equity investments by many Chinese companies. A prominent example is that Ping An, China's second largest life insurance company, cross-listed in Shanghai and Hong Kong, suffered a major loss of CNY 22.79 billion (roughly USD3.3 billion) from its ill-fated investment in the Belgian–Dutch financial group Fortis.

1.64 It should be noted that although China's financial markets and institutions have been affected by the GFC, the impact appears less direct and less severe than is the case with overseas markets. To date, the Chinese financial system as a whole has survived the crisis in relatively good shape: no major financial institutions have fallen and no major scandals over transactions of complex financial products have occurred. The losses suffered by Chinese financial institutions, as noted above, are essentially the consequence of their ill-fated investment in overseas markets rather than in domestic markets. Further, the overall risk exposure of China's financial institutions and listed companies in overseas markets is quite limited and manageable. For example, the above-mentioned Lehman bond investment by the ICBC accounted for just 0.03 per cent of its total bond portfolio and 0.01 per cent of its total assets. In short, the GFC has had only a limited impact on China's financial markets.[34]

---

[33] From the website of Shanghai Stock Exchange, http://www.sse.com.cn.
[34] Hui Huang, 'China's Legal Responses to the Global Financial Crisis: From Domestic Reform to International Engagement' (2010) 12(2) *Australian Journal of Asian Law* 157.

1.65 Although the impact of the GFC on China's financial system has been relatively mild, one would be wrong to believe, in considering the relatively good health of the Chinese financial markets throughout the financial storm, that China's financial regulatory system is advanced and problem-free. Rather, a closer examination reveals the irony that the positive functioning of China's financial system in this financial crisis is largely attributable to its lack of sophistication and its isolation from the global economy.

1.66 To begin with, the Chinese financial markets are still underdeveloped. At present, the financial products traded on the Chinese financial markets are quite limited and the technology of securitization is yet to become widely used. There are some traditional financial derivatives in China, such as options and warrants, but they are far lower in number than those found in overseas markets and far less sophisticated than their overseas counterparts, such as collateralized debt obligations (CDOs), collateralized loan obligations (CLOs), and synthetic CDOs. As securitization and complex financial instruments have been identified as one of the core causes of the current financial crisis, it is not hard to understand why China's financial system has not suffered any home-grown problems.

1.67 In addition, the Chinese financial system's isolation from the outside world has helped to stop the effects of the financial crisis flowing on to China. Although China has worked to open up its financial markets since its accession to the WTO, this process is gradual, cautious, and ongoing. For the time being, foreigners have only limited access to the Chinese financial markets. For example, foreign investors cannot trade in China's stock market except through several designated means, such as the QFII method. Further, the Chinese government still exerts tight control over its currency policy. For instance, there are restrictions on capital accounts; the Chinese currency, the RMB or CNY, is not fully convertible yet; the exchange rate is set within a managed floating range. All these measures have collectively operated as a firewall to insulate China's financial system from the spills of the financial crisis overseas.

1.68 China can take some comfort from the fact that its financial system has sustained relatively modest losses in the current financial crisis; however, it should not be overjoyed about its lucky escape and overlook the real problems it faces. Indeed, the financial crisis has clearly exposed that China has lagged behind the rest of the world in terms of financial innovation and modernization.

1.69 China's financial system cannot afford to remain primitive and closed to the outside world forever. The techniques of securitization and financial derivatives, if used and regulated properly, can make the market more efficient and effective. In fact, China has successfully used securitization, on a trial basis, to deal with its massive amount of non-performing loans in the banking sector. Although securitization has the potential to be abused, it remains an ingenious financial innovation capable of performing important economic functions. This is particularly so for

Introduction

China, where the banks still have a relatively high level of bad loans and the home mortgage market is huge and rapidly growing. It would seem to follow that China will not—nor should it—abandon efforts at financial innovation in the face of the GFC. China is thus best advised to further develop its financial markets by introducing those financial tools while at the same time strengthening its regulatory system to avoid abuse.

1.5.2. Shanghai: toward a new global financial centre

1.70 China is now the world's second largest economy, but its financial system is nowhere close to this ranking. According to the recent Global Financial Centers Index, which ranks the competitiveness of financial centres, Mainland China does not have a centre in the top 20: Shanghai ranks 21st and Shenzhen 30th, compared to the third place Hong Kong occupies.[35] Clearly, China needs to develop a more efficient financial system, with at least one or two world-class financial centres, to support its continued economic growth.

1.71 On 25 March 2009, the Chinese central government approved a programme proposed by the Shanghai municipal government to build Shanghai into a major global financial centre by 2010.[36] Under the 12th Five-Year Plan of Financial Industry Development and Reform, one of the key tasks is to accelerate the development of Shanghai as a global financial centre.[37] With strong governmental support at both the national and local levels, the financial services industry in Shanghai has made rapid progress in recent years. In fact, as early as 2001, Shanghai surpassed Hong Kong in terms of stock market capitalization, though this was subsequently reversed. And in 2007, Shanghai replaced Hong Kong as the world's largest centre for initial public offerings.

1.72 There has been ongoing debate as to how Shanghai will rise as China's global financial centre and how Hong Kong should respond to this. For a long time, Hong Kong has served as a powerful financing source for Mainland companies, which has in turn helped Hong Kong maintain its status as one of the leading financial centres in the world. The emergence of Shanghai as a financial centre is seen by many as a direct threat to Hong Kong. In this regard, Shanghai and Hong Kong both have competitive advantages. For Shanghai, the key advantages include the powerful underlying national economy and strong Chinese government support. Hong Kong, on the other hand, also has its own advantages, the most important

---

[35] The ranking is an aggregate of indices from five key areas: people, business environment, market access, infrastructure, and general competitiveness. It is compiled and published twice a year by Z/Yen Group, which is a commercial think-tank, consultancy, and venture firm headquartered in the City of London. For more details, see http://www.zyen.com/activities/gfci.html.

[36] Zhang Ran, 'Shanghai Aims at International Financial and Shipping Center', *China Daily* (26 March 2009).

[37] People's Bank of China et al, *12th Five-Year Plan of Financial Industry Development and Reform* (17 September 2012), 32.

of which are rule of law, a free market economy, and integration into the Chinese economy under the 'One Country, Two Systems' arrangement.

1.73 However, the relationship between Shanghai and Hong Kong should have more options than simply competition. A big country such as China could and should have more than one global financial centre—considering that the US has several financial centres, including New York, Chicago, Boston, San Francisco, and Washington DC, all of which are ranked in the top 20 in the recent Global Financial Centers Index. This is particularly so in China's current context of political economy. Hong Kong is uniquely positioned to act as a gateway to China, whose financial market is still quite restricted in many aspects with regard to the rest of the world due to issues such as foreign exchange control. The Chinese government's recent support for Hong Kong's development into an offshore RMB centre is a good example of the complementary relationship Hong Kong can have with financial centres in the Mainland.

2

FINANCIAL REGULATORY FRAMEWORK

2.1. Introduction	2.01	2.3.2. Resource constraints and regulatory capture	2.48
2.2. The Current Financial Regulatory Structure	2.03	2.3.3. Challenges of financial modernization and innovation	2.55
2.2.1. Central banking	2.06	2.4. The Future of China's Financial Regulatory Framework	2.60
2.2.2. Banking Regulation	2.12		
2.2.3. Insurance regulation	2.19	2.4.1. Major structural models of financial regulation	2.61
2.2.4. Securities regulation	2.22		
2.3. Characteristics and Problems	2.39	2.4.2. The way forward for China	2.66
2.3.1. Lack of regulatory independence	2.39	2.5. Conclusion	2.85

2.1. Introduction

2.01 This chapter examines the legal and institutional regulatory framework for China's financial markets, and evaluates how China may need to restructure its regulatory regime in order to keep up with market developments.

2.02 It first provides a detailed discussion of the current Chinese financial regulatory framework. In light of the recent global financial crisis that began in 2008, this chapter identifies several major structural problems of the Chinese regulatory regime. It then conducts a comparative analysis of financial regulatory structure in overseas jurisdictions, as well as a contextual consideration of China's local conditions, with a view to setting forward an appropriate agenda for reform of China's financial regulatory structure.

2.2. The Current Financial Regulatory Structure

2.03 The current financial regulatory structure in China has the defining feature of being sector-based. As the central bank, the PBC assumes responsibility for monetary policy and the stability of the financial system generally. The CBRC, the CSRC, and the China Insurance Regulatory Commission (CIRC) are the authorities responsible for regulating the banking, securities, and insurance sectors respectively. These regulatory bodies will be examined in detail later in the chapter.

It should be noted however that certain other government agencies also perform important regulatory functions in the financial markets. For instance, the Ministry of Finance has the authority to make strategic and policy decisions on finance and taxation, set accounting standards, and issue treasury bonds; the National Development and Reform Commission is empowered to approve the issuance of enterprise bonds and get involved in making financial and monetary policies; and the National Audit Office has responsibility to audit the financial accounts of state-owned banks, securities firms, and insurance companies. It is worth noting that the above government agencies, along with the PBC, the CBRC, the CSRC, and the CIRC, are all ranked equally under the direct leadership of the State Council.[1]

Apart from governmental agencies, there exist a variety of self-regulatory organizations (SROs) which are subject to the regulatory oversight of the relevant governmental regulatory agencies and have varying levels of responsibility for their respective markets and the conduct of their members. These include the China Banking Association (CBA), Insurance Association of China (IAC), Securities Association of China (SAC), China Futures Association (CFA), and China Trustee Association (CTA). In addition, the market operators, including the two stock exchanges and the four futures exchanges, play an important self-regulatory role, subject to the oversight of the CSRC.

2.2.1. Central banking

2.2.1.1. People's Bank of China (PBC)

The PBC is the central bank in the People's Republic of China (China), a role legally confirmed by the Law of PRC on the People's Bank of China (PBC Law).[2] Pursuant to the PBC Law, the PBC must formulate and implement monetary policies, guard against financial risks and maintain financial stability under the leadership of the State Council.[3]

As with most central banks in the world, the PBC has a threefold role as the currency-issuing bank, the bank of banks, and the government bank. More specifically, the PBC performs the following functions: (1) promulgating and implementing orders and regulations in relation to its functions; (2) formulating and implementing monetary policies in accordance with the law; (3) issuing the Chinese

---

[1] Guowuyuan Guanyu Jigou Shezhi de Tongzhi [Notice on the Institutional Structure of the State Council] (promulgated by the State Council on 21 March 2008).
[2] Zhonghua Renmin Gongheguo Zhongguo Renmin Yinhang Fa [The Law of PRC on the People's Bank of China] (adopted at the 3rd session of the Standing Committee of the 8th National People's Congress of the PRC on 18 March 1995, amended on 27 December 2003), Art 2.
[3] PBC Law, Art 2.

currency, namely Renminbi (RMB), and controlling its circulation; (4) supervising the interbank borrowing or lending markets and interbank bonds markets; (5) administering foreign exchange and supervising the interbank foreign exchange market; (6) supervising the gold market; (7) holding, controlling, and managing the state foreign exchange reserve and gold reserve; (8) managing the state treasury; (9) maintaining the normal operation of the systems for payments and settlements of accounts; (10) directing and disposing the anti-money-laundering work of the financial industry, being responsible for capital supervision and measurement over anti-money-laundering measures; (11) being responsible for statistics, investigation, analysis, and forecasting of the financial industry; (12) undertaking the relevant international banking operations as the central bank of the state; and (13) other functions assigned to it by the State Council.[4]

2.08 As noted earlier, in 2003, the PBC was divested of its direct banking supervisory powers. These powers were transferred to the newly established CBRC in order to provide the PBC with the necessary independence to implement the nation's monetary policy. The PBC now seeks to stabilize the currency and the financial system by indirect, macroeconomic means rather than through a direct, interventionist approach as was the case in the planned economy era. It therefore exercises macroeconomic control over the financial markets primarily through a range of monetary tools such as deposit reserves, rediscount rates, interest rates, and open market operations.

2.2.1.2. Exchange rate

2.09 The Chinese currency, the Renminbi or yuan, had long been fixed to the US dollar, but on 21 July 2005 China introduced the so-called managed floating mechanism of exchange rate. Under this mechanism, China allows its currency to float within a managed range. At the same time, the fixed peg to the US dollar is replaced with a basket of currencies of China's major trading partners. Since then, the Chinese current has appreciated by about 25–30 per cent against the US dollar. The appreciation of the Chinese currency has had significant impact on, among other things, its financial markets.

2.2.1.3. Interest rate

2.10 Historically, China has adopted the policy of interest rate control, under which the PBC as the central bank sets the base interest rates and commercial banks cannot freely depart from the official rates. One of the consequences of this policy is that there is limited scope for banks to compete by way of interest rates, and thus the banking industry as a whole can easily make profits from the traditional business of lending. Indeed, Chinese banks' main source of revenue is the spread between

---

[4] PBC Law, Art 4. It should be noted that the State Administration of Foreign Exchange is a government agency under the leadership of the PBC, and it acts as the implementation branch of the PBC in relation to foreign exchange administration and supervision.

its average borrowing and lending rates. The net interest rate income of Chinese banks generally accounts for more than 80 per cent of their total revenue, while this figure is less than 60 per cent for banks in developed economies.[5] This means Chinese banks rely too heavily on the traditional business of lending and need more fee-based income.

As the financial reform deepens, interest rate liberalization has been listed as one of the reform priorities. Since 2004, deposit and loan interest rate control has been gradually relaxed. On the one hand, the loan rate was allowed to fluctuate within 10 per cent of the official rate in 2004, increased to 20 per cent in June 2012 30 per cent in July 2012, and at last freely in July 2013; on the other, 10 per cent fluctuation was allowed in the deposit rate for the first time in June 2012. The process of interest rate liberalization will undoubtedly lead to greater competition among banks and thus a smaller spread between borrowing and lending rates, making it more difficult for banks to make money through their traditional lending business. Given Chinese banks' heavy reliance on net interest rate income, the liberalization process is seen as—in the words of the president of the Merchant Bank—'a life or death test for China's banking industry'.[6] 2.11

2.2.2. Banking regulation

2.2.2.1. China Banking Regulatory Commission (CBRC)

In 2003, the CBRC came into existence as the banking 'watchdog', taking over the role previously performed by the PBC. The legal and regulatory framework for banking regulation comprises the Law of the PRC on Commercial Banks[7] and the Law of the PRC on Banking Regulation and Supervision.[8] Like its peers in the securities and insurance markets, the CBRC is a ministry rank unit under the direct leadership of the State Council. 2.12

The main objectives of the CBRC as banking regulator are to: (1) promote the lawful, smooth, and sound operations of the banking industry, and maintain the confidence of the general public in the banking industry; (2) ensure fair competition in the banking market and improve the competiveness of the banking industry.[9] It should be noted that the CBRC regulates not only banks, but also a variety of specified non-bank financial institutions. The former group covers those banks 2.13

---

[5] Website of the CBRC, http://www.cbrc.gov.cn.
[6] 'Ma Weihua: Interest Rate Liberalization is a Life or Death Test for China's Banking Industry' *Jinrong Shibao* [*Financial Times*], 7 August 2012.
[7] Zhonghua Renmin Gongheguo Shangye Yinhang Fa [Law of the PRC on Commercial Banks] (adopted at the 13th session of the Standing Committee of the 8th National People's Congress of the PRC on 10 May 1995, amended on 27 December 2003).
[8] Zhonghua Renmin Gongheguo Yinhangye Jiandu Guanli Fa [Law of the PRC on Banking Regulation and Supervision (Banking Regulation and Supervision Law)] (adopted at the 6th session of the Standing Committee of the 10th National People's Congress of the PRC on 27 December 2003, amended on 31 October 2006).
[9] Banking Regulation and Supervision Law, Art 3.

Introduction

discussed in Chapter 1, such as commercial banks, policy banks, urban/rural credit unions, and other financial institutions engaged in taking deposits from the general public. The latter group includes financial asset management companies, trust investment companies, financing companies, financial lease companies, and other financial institutions established with the approval of the CBRC.[10] As trust investment companies are subject to CBRC regulation, approval is needed for the establishment of private equity funds which usually take the legal structure of trust.

2.14 In its regulatory role under the relevant law, the CBRC is responsible for both market conduct regulation and prudential regulation. Under Article 16 of the Law of the PRC on Banking Regulation and Supervision, the CBRC is responsible for the examination and approval of the establishment, modifications, termination, and operational scope of the financial institutions it regulates.[11] Article 18 provides that certain types of financial operation, as prescribed by the rules of the CBRC, need to be examined and approved by the CBRC before the financial institutions can carry out those operations.[12] Under Article 21, the CBRC has powers to make and enforce rules regarding prudential regulation.[13] In this way the CBRC exercises its supervisory function through prudential standards such as asset/liability ratio requirement, capital adequacy ratio, and risk management, as opposed to the more interventionist means, such as imposition of loan quotas, used under the planned economy.

2.2.2.2. Regulatory issues: non-performing loans

2.15 In general, the CBRC has done a great job of supervising China's banking industry in a relatively short period of time. In 2003, when the CBRC was established, China's banking industry was described as 'technically bankrupt', with the non-performing loans (NPL) of the 'Big Four' state-owned banks amounting to 17.9 per cent of all loans; before 1998, this figure was as high as 25 per cent.

2.16 In recognition of this issue, in 2003 the Chinese government established Central Huijin Investment Ltd (Central Huijin), which is wholly state-owned and authorized by the State Council to exercise rights and obligations as an investor in major state-owned financial enterprises on behalf of the State. Through Central Huijin, money from China's foreign exchange reserve was injected into the then financially ailing banks. Moreover, a total amount of about CYN 1.19 trillion worth of NPLs from the state-owned banks were spun off to four financial asset management companies: Xinda, Huarong, Changcheng, and Dongfang. These measures combined to have the effect of bringing the banks' capital adequacy ratio in line with

---

[10] Banking Regulation and Supervision Law, Art 2.
[11] Banking Regulation and Supervision Law, Art 16.
[12] Banking Regulation and Supervision Law, Art 18.
[13] Banking Regulation and Supervision Law, Art 21.

the regulatory standard of 8 per cent. After this exercise, the banks were required to operate on a market-oriented basis and their regulation improved progressively.

2.17 In the face of rapid changes in the financial markets, the CBRC's regulatory strategy is to adhere to clear prudential supervisory policies and focus on traditional indicators, such as capital adequacy ratio (CAR), large items of risk exposure, rate of non-performing assets, and provisioning adequacy and coverage. This has resulted in significant improvement in key aspects of China's banking industry, including quality of assets and risk resilience. For instance, the CAR of all commercial banks in China increased to 13.25 per cent in 2012, up from minus 2.98 per cent at the end of 2003; the NPL rate, meanwhile, has been declining steadily, from 17.9 per cent in 2003 to 0.95 per cent in 2012.[14]

2.18 Despite the remarkable achievements outlined above, some worrying problems loom for Chinese banking regulation. One of the major sources of bank loan risk is the high volume of housing mortgages. As China's housing market has continued to develop at a rapid rate in the past decade, so has the demand for mortgages, giving rise to a sharp increase in the ratio of housing loans to all bank loans to a level widely judged to be too high for the safety of the banks. The problem is exacerbated by the increasing bubble in the housing market. The government has been trying to cool the overheated property market with a series of measures, such as a tightened housing loan policy and a limit on the number of properties one can buy in the same city. This may cause significant housing price fluctuations, which in turn will put pressure on the balance sheets of Chinese banks. Mr Liu MinKang, the former Chairperson of the CBRC, has expressed concern that after a steady decrease in the bad loan rate since 2003, bad loans may start to grow in the years ahead.[15]

2.2.3. Insurance regulation

2.19 Against the backdrop of the fast-growing insurance market, the regulatory regime has been reformed over the years. The CIRC was set up in 1998 to assume regulatory responsibility for the insurance industry in China under the Insurance Law of the PRC.[16] The principal duties and responsibilities of the CIRC are to supervise and administer the insurance sector in accordance with the principles of legality, openness, and fairness, with the aim of maintaining the order of the insurance market and protecting the legitimate rights and interests of insurance purchasers, insurants, and beneficiaries.

---

[14] Website of the CBRC, http://www.cbrc.gov.cn.
[15] For more discussion of Chinese banks' non-performing loans, see Hui Huang, 'China's Legal Responses to the Global Financial Crisis: From Domestic Reform to International Engagement' (2010) 12(2) *Australian Journal of Asian Law* 157.
[16] Zhonghua Renmin Gongheguo Baoxian Fa (Insurance Law of the PRC (Insurance Law)) (adopted at the 14th session of the Standing Committee of the 8th National People's Congress of the People's Republic of China on 30 June 1995, amended 28 October 2002 and 28 February 2009), Art 9.

2.20 As with the CBRC, the CIRC is charged with both market conduct regulation and prudential regulation in relation to insurance companies. The Insurance Law of the PRC devotes a whole chapter to the making and enforcement of insurance contracts.[17] In China, life insurance is separated from property insurance, and thus one insurance company cannot conduct both concurrently.[18] The CIRC is also tasked with licensing and regulating insurance agents and brokers to make sure that financial intermediaries operate in a fair and efficient manner.

2.21 On the prudential regulation front, the CIRC needs to ensure the compliance of insurance companies with various prudential requirements, including the requirement to draw guarantee funds, liability reserve funds, capital reserves, and insurance protection funds. In addition, the CIRC is required to set up and improve a system to monitor the solvency of insurance companies. Particular regulatory attention will be paid to those insurance companies whose ability to pay indemnity is regarded as inadequate, and the CIRC has power to take a variety of measures to deal with the issue, such as ordering an increase of capital or reinsurance; limiting the scope of business; restricting the payment of dividends to shareholders; restricting the purchase of fixed assets or the scale of operation costs; and restricting the salary level of directors, supervisors, and senior managers.[19]

2.2.4. Securities regulation

2.2.4.1. *China Securities Regulatory Commission (CSRC)*

2.22 The legal and regulatory framework for the securities market in China is largely based on the Securities Law of the PRC (Securities Law).[20] Established in 1992 and upgraded in 1998, the CSRC is, as previously noted, the oldest of the three industry-specific regulatory bodies in the financial markets. Since then, the CSRC has assumed responsibility for securities regulation in China. It should be noted that the coverage of the Securities Law and therefore the authority of the CSRC is so broad as to include the regulation of shares, corporate bonds, treasury bonds, securities investment funds, and derivative products such as futures contracts, options, and warrants.[21] Thus, in terms of regulatory area, the CSRC is roughly equivalent to a combination of the Securities and Exchange Commission (SEC) and the Commodity Futures Trading Commission (CFTC) in the US. However,

---

[17] Insurance Law, Ch 2.
[18] Insurance Law, Art 95.
[19] Insurance Law, Art 139.
[20] Zhonghua Renming Gongheguo Zhengquanfa (Securities Law of the PRC (Securities Law)) (promulgated by the 6th session of the Standing Committee of the 9th National People's Congress of the PRC on 29 December 1998 and effective from 1 July 1999, amended in 2004, 2005, and 2013).
[21] Securities Law, Art 2.

the CSRC's regulatory territory is narrower than that of its Australian counterpart, namely the Australian Securities and Investment Commission, which acts as both securities regulator and corporate regulator.

2.23 The principal function of the CSRC is to 'carry out supervision and administration of the securities market according to law so as to preserve the order of the securities market and ensure the legitimate operations thereof'.[22] More precisely, the CSRC performs the following regulatory duties: (1) formulating relevant rules and regulations on supervision and administration of the securities market and exercising the power of examination or verification according to law; (2) carrying out supervision and administration of the issuance, listing, trading, registration, custody, and settlement of securities according to law; (3) carrying out supervision and administration of the securities activities of securities issuers, listed companies, stock exchanges, securities companies, securities registration and clearing institutions, securities investment fund management companies, and securities trading service institutions according to law; (4) formulating the standards for securities practice qualification and code of conduct and carrying out supervision and implementation according to law; (5) carrying out supervision and examination of information disclosure regarding the issuance, listing, and trading of securities; (6) offering guidance for and carrying out supervision of the activities of the securities industrial associations according to law; (7) investigating and punishing any violation of any law or administrative regulation regarding the supervision and administration of the securities market according to law; and (8) performing any other functions and duties as prescribed by any law or administrative regulation.[23]

2.24 In discharging its duties, the CSRC has a number of important semi-legislative, investigative, and adjudicative powers. First, it is empowered to make relevant rules and regulations. Second, it can take a range of investigative measures. For instance, it has power to undertake on-the-spot examination of securities intermediaries; to enter into the place of occurrence of misconduct to investigate and collect evidence; to question the parties concerned or any entity or individual relating to a case, requiring them to give explanations on relevant matters; to examine the capital account, security account, or bank account of any relevant party concerned in or any entity or individual relating to a case under investigation; to freeze or seal up relevant assets and/or evidence which is in jeopardy of dissipation, waste, or improper removal, with the approval of the responsible officer of the CSRC; to restrict the securities transactions of the parties concerned in a case under investigation when investigating any major securities irregularity such as manipulation of the securities market or insider trading, with the approval of the responsible officer of the CSRC.

---

[22] Securities Law, Art 178.
[23] Securities Law, Art 179.

2.25 It is remarkable that, unlike its counterparts in many overseas jurisdictions, the CSRC can take the above investigative measures as deemed necessary without the need to apply to the court. In fact, before the 2005 revision of the Securities Law, the CSRC was required to apply to courts to take those measures. However, this mechanism was proven ineffective, because in practice the courts always failed to efficiently respond to the application of the CSRC, due to factors such as the following: (1) localism—courts at local levels are generally amenable to local governments, who often protect their listed companies from the CSRC; (2) endemic judiciary corruption; and (3) red tape and bureaucracy. This situation made it very difficult for the CSRC to carry out its investigative work and thus the 2005 Securities Law empowers the CSRC to take those measures on its own.

2.26 The CSRC, according to the results of an investigation, can decide to impose administrative sanctions for relevant securities irregularity. The usual weapons in the CSRC's arsenal include warning, fine, suspension, and cancellation of licences. Further, the CSRC can issue a barring order (*shichang jinru*), under which a person is prohibited from undertaking any securities practice or holding any post as director, supervisor, or senior manager of a listed company within a prescribed term or for life. Finally, if the case is serious enough to warrant criminal sanction, the CSRC will refer the case to the procuratorate to bring criminal charges.

2.27 As an administrative body, the CSRC's administrative decisions on various issues such as securities offerings and administrative punishment are subject to administrative review (*xingzheng fuyi*) and administrative litigation (*xingzheng susong*). As the CSRC is a very powerful agency, bringing administrative litigation to challenge the CSRC is certainly not a decision to be taken lightly by market participants.

2.28 The first administrative litigation against the CSRC did not come until 2000, involving a company named Hannan Kaili (Kaili). The CSRC rejected Kaili's application for securities offering on the grounds that Kaili's financial reports were fraudulent. More importantly, Kaili was barred from reapplying in future. In light of this life ban, Kaili had nothing to lose and thus decided to take the CSRC to court. The court of first instance, namely the First Intermediate Court of Beijing, held on 18 December 2000 that the CSRC's decision to impose a life ban on Kaili had no legal basis and that the issue of whether Kaili's financial reports were fraudulent should be decided by professionals. The CSRC appealed to the High Court of Beijing and on 5 July 2001, the judgment of the court of first instance was affirmed. This case has had far-reaching implications for Chinese securities regulation, in that it acted as a check on the CSRC.

2.2.4.2. Stock exchanges

2.29 Self-regulation by stock exchanges is a necessary and important supplement to governmental regulation by the CSRC. The two stock exchanges in Shanghai and

Shenzhen are assigned the role of front-line regulator in the respective markets they operate.

2.30 More specifically, the securities exchanges can make and enforce their rules, such as listing rules and business rules;[24] they have discretion concerning the admission of an entity to the official list (and its removal) and quotation of its securities (and their suspension).[25] Further, the securities exchanges shall exercise the real-time monitoring of securities trading and report certain abnormal trading to the CSRC; they also need to carry out supervision over information disclosure by listed companies or relevant disclosing entities, so as to ensure information is disclosed in a timely and accurate manner.[26]

2.31 It is important to note that the securities exchanges are subject to the oversight of the CSRC. The CSRC supervises and monitors the activities of securities exchanges, approves their constitutions and amendments,[27] approves their operating rules and amendments,[28] and administers and enforces the relevant applicable legislation.[29]

2.32 The stock exchanges perform their front-line regulatory functions principally through the promulgation and enforcement of operating rules, which include, but are not limited to, listing rules (*shangshi guize*) and trading rules (*jiaoyi guize*). The trading rules basically regulate the machinery of stock exchange transactions and the conduct of securities business by market participants. The provisions are internal to the stock exchange, relating to issues such as prudential controls and supervision over member organizations, as well as the clearing and settlement of dealings.

2.33 The listing rules, on the other hand, mainly govern the admission of companies to the official lists maintained by the stock exchanges and the conduct of companies whose securities are granted quotation. The provisions specify criteria for companies to be listed and impose continuing obligations, particularly with regard to disclosure, upon listed companies. The listing rules can set out more stringent requirements than those prescribed by the Securities Law for quotation of securities on the stock exchanges.[30]

2.34 If a person who is under an obligation to comply with the stock exchange's operating rules fails to meet the obligation, the stock exchange can take relevant measures, including notices of criticism (*tongbao piping*), public censure (*gongkai qianze*),

---

[24] Securities Law, Art 118.
[25] Securities Law, Arts 48, 55, 56. Before the 2005 amendment to the Securities Law, the CSRC had the power (or delegate the power to securities exchanges) to decide on matters relating to listing, trading suspension and delisting.
[26] Securities Law, Art 115.
[27] Securities Law, Art 103.
[28] Securities Law, Art 118.
[29] Securities Law, Arts 116, 117 (providing that securities exchanges must draw a risk fund and deposit it into a special bank account).
[30] For more discussion of this, see Chapter 4.

Introduction

and disqualification of individuals from serving as directors, senior managers, and secretaries of the board of directors.[31] As notices of criticism and public censure are reputational sanctions in nature and are not backed by legal liabilities, it is not entirely clear how effective they are.[32] However, there are more powerful weapons in the arsenal of the stock exchange. For instance, in the case that a listed company breaches the listing rules, the stock exchange has power to suspend quotation of the company's securities or even remove the company from the official list.[33]

2.35 An interesting issue here is whether the decisions of the stock exchange, particularly those relating to admission, suspension, and removal of a company to the official list, are subject to judicial review. Under the Chinese legal system, administrative litigation can be brought against specific illegal administrative acts such as licensing decisions and penalty decisions made by administrative bodies.

2.36 According to a judicial interpretation issued by the Supreme People's Court of the PRC in 2005, the stock exchange may be subject to either civil or administrative litigation for acts in relation to its regulatory functions, including decisions towards securities issuers and the relevant personnel thereof or stock exchange members and the relevant personnel thereof, or regarding the listing of securities and transaction activities.[34] The judicial interpretation does not, however, provide clear guidance on what acts of stock exchanges give rise to what kinds of litigation. Further, it is stated:

> The people's court shall not accept the lawsuits brought by investors against stock exchanges due to their acts upon securities issuers or the relevant personnel thereof, stock exchange members or the relevant personnel thereof, or regarding the listing of securities or transaction activities, which are conducted in the process of their implementation of regulatory duties but do not *directly* impact on the investors' interests.[35]

2.37 On one view, the above provision suggests that investors cannot sue, either civilly or administratively, against decisions made by stock exchanges in relation to securities listing, trading suspension, and delisting. But the validity of this view depends on how to interpret the phrase 'do not *directly* impact on the investors' interests'. Indeed, it could be argued that listing decisions have a direct bearing on investors. Thus, the Chinese law is quite ambiguous on this important issue. An

---

[31] See eg Shanghai Stock Exchange Listing Rules, Ch 17.
[32] An empirical study suggests that Shenzhen Stock Exchange has used the measure of public criticism more often than Shanghai Stock Exchange, and overall the measure seems to be effective. See Benjamin L Liebman and Curtis J Milhaupt, 'Reputational Sanctions in China's Securities Market' (2008) 108 *Columbia Law Review* 929.
[33] For more discussion of this, see Chapter 5.
[34] Guanyu dui yu Zhengquan Jiaoyisuo Jianguan Zhineng Xiangguan de Susong Anjian Guanxia yu Shouli Wenti de Guiding [Rules on the Jurisdiction and Acceptance of Cases Relating to the Regulatory Function of Stock Exchanges] (issued by the Supreme People's Court in 2005) (SPC Rules on Stock Exchanges), Arts 1, 2.
[35] SPC Rules on Stock Exchanges, Art 3 (emphasis added).

empirical study by this author has not found any case against listing decisions of stock exchanges by way of administrative litigation in China.

2.38 This is actually a subject of international debate, which depends essentially on the nature of stock exchanges and the listing rules they issue. In many overseas jurisdictions, judicial reviews are usually not conducted with regard to stock exchanges' enforcement of their listing rules, because stock exchanges are considered private bodies; listing rules are seen as contractual arrangements between the listed company and the stock exchange, not as administrative acts. The international experience may not be readily applicable in China, however, given the special nature of the Chinese securities market, and in particular the quasi-administrative role of stock exchanges there. It thus remains debatable whether China's stock exchanges exercise powers of administrative character and thus should be subject to judicial review.

2.3. Characteristics and Problems

2.3.1. Lack of regulatory independence

2.39 Lack of regulatory independence is a long-standing issue plaguing financial regulation in China. Although the PBC Law seeks to preserve some measure of independence for the PBC, it is in essence a ministry-ranking constituent department directly under the leadership of the State Council—the Chinese central government. The PBC has one governor and a certain number of deputy governors. The governor of the PBC is appointed or removed by the President of the PRC upon nomination by the Premier of the State Council and also with approval from the National People's Congress. Whereas the National People's Congress is not in session, he or she should be affirmed by the Standing Committee of the National People's Congress. But the deputy governors of the PBC are appointed or removed directly by the Premier of the State Council.[36] The PBC is required to submit working reports to the Standing Committee of the National People's Congress.[37]

2.40 The lack of independence of the PBC from the central government is further illustrated in the way it performs its functions: under the PBC Law, the PBC shall, *under the leadership of the State Council*, independently implement monetary policies, perform its functions, and carry out its operations according to law free from any intervention of local governments, departments of governments at all levels, public organizations, or individuals.[38] Article 5 of the PBC Law further provides that the PBC must obtain the approval of the State Council before it is able to take

---

[36] PBC Law, Art 10.
[37] PBC Law, Art 6.
[38] PBC Law, Art 7.

actions on certain important matters such as the annual supply of currency, interest rates, and foreign exchange rates.[39]

2.41 The three specialist regulatory commissions, namely the CBRC, the CSRC, and the CIRC, may have even less independence from the government. Take the CBRC as an example. To begin with, the CBRC is formally an instrument of the central government and is subject to the direct leadership of the State Council. In the relevant law, the CBRC is referred to as 'the banking supervision institution of the State Council'.[40] All the chairpersons of the CBRC are appointed by the State Council and are accountable to the Premier. This is also the case with the CSRC and CIRC.

2.42 Second, the authority of the CBRC is further undermined due to the role of the state in the financial markets. As previously discussed, the Chinese financial system exhibits a high degree of concentration, with state ownership taking a dominating position. Traditionally, the State Council appoints the presidents and other senior officers of the Big Four state-owned banks. Those people have a dual role: on the one hand, they are businesspersons in the sense that they work in the industry; on the other, they are government staff in the sense that they still have relevant administrative ranks and are subject to the administrative system. Simply put, they are quasi-governmental officials, and may even rank equally with the Chairman of the CBRC in the hierarchy of China's administrative system. This feature largely remains even after those banks started to undertake reform and went public over the past several years, as the state is still able to appoint senior officers of banks in its capacity as the controlling shareholder. This has affected the authority of the CBRC vis-à-vis the major state-owned/controlled banks it regulates. Given that the securities and insurance markets are less influential than the banking sector, the above 'too big to regulate' problem is less severe, but nevertheless exists to a certain extent.

2.43 The strong position and governmental background enjoyed by the presidents of state-owned banks has also caused corporate governance problems. On the surface, the state-owned banks have put in place relevant corporate organs in accordance with modern corporate governance requirements, but the practical effects of those mechanisms are far from satisfactory. For instance, the risk management department and the audit department are supposed to be accountable to the risk management committee and the audit committee established under the board of directors. In reality, however, the two departments must first report to the president, and the relevant information can only reach the board of directors after it has been screened and approved by the president. Needless to say, without relevant

---

[39] PBC Law, Art 5.
[40] Zhonghua Renmin Gongheguo Yinhangye Jiandu Guanli Fa [Law of the PRC on Banking Regulation and Supervision] (adopted at the 6th session of the Standing Committee of the 10th National People's Congress of the PRC on 27 December 2003, amended on 31 October 2006), Art 2.

Financial Regulatory Framework

reliable information, the board of directors is not able to effectively perform its monitoring role.

2.44 Moreover, the issue of lack of independence is manifested in the relationship between the governmental regulators and self-regulatory bodies. Indeed, although securities exchanges are referred to as self-regulatory legal persons and are given a range of self-regulatory powers, they are not suitably structured and constituted so as to ensure an adequate level of independence.

2.45 The two stock exchanges in Shanghai and Shenzhen are both membership-based mutual organizations, and the right to trade upon the exchange is confined to brokers who have been admitted to exchange membership.[41] Under the Securities Law, the securities exchange shall have a council,[42] and it is further clarified that the council is the decision-making organ of the securities exchange.[43] The council of a stock exchange consists of 7–13 persons, with the number of non-membership council members being no less than one third but no more than one half of the total of the council members. The membership council members shall be elected by the membership congress and the non-membership council members shall be appointed by the CSRC.[44] This has meant that the CSRC can appoint up to half of the members of the council of the securities exchange.

2.46 Further, the council shall have a president and one or two vice-presidents, all of whom shall be elected by the council upon the nomination of the CSRC.[45] In other words, the CSRC exerts control over who can become presidents and vice-presidents of securities exchanges. Finally, a stock exchange shall have one general manager and one to three deputy general managers. The general manager and deputy managers are appointed and dismissed by the CSRC.[46] The appointment and dismissal of middle-level officers of the stock exchanges shall be registered with the CSRC for record-keeping purposes, but the appointment and dismissal of the heads of departments of finance and personnel need the approval of the CSRC.[47]

2.47 In short, the CSRC has a tight grip over the personnel of all ranks in securities exchanges, from council presidents to council members and from general managers to mid-level officers. This makes a mockery of the members' meeting of

---

[41] This is in contrast with the international trend of stock exchange demutualization and self-delisting. In 1998, the Australian Stock Exchange decided to simultaneously demutualize and self-list, being the first stock exchange to do so in the world; it was soon followed by many other prominent stock exchanges, including the Singapore Stock Exchange, Hong Kong Stock Exchange, London Stock Exchange, Toronto Stock Exchange, Deutsche Boerse, and New York Stock Exchange.

[42] Securities Law, Art 106.

[43] Zhengquan Jiaoyisuo Guanli Banfa [Measures for the Administration of Securities Exchanges (Exchange Administration Measures)] (promulgated by the China Securities Regulatory Commission on 10 December 1997, amended on 12 December 2001).

[44] Exchange Administration Measures, Art 21.

[45] Exchange Administration Measures, Art 22.

[46] Exchange Administration Measures, Art 24.

[47] Exchange Administration Measures, Art 25.

Introduction

securities exchanges, which is on paper said to be the highest organ of the securities exchange.[48] This organizational structure renders the relationship between the CSRC and securities exchanges one of superior and subordinate, or has the effect that the securities exchange is essentially a department of the CSRC.

2.3.2. Resource constraints and regulatory capture

2.48 The issue of regulatory resource constraints is another problem associated with China's financial regulation. Take the CSRC as an example. The CSRC is hampered by a lack of resources, including funding and staffing, though on the surface, compared to other government agencies of the same rank, the CSRC enjoys more resources in terms of funding and staffing.

2.49 The CSRC, in its annual report, is usually silent on its funding and accounting issue, except for a simple sentence to the effect that its regulatory costs and incomes are totally managed within the state fiscal budget system. Anecdotal evidence suggests, however, that CSRC officials generally receive more perks than their counterparts in other departments. Hence there is more intense competition for positions in the CSRC.

2.50 As a specialist commission, the CSRC has many technocrat staff who are young, energetic, and well-educated. According to its 2012 annual report, the average age of a member of CSRC staff was 36.3; 97.5 per cent of staff had Bachelor's degrees, 76.1 per cent Master's degrees, and 16.4 per cent PhD degrees.[49] The CSRC is also quite international in terms of the profile of its staff, with 10.8 per cent of its employees having overseas education and even work experience. Mr Anthony Neoh, the former chief advisor of the CSRC and a current member on the CSRC's International Advisory Committee, is the former chairman of the Securities and Futures Commission of Hong Kong (SFCHK); Ms Laura Cha, one of the former deputy chairmen of the CSRC, previously served as a deputy chairman of the SFCHK; Mr Gao Xiqing, the former executive deputy chairman of the CSRC, is a prominent professional who was educated in the US and had worked on Wall Street; Mr Yao Gang, the current deputy chairman of the CSRC, studied and worked in Japan.

2.51 Nevertheless, the CSRC still suffers from big problems in the area of funding and staffing. Resource constraints are a universal problem faced by regulatory bodies worldwide, including the US's SEC;[50] however, this problem is particularly severe for the CSRC. As of the end of 2012, the CSRC had 2,891 staff members.[51] As such, the regulatory staffing level per million of China's population was about

---

[48] Exchange Administration Measures, Art 17.
[49] CSRC, *CSRC Annual Report 2012*, 7.
[50] Donald C Langevoort, *Insider Trading: Regulation, Enforcement, and Prevention* (1991) §1.04, 1–24.
[51] CSRC, *CSRC Annual Report 2012*, 7.

2.02, compared with 23.75 in the US, 19.04 in the UK, 34.44 in Australia, and 59.59 in Hong Kong.[52] As the budget figure is not disclosed in the CSRC's annual report, it is not possible to compare the ratio of budget to national gross domestic product (GDP) in China with that in other jurisdictions.

2.52 In practice, the CSRC has difficulties in retaining good staff. Anecdotally, many people choose to work with the agency to gain experience and establish networks, in the hope that it will help them to find a much better paid job in the private sector. Over the years, a large number of CSRC staff have left to work in the industry—in particular moving to securities firms and securities investment fund management companies—which they regulate at the CSRC. The recent high-profile case of Mr Lin Haizhong is a good example in point. Mr Lin started working with the CSRC in 2002, and moved up through the ranks to become a director in the CSRC's Department of Fund Supervision. This is an important post in an important department, but on 22 August 2012, a fund management company made a public announcement that Mr Lin had joined it as Chief Supervision Officer, with responsibility for overseeing all risks in its management and operation.

2.53 The above situation, where senior officers of private companies in the financial sector are former regulatory officials, is dubbed the 'revolving door phenomenon'. To be sure, it is a global phenomenon, and is in no way unique to China. The worrying issue, though, is the scale of the phenomenon in China and the lack of an effective regime to regulate it. The revolving door phenomenon is said to present conflicts of interest and, if not properly regulated, may lead to the problem of regulatory capture, a term used to refer to a situation in which the regulator becomes captive to the objects it regulates. On the one hand, as the incumbent regulatory officials hope to work in the private sector in future, they will not rigorously regulate the industry, particularly the firms which may be their future employers. On the other, after the regulatory officials leave for the private sector, they can take advantage of their personal networks at the regulatory agency to get favourable treatment for their new employers.

2.54 China has had in place some laws in relation to the revolving door issue, but there are problems. As it is a government instrument, the leaders of the CSRC are public servants and thus are subject to the 2005 Civil Servant Law.[53] Under Article 102 of this law, where a civil servant resigns his post or retires and was a leading member before resignation, he shall not take any post in an enterprise or any other profit-making organization that is directly related to his original post, or shall not engage in any profit-making activity directly related to his prior work within three years after he leaves his post. In November 2009, the CSRC issued the Code of

---

[52] Howell E Jackson and Mark J Roe, 'Public and Private Enforcement of Securities Laws: Resources-based Evidence' (2009) 93 *Journal of Financial Economics* 207, 214–15.
[53] Zhonghua Renmin Gongheguo Gongwuyuan Fa [Civil Servant Law of the People's Republic of China] (issued 27 April 2005, effective 1 Jan 2006).

Conduct for CSRC Officials, further stipulating that the cooling-off period for the CSRC leaders is three years and for ordinary staff is one year.[54] There is a huge loophole in this regime, however: according to the CSRC, the restriction does not apply if the post in the private sector is Chief Supervision Officer, Chief Counsel, or Chief Risk Officer, because these are special posts and do not involve business management responsibilities. Thus, in practice, this loophole has become the main route through which CSRC officials comfortably enter the private sector without being subject to the cooling-off period restriction. Further, in some cases, the restriction is not applied even though the posts in question are not the special posts noted above.

2.3.3. Challenges of financial modernization and innovation

2.55 Another key issue with regard to China's financial regulation lies in its traditional sectoral regulatory structure. Over recent years, China's financial regulation has come under increasing pressure from the latest developments in the Chinese financial markets. China has followed the international trend of gradually removing structural restraints which segment financial markets and confine institutions to specific business lines, a process sometimes dubbed financial modernization. As a result, the once clear boundaries between different types of financial institutions are increasingly blurred.

2.56 To start with, the Law of the PRC on Commercial Banks was revised in 2003 to add the clause 'unless the State Council provides otherwise' to the traditional prohibition on banks engaging in securities business activities.[55] Before long, the amendment to the Securities Law of the PRC in 2005 provided an exception to traditional sectoral segregation through the same clause, 'unless the State Council provides otherwise'.[56] Finally, the Insurance Law of the PRC has recently been amended and a number of significant changes made, including the dismantling of the previous rule strictly segregating insurance companies from other financial businesses. Article 8 of the Insurance Law of the PRC now provides that insurance shall be segregated from banking, securities, and trust sectors, *unless it is otherwise provided for by the state*.[57] This leaves the door open for insurance companies branching into other kinds of financial services. Under Article 106, insurance companies now have a broader range of investment forms. Apart from those previously allowed investment forms such as bank deposits, treasury bonds, and financial bonds, insurance companies now can also invest in shares, units of securities investment funds, real estate, and other forms prescribed by the State Council.[58] The legislative memorandum to the amendment

---

[54] CSRC, Zhongguo Zhengjianhui Gongzuo Renyuan Xingwei Zhunze [Code of Conduct for CSRC Officials] (issued in November 2009).
[55] Zhonghua Renmin Gongheguo Shangye Yinhang Fa [Law of the PRC on Commercial Banks] (promulgated on 10 May 1995, amended on 27 December 2003), Art 43.
[56] Securities Law, Art 6.
[57] Insurance Law, Art 8.
[58] Insurance Law, Art 106.

states that the change is in line with the international trend and is also suited to China's local economic conditions.

2.57 The above legislative amendments have formalized and encouraged the ongoing process of financial modernization in China. As discussed before, traditionally, strict segregation was enforced among the major sectors of the financial markets, namely banking, securities and insurance. Since China's entry to the World Trade Organization (WTO), financial modernization has been carried out on a trial basis and has made significant progress. The development is exemplified by the emergence of some large financial conglomerates, such as China Everbright Group, CITIC Group, and China PingAn Group, which involve a diversity of institutions operating in a range of different sectors, including banking, securities, insurance, trusts, and asset investment. This gives rise to what is called the business model of *Hunye Jingying* (combining the business activities of banking, securities, and insurance), representing a departure from the traditional model of *Fenye Jingying* (separating financial services and markets). With the legislative backing previously mentioned, the process of financial modernization is set to accelerate, and there will be progressively more large financial groups.

2.58 Further, financial innovation has created products such as sophisticated derivatives which cannot be easily accommodated within the traditional contractual forms of debt, equity, and insurance. This development has resulted in significant changes to the nature and distribution of risk in the financial system, with the risk profiles of different financial institutions having begun to converge. A prime example is securitization, whereby securities firms become exposed to banking-type risks by holding mortgage-backed securities or securitized bank loans. China has used this financial technique, with considerable success, to deal with the massive amount of NPLs in its banking sector. As previously discussed, although securitization has the potential to be abused, it remains an ingenious financial innovation capable of performing important economic functions, provided it is regulated properly. This is particularly so for China, where the banks still have a relatively high level of bad loans and the home mortgage market is huge and rapidly growing. It would seem to follow that China will not, nor should it, abandon efforts at financial innovation in the face of the global financial crisis. Hence, there will likely be more financial products that straddle the traditional boundaries of financial sectors.

2.59 Therefore, the ongoing process of financial modernization and innovation—as symbolized by the emergence of large multiservice financial conglomerates and complex cross-sectoral financial products—has significantly changed the way in which the financial markets operate in China. These market developments pose a serious challenge to China's traditional sectoral regulation, under which regulatory responsibility is divided along the traditional lines of banking, securities, and insurance. Not surprisingly, China's current regulatory structure has shown significant inadequacies in response to the changing financial landscape. For

Introduction

instance, it is difficult to take the system-wide perspective necessary to obtain an adequate supervisory overview of the large financial groups, as separate regulators are responsible for supervising different lines of business of those multiservice financial groups: the CSRC for the securities arm, the CIRC for the insurance arm, and the CBRC for the banking arm. Furthermore, some of the innovative financial products do not fit neatly into the traditional classification of banking, securities, and insurance businesses which underpin China's current sector-based regulation. In short, the mismatch between China's regulatory structure and the underlying market that it regulates has increased the regulatory costs and, more importantly, has led to overlaps and gaps in regulatory coverage. The following part will explore this issue in detail and seek to find an appropriate solution from a comparative perspective.

2.4. The Future of China's Financial Regulatory Framework

2.60 As discussed in the preceding section, the new financial landscape, as brought about by financial modernization and innovation, demands suitably designed reforms to China's current financial regulatory restructuring which are based on the traditional segmentation of financial services and markets. Added to this picture is the long-standing problem of structural imbalance in China's financial system, which requires a regulatory framework better able to take concerted action across the financial sectors. In the quest for a solution to the above problems, a comparative analysis of the financial regulatory structure in various jurisdictions will be conducted. The US, the UK, and Australia are chosen for comparison due to the fact that they are all advanced economies and, more importantly, each is typical of one of three major regulatory models currently in use around the world.[59]

2.4.1. Major structural models of financial regulation

2.4.1.1. 'Sectoral regulation' model

2.61 The US financial regulation is typical of this model, under which the different financial sectors of banking, securities, and insurance are subject to separate statutes and supervised by separate regulatory agencies. In brief, the US sectoral regulatory framework includes: (1) five federal depository institution regulators in addition to state-based supervision, including the famous Federal Reserve, which also serves as the central bank in the US; (2) one federal securities regulator, namely the SEC, and one federal futures regulator, namely the CFTC—the US has additional state-based supervision of securities firms as

---

[59] For a more detailed discussion, see Hui Huang, 'Institutional Structure of Financial Regulation in China: Lessons from the Global Financial Crisis' (2010) 10(1) *The Journal of Corporate Law Studies* 219.

well as SROs with broad regulatory powers; and (3) almost wholly state-based insurance regulation, with more than 50 regulators. As this regulatory structure consists of separate agencies responsible for different financial sectors, with the boundaries divided institutionally or functionally, it can be termed a 'sectoral regulation' model.

In response to the global financial crisis of 2008, the US adopted the Dodd–Frank **2.62** Wall Street Reform and Consumer Protection Act (Dodd–Frank Act). It does make some structural changes to the US financial regulatory framework, eliminating one financial regulatory agency (the Office of Thrift Supervision) and creating two agencies (the Financial Stability Oversight Council and the Office of Financial Research) in addition to several consumer protection agencies, including the Bureau of Consumer Financial Protection. However, the reform does not fundamentally change the 'sectoral regulation' model.

2.4.1.2. 'Integrated regulation' model

This model was best represented by the UK until its recent reforms.[60] The UK was **2.63** the first jurisdiction in the world—soon followed by countries including Germany, Japan, and South Korea—to adopt this model in setting up a powerful and nearly universal regulator for its financial services industry, namely the Financial Services Authority (FSA), to integrate regulatory and supervisory functions previously carried out by nine bodies in the UK.[61] The FSA was a super-regulator in terms of its unusually broad regulatory mandate: it was mandated not only to regulate a diversity of businesses, including banking, securities, and insurance, but was also charged with both prudential and business conduct regulation. Thus, this regulatory structure is called the 'integrated regulation' model.

2.4.1.3. 'Twin peaks' model

Australia is the champion of this model, having been the first to establish a finan- **2.64** cial regulatory framework comprising two main regulators. The first regulator, the Australian Securities and Investment Commission (ASIC), has responsibility for business conduct regulation across banking, securities, and insurance.[62] Unlike the US SEC, whose responsibilities are limited to regulating the markets for corporate securities, the ASIC's power extends to a wide range of financial products. However, the authority of the ASIC is not as extensive as that of the FSA in the UK due to the existence of a second regulator in the Australian regime, namely the Australian Prudential Regulatory Authority (APRA). As the name suggests, the APRA is responsible for prudential regulation, ensuring the financial soundness of all licensed financial institutions except for securities firms, which are regulated by the ASIC.

---

[60] The recent reform of the FSA will be discussed later: see para 2.84.
[61] Eilis Ferran, 'Examining the UK's Experience in Adopting the Single Financial Regulator Model' (2003) 28 *Brooklyn Journal of International Law* 257.
[62] Australian Securities and Investments Commission Act 2001.

Introduction

2.65 As the Australian regulatory regime consists of two separate regulators with different mandates in relation to prudential regulation and business conduct regulation respectively, it is vividly named the 'twin peaks' model, or the 'objectives-based regulation' model. It is noteworthy that in addition to the ASIC and the APRA, some other agencies perform certain regulatory functions in the financial markets, most notably the Reserve Bank of Australia, the central bank in Australia— this is responsible for monetary policy and financial stability, but no longer has any direct banking regulatory responsibilities.[63]

2.4.2. The way forward for China

2.66 As shown above, there are three major structural models of financial regulation at the international arena: (1) the 'sectoral regulation' model; (2) the 'integrated regulation' model; and (3) the 'twin-regulators' model. While the first model has a multiplicity of financial regulators segregated on the basis of the type of financial institution or activities, the second model sits at the other end of the spectrum, with only one universal regulator for most of its financial markets. The third model lies somewhere in between, dividing responsibility for financial regulation into two agencies.

2.4.2.1. A comparison of structural models

2.67 Naturally, each regulatory model has its own advantages and disadvantages. The merits of one model are always the demerits of another, and vice versa. The sectoral regulation model has significant problems. First, it is essentially a model designed for the traditional segmented financial markets, and thus is ill-suited to the new financial landscape brought about by the tide of financial modernization, with aspects such as the emergence of large financial conglomerates and innovative financial derivatives. As each regulator is focused on its designated part of the financial system, each often fails to see the wood for the trees. In other words, no single regulator possesses all of the information and authority necessary to monitor systemic risk. By contrast, a unified regulator is able to approach financial

---

[63] In this sense, the Australian financial regulatory system is composed of three regulators, namely the ASIC, the APRA, and the Reserve Bank of Australia, and therefore it is sometimes classified as not two but 'three-peaked'. This is in contrast with the Netherlands, the other country with the 'twin peaks' model. In the Netherlands, prudential regulation is combined with financial stability regulation in a single agency (ie the Dutch central bank, 'De Nederlandsche Bank'), with conduct of business regulation being assigned to a separate agency called 'Autoriteit Financiele Markten' (Financial Markets Authority). There are three major reasons behind the Australian decision to separate prudential responsibilities from the central bank. First, the central bank is ill-equipped to deal with institutions other than banks; second, it avoids the expectation that the central bank would automatically provide liquidity support in the event of a crisis; third, separation of the central banking and prudential functions would enable each institution to become more focused and efficient. In recognition of the view that there is some degree of connection between prudential regulation and systemic stability and that the information gathered through prudential regulation is important for effective systemic regulation, the Reserve Bank of Australia has power to request the APRA to collect financial sector data for it.

regulation from a wider perspective, dealing with regulatory hazards in a holistic fashion.

Second, the demarcation of responsibilities between various regulators is not always clear-cut or logical for historical and political reasons; this gives rise to regulatory gaps and at the same time regulatory overlaps. In some circumstances involving thorny problems, regulators may rationally shirk their responsibilities as much as they can, leaving the markets regulated by nobody. In other cases, regulators may fight hard over turf, resulting in regulatory duplication, causing significant costs for both regulators and regulatees. **2.68**

Although the integrated regulation model addresses the above problems facing the sectoral regulation model, it does not come without its own shortcomings. First, while the integrated regulation model has the advantage of economy of scale, it is a legitimate concern that the single universal regulator is far too powerful. This problem is somewhat mitigated under the twin peaks model. Second, the broad scope of regulatory responsibilities assigned to a single regulator may be such that the senior management of the regulator is overloaded and regulatory efficiency reduced. In contrast, the division of regulatory tasks across a number of regulators allows regulatory diversity and specialization. Third, a unified agency may be susceptible to reputational contagion, as a mistake in one part of the agency may undermine their credibility over the broad range of their responsibilities. **2.69**

Finally, and most importantly, one should be wary of the one-size-fits-all approach under the single-regulator model. Although the distinctions between financial industries may be increasingly blurred at the fringes, the core businesses of banking, insurance, and securities remain separate. It would be dangerous if insufficient attention was paid to the differences between financial industries. **2.70**

Moreover, it is very difficult for one single regulator to discharge all regulatory responsibilities and meet various regulatory objectives, as they may be different in nature and even conflict with each other. For example, prudential regulation is concerned with the financial soundness of regulated institutions, whereas business conduct regulation is concerned with the way in which financial products are marketed and sold. It follows that the two types of regulation are so different that they are best carried out by two separate agencies, as is the case under the twin peaks model. **2.71**

2.4.2.2. Short and long-term reform suggestions for China

The foregoing discussion reveals the respective strengths and weaknesses of each of the three regulatory models. However, an objective assessment of each approach, in isolation from their jurisdictional financial landscapes, is hardly meaningful. Thus, this section will put the assessment into the Chinese context, with a view to finding an appropriate solution to the problems confronting China's financial regulation. **2.72**

2.73 As shown earlier, the Chinese financial regulatory regime is broadly similar to the US—both adopt the traditional sectoral structure with a multiplicity of regulators. One major difference is that unlike the US, China has removed the responsibility for regulating individual banks from the central bank, ie the PBC. This is in line with the international trend to divest central banks of a direct role in banking supervision.

2.74 In response to the problems with China's sectoral financial regulation, some have suggested that China should make an immediate transfer towards the UK model by merging the existing three sector-specific regulatory agencies, namely the CSRC, the CBRC, and the CIRC, into a single financial regulator. While there is merit in this suggestion, it does not adequately consider other options and the Chinese local conditions. It is necessary to perform a cost-benefit analysis of transferring to another system. An immediate and wholesale shift for China across to the UK model will not be cost-effective, as it would involve large costs which may well outweigh the corresponding benefits. China would be best advised to adopt a staged reform agenda for its financial regulation in line with the gradual growth of the underlying markets.

2.75 In the short term, China may learn from the US practice to improve its financial regulation without radically changing the overarching structural model. In the US, the Federal Reserve is given umbrella regulatory authority over bank holding companies. Under the Dodd–Frank Act, the Federal Reserve will have new authority to supervise all firms that could pose a threat to financial stability, even those that do not own banks.[64] This effectively extends the Federal Reserve's consolidated supervision to all large, interconnected financial groups whose failure could have serious systemic effects. As a result, financial firms will not be able to escape regulatory oversight simply by manipulating their legal structure. Moreover, a new Financial Services Oversight Council of financial regulators is to be created to improve interagency co-operation and prevent things falling through the cracks when it comes to the various regulators.

2.76 The above reforms seem to be a pragmatic response to the problems of US financial regulation as highlighted by the 2008 global financial crisis. Indeed, the Dodd–Frank Act stops short of holistically addressing the structural inadequacies of US financial regulation, and its structural model remains sector-based, with separate regulators responsible for each financial sector. But the reform has the advantage of being quick and measured, in order to deal with the pressing issues in practice.

2.77 The US approach merits consideration in the context of China. On the one hand, the PBC can be authorized to supervise the consolidated operations of large financial groups; on the other hand, an interagency oversight council can be created to bring together regulators across markets and other relevant agencies to co-ordinate

---

[64] H.R. 4173 §§ 162(a), 163.

and share information, and to identify gaps in regulation. In order to promote efficiency and continuity, the council may set up a standing committee composed of the PBC and the three sector-specific regulatory agencies, namely the CBRC, the CSRC, and the CIRC. As with the case of the Dodd–Frank Act, this solution can be a practical expedient for China in the short term.

2.78 More importantly, the short-term recommendation is based on a realistic appraisal of the present needs of China's financial markets. While the US current regulatory regime is said to be sub-optimal for its financial markets, it may well be a suitable model for the less developed Chinese markets. Despite the rapid progress in recent years, China's financial markets are still largely segmented along the traditional banking, securities, and insurance lines. Financial innovation and modernization are relatively limited in extent and cautiously carried out at an experimental stage. Thus, the US model will be adequate to meet the challenges which China's financial regulatory regime currently faces due to the emergence of financial conglomerates and financial innovation.

2.79 After all, China's current financial regulatory regime was shaped just several years ago, and should be given a period of time to demonstrate its ability to adapt to the recent market developments. More importantly, although the Chinese financial regulators are suffering teething problems associated with maintaining independence from the government, they have done a great job of managing financial risks, as shown in the recent global financial crisis which began in 2008. It follows that the current Chinese financial regulatory system is functioning reasonably well and radical structural changes are not warranted at this stage.[65]

2.80 In the intermediate or long run, however, China cannot rely on the US experience, but instead needs to consider the twin peaks model—or, to a lesser extent, the integrated regulation model. The US reform under the Dodd–Frank Act does little more than fine-tune regulatory authorities within the pre-existing regulatory framework, which has proven an antiquated system for a well-developed economy such as the US. By contrast, the twin peaks and integrated regulation models attempt to thoroughly overhaul the regulatory structure, taking a novel approach to financial regulation. They are better adapted to the realities of modern financial markets than the sectoral structure, dispensing with the traditional boundaries between banking, securities, and insurance. Both represent genuine efforts to modernize financial regulation to deal with the issues created by the formation of financial conglomerates and the blurring of distinctions between financial

---

[65] The Chinese government appears to have proceeded in line with the short-term reform strategy discussed here. On 20 August 2013, the Chinese government announced the establishment of a financial regulatory interagency co-ordination mechanism which will be led by the PBC and will include representatives from the CBRC, the CSRC, and the CIRC, as well as the State Administration of Foreign Exchange. See Bettina Wassener and Chris Buckley, 'New Chinese Agency to Increase Financial Coordination', *The New York Times*, 21 August 2013.

products. In this sense, they point to the right direction for future financial regulatory reforms.

2.81 The key difference between the integrated regulation and the twin peaks models is that while the former assigns all regulatory responsibilities to a single regulator, the latter divides responsibilities and creates two separate regulators: one for prudential regulation and the other for business conduct regulation. Compared to the twin peaks model, the integrated regulation model has a number of disadvantages.

2.82 First, prudential regulation and business conduct regulation deal with different forms of market failure and therefore require different approaches to be taken. Indeed, there are significant differences in the focus of their work and the ways in which it is carried out between prudential regulators and business conduct regulators. The former is focused on the soundness of financial institutions while the focus of the latter is on protection of consumer interests. What this means is that prudential and conduct-of-business regulators require different skill sets and different tools to do their respective jobs. This is broadly mirrored in the fact that prudential regulators are typically from an economics background while business conduct regulators are often selected from among lawyers.

2.83 Second, it is difficult to reconcile the competing demands of prudential and conduct-of-business regulation. There is a risk that if both prudential regulation and business conduct regulation are housed within one entity, one of them may be prioritized at the expense of the other. Potential conflicts of interest may arise between prudential and conduct-of-business regulation because of the different nature of their objectives. A good example is that a business conduct regulator might argue for early and full disclosure of a firm's problems, while a prudential regulator might place greater weight on the potential threat to the solvency of the institution caused by an early announcement. Finally, there are a number of other considerations in favour of a 'twin peaks' model, such as clear mandates and accountability, avoiding the problem of reputational contagion.

2.84 Due to its strengths, the twin peaks model has attracted increasing attention as a template for reform in many countries, particularly after the global financial crisis that began in 2008. The US government carried out a thorough investigation into its financial regulatory regime in 2008, concluding that the ultimate reform goal for financial regulation in the US is not the integrated regulation model, but rather the twin peaks model.[66] Most interestingly, the UK, the pioneer and symbol of the integrated regulation model, has recently carried out reform in line with the twin peaks model: as of 1 April 2013, the FSA was abolished and its responsibilities split between two agencies—(1) the Financial Conduct Authority, which

---

[66] US Department of the Treasury, *Blue Print for a Modernized Financial Regulatory Structure* (2008).

watches how financial institutions treat their customers, and (2) the Prudential Regulatory Authority, which conducts prudential regulation of financial institutions. Moreover, the South African government issued the National Treasury Policy Document in February 2011, which set out proposals for strengthening its financial regulatory system by adopting the twin peaks model.[67] These latest international developments should shed light on the debate over the future development of China's financial regulation.

2.5. Conclusion

This chapter has shown that the current Chinese regulatory regime is broadly similar to its US counterpart, adopting a traditional sectoral regulatory structure. It comprises the PBC as the central bank and three sector-specific regulators, namely the CBRC, the CSRC, and the CIRC, responsible for banking, securities, and insurance, respectively. This regulatory framework exhibits several inadequacies in the face of recent market developments such as financial globalization, financial innovation, and the emergence of financial conglomerates. **2.85**

From a comparative perspective, there are three main approaches to financial regulation at the international arena, including the 'sectoral regulation' model, the 'integrated regulation' model, and the 'twin peaks' model. When looking to these models for guidance, China should have regard not only to their objective merits, but also to its local conditions. There is no urgent need for China to scrap its current sectoral regulation model in the short term, but with the further growth of its financial markets in the long run, China should adopt the twin peaks model. **2.86**

---

[67] South Africa Department of National Treasury, *A Safer Financial Sector to Serve South Africa Better* (February 2011).

Part II

REGULATION OF SECURITIES OFFERINGS AND LISTINGS

3

SECURITIES OFFERINGS

3.1. Regulatory Model: Disclosure-based vs Merits-review	3.01	3.4. China Securities Regulatory Commission (CSRC) Approval Regime	3.31
3.1.1. Overview	3.02	3.4.1. Overview	3.31
3.1.2. The evolution of China's fundraising regulation	3.04	3.4.2. The Issuance Examination Committee (IEC)	3.34
3.1.3. Future development	3.09	3.4.3. Comments	3.46
3.2. Disclosure and Market Efficiency	3.14	3.5. Securities Offerings by Listed Companies	3.48
3.2.1. Efficient Capital Market Hypothesis (ECMH)	3.14	3.5.1. Public offerings	3.50
3.3. Regulatory Structure: Public Offerings vs Private Placement	3.23	3.5.2. Private placement	3.70
3.3.1. Public offerings	3.25	3.5.3. The procedure for offering securities	3.74
3.3.2. Private placement	3.27		
3.3.3. Comments	3.29	3.5.4. Disclosure requirements	3.85

3.1. Regulatory Model: Disclosure-based vs Merits-review

Corporations raise funds through the issue of their securities, including equity securities and debt securities. The process by which corporations solicit investments in their securities has long been a central concern of corporate regulation. Internationally, there are two main models of fundraising regulation. This part will first have a brief overview of the two models, and then discuss the model China has adopted from a historical perspective, as well as the likely course of future development in this area. **3.01**

3.1.1. Overview

The first model is so-called 'disclosure-based' regulation, under which the state adopts a limited form of interventionism by requiring adequate information disclosure from the company and imposing sanctions for false or misleading statements. As long as the information disclosure is adequate, it is the responsibility of the investors to decide whether the securities being offered are investment-worthy. This disclosure philosophy is vividly reflected in the telling phrase of the former **3.02**

US Justice Brandeis: 'Sunlight is said to be the best of disinfectants, electric light the most efficient policeman.'[1]

3.03 The other model, known as 'merits-review' regulation, goes beyond the mere requirement of information disclosure to include merit review in terms of the state of the efficacy and equity of the securities being offered. The model contains, in addition to information disclosure requirements as found under the disclosure-based model, a merit-review mechanism whereby an offering is subject to various merits tests carried out by the state. In more extreme cases, the state not only examines the terms of securities offerings, but also controls the number of securities offerings under a quota system.

3.1.2. The evolution of China's fundraising regulation

3.1.2.1. 1990–1999: Pei E Zhi (quota system)

3.04 During the 1990s China's securities market was in its infancy, with the mission to rescue many financially distressed state-owned enterprises (SOEs) and facilitate the state's transition from a planned economy to a market-oriented one. Against this background, the regulation of securities offerings was characterized by a high level of governmental control, reminiscent of the planned economy era. This phase of regulation is aptly termed Pei E Zhi (quota system); not only did it require governmental approval, but a quota system was also implemented to control the flow of total funds raised or the total number of offerings on an annual basis. Under this system, the central government first set the maximum number of offerings every year and then allocated the quotas to different provinces and ministries. This meant that the issuer had first to get the quota from the local government of the province where it was located, and then to make an application for approval from the relevant regulator at the central level.

3.05 Hence, irrespective of the quality of the proposed offerings, the issuer could not get approval if, for whatever reason, it failed to get the quota from the local government. This effectively represented a double approval requirement, namely approval from the local government as well as from the central government. In this sense, the quota system involved more governmental intervention than the merit-review system which has replaced it since 1999.

3.1.2.2. 1999–present: He Zhun Zhi (approval system or merit-review system)

3.06 The year of 1999 marked a major milestone in the history of China's securities regulation. In July 1999, the long-awaited Securities Law came into force, substantially improving the previous situation, in which there had been no national legislation on securities matters and China's securities regulation had been based on a

---

[1] Louis Dembitz Brandeis, *Other People's Money: And How the Bankers Use it* (F.A. Stokes, 1914) Ch 5.

bewildering array of governmental rules. A significant change brought about by the legislation in 1999 was that the regulation of securities offerings was changed from the quota system to the so-called He Zhun Zhi (approval system or merit-review system).

3.07 Under this new regime, the government no longer put a cap on the number of offerings allowed to be made every year, but rather, in theory, the CSRC could approve any offering application as long as it fits the relevant merits test. To facilitate the running of the new regime, the CSRC introduced a number of supporting systems—notably the Tuijian Zhi (recommendation system), where prospective offerings must be recommended to the CSRC by qualified securities firms for approval. In order to encourage securities firms to properly perform their role in recommending worthy offerings, the CSRC came up with the TongDao Zhi (channel system), under which the CSRC gave every qualified securities firm a certain number of so-called 'channels' used to recommend prospective offerings at the same time. In practice, the number of recommendations each firm could make varied from one to eight, depending on the capacity of the particular securities firm. One 'channel' was to be used for one offering, and only after the offering recommended through a channel had been approved could the same channel be reused for a new offering. In this way, qualified securities firms had strong incentives to recommend those offerings which in their view were of high quality, and thus likely to gain CSRC approval.

3.08 As the channel system was still under strong administrative control, it proved inadequate to meet the market demand. In 2004, the CSRC introduced the Baojian Zhi (sponsorship system) from Hong Kong to phase out the channel system. The sponsorship system is very similar to the channel system in many aspects, such as the role, function, and qualification of the intermediaries, but the key difference is that under the sponsorship system there is no ceiling on the number of offerings that can be sponsored concurrently by the same sponsor. It is a matter of business judgement for the sponsor to decide whether to sponsor a particular offering and how many offerings to be sponsored simultaneously. This has the virtue of promoting market competition among sponsors and thus improving the quality of sponsorship services.

3.1.3. Future development

3.09 China's current regulation of securities offerings is merits-review based, having evolved over time in the context of China's emerging securities market. As the underlying market grows at a rapid pace, China faces an ongoing challenge to improve its securities offerings regulation to keep up with market developments.[2]

---

[2] For more detailed discussion, see Hui Huang, 'The Regulation of Securities Offerings in China: Reconsidering the Merit Review Element in Light of the Global Financial Crisis' (2011) 41(10) *Hong Kong Law Journal* 261.

3.10 The merit-review element of China's fundraising regulation has attracted considerable criticisms based on both philosophical and practical considerations. To begin with, merit review essentially represents a form of state 'paternalism' in that it replaces investors' value judgements with those of the regulator with respect to the securities and the issuing corporation. Second, merit review has generated huge expenses for both the regulator and the entities subject to the review. The third defect lies with the inherent difficulties in conducting merit review. Fourth, cronyism and favouritism may arise in the conduct of the merit review. Last but not least, merit regulation has also provided a fertile breeding ground for rent seeking and corruption by regulators.

3.11 Internationally, most advanced economies—such as the United States,[3] the United Kingdom, Australia, and Hong Kong—have adopted disclosure-based regulation. One may naturally be tempted to jump to the conclusion that China should simply switch to disclosure-based regulation in line with international best practice, as seen in those developed markets. This requires careful consideration, however. Indeed, disclosure-based regulation is largely free of the problems associated with China's merits-based regulation—but, as illustrated in the recent global financial crisis, it has its own weaknesses.

3.12 One of the biggest lessons to emerge from the global financial crisis of 2008 is that, as a method of investor protection, disclosure-based regulation falters where investors are unable or unwilling to make rational choices on the basis of the information disclosed. This is more likely to be the case in China, where the securities market is still underdeveloped and investors as a whole are less sophisticated than their counterparts in advanced economies.

3.13 It is not advisable for China to immediately change to the disclosure-based regulation. Rather, China should take a gradualist approach, and only switch to disclosure-based regulation when the market and institutional preconditions necessary for success are present. These conditions include an appropriate level of financial sophistication of investors, access to financial advisory services supplied by a full-fledged investment community, and a well-developed legal system to sanction misrepresentation.

3.2. Disclosure and Market Efficiency

3.2.1. Efficient Capital Market Hypothesis (ECMH)

3.14 Under both the disclosure-based model and the merit-review model, information disclosure is an integral part of the regulatory regime. The theoretical foundation

---

[3] The US securities law at the federal level adopts the disclosure-based model, but this is not the case for the state law. In fact, the most influential and renowned system of merit regulation is found in the so-called 'blue sky' laws adopted by some states in the United States.

of disclosure is supplied by the ECMH. Under the ECMH, an efficient market will operate to factor information about particular securities into the price, and thus the need for information disclosure—information about securities should be discovered and put into the market as efficiently as possible.

Economists have generated three alternative versions of the ECMH. Each version makes a different claim about how efficient the market is, and about what type of information is reflected in the price of securities. Therefore, each version implies a different conclusion about the need for information disclosure. **3.15**

First, according to the weak form of the ECMH, all historical information is reflected in the current price of securities. Thus, there is no reason to include historical information in prospectuses. Moreover, the future price of securities cannot be predicted by studying previous price movements, because security prices move randomly in response to market events. Second, the semi-strong form of the ECMH claims that security price will react rapidly to reflect all publicly available information about those securities. Information can become public either through disclosure by a company, or through the trading activities of investors. Third, the strong form of the ECMH states that even non-public information will be incorporated quickly into securities prices. Thus, it will be rare for an investor to make a profit out of inside information. **3.16**

3.2.1.1. Mandatory disclosure

Despite the differences in their claims about the market efficiency level, each of the three versions of the ECMH has a common element of information disclosure. Hence, it is widely accepted that information disclosure is needed in order for the securities market to function efficiently, but the further—and more difficult—question is whether disclosure should be mandatory. **3.17**

The need for a mandatory disclosure regime has been the subject of considerable theoretical debate. On the one hand, several arguments have been advanced to support mandatory disclosure.[4] First, it helps all investors to have equal access to relevant information, and works to simplify or standardize presentation so that information can be more readily understood. Second, information about a company's securities and its financial situation can be thought of as a 'public good', and thus companies will tend to under-produce such information unless required to do so by the state. On the other hand, it has been argued that market forces would be capable of producing the optimal level of disclosure.[5] To start with, silence is not golden, as the argument goes, because investors will treat a firm that fails to disclose information with suspicion. Thus, a firm that wants to attract investors has **3.18**

---

[4] See eg J Coffee, 'Market Failure and the Economic Case for a Mandatory Disclosure System' (1984) 70 *Virginia Law Review* 717.
[5] See eg F Easterbrook and D Fischel, *The Economic Structure of Corporate Law* (Harvard: Harvard University Press, 1991), Ch 11.

sufficient incentives to disclose information. Further, mandatory disclosure laws typically require the production of more information than is cost-efficient.

3.19 A number of empirical studies in the US have attempted to assess the desirability of mandatory disclosure rules, but the overall empirical findings are inconclusive.[6] This outcome is not surprising, given the difficulties in measuring the costs and benefits of disclosure regulation.

3.2.1.2. Forms of disclosure

3.20 In securities regulation, mandated disclosure takes several forms with differing contents. The first form of disclosure is new issue disclosure, which applies when securities are offered to investors for the first time. The prospectus, as the most common disclosure document, must contain all material information prospective investors would need to make an informed decision on the securities being offered. The following parts will provide a detailed discussion of various issues of prospectus disclosure in China, such as when disclosure is required, what must be disclosed and how disclosure should be made.

3.21 Second, after the securities are issued and then, in most cases, are also quoted on stock exchanges, the company is required to make disclosure of price-sensitive information in relation to those securities on a periodic basis or even in a continuous manner.[7]

3.22 Finally, disclosure requirements are imposed in the context of some specific corporate transactions. This form of transaction-specific disclosure applies to transactions which typically involve conflicts of interest and have a major impact on the company, such as related party transactions or takeovers or other corporate control transactions.[8]

3.3. Regulatory Structure: Public Offerings vs Private Placement

3.23 China adopts the traditional public offer/private placement divide as the foundation of its fundraising regime. Under this paradigm, a public offer is an offer to take up securities made to the public or a section of the public. Due to the public character of the offerees, there is a need for legal protection through mandatory information disclosure in a registered document such as a prospectus. The residual group of private placements is judged not to call for such protection, and thus prospectus disclosure is not legally mandated.

---

[6] See eg George J Stigler, 'Public Regulation of the Securities Markets' (1964) 37 *Journal of Business* 117; George J Benston, 'The Value of the SEC's Accounting Disclosure Requirements' (1969) 44 *Accounting Review* 515.

[7] For more discussion of this, see Chapter 5.

[8] For discussion of takeovers, see Part 4.

Compared with public offerings, private placement has some advantages. As there 3.24
is no public disclosure requirement, private placement can be done with confidentiality and speed. Without the need to prepare a prospectus, the cost of private placement can also be reduced. On the other hand, private placement has some disadvantages. It is legally required to be limited to specified investors, and the market for the securities placed has a relatively low level of liquidity. In most cases, the securities issued through private placement are subject to certain restrictions, such as lock-up requirements and transfer restrictions.

3.3.1. Public offerings

The concept of public offering is found in Article 10(2) of the Securities Law, which 3.25
states:

> It shall be deemed as a public issuance under any of the following circumstances:
> a. securities are issued to unspecified objects;
> b. securities are issued to accumulatively more than 200 specified objects;
> c. making a public issuance as prescribed by any law or administrative regulation.

Thus, there are two main types of public offerings in China: namely, offerings made to the general public and offerings to cumulatively no more than 200 specified objects. The first type is quite straightforward; the second is more complicated, and two important points need to be noted. First, the number limit is calculated cumulatively not for a single round of offering, but for the whole life of the company. Second, the term 'specified objects' is not clearly defined.

Under Article 10(1) of the Securities Law, a public offering of securities shall meet 3.26
the requirements of the relevant laws and administrative regulations and shall be reported to the securities regulatory authority under the State Council or a department as authorized by the State Council for examination and approval according to law. No entity or individual may make a public issuance of any securities without any examination and approval according to law. Contravention of the above prohibition is a serious matter, which may attract administrative, civil, and criminal liabilities. According to Article 188 of the Securities Law, a company conducting public offerings without governmental approval shall be ordered to cease the issuance, return the funds raised plus a deposit interest to the investors, and pay a fine of between 1 per cent and 5 per cent of the funds it has illegally raised. Article 179 of the Criminal Law of the PRC provides that any person issuing securities without governmental approval may be sentenced to a fixed term of imprisonment of up to five years and be fined between 1 per cent and 5 per cent of the funds illegally raised.

3.3.2. Private placement

If a securities offering is not a public one, then it falls into the residual category 3.27
of private placement. Article 10(3) of the Securities Law stipulates that, for any

securities that are not issued in a public manner, the means of advertising, public inducement or public issuance in any disguised form shall not be adopted thereto. This prohibition on general solicitation is in line with the international practice in relation to private placement.

3.28 In the case of private placement, a disclosure document such as prospectus is not required. Under Article 13(2) of the Securities Law, however, private placement by listed companies is still subject to merits-review—that is, it shall meet the substantive requirements as prescribed by CSRC, and shall be reported to the CSRC for examination and approval.

3.3.3. Comments

3.29 Conceptually, the public offer/private placement paradigm is not hard to understand; its difficulty, however, lies in its application. In determining whether a particular group of offerees constitutes a section of the public, one needs to have regard to a variety of factors, including the number of persons comprising the group, the relationship between the offeror and the members of the group, the nature and content of the offer, the characteristics of the members of the group, the connection between the offer and the members of the group, and so on. Hence, the public offer test is not clear-cut, and in some cases an offer confined to a particular group may not be a public offer.

3.30 As the generality of the public offer test promotes confusion and evasion, the Chinese law defines public offering almost exclusively by reference to the number of offerees, including even specified objects. This has the virtue of being clear, but it is too rigid to suit the commercial reality. In overseas jurisdictions, when securities are offered to professional, sophisticated, and experienced investors, the offerings are exempted from the mandatory disclosure regime, regardless of the number of such investors. Also, small-scale offerings are often exempted in overseas jurisdictions, as it is not cost-effective to require a disclosure document for such offerings.

3.4. China Securities Regulatory Commission (CSRC) Approval Regime

3.4.1. Overview

3.31 Under the merits review regulation of fundraising in China, the CSRC is empowered to conduct the merits review. In practice, the merits review can be broadly divided into two stages. The first stage is the preliminary review, which is carried out by a functional department of the CSRC, namely the Issuance Supervision Department. At this stage, the CSRC staff will check whether the application contains all relevant materials and seek comments from the relevant government of the locality where the applicant company is registered, as well as from the National Development and Reform Commission.

The second stage of the review is then more focused on the substance of the issuance application. To this end, the CSRC has established a special committee, namely the IEC, which is composed of some CSRC staff members and external experts who possess notable expertise in the relevant fields of securities, accounting and law.[9] The IEC performs its function by holding meetings and casting votes. It should be noted that the IEC is an advisory body in nature and the final approval decision rests with the CSRC. In practice, however, the CSRC always makes its final approval decision on the basis of the IEC's review opinions.   3.32

The CSRC has issued a regulation, namely the Measures of China Securities Regulatory Commission for the Issuance Examination Committee (Measures for the IEC), to provide more details on the membership, tenure of members, and work procedures of the IEC.[10]   3.33

3.4.2. The Issuance Examination Committee (IEC)

In China, initial public offerings always go hand in hand with listings, and thus the CSRC merits review process varies according to the place where the securities are to be listed. In 2009, as the Shenzhen Stock Exchange established the Growth Enterprise Market, also called Second Board Market, the CSRC revised the Measures for the IEC to set up two IECs: the Main Board Market Issuance Examination Committee ('Main Board IEC') and the Second Board Market Issuance Examination Committee ('Second Board IEC'). Apart from the way in which the two IECs are constituted, they are subject to the same set of rules in other aspects such as term, powers and duties, and work procedures.   3.34

3.4.2.1. Constitution and term

Under Article 6 of the Measures for the IEC, the number of Main Board IEC members shall be 25, some of whom may be full-time staff members. In particular, five Main Board IEC members shall come from the CSRC, and the other 20 members shall come from outside the CSRC. The number of Second Board IEC members shall be 35, some of whom may be full-time staff members. In particular, five Second Board IEC members shall come from the CSRC, and the other 30 members shall come from outside the CSRC.   3.35

The tenure of an IEC member shall be one year; upon the expiration of the term, he may be reappointed, but shall not serve for more than a maximum of three terms.   3.36

---

[9] Art 22 of the Securities Law.
[10] Zhongguo Zhengquan Jiandu Guanli Weiyuanhui Faxing Shenhe Weiyuanhui Banfa [Measures of China Securities Regulatory Commission for the Issuance Examination Committee] (promulgated by the CSRC in 2006, amended in 2009).

It should be noted that the members of the Main Board IEC and the Second Board IEC may not hold concurrent posts in both boards.[11]

3.37 Given the important role played by the IEC, the Measures for the IEC set out clear selection and dismissal criteria for IEC members. The selection criteria include:

(1) Sticking to the principles, being impartial and clean, devoted to one's duties and posts, and strictly abiding by the laws, administrative regulations and rules.
(2) Being familiar with the securities and accounting business as well as the relevant laws, administrative regulations and rules.
(3) Being proficient in the special knowledge of one's profession, and enjoying a high reputation in one's field of practice.
(4) Having no records of violation of any law or discipline.
(5) Other requirements as regarded necessary by the CSRC.[12]

In the case that the following circumstances befall any IEC member, the CSRC shall dismiss him:

(1) Violating any law, administrative regulation, rule or discipline regarding the work of issuance examination.
(2) Failing to fulfil due diligence in accordance with the relevant provisions of the CSRC.
(3) Filing an application for resignation.
(4) Failing to attend IEC meetings without reason twice or more.
(5) Other circumstances under which the CSRC thinks the member is unsuitable for assuming the post of IEC member after examination.[13]

3.4.2.2. Powers and duties

3.38 To ensure that the IEC properly performs its role, the Measures for the IEC stipulate powers and duties for the IEC and its members. Under Article 10, the IEC is empowered to perform the following matters:

(1) Examine whether applications for stock issuance meet the relevant requirements.
(2) Examine the relevant materials and letters of opinions as issued by the recommendation institutions, accounting firms, law firms, asset valuation institutions, and other securities intermediary institutions, as well as the relevant personnel thereof for the stock issuance.
(3) Examine the preliminary examination reports issued by the relevant functional departments of the CSRC.
(4) Give examination opinions on the applications for stock issuance.

---

[11] Measures for the IEC, Art 7.
[12] Measures for the IEC, Art 8.
[13] Measures for the IEC, Art 9.

3.39 In performing its duties, the IEC member is required to observe the following provisions:

(1) Attending the IEC meetings as required, and fulfilling due diligence in the examination work.
(2) Keeping state secrets and the business secrets of the issuers.
(3) Prohibition from disclosing any contents discussed in the IEC meetings, the voting information, or any other relevant information.
(4) Prohibition from taking advantage of one's position as an IEC member or of the non-public information accessed in performing one's duties in the direct or indirect interest of oneself or any other people.
(5) Prohibition from having any interest in any applicant, from directly or indirectly accepting any gift such as money, goods, or any other benefits offered by the issuer or any other related entities or individuals, from holding stocks whose issuance applications are subject to his examination, and from privately contacting any of the issuers or any other related entities or individuals.
(6) Prohibition from colluding with any other IEC member to cast votes or inducing any other IEC member to cast votes.
(7) Other relevant provisions of the CSRC.[14]

The IEC member has the duty to report to the CSRC any issuer or any other related entity or individual that impose influence on them by illicit means.

3.40 Further, where any of the following circumstances befall any IEC member in the examination of the application documents for stock issuance, the member shall offer to withdraw before problems arise:

(1) The IEC member or any of the member's relatives is the issuer or director (including independent director, the same hereinafter), supervisor, manager, or any other senior executive member of the recommendation institution.
(2) The IEC member, any of the member's relatives, or the entity where the member works holds shares of the issuer, which may influence his fair performance of duties.
(3) The IEC member or the entity where the member works has provided such services as recommendation, underwriting, auditing, appraisal, legal service, consultation, etc, in the past two years, which may hamper the member's fair performance of duties.
(4) The company in which the IEC member or the member's relative is a director, supervisor, manager, or other senior executive has any trade competition with the issuer or the recommendation institution, which may affect the member's fair performance of duties after verification.

---

[14] Measures for the IEC, Art 13.

(5) Before the IEC convenes a meeting to examine an application for securities offerings, the IEC member who will vote in the meeting has been contacted by the applicant or other related entity or individual, and as such, his ability to discharge duties fairly may be impaired.

(6) Other circumstances as determined by the CSRC to have the possibility of leading to conflicts of interest, or as regarded by the IEC as having the possibility to affect the member's fair performance of duties.[15]

3.41 Where an issuer or other related entities or individuals believe that any IEC member has any conflicts of interest or potential conflicts of interests with them, which may affect the fair performance of duties of the IEC member, they may file a written application to the CSRC demanding the withdrawal of the relevant IEC member and providing an explanation when they submit the application documents on stock issuance to the IEC for examination. The CSRC shall, according to the written application filed by the issuer and other related entities or individuals, decide whether the relevant IEC member shall withdraw.[16]

3.4.2.3. Work procedure

3.42 The IEC carries out the examination through convening IEC meetings. Before the formation of examination opinions on an issuer's application for stock issuance, the IEC meeting may invite the representatives of the issuer and the recommendation representatives to the meeting to face the inquiries of the IEC members. Open ballots shall be adopted for voting at the IEC meetings, and votes shall include concurring and negative votes. No IEC member may waive their voting right and members shall explain the reasons for their vote at the time of voting. The IEC meeting normally carries out only one examination on the application of an issuer for stock issuance.

3.43 Depending on the type of securities issuance application, the IEC has two different work procedures: namely, ordinary procedure and special procedure.

3.44 The ordinary procedure shall be applied when the IEC meeting examines the issuers' applications for public offerings of shares or convertible corporate bonds, or any other public securities offerings as classified by the CSRC.[17] The relevant functional departments of the CSRC shall, five days before an IEC meeting is convened, serve notice of the meeting, the application documents for stock issuance, and the preliminary examination report of the relevant functional departments of the CSRC to the IEC members attending the meeting, and shall publicize the list of names of issuers being examined by the IEC, the time of the meeting, and the

---

[15] Measures for the IEC, Art 15.
[16] Measures for the IEC, Art 16.
[17] Measures for the IEC, Art 27. For a detailed discussion of convertible corporate bonds, see Part V.A.

letters of commitment of the issuers, as well as the list of names of the IEC members attending the meeting, on the CSRC website.[18] The number of IEC members who take part in each IEC meeting shall be seven: five concurring votes may be deemed as a pass; less than five concurring votes will be deemed as a failure.[19] The result of voting on an issuer's application for stock issuance shall be publicized on the CSRC website after voting at the IEC meeting.[20]

A special procedure shall be applied when the IEC meeting examines issuers' applications for non-public offerings of shares, or any other non-public securities offerings as classified by the CSRC.[21] The number of IEC members who take part in each IEC meeting shall be five, of which three concurring votes may be deemed as a pass; less than three concurring votes will be deemed as a failure.[22] Unlike the ordinary procedure as noted above, the CSRC shall not publicize the list of names of issuers being examined by the IEC meeting, the time of the meeting, the issuers' letters of commitment, the list of names of the IEC members attending the meeting, or the voting result.[23] **3.45**

3.4.3. Comments

The IEC regime is a distinctive feature and key element of China's regulation of securities offerings. It was first set up by the 1998 Securities Law. Before 2003, in order to insulate the IEC from outside interference, the identities of the IEC members were kept confidential. It turned out however that this confidentiality rule gave rise to many problems. This is well illustrated in a high-profile case which involved Mr Wang Xiaoshi, then a low-level CSRC official who was responsible for the compilation of the list of IEC members and had no power to express views as to issuance applications. By virtue of his position, however, he knew who would be chosen as the panel members to review a specific application. In 2002, Mr Wang sold to an applicant for an initial public offering (IPO) information about the identities of the panel members for its application, so that the applicant could privately contact the panel members and, through illegal means such as bribery, try to get favourable treatment from them. This was later discovered and Mr Wang was sentenced to three years in prison. This case provided impetus for the CSRC to reform the IEC regime to make it more open and transparent. **3.46**

As discussed, in order to maintain the integrity of IEC decisions, the Measures for the IEC have now provided for a series of mechanisms in relation to IEC members' appointment and removal, duties, and work procedures. For instance, the identities of IEC members are now publicly disclosed and members are subject to **3.47**

---

[18] Measures for the IEC, Art 28.
[19] Measures for the IEC, Art 29.
[20] Measures for the IEC, Art 31.
[21] Measures for the IEC, Art 33.
[22] Measures for the IEC, Art 35.
[23] Measures for the IEC, Art 37.

more stringent duties, particularly in circumstances where there may be issues of conflicts of interest. Those mechanisms represent a substantial improvement on the previous regime, but it remains to be seen how effective they are in practice.

3.5. Securities Offerings by Listed Companies

3.48 Depending on the status of the issuer company, securities offerings can be broadly divided into two categories: offerings by unlisted companies and offerings by listed companies. They are governed by two different regulatory regimes. In China, IPOs—the process by which a company publicly issue securities for the first time—always go hand in hand with stock exchange listings. Thus, IPOs will be discussed in Chapter 4, which deals with the issue of securities listings. In line with international practice, private placement by unlisted companies is subject to neither merits review nor disclosure rules. However, this is not the case for private placement by listed companies in China. This section therefore discusses the regulatory regime for subsequent offerings by listed companies, including public offerings and private placement.

3.49 After IPO and listing, the company may need to raise further capital from time to time by issuing securities. In China, the securities issued by a listed company for subsequent fundraising are mainly shares and convertible bonds. As the issuer company is already listed and subject to periodic and continuous disclosure, the regulatory regime for subsequent fundraising by listed companies is different from that for IPO in terms of merits review criteria, information disclosure rules, and the offering procedure.

3.5.1. Public offerings

3.5.1.1. General merits review criteria

3.50 Article 13 of the Securities Law sets out general merits review criteria for public offerings, which apply to both IPOs and public offerings by listed companies. The criteria include:

(1) The issuer must have a complete and well-functioning organizational structure.
(2) The issuer must have the capability to make profits continuously and have sound financial status.
(3) The issuer must have no false records in its financial statements over the preceding three years, nor any other major irregularity.
(4) Other requirements as prescribed by the CSRC.

3.51 Clearly, the above provision is too general to be implemented in practice. In recognition of this, coupled with concern arising from the stiff liability attached to the regime, the CSRC has promulgated some administrative regulations to flesh out the merit-review requirements, the most important of which is the Administrative Measures for Securities Offerings by Listed Companies (hereinafter Measures for Subsequent Offerings).[24]

Article 6 of the Measures for Subsequent Offerings explains what is meant by 'a complete and well-functioning organizational structure', stating that: **3.52**

> A listed company which satisfies the following provisions shall be deemed that it has a sound and well-operated organizational structure:
> (1) The articles of association shall be lawful and effective, and there are sound bylaws for the shareholders' assembly, the board of directors, the board of supervisors, and independent directors, who are able to perform their respective functions in accordance with the law;
> (2) The company has its internal control bylaws, which can ensure the operating efficiency, lawfulness and regulation compliance of the company, and the reliability of its financial reports. There is no serious defect in regard to the completeness, reasonableness and validity of the internal control bylaws;
> (3) The incumbent directors, supervisors and senior management members are qualified for their posts and can faithfully and diligently perform their duties. None of them has committed any act in violation of Article 148 or Article 149 of the Company, or has been given any administrative punishment by the CSRC within recent 36 months, or is publicly condemned by the stock exchange within 12 months;
> (4) The listed company separates its personnel, assets and financial affairs from those of the controlling shareholder or the actual controller, it is independent in terms of its institutions and business operations and can carry out business operations and management independently;
> (5) The listed company has not provided any illegal guaranty to any outsider within the recent 12 months.

Article 7 of the Measures for Subsequent Offerings provides guidance on the meaning of 'the capability of making profits continuously', stating that: **3.53**

> A listed company which meets the following provisions shall be deemed to have a sustainable profit-making ability:
> (1) It has a favorable balance for the recent 3 consecutive fiscal years as calculated on the basis of the net profits after deducting the non-regular profits and losses or the pre-deduction net profits, whichever is smaller;
> (2) It has relatively stable sources of businesses and profit and it does not substantially rely on its controlling shareholder or actual controller;
> (3) It can continue its present primary business or investment trend in a sustainable manner. It has a sound business operation mode and investment plan, and has a good market prospect for its main products or services.

---

[24] Shangshi Gongsi Zhengquan Faxing Guanli Banfa [Administrative Measures for Securities Offerings by Listed Companies] (promulgated by the CSRC in 2006, amended later).

There is no seriously unfavorable imminent or foreseeable change in the business operation environment and market demands;
(4) The senior management members and the core technicians are stable and there is no seriously unfavorable change in the recent 12 months;
(5) The important assets, core technologies or other important interests have been lawfully obtained, and can be continuously utilized, and there is no seriously imminent or foreseeable unfavorable change therein;
(6) There is no guaranty, lawsuit, arbitration or any other important matter that is likely to seriously affect the sustainable business operations of the company; and
(7) Where it has ever issued any securities publicly within the recent 24 months, there is no such thing as decrease in the business profits of the current year of the issuance decrease by 50% or more as compared to the previous year.

3.54 Article 8 of the Measures for Subsequent Offerings elaborates on the phrase 'a sound financial status', stating that:

A listed company which satisfies the following provisions shall be deemed that it has a good financial status:
(1) Its basic accounting work is standard and it strictly complies with the uniform accounting system of the state;
(2) For the financial statements of the recent three years and the recent 1 period, there is no audit report with reserved opinions or negative opinions as issued by certified accountants or on which it is difficult for certified accountant to express their opinions. If an audit report with no reserved opinions but with emphasized matters is issued by a certified public accountant, the matters involved shall have no seriously unfavorable effect on the issuer of securities or the seriously unfavorable effect has been eliminated prior to the issuance of securities;
(3) The assets are of good quality. The non-performing assets cannot result in any seriously unfavorable effect on the financial status of the company;
(4) Its business outcomes are genuine and the cash flows are normal. It has strictly complied with the relevant accounting standards of the state in the recognition of its business incomes, costs and expenses. It has made full and reasonable provisions for asset impairment in recent three years and has never manipulated its business performances; and
(5) The profits which it has accumulatively distributed in cash or in stocks are not less than 20% of the average annual distributable profits realized in the recent 3 years.

3.55 Article 9 of the Measures for Subsequent Offerings sheds light on the criterion of 'no false record', stating that:

A listed company has no false record in its financial and accounting documents within the recent 36 months and has not committed any of the following serious illegal acts:
(1) Due to violating any securities law, administrative regulation or rules, it has been subject to any administrative punishment of the CSRC or has been given any criminal punishment;
(2) Due to violating any law, administrative regulation or rules on the industry and commerce, tax, land, environmental protection or customs, it has been

subject to any administrative punishment very serious circumstance, or has been subject to any criminal punishment; or
(3) Other acts in violation of other laws or administrative regulations of the state, of which the circumstances are serious.

3.56 Article 15 of the Securities Law sets out a further requirement about the usage of funds raised from securities offerings, providing that:

> The funds as raised through public offer of stocks as made by a company shall be used according to the purpose as prescribed in the prospectus. Any alteration of the use of funds as prescribed in the prospectus shall be subject to a resolution of the general assembly of shareholders. Where a company fails to correct any unlawful alteration of its use of funds or where any alteration of its use of funds fails to be adopted by the general assembly of shareholders, the relevant company shall not make any public offerings.

3.57 Again, Article 10 of the Measures for Subsequent Offerings provides further guidance on the above provision, stating that:

> The amount and utilization of the funds raised by a listed company shall satisfy the following provisions:
> (1) The amount of funds raised shall not exceed the required amount of the project;
> (2) The purposes of use of the fund raised are in line with the industrial policies of the state as well as the laws and administrative regulations on environmental protection and land management;
> (3) Except for a financial enterprise, the fund raised at the present time shall not be used as financial investments such as holding transactional financial assets or financial assets available for sale, or lending it to others or use it as entrusted financing, nor may it be used to invest directly or indirectly in any company which mainly engages in the buying and selling securities;
> (4) The investment project will not result in competition with the controlling shareholder or the actual controller, nor will it affect the company's independence in production and business operations; and
> (5) It shall formulate rules on the special deposit of the raised funds and shall deposit the raised funds in the special account as decided by its board of directors.

3.58 Article 11 of the Measures for Subsequent Offerings provides for certain circumstances where a listed company shall be deprived of the right to carry out public offerings, stating that:

> Where any listed company is under any of the following circumstances, it shall not issue any securities publicly:
> (1) The application documents for the present issuance have any false record, misleading statement or serious omission;
> (2) The listed company illegally changes the purposes of use of the funds raised in the previous public issuance of securities and fails to make a correction;

(3) The listed company has ever been publicly condemned by the stock exchange within the recent 12 months;

(4) The listed company and its controlling shareholder or actual controller fail to the perform their public commitments to the investors within the recent 12 months;

(5) The listed company or any of its incumbent directors, senior management members is being investigated by the judicial organ due to any suspected crime or is being investigated by The CSRC due to any suspected violation; or

(6) Other circumstances under which the legitimate rights and interests of the investors or the social and public interests are severely impaired.

3.5.1.2. Special requirements for offerings of shares

3.59 Apart from the general merits review criteria as noted above, there are special requirements which are applicable to different types of offerings respectively. Under the Measures for Subsequent Offerings, public offerings by listed companies are further divided into so-called additional issues (*zeng fa*) and rights issues (*pei gu*). Additional issues are post-IPO securities offerings made by listed companies to unspecified objects, while rights issues are offers to all holders of a listed company's securities to issue new securities in proportion to their existing holdings where the offer is made in the same terms to all holders (the offers may be renounceable in favour of others).

3.60 Under the Measures for Subsequent Offerings, rights issues shall not only meet the general merits review criteria as discussed above, but also satisfy the following provisions:

(1) The amount of the shares to be allotted shall not exceed 30 per cent of the total capital stock prior to the present allotment of shares;

(2) The controlling shareholder shall make a public commitment to subscribe to the number of shares to be allotted to it; and

(3) The stocks shall be issued by way of proxy sale under the Securities Law.

3.61 If the controlling shareholder fails to perform its commitment to subscribe to the shares allotted to it, or if the number of shares subscribed to by the existing shareholders does not reach 70 per cent of the number of shares to be allotted at the expiration of the term of issue, the issuer company shall refund the issuing price plus interest, as calculated at the bank deposit rate for the same period, to the shareholders who have subscribed to the shares allotted to them.[25]

3.62 Additional issues are also subject to special requirements as follows:

(1) The average of the weighted average net asset yield rates for the preceding three years is not lower than 6 per cent as calculated on the basis of the net

---

[25] Measures for Subsequent Offerings, Art 12.

profits after deducting the non-regular profits and losses or the pre-deduction net profits, whichever is smaller;
(2) At the end of the recent period, there is no financial investment in the listed company as holding any relatively large sum of transactional financial assets or financial assets available for sale, lending it to others, or making any entrusted financing, with the exception of financial enterprises;
(3) The issuance price shall not be lower than the average price of the company's stock prices during the 20 transaction days prior to the announcement of the prospectus or the average price of the transaction on the day prior to the issuance.[26]

3.5.1.3. *Special requirements for offerings of convertible corporate bonds*

3.63 The term 'convertible corporate bonds' refers to corporate bonds which are issued by an issuing company pursuant to law and which may be converted to shares during a certain period and under stipulated conditions. A bond holder has the option to convert the corporate bonds into stocks or not to convert them into stocks, and they will become a shareholder of the issuing company on the day following the conversion day.[27]

3.64 In addition to the general merits review criteria discussed above, special requirements are imposed on the issuance of convertible corporate bonds. Article 14 of the Measures for Subsequent Offerings stipulates the following substantive requirements:

(1) The average of the weighted average net asset yield rates for the preceding three years is not lower than 6 per cent as calculated on the basis of the net profits after deducting the non-regular profits and losses or the pre-deduction net profits, whichever is smaller.
(2) After the present issuance, the balance of the accumulative corporate bonds shall not exceed 40 per cent of the amount of net assets at the end of the recent period.
(3) The annual average amount of distributable profits realized in the preceding three years is not less than the annual amount of interest of the corporate bonds.

3.65 Convertible corporate bonds are also subject to other relevant rules under the Measures for Subsequent Offerings. For instance:

(1) The minimum time period of convertible corporate bonds shall be one year, and the maximum shall be six years (Article 15).

---

[26] Measures for Subsequent Offerings, Art 13.
[27] Measures for Subsequent Offerings, Art 21.

(2) The face value of each convertible corporate bond shall be 100 yuan. The interest rate of a convertible corporate bond shall be determined by the issuing company and the leading underwriter through negotiations, but it shall satisfy the relevant provisions of the state (Article 16).

(3) To publicly issue convertible corporate bonds, a company shall entrust a qualified credit rating agency to make credit ratings and follow-up ratings. A credit rating institution shall at least announce one follow-up rating report every year (Article 17).

(4) A listed company shall, within five working days after the expiration of the term of convertible corporate bonds, pay off the principal and interest of the balance of the bonds (Article 18).

(5) To publicly issue convertible corporate bonds, a company shall stipulate the measures for protection of the rights of the bond holders, the rights and procedures of the bondholders' meetings, as well as the conditions for the effectiveness of the resolutions made at the meetings of bond holders (Article 19).

(6) To publicly issue convertible corporate bonds, a guaranty shall be provided unless the company's unaudited net assets at the end of the recent period amounted to RMB 1.5 billion yuan or more (Article 20).

(7) The convertible corporate bonds shall not be converted into corporate stocks unless six months have elapsed since the end of the issuance thereof. The time limit for the conversion shall be determined according to the existence period of the corporate bonds as well as the financial status of the company (Article 21).

(8) The conversion price shall not be lower than the average price of the company's stock prices over the 20 transaction days prior to the announcement of the prospectus or the average price on the transaction day prior to the conversion (Article 22).

(9) The conversion price can be adjusted. The prospectus shall stipulate the principle and method for adjusting the conversion price (Article 25).

3.66 Importantly, the Measures for Subsequent Offerings allow convertible corporate bonds to design some special mechanisms. First, they can be redeemable. The prospectus may include redemption clauses, stating that the listed company may redeem the convertible corporate bonds which have not been converted into stocks according to the conditions and prices given in advance.[28]

3.67 Second, they can be sold back to the issuer company. The prospectus may include sell-back clauses, stating that the bond holders may sell the bonds back to the listed company under the conditions and price given in advance. The prospectus shall stipulate that if the listed company changes any of the announced purposes of use of the raised funds, the bond holders will have the sell-back right for one time.[29]

---

[28] Measures for Subsequent Offerings, Art 23.
[29] Measures for Subsequent Offerings, Art 24.

Finally, convertible corporate bonds can be bonds with attached warrant (also called equity warrant bonds), where the transaction of warrants is separated from the transaction of bonds. To issue such bonds, the listed company shall not only meet the general merits review criteria discussed earlier, but also satisfy the following special requirements: **3.68**

(1) The company's unaudited net assets at the end of the recent period have amounted to no less than 1.5 billion yuan.
(2) The average annual distributable profits realized in the preceding three years is not less than the annual amount of interest of the corporate bonds.
(3) The average annual net amount of the cash flows brought about by its business operations within the preceding three accounting years is not less than the annual amount of the interest of corporate bonds, excluding those companies which meet the provisions of Article 14(1) of these Measures.
(4) After the present issuance, the balance of the cumulative corporate bonds shall not exceed 40 per cent of the amount of the net assets at the end of the recent period and the expected total amount of funds raised by the exercise of all related warrants shall not exceed the amount of the convertible corporate bonds to be issued.[30]

Bonds with attached warrant are also subject to other provisions under the Measures for Subsequent Offerings in relation to the listing and trading of bonds and warrants, the term period, face value, interest rate, protection of bond holders, and so on.[31] **3.69**

3.5.2. Private placement

Listed companies can also issue securities to specified objects in a private manner. Under Article 13(2) of the Securities Law, private placement by listed companies is also subject to merits-review: that is, it shall meet the substantive requirements as prescribed by CSRC, and shall be reported to the CSRC for examination and approval. **3.70**

3.5.2.1. Definition of private placement

Under Article 37 of the Measures for Subsequent Offerings, the specified objects of private offering of securities shall satisfy the following provisions: **3.71**

(1) The specified objects shall meet the conditions as given in the resolution of the shareholders' assembly.
(2) The number of specified objects shall not exceed 10.

Further, if a specified object is an overseas strategic investor, it shall be subject to the prior approval of the relevant department of the State Council.

---

[30] Measures for Subsequent Offerings, Art 27.
[31] Measures for Subsequent Offerings, Arts 28–35.

3.5.2.2. Merits review criteria

3.72 To make a private offering of securities, a listed company shall meet a number of substantive requirements relating to the issue price, transfer restrictions, use of the fund, and so on:

(1) The issuance price shall not be lower than 90 per cent of the average price of the company's stocks of the 20 transaction days prior to the date of benchmark pricing.
(2) The shares presently issued shall not be transferred to any other person within 12 months as of the end of issuance. The shares subscribed to by the controlling shareholder or actual controller and the enterprises it controls shall not be transferred to any other person within 36 months.
(3) The utilization of the raised funds shall satisfy the provisions of Article 10 of these Measures.
(4) If the present issuance will result in any change in the controlling power of the listed company, it shall meet other provisions of the CSRC.[32]

3.73 According to Article 39 of the Measures for Subsequent Offerings, a listed company shall not make any private offering of stocks in any of the following circumstances:

(1) The application documents for the present issuance contain any false record, misleading statement, or serious omission.
(2) The rights and interests of the listed company were severely injured by its controlling shareholder or actual controller and the impairment has not been eliminated.
(3) The listed company or its subsidiary company has illegally provided any guaranty to any other person and the guaranty has not been cancelled.
(4) Any of the incumbent directors or senior management members of the listed company has been given any administrative punishment by the CSRC within the past 36 months or has been condemned publicly by the stock exchange within the past 12 months.
(5) The listed company or any of its incumbent directors or senior management members is being investigated by the judicial organ due to any suspected crime or is being investigated by the CSRC due to any suspected violation.
(6) The listed company has been issued by a certified accountant with an audit report where the accountant expresses reserved opinions or adverse opinions, or cannot provide any opinion, on the company's financial reports in the preceding one year and in the most recent reporting period, unless the consequences of the events involved therein have been eliminated or unless the present offering involves significant restructuring.

---

[32] Measures for Subsequent Offerings, Art 27.

Securities Offerings

(7) Other circumstances under which the legitimate rights and interests of the investors and social and public interests are severely injured.

3.5.3. The procedure for offering securities

3.74 There are three distinct stages in the offering process, namely approval by the shareholders, approval by the CSRC, and the actual issuance.

3.5.3.1. Shareholder resolution

3.75 The offering process starts within the listed company. The board of directors of the listed company shall make a proposal for securities offerings, and then submit it to the shareholders' assembly for approval. The proposal should cover the following matters:

(1) A plan for the present issuance of securities.
(2) A feasibility report about the purposes of use of the funds to be raised by the present issuance.
(3) A report about the purposes of use of the funds raised in the previous issuance.
(4) Other matters that must be specified explicitly.[33]

3.76 The shareholders' assembly shall then make a resolution on the offering and, depending on the type of the securities to be offered, the resolution shall contain different matters. For instance, in the case of share offering, the shareholder resolution shall at least include the following matters:

(1) The type and number of securities of the present issuance.
(2) The issuance method, issuance objects, and the arrangement about the allotment to original shareholders.
(3) The pricing method or the range of price.
(4) The purposes of use of the funds to be raised.
(5) The valid period of the resolution.
(6) Authorization to the board of directors to deal with the concrete matters relating to the present issuance.
(7) Other matters that must be specified explicitly.[34]

3.77 If convertible corporate bonds are to be offered, the shareholder resolution should cover not only the matters required for share offerings as noted, but also other matters, as follows:

(1) The interest rate of the bonds.
(2) The term of the bonds.

---

[33] Measures for Subsequent Offerings, Art 40.
[34] Measures for Subsequent Offerings, Art 41.

(3) The guaranty-related matters.
(4) The sell-back clauses.
(5) The time limit and method for the repayment of principal and interest.
(6) The conversion period.
(7) The determination and revision of the conversion price.[35]

3.78 There are also rules to govern the ways in which shareholders should meet and vote. A resolution made by the shareholders' assembly regarding the issuance of securities shall be subject to adoption by two thirds of voting rights of the shareholders attending the meeting. If the listed company is to issue securities to specific shareholders and their connected parties, when the shareholders' assembly takes a vote on the issuance plan, the connected shareholders shall disqualify themselves.

3.79 If a listed company convenes a shareholders' assembly regarding the issuance of securities, it shall facilitate the shareholders attendance at the shareholders' assembly by providing them with network access or otherwise.[36]

3.5.3.2. CSRC approval

3.80 Where a listed company applies for the public issuance of securities or private offering of new shares, it shall be recommended by a sponsor, and it is the sponsor who shall prepare and submit the application documents according to the relevant provisions of the CSRC.[37]

3.81 The CSRC shall examine a securities issuance application according to the following procedures:

(1) It shall decide whether or not to accept the application documents within five working days after it receives them.
(2) It shall conduct a preliminary examination over the application documents after it accepts them.
(3) Its Issuance Examination and Approval Commission shall review the application documents.
(4) It shall make a decision of approval or disapproval.[38]

3.82 A listed company shall issue securities within six months from the day when it is granted an approval of issuance by the CSRC. If it fails to do so, the approval document shall be invalidated and it shall not issue any securities unless it is granted a new approval by the CSRC.[39]

---

[35] Measures for Subsequent Offerings, Art 42.
[36] Measures for Subsequent Offerings, Art 44.
[37] Measures for Subsequent Offerings, Art 45. For more discussion of the sponsor issue, see Chapter 4.
[38] Measures for Subsequent Offerings, Art 46.
[39] Measures for Subsequent Offerings, Art 47.

On the other hand, for a listed company whose securities issuance application is disapproved, it shall not file any new securities issuance application unless six months have elapsed from the day when the CSRC makes a decision of disapproval.[40] **3.83**

3.5.3.3. Issuance

Under Article 49 of the Measures for Subsequent Offerings, the securities to be issued by a listed company shall be underwritten by securities companies. For private offering stocks, if the offerings are made to the existing ten largest shareholders of the listed company, the stocks may be sold by the listed company itself.[41] **3.84**

3.5.4. Disclosure requirements

3.5.4.1. General requirements

Apart from the merit-review requirements, the issuer company must also comply with relevant information disclosure rules. In principle, when a listed company issues securities, it shall, according to the procedures, contents, and formats as prescribed by the CSRC, prepare a prospectus for the public issuance of securities or other information disclosure documents, and shall perform the information disclosure obligation.[42] **3.85**

A listed company shall ensure that investors have access to the statutory disclosure information in a timely, adequate, and fair manner. The words in the information disclosure documents shall be concise, simple, and understandable. The contents as prescribed by the CSRC are the minimum requirements for the information disclosure. A listed company shall fully disclose any information which has significant effects on investors' investment decisions.[43] **3.86**

The Measures for Subsequent Offerings then set out specific disclosure requirements for each of the three stages of the procedure for offering securities, namely shareholder resolution, CSRC approval, and actual issuance. These will now be discussed in turn. **3.87**

3.5.4.2. Disclosure relating to shareholder resolution

After the securities issuance plan has been adopted by the board of directors upon voting, the listed company shall report it to the stock exchange within two working days and announce notice to hold a meeting of the shareholders' assembly. If the listed company intends to use any of the funds to be raised to purchase any asset or stock right, when it announces the notice to hold a meeting of the shareholders' assembly it shall disclose basic information about the asset or stock right, the **3.88**

---

[40] Measures for Subsequent Offerings, Art 50.
[41] For more discussion on the underwriting issue, see Chapter 4.
[42] Measures for Subsequent Offerings, Art 51.
[43] Measures for Subsequent Offerings, Art 52.

transaction price, the pricing basis, and whether or not the shareholders or other connected parties of the company have any interests therein.[44]

3.89 A listed company shall, within two working days from the day when the shareholders' assembly adopts the plan on the present issuance, announce the resolution of the shareholders' assembly.[45]

3.5.4.3. Disclosure relating to CSRC approval

3.90 A listed company shall, on the next working day after it receives any of the following decisions about the application for the present issuance, make an announcement of:

(1) Rejection or termination of the examination.
(2) Disapproval or approval.

3.91 If the listed company decides to withdraw its securities issuance application, it shall make an announcement on the next working day after it withdraws its application documents.

3.5.4.4. Disclosure relating to issuance

3.92 Within 2–5 working days prior to the public issuance of securities, a listed company shall publish an abstract of the prospectus or of the letter of intent for raising funds as examined and approved by the CSRC in at least one newspaper or periodical as designated by the CSRC, publish the full text of the prospectus on the internet website as designated by the CSRC, and place it in a place as designated by the CSRC for public consultation.[46]

3.93 A listed company shall, after making a private offering of new shares, at least publish the issuance information report in a newspaper or periodical as designated by the CSRC, publish the full text of the report on the internet website as designated by the CSRC, and place it in a place designated by the CSRC for public consultation.[47]

3.5.4.5. Comments

3.94 In general, the Chinese information disclosure regime for securities offerings by listed companies is clear and comprehensive. It works to ensure that the investors would have adequate information to make an informed investment decision. However, as information disclosure involves significant costs, it is not simply a case of the more disclosure, the better. Rather, a disclosure regime should be assessed from a cost-efficient perspective. In this regard, two broad observations can be made about the Chinese regime.

---

[44] Measures for Subsequent Offerings, Art 53.
[45] Measures for Subsequent Offerings, Art 54.
[46] Measures for Subsequent Offerings, Art 61.
[47] Measures for Subsequent Offerings, Art 62.

3.95 First, both public offerings and private placement are subject to disclosure requirements, even though there are some important differences in the requirements. True, a prospectus is required for public offerings and not private placement, which is in line with the international practice. However, private placement requires the publication of the issuance information report, and more generally is also subject to the aforementioned disclosure rules relating to shareholder approval, CSRC approval, and issuance.

3.96 Second, even for public offerings, the disclosure regime applies a one-size-fits-all approach and does not take into consideration certain special circumstances where investors may not need protection through prospectus disclosure, or at least may need this to a lesser extent. For instance, in many overseas jurisdictions, rights issues are exempted from disclosure requirements, because the issue is proportional and investor protection is considered to be achieved through the original prospectus disclosure, coupled with the continuous disclosure obligation upon listed companies.

4

SECURITIES LISTINGS

4.1. Overview	4.01	4.4.1. IPO and listing on the main board	4.88
4.1.1. Listings vs offerings	4.01	4.4.2. IPO and listing on the second board	4.96
4.1.2. The benefits and costs of listing	4.06		
4.2. Criteria for Initial Public Offering (IPO)	4.10	4.5. Sponsorship	4.107
		4.5.1. Overview	4.107
4.2.1. Securities Law	4.10	4.5.2. Qualifications of sponsors and sponsor representatives	4.112
4.2.2. China Securities Regulatory Commission (CSRC) regulation	4.15	4.5.3. Sponsor responsibilities	4.114
4.2.3. Stock exchange listing rules	4.69	4.5.4. Procedures for the sponsorship business	4.128
4.3. The Procedure	4.76	4.5.5. Supervisory measures and legal liabilities	4.134
4.3.1. IPO and listing on the main board	4.76		
4.3.2. IPO and listing on the second board	4.87	4.6. Pricing and Underwriting	4.142
4.4. Information Disclosure Requirements	4.88	4.6.1. Pricing	4.143
		4.6.2. Underwriting	4.161

4.1. Overview

4.1.1. Listings vs offerings

4.01 Conceptually, securities offerings and listings are two distinct processes involving different issues. In theory, one company can conduct securities offerings but not get the securities quoted on stock exchanges. Conversely, listing matters may arise without an accompanying process of securities offerings—for instance, a listed company migrates from one stock exchange to another, or the holder of convertible bonds in a listed company exercises the right to convert their bonds into shares.

4.02 Indeed, securities offerings and listings are different in several important aspects. First, the process of securities offerings seeks to achieve the purposes of fundraising or capital formation, which can be carried out without the involvement of the stock exchange. In contrast, the process of listing seeks to get the securities quoted on a stock exchange, which can provide liquidity for their trading. Second, the legal document required for securities offerings is usually a prospectus, while that for securities listings is a listing document.

Third, in the strict sense, securities offerings are a corporate finance matter, and thus are usually regulated by company law in those jurisdictions which have a company law/securities law divide. The US and Hong Kong are good examples of this legislative pattern, and it was also the case for China until the overhaul of its company and securities law in 2005.[1] As discussed in the previous chapter, the rules governing securities offerings are now contained in the 2005 Securities Law. Securities listings, however, are mainly dealt with by the listing rules of the stock exchange. Again, China is an exception in that, as shall be discussed later, in addition to stock exchanges' listing rules, the Securities Law and CSRC regulations set out relevant rules on securities listings.

4.03

Finally, securities offerings are usually supervised by securities regulators. In China, the securities regulator, namely the CSRC, conducts merits review of securities offerings in addition to enforcing information disclosure rules; in many developed markets, only the latter is the case. Securities listings, on the other hand, are traditionally regarded as contractual arrangements between the listed company and the stock exchange.[2]

4.04

In the context of IPOs, however, securities offerings always go hand in hand with company listing and securities quotation. IPO stands for 'initial public offering', and it is possible for a company to conduct an IPO but not seek listing on a stock exchange. In China, due to reasons such as the underdevelopment of off-exchange markets, IPO is almost invariably coupled with a following listing process. Thus, strictly speaking, this two-in-one process should be called 'IPO plus listing', and not just IPO. For brevity, however, the term 'IPO' will be used to mean 'IPO and listing' in this chapter.

4.05

4.1.2. The benefits and costs of listing

In China, there are two types of companies, namely limited liability companies and joint-stock companies. They roughly correspond to private companies and public companies in many British Commonwealth jurisdictions such as Hong Kong, or privately held corporations and publicly held corporations in the US. Limited liability companies do not issue shares, let alone get listed. Joint-stock companies issue shares, and can be listed or unlisted. Thus, limited liability companies which want to pursue IPO must first become joint-stock companies.

4.06

---

[1] Baoshu Wang and Hui Huang, 'China's New Company Law and Securities Law: An Overview and Assessment' (2006) 19(2) *Australian Journal of Corporate Law* 229.

[2] In recent years, there has been an international trend of stock exchanges getting demutualized and self-listed, since the Australian Stock Exchange first did so in the world in 1998. Due to concerns over conflicts of interest this may bring about for stock exchanges as frontline regulators, some jurisdictions, such as the UK and Australia, have transferred the power over listing decisions from the stock exchange to the government regulator.

4.07 Whether to get listed on a stock exchange is a business decision to be made by a company in light of its particular circumstances. Indeed, listing may bring both benefits and costs for the company.

4.08 There are five main advantages of listing and quotation upon a stock exchange. First, it makes it easier for companies to raise funds through the new issue facilities of securities markets. Floating a company gives access to wider sources of equity capital than is generally available through private placement of its securities. Stock exchange listing also facilitates the raising of additional capital through rights issues. Second, listing secures liquidity for corporate securities, which enhances the appeal of the security to investors. This provides inducement to investment in the first place, and also facilitates the raising of further funds. Third, listing enables proprietors whose capital has been effectively locked up in their shareholdings to realize the value of their investment through sale on a public market. This is particularly important for venture capitalists, whose business model is typically to first invest in a start-up company and then, once the company grows and is listed, exit with profits from selling their investment on the stock exchange. Fourth, the stock exchange promotes investor confidence through its monitoring of trading in securities and reduces transaction costs through its standard-form governance and transaction settlement rules. Finally, as listed companies must meet certain listing criteria, listing generally brings a reputational benefit for the listed company. This positive reputational signal is of potential value for the listed company in doing business.

4.09 On the other hand, listing is not an unqualified good, as it does involve costs. First, listing is a time-consuming and costly process. Second, after getting listed, the company is also subject to considerable expense for matters such as listing fee, share registry, and information disclosure. Third, as a listed company, it faces greater regulation of conduct through higher governance standards and trading restraints. Fourth, the listed company also suffers a loss of privacy to the extent that they are subject to many information disclosure requirements. Finally, the controller of the listed company may be exposed to the threat of loss of control through takeover due to the public market facility for the company's shares.

4.2. Criteria for Initial Public Offering (IPO)

4.2.1. Securities Law

4.10 To start with, as a form of public offering, IPOs are subject to the general merits review criteria for public offerings under Article 13 of the Securities Law, which state that:

> (1) A company conducting public offerings of new shares shall meet the following requirements:
> (2) the issuer must have a complete and well-functioning organizational structure;

(3) the issuer must have the capability of making profits continuously and a sound financial status;
(4) the issuer must have no false record in its financial statements over the last three years and have no other major irregularity; and
(5) other requirements as prescribed by [the CSRC].

4.11 Further, Article 15 of the Securities Law sets out requirements about the usage of funds raised through securities offerings, providing:

> The funds as raised through public offer of stocks as made by a company shall be used according to the purpose as prescribed in the prospectus. Any alteration of the use of funds as prescribed in the prospectus shall be subject to a resolution of the general assembly of shareholders. Where a company fails to correct any unlawful alteration of its use of funds or where any alteration of its use of funds fails to be adopted by the general assembly of shareholders, the relevant company shall not make any public offerings.

4.12 Finally, Article 50 of the Securities Law sets out criteria for share listings, including:

(1) The stocks shall have been publicly issued upon the approval of the securities regulatory authority under the State Council;
(2) The total amount of capital stock of the company shall be no less than RMB 30 million yuan;
(3) The shares as publicly issued shall reach more than 25% of the total amount of corporate shares; where the total amount of capital stock of a company exceeds RMB 0.4 billion yuan, the shares as publicly issued shall be no less than 10% thereof; and
(4) The company shall not have any major irregularity over the latest three years and there are no false records in its financial statements.

4.13 It is also made clear that a stock exchange may prescribe requirements of listing that are more strict than those prescribed in the above provision, which shall be reported to the CSRC for approval.

4.14 With the respective powers delegated under Articles 13 and 50 of the Securities Law, the CSRC and stock exchanges have promulgated rules to provide more guidance and further requirements for IPO.

4.2.2. China Securities Regulatory Commission (CSRC) regulation

4.15 Depending on whether the securities are to be listed on the main board market or the second board market of the stock exchange, the CSRC has promulgated two separate regulations. More specifically, the process of IPO and listing on the main board market is covered by the Measures for the Administration of Initial Public Offerings and Listing of Stocks' (Measures for IPO and Listing),[3] while the process

---

[3] Shouci Gongkai Faxing Gupiao bing Shangshi Guanli Banfa [Measures for the Administration of Initial Public Offering and Listing of Stocks] (promulgated by the CSRC in 2006).

of IPO and listing on the second board market is dealt with by the Measures for the Administration of Initial Public Offerings and Listing on the Second Board Market (Measures for IPO and Listing on Second Board).[4]

4.2.2.1. IPO and listing on the main board market

4.16 The Measures for IPO and listing provide more details on the requirements for IPO and listing on the main board market, which can be broadly divided into five categories: qualification for issuers, independence, standardized operation, finance and accounting, and utilization of raised funds.

(1) Qualification for issuers

4.17 An issuer shall be a joint-stock limited company that has been legally established and lawfully exists.[5] Further, the joint stock limited company must have operated its business for at least three years, unless it gets special approval from the State Council. Where a limited liability company is transformed into a joint-stock limited company by converting the entirety of its original net book value of assets, the term of its business operations may be calculated as of the day when the limited liability company is established.[6]

4.18 It is further required that the issuer's registered capital has been fully paid, that the formalities for transferring the property right of the assets that the promoter or shareholders apply as contributions have been concluded, and that there is no substantial dispute over ownership of the issuer's major assets. The business operation of the issuer shall comply with the relevant provisions of the laws, administrative regulations, and company constitution, and meet the relevant industrial policies of the state.

4.19 There is no major change regarding the issuer's main business, directors, and senior managers, as well as its actual controller. The issuer's shareholding structure is well-defined, and there is no substantial dispute over the ownership of the issuer's shares held by its controlling shareholders, or the shareholders under the control of its controlling shareholders or the actual controller.

(2) Independence

4.20 In general, an issuer shall have a complete set of operations and be capable of independently conducting market-based business operations.[7] The independence requirement is reflected in five main aspects of the company: assets, personnel, finance, organization, and business.[8]

---

[4] Shouci Gongkai Faxing Gupiao bing zai Chuangyeban Shangshi Guanli Zanxing Banfa [Measures for the Administration of Initial Public Offerings and Listing on the Second Board Market] (promulgated by the CSRC in 2009).
[5] Measures for IPO and Listing, Art 8.
[6] Measures for IPO and Listing, Art 9.
[7] Measures for IPO and Listing, Art 14.
[8] Measures for IPO and Listing, Arts 15–19.

First, an issuer shall have integrated assets. A production enterprise shall be equipped with the relevant production system, auxiliary production system, and supporting facilities corresponding to its business operations; have the right to own or use the land, workshops, and machines and facilities relating to its business operations as well as the ownership or use right to its trade marks patent technologies, and know-how; and have an independent purchase system of raw materials and sales system of products. A non-production enterprise shall be equipped with a set of operations as well as the relevant assets relating to its business operations.

4.21

Second, an issuer shall have personnel independence. Such senior managers as the general manager, deputy manager, financial principal, and secretary of the board of directors shall not hold any post other than director or supervisor in, or collect any salary from, its controlling shareholder, actual controller, or any other enterprise under its control. The financial staff of an issuer shall not hold any part-time post in its controlling shareholder, actual controller, or any other enterprise under its control.

4.22

Third, an issuer shall enjoy financial independence. An issuer shall establish an independent financial verification system, be capable of making independent decisions, and have a standardized financial accounting system as well as financial management of its branches and subsidiary companies. An issuer shall not share any bank account with its controlling shareholder, actual controller, or any other enterprise under its control.

4.23

Fourth, an issuer shall enjoy organizational independence. An issuer shall establish and improve an internal operating and management system, independently exercise its power of business operation and management, and shall not mix up its organizational system with that of its controlling shareholder, actual controller, or any other enterprise under its control.

4.24

Fifth, an issuer shall enjoy business independence. An issuer shall carry out its business operations independently from its controlling shareholder, actual controller, or any other enterprises under its control, and shall not have any intra-trade competition or obviously unfair associated transactions with its controlling shareholder, actual controller, or any other enterprise under its control.

4.25

(3) Standardized operation

This requirement is actually a clarification of the requirements under Article 13 of the Securities Law that 'the issuer must have a complete and well-functioning organizational structure' and that 'the issuer must. . . have no other major irregularity'.[9]

4.26

An issuer shall establish and improve relevant rules governing the shareholders' assembly, board of directors, board of supervisors, independent directors, and a secretary system for the board of directors according to law. The relevant organizations

4.27

---

[9] Measures for IPO and Listing, Arts 21–7.

and personnel shall be capable of performing their functions and duties according to law.

4.28 The directors, supervisors, and senior managers of an issuer shall have good knowledge of the relevant laws and regulations on the stock IPO and listing, as well as the statutory obligations and duties of a listed company and the directors, supervisors, and senior managers thereof.

4.29 The directors, supervisors, and senior managers of an issuer shall meet the qualification requirements for holding their positions as prescribed by laws, administrative regulations, and rules, and shall not be subject to any of the following circumstances:

(1) Having been banned from entering into the market by the CSRC and the ban is still valid.
(2) Having been given an administrative punishment by the CSRC within the preceding 36 months or having been given a public reprimand by a stock exchange within the preceding 12 months.
(3) Being subject to a case investigation of the judicial organ for involvement in a suspected crime or suspected violation of any law or regulation, and yet there being no clear conclusion.

4.30 An issuer shall have an improved and effectively implemented internal control system and shall ensure the reliability of its financial statements, legality of its business operations, and efficiency and efficacy of its business performances.

4.31 An issuer shall not be under any of the following circumstances:

(1) Having publicly offered, unlawfully or in disguise, any securities without obtaining an approval from the statutory organ in the preceding 36 months; or having been involved in any law-breaking act that started 36 months ago but lasts up to the present time.
(2) Having been given an administrative punishment for violation of any provision on industry and commerce, taxation, land, environmental protection or customs, or any other law or administrative regulation, with serious circumstances.
(3) Having filed an application with the CSRC in the preceding 36 months but the submitted application materials having any false record, misleading statement, or major omission; or failing to meet the requirements for issuance and thus cheating for an approval by any fraudulent means; or disturbing the examination as conducted by the CSRC or the Issuance and Verification Committee thereof, or fabricating or altering the seal or signature of an issuer or any director, supervisor, or senior manager thereof.
(4) Its application materials submitted this time for issuance having any false record, misleading statement, or major omission.

(5) Being subject to a case investigation of the judicial organ for its involvement in a suspected crime without explicit conclusion.
(6) Being under any other circumstance where the legitimate rights and interests of investors or social and public interests are seriously injured.

An issuer's constitution shall clarify the authority of examination and approval of its external guaranty as well as the relevant procedures for deliberation thereabout. There shall be no rule-breaking guaranty as provided for its controlling shareholder, actual controller, or any other enterprise under its control. **4.32**

An issuer shall have strict rules for capital management and shall not be under any circumstance where its capital is embezzled by any controlling shareholder, actual controller, or any other enterprise under its control by loaning, compensatory repayment, advance payment, or any other method. **4.33**

(4) Finance and accounting

Similar to the nature of the preceding section, this section fleshes out more detail on the requirement under Article 13 of the Securities Law that 'the issuer must have the capability of making profits continuously and a sound financial status'.[10] It sets out the most important set of the approval criteria, which is characteristic of merit regulation. **4.34**

An issuer shall have a sound asset quality, reasonable structure of assets and liabilities, comparatively strong profit-making capacity, and normal cash flows. Further, the issuer shall have an effective internal control in all substantial aspects, for which an authentication report on internal control shall be produced by an accounting firm, carrying an unreserved conclusion thereon. **4.35**

An issuer shall have standardized accounting rules. The formulation of its financial statements shall satisfy the provisions on enterprise accounting standards as well as the relevant accounting rules, which shall, in all substantial aspects, reflect its financial status, business achievements, and cash flows thereof at arm's length. An auditing report shall be produced by an accounting firm, carrying an unreserved conclusion thereon. **4.36**

An issuer shall formulate its financial statements based on the transactions and issues that have actually occurred and shall be prudent in its accounting recognition, measurement, or reporting, and shall apply a uniform accounting policy for a same or identical business operation, which shall not be altered at random. **4.37**

An issuer shall fully disclose its relationship with associated parties and shall, according to the principles of importance, disclose their associated transactions. **4.38**

---

[10] Measures for IPO and Listing, Arts 28–37.

The prices in associated transactions shall be at arm's length and there shall be no manipulation of profits through associated transactions.

4.39 An issuer shall meet the following requirements:

(1) Having a positive net profit of over 30 million yuan cumulatively for the preceding three accounting years, which are calculated on the basis of the comparatively low net profits upon deduction of non-regular profits/losses.
(2) Having a net cash flow of over 50 million yuan cumulatively, or having a business income of over 0.3 billion yuan cumulatively for the preceding three accounting years.
(3) Having a total amount of stock capital of not less than 30 million yuan before issuance.
(4) The proportion of its latest intangible assets (upon deduction of its land use right, right to aquatic breeding, and right to mining) in its net assets not being higher than 20 per cent.
(5) Having no uncovered deficit in the latest period.

4.40 An issuer shall pay taxes according to law, for which all tax preferences shall meet the provisions of the relevant laws and regulations. An issuer's business achievements shall not overly depend on tax preferences.

4.41 An issuer shall not have any major debt-paying risk or be involved with any major contingent issue such as guaranty, litigation, or arbitration that may negatively affect its business operations.

4.42 An issuer's documents on application shall not:

(1) Omit or make up, purposely, any transaction, item, or any other important information.
(2) Abuse any accounting policy or accounting estimate.
(3) Manipulate, fabricate, or tamper with the relevant accounting records or credentials that form the basis of financial statements.

4.43 An issuer shall not be under any of the following circumstances where its capability to make profits continuously is negatively affected:

(1) Where its operational mode or variety structure of products and services has been or will be greatly changed, thereby inflicting a major negative impact on its capability to make profits continuously.
(2) Where its industrial status or business environment has or will greatly change, thereby inflicting a major negative impact on its capability to make profits continuously.
(3) Where its business income or net profit in the latest accounting year largely depends on its associated party or on any client and there is great uncertainty.

(4) Where its net profit in the latest accounting year mainly comes from the proceeds generated from investment beyond the scope of consolidated financial statements.
(5) Where it takes risks of negative change in obtaining or utilizing such important assets and technologies as trade mark, patent, exclusive technologies, and franchise.
(6) Where it is under any other circumstance in which its capability of making profits continuously is negatively affected.

(5) Utilization of raised funds

This section contains six articles, providing more guidance on Article 15 of the Securities Law which regulates the utilization of raised funds.[11] Basically, the funds raised must be used for the specified purposes as clearly indicated in the application documents, and there are restrictions on the use to which the funds can be put. This requirement is very important in China as in practice the funds raised are often misused or diverted to unauthorized destinations, such as the property and equity markets.

4.44

The funds raised shall be utilized for specified purposes and shall be used in the issuer's main business operations, as is the general principle. Except for financial enterprises, no funds raised may be utilized in such financial investments as the holding of transactional financial assets or saleable financial assets, loaning to others, and entrusted financial management, or be directly or indirectly invested in any company that mainly engages in the purchase and sale of securities.

4.45

The projects as invested by raised funds shall comply with the relevant state industrial policies, investment management, environmental protection, land administration, as well as the provisions of other relevant laws, regulations, and rules. The board of directors of an issuer shall carry out an earnest analysis on the feasibility of a project as invested by raised funds so as to ensure that the investment project may have a good market perspective and profit-making capability, to effectively prevent any investment risk and to elevate the benefits as generated from the use of the raised funds.

4.46

Where a project invested in by raised funds is implemented, it shall not incur any intra-trade competition or have any negative impact on the issuer's independence. An issuer shall establish a special reserve system for raised funds, which shall be deposited in a special account, as decided by the board of directors.

4.47

4.2.2.2. IPO and listing on the Second Board market

The Measures for IPO and Listing on the Second Board are drafted on the basis of the Measures for IPO and Listing, but reduces the criteria to suit the needs of second board listing.

4.48

---

[11] Measures for IPO and Listing, Arts 38–43.

4.49 In general, to apply for IPO of stocks, an issuer shall meet the following conditions:

(1) It shall be a joint-stock company legally established and having been operating continuously for three years or more. For a limited liability company, which is totally changed into a joint-stock company by converting its net asset value as shown in its account book into shares, the time of continuous operation may be calculated from the date at which the limited liability company is established.

(2) Its profits have been increasing for the preceding two consecutive years, and its cumulative net profits gained in the preceding two years are 10 million yuan or more and have been growing continuously; or it made profits in the latest year and the net profits are 5 million yuan or more, and its business income in the latest year is 50 million yuan or more, and the growth rate of its business income in the latest two years is 30 per cent or more (the net profits shall be calculated on the basis of the amount before or after deducting the non-recurring profit and loss, whichever is smaller).

(3) Its net asset value is 20 million yuan or more and it has no loss to cover in the latest period.

(4) The total amount of capital stock after offering is over 30 million yuan.[12]

4.50 Similarly, other provisions can be grouped into the same five categories as is the case for IPO and listing on the main board market, namely qualification for issuers, independence, standardized operation, finance and accounting, and utilization of raised funds.

4.51 **(1) Qualifications for issuers**[13]
The issuer shall have paid the registered capital in full and shall have finished the formalities for the transfer of property rights over the assets contributed by promoters or shareholders as investment. There is no gross ownership dispute over the major assets of the issuer.

4.52 The issuer shall focus on one business, and the production and operating activities shall conform to laws, administrative regulations, and the bylaws of the company and be in line with the state's industrial policies and environmental protection policies.

4.53 There is no major change in the principal business, directors, or senior managers of the issuer in the preceding two years, nor any change in the actual controller of the issuer.

4.54 **(2) Finance and accounting**[14]
The issuer shall have sustained profitability and not fall under any of the following circumstances:

(1) Its business mode or product or service structure has changed or is about to change to a large extent, which exerts great adverse influence upon its sustained profitability.

---

[12] Measures for IPO and Listing on Second Board, Art 10.
[13] Measures for IPO and Listing on Second Board, Arts 11–13.
[14] Measures for IPO and Listing on Second Board, Arts 14–17.

(2) Its position in the industry or the business environment of its industry has changed or is about to change to a large extent, which exerts great adverse influence upon its sustained profitability.
(3) There exist risks that great adverse changes would occur in its acquisition or use of such important assets or technologies as trade mark, patent, proprietary technology, and franchise rights, etc.
(4) Its business incomes or net profits in the latest year are greatly dependent on any affiliated party or client about which there are many uncertainties.
(5) Its net profits in the latest year are mainly from investment yields beyond the consolidated financial statements.
(6) Other circumstances which would exert great adverse influence upon its sustained profitability.

The issuer shall pay taxes according to law, and enjoy tax preferences in accordance with the relevant legal provisions. The business performance of the issuer shall not be greatly dependent on tax preferences. **4.55**

The issuer does not have great debt redemption risks, and has no major contingent issues such as guarantee, litigation, or arbitration that would affect its sustained operation. **4.56**

The stock equity of the issuer is clear, and there is no major dispute over the ownership of shares of the issuer held by the controlling shareholder and shareholders under the control of the controlling shareholder or actual controller. **4.57**

(3) Independence[15] **4.58**
The assets of the issuer are complete, its business, personnel, finance and institution are independent from each other, and it has a complete business system and the capability of market-oriented independent business operation. It has no horizontal competition with its controlling shareholder, actual controller, or any other enterprise controlled by the controlling shareholder or actual controller, nor any affiliated transactions that seriously affect the independence of the company or are obviously unfair.

(4) Standardized operation[16] **4.59**
The issuer has a good corporate governance structure, and has established such systems as the general meeting of shareholders, the board of directors, the board of supervisors, independent directors, secretary of the board of directors and the audit committee. The related institutions and personnel can perform their duties according to law.

The basic accounting work of the issuer is standardized. Its financial statement is prepared in accordance with the accounting standards for enterprises and **4.60**

---

[15] Measures for IPO and Listing on Second Board, Art 18.
[16] Measures for IPO and Listing on Second Board, Arts 19–26.

other relevant accounting systems and fairly reflects the financial status, business achievements, and cash flow of the issuer in all important aspects. A certified public accountant has issued an auditing report with a clean opinion for such statement.

4.61 The internal control system of the issuer is sound, has been effectively executed, and can reasonably guarantee the reliability of the company's financial report, the legality of production and business operations, and the efficiency and effects of operation. A certified public accountant has issued an internal control verification report with a clean opinion.

4.62 The issuer has a strict capital management system, and no funds are possessed by the controlling shareholder, the actual controller, or other enterprises under the control of the controlling shareholder or actual controller by way of loan, repayment of debts for the issuer, advance money for the issuer, or any other matter.

4.63 The bylaws of the issuer have expressed the limits of examination and approval authority and deliberation procedures for outside guarantee, and no illegal guarantee has been provided for the controlling shareholder, the actual controller, or other enterprises under the control of the controlling shareholder or actual controller.

4.64 The directors, supervisors, and senior managers of the issuer know the relevant laws and regulations on offering and listing stocks and are fully informed of the legal duties and responsibilities of listed companies and of the directors, supervisors, and senior managers thereof.

4.65 The directors, supervisors and senior managers of the issuer shall be loyal and diligent and have the corresponding post-holding qualification as specified by laws, administrative regulations and rules, and may not fall under any of the following circumstances:

(1) Being prohibited by the CSRC from accessing the securities market for a certain period, and being still within the prohibited period.
(2) Having been subject to administrative penalty by the CSRC in the preceding three years, or having been publicly decried by a securities exchange in the one preceding year.
(3) Being suspected of being involved in a crime where a case has been placed on file by the judicial organ for investigation and prosecution for that purpose, or being suspected of being involved in a violation where a case has been placed on file by the CSRC for investigation for that purpose, for which there is no express conclusion or opinion as yet.

4.66 The issuer and its controlling shareholder or actual controller do not commit any major illegal acts damaging the legitimate rights and interests of investors or the public interests in the latest three years. The issuer or its controlling shareholder or actual controller has not publicly offered securities without approval either directly or in any disguised form in the latest three years. Or, if it did publicly offer securities either directly or in any disguised form without approval three years ago, it is not doing it at present.

(5) Utilization of raised funds[17]

Funds raised by the issuer shall be mainly used for its principal business and have specific purposes. The amount of funds raised by it and the investment projects for which they are used shall be suitable for its current production and operation scale, financial status, technical level, management ability, etc. **4.67**

The issuer shall establish a system of storing funds raised for special purposes, and funds raised shall be deposited into the special account determined by the board of directors. **4.68**

4.2.3. Stock exchange listing rules

In line with international practices, the two national stock exchanges in China have each made their listing rules to set out listing criteria. **4.69**

4.2.3.1. Shanghai Stock Exchange

Under Article 5.1.1 of the Shanghai Stock Exchange Shares Listing Rules, an issuer that applies to the Shanghai Stock Exchange to list its IPO shares shall meet the following conditions: **4.70**

(1) Its shares have been issued to the public with the approval of the CSRC.
(2) Its total amount of share capital shall not be less than RMB 50 million.
(3) Its shares issued to the public account for 25 per cent or more of its total shares; for an issuer whose total share capital exceeds RMB 400 million, the aforesaid percentage shall be 10 per cent.
(4) It has not committed any serious illegal act and there has been no falsehood in its financial reports in the most recent three years.
(5) Other conditions as required by the Shanghai Stock Exchange.[18]

The above provision basically reproduces the listing requirements under Article 50 of the Securities Law, but with one important difference—it raises the total amount of share capital of the issuer from RMB 30 million to RMB 50 million. **4.71**

4.2.3.2. Shenzhen Stock Exchange

As Shenzhen Stock Exchange operates both main board and second board markets, it has promulgated two sets of listing rules for the two submarkets respectively. **4.72**

---

[17] Measures for IPO and Listing on Second Board, Arts 27–28.
[18] Shanghai Zhengquan Jiaoyisuo Gupiao Shangshi Guize [Shanghai Stock Exchange Shares Listing Rules] (2012 edition), Art 5.1.1.

4.73 For the main board market, the listing requirements are identical to those prescribed by the Shanghai Stock Exchange as discussed above, in terms of both the content and numbering of the relevant provision.[19]

4.74 The listing requirements for the second board market are contained in Article 5.1.1 of the Shenzhen Stock Exchange Second Board Shares Listing Rules, which include:

(1) Its shares have been issued to the public.
(2) Its total amount of share capital shall not be less than RMB 30 million.
(3) Its shares issued to the public account for 25 per cent or more of its total shares; for an issuer whose total share capital exceeds RMB 400 million, the aforesaid percentage shall be 10 per cent.
(4) The number of shareholders of the issuer is not less than 200.
(5) It has not committed any serious illegal act and there has been no falsehood in its financial reports in the preceding three years.
(6) Other conditions as required by the Shenzhen Stock Exchange.[20]

4.75 Compared with its counterpart for the main board, the above provision has two notable differences: first, it sets the minimum amount of share capital as RMB 30 million, rather than RMB 50 million; second, it adds a requirement for the minimum number of shareholders.

4.3. The Procedure

4.3.1. IPO and listing on the main board

4.76 The procedure for carrying out IPO and listing on the main board can be divided into the following stages.

4.3.1.1. Shareholder resolution[21]

4.77 The board of directors of an issuer shall make a resolution on the specific plans of stock issuance, on the feasibility regarding the utilization of the raised funds, and on any other item that shall be clarified, and shall submit them to the shareholders' assembly for approval.

4.78 A resolution as made by the shareholders' assembly of an issuer shall at least include the following items:

(1) Varieties and quantity of the stocks as publicly offered.

---

[19] Shenzhen Zhengquan Jiaoyisuo Gupiao Shangshi Guize [Shenzhen Stock Exchange Shares Listing Rules] (2012 edition), Art 5.1.1.
[20] Shenzhen Zhengquan Jiaoyisuo Chuangyeban Gupiao Shangshi Guize [Shenzhen Stock Exchange Second Board Shares Listing Rules] (2012 edition), Art 5.1.1.
[21] Measures for IPO and Listing, Arts 44–5.

(2) Issuance targets.
(3) Price range or method of pricing.
(4) The purposes of utilization of the funds raised.
(5) A distribution plan of the accumulated profits before issuance.
(6) The effective term for the resolution.
(7) Authorization of specific matters in the issuance by the board of directors.
(8) Any other matter that requires clarification.

4.3.1.2. Sponsor and application[22]

4.79 An issuer shall, according to the relevant provisions of the CSRC, formulate its documents of application, which shall be recommended and reported to the CSRC by its sponsor.[23]

4.3.1.3. CSRC approval[24]

4.80 The CSRC shall, after receiving any application material, make a decision on whether to accept it within five working days. After the CSRC accepts any application document as reported by an issuer, the relevant functionary department thereof shall carry out a preliminary examination thereon, and the Issuance and Verification Committee shall carry out an examination thereon as well.

4.81 Where the CSRC carries out a preliminary examination, it shall inquire of the provincial people's government where the relevant issuer is registered whether the government agrees to the stock issuance or not, and shall inquire of the National Development and Reform Commission whether the project invested in by the funds raised meets the state industrial policies and the relevant provisions on investment management.

4.82 The CSRC shall, according to the statutory requirements, decide whether to approve an issuer's application for issuance, and produce the relevant documents as well.[25] In the case of disapproval an issuer may, six months after the CSRC makes a decision on disapproval, again file an application for stock issuance.

4.3.1.4. Issuance[26]

4.83 The relevant issuer shall make the stock IPO within six months as of the day when the CSRC approves an issuance. Where it fails to do so within six months, the relevant approval document shall be deemed as invalid, and therefore it shall reapply for the CSRC's approval before any IPO is conducted.

---

[22] Measures for IPO and Listing, Art 46.
[23] For detailed discussion of the sponsorship system, see Part 4.5.
[24] Measures for IPO and Listing, Arts 47–50, 52.
[25] For detailed discussion of the CSRC approval matter, see Chapter 3.
[26] Measures for IPO and Listing, Arts 50–1.

4.84 After an application for issuance is approved and before the stock issuance is concluded, in the case that any major event occurs to the relevant issuer, it shall suspend the stock issuance, report the situation to the CSRC in a timely manner, and also perform its obligation of information disclosure. Where any requirement for issuance is thus affected, the procedures for verification shall be carried out again.

4.3.1.5. Listing

4.85 Under Article 48 of the Securities Law, an application for the listing of any securities shall be filed with a stock exchange and shall be subject to the examination and approval of the stock exchange according to law, and a listing agreement shall be concluded by both parties.

4.86 The listing procedure is prescribed by stock exchange listing rules and other relevant rules issued by the stock exchange.

4.3.2. IPO and listing on the second board

4.87 The procedure for IPO and listing on the second board is broadly similar to that for IPO and listing on the main board as previously discussed. Relevant rules can be found in the Measures for IPO and Listing on Second Board, as well as the Shenzhen Stock Exchange Second Board Shares Listing Rules.

4.4. Information Disclosure Requirements

4.4.1. IPO and listing on the main board[27]

4.88 An issuer shall, according to the relevant provisions of the CSRC, formulate and disclose a prospectus. The Rules on the Contents and Format of Prospectuses shall be the minimum requirements for information disclosure. Whether the previously discussed Rules contain explicit requirements or not, any information that may have any major impact on the investors' decisions on investment shall be disclosed.

4.89 An issuer, as well as all the directors, supervisors, and senior managers thereof, shall affix its seal and their signatures to its prospectus so as to ensure the authenticity, accuracy, and integrity of the contents thereof. The relevant recommender as well as the representative of recommendation thereof, shall carry out an examination of the authenticity, accuracy, and integrity of the prospectus and shall affix its seal and the representative's signature to the opinions on examination.

4.90 The financial statements as cited in a prospectus shall be effective within six months of expiration of the latest accounting term. Under any special circumstance, an issuer may apply for proper extension, which shall not exceed one month at most.

---

[27] Measures for IPO and Listing, arts 53–63.

The day of expiration for financial statements shall be based on the end of a year, six months or a quarter. The effective term for a prospectus shall be six months, which shall be calculated as of the last day of signature when the CSRC approves an application for issuance.

4.91 After an application document is accepted and before the Issuance and Verification Committee carries out an examination, an issuer shall disclose in advance its prospectus (for-application version) on the CSRC's website (www.csrc.gov.cn). An issuer may publicize its prospectus (for-application version) on its enterprise website, on which the disclosed contents shall be identical to those disclosed on the CSRC's website, and the time of disclosure shall not be earlier than that on the CSRC's website.

4.92 An issuer as well as all the directors, supervisors, and senior managers thereof shall ensure the authenticity, accuracy, and integrity of its prospectus (for-application version) as disclosed in advance. A prospectus (for-application version) as disclosed by an issuer in advance is not an official document for stock issuance, which shall not include any information on price. The relevant issuer shall not take it as a basis for stock issuance. An issuer shall announce in an eye-catching position in its prospectus (for-application version), as disclosed in advance: 'The CSRC has not granted an application for this issuance. This Prospectus (for-application version) shall not be applied as a legal ground for stock issuance and is merely used for advance disclosure. The relevant investors shall make their investment decisions on the basis of the full text of the Prospectus as officially announced.'

4.93 An issuer shall, before making any stock issuance, publicize an extract of its prospectus in at least one of the newspapers or periodicals as designated by the CSRC, publicize the full text of its prospectus on the websites designated by the CSRC, and post the full text of its prospectus in its domicile, in the stock exchange for its stock IPO, and in the domiciles of its recommender, major underwriter, and any other underwriting institution, for public reference.

4.94 A Recommendation Letter of Issuance as produced by a recommender, as well as the relevant documents produced by a securities trading service institution, shall be deemed as reference to the relevant prospectus, which shall be disclosed on the websites as designated by the CSRC and be posted in the relevant issuer's domicile, in the stock exchange for stock IPO, and in the domiciles of the relevant recommender, major underwriter, and any other underwriting institution, for public reference.

4.95 An issuer may publicize an extract and the full text of its prospectus as well as the relevant documents of reference in any other newspaper or website, in which the disclosed contents shall be identical to those as disclosed on the CSRC's website and the time of disclosure shall not be earlier than that on the CSRC's website.

4.4.2. IPO and listing on the second board[28]

4.96 Due to the higher risk profile of the second board market, the information disclosure requirement is more stringent than that for IPO and listing on the main board as previously discussed.

4.97 The issuer shall prepare and disclose the prospectus in accordance with the relevant provisions of the CSRC. The information disclosure provisions the CSRC sets out for the content and format of prospectus shall be taken as the minimum requirements on information disclosure. All information that has great influence upon investors' investment decision-making, whether expressly specified in the standards or not, shall be disclosed.

4.98 The issuer shall note at a prominent place of its prospectus the following:

> The stocks issued hereby are to be listed on the second board, which has a relatively high investment risk. Companies listed on the second board share such characteristics as instability in performance and high risk in business operations, and investors will face relatively big market fluctuations. Investor shall well know the investment risks in the second board market and the risk factors disclosed by this Company, and make investment decisions in a prudent manner.'

4.99 The issuer and all its directors, supervisors, and senior managers shall affix their signatures and seals to the prospectus so as to ensure the authenticity, accuracy, and integrity of the content of the prospectus. The sponsor and its representative shall check and examine the authenticity, accuracy, and integrity of the prospectus and affix their signatures and seals to the examination opinion. The controlling shareholder of the issuer shall issue an affirmative opinion for the prospectus, and affix their signature and seal to the opinion.

4.100 The financial statements cited in the prospectus shall be valid for six months from the expiry date of the latest issue. Under special circumstances, the issuer may apply to extending the valid period for one month at most. The expiry date of a financial statement shall be the end of a year, the end of half a year, or the end of a quarter. The prospectus shall be valid for six months from the date at which it is last signed and before it is approved by the CSRC.

4.101 After the application document is accepted but before the issuance review committee starts review, the issuer shall make advance disclosure of the prospectus (draft for examination and approval) on a website designated by the CSRC. The issuer may publish the prospectus (draft for examination and approval) on its website, but the information disclosed shall be consistent with that disclosed on the website designated by the CSRC and the publication shall be after the disclosure on the website designated by the CSRC.

---

[28] Measures for IPO and Listing, Arts 38–50.

The prospectus (draft for examination and approval) disclosed in advance may not contain any information about issue price. The issuer shall declare at a prominent place of the prospectus (draft for examination and approval) disclosed in advance that: 'The application for issuance of this Company has not been approved by the CSRC yet. This Prospectus (draft for examination and approval) does not have the legal force for issuing stocks. This Prospectus is for advance disclosure only. Investors shall make investment decisions based on the officially announced prospectus.' 4.102

The issuer and all its directors, supervisors and senior managers shall undertake to confirm the authenticity, accuracy, and integrity of the content of the prospectus (draft for examination and approval) disclosed in advance. 4.103

Before issuing stocks, the issuer shall publish the prospectus in full text on a website designated by the CSRC, and publish an announcement in a newspaper designated by the CSRC to notify investors of the address of the website where the prospectus is published and ways of obtaining the document. The issuer shall disclose the prospectus on its website after publishing it on a CSRC-designated website. 4.104

The sponsoring paper for issuance issued by the sponsor, the document issued by the securities service agency, and other important documents related to the issuance shall be taken as documents for future reference to the prospectus and be disclosed on a CSRC-designated website and the website of the issuer. The issuer shall provide its prospectus and the documents for future reference in the domiciles of the issuer, the stock exchange where it is to be listed, the sponsor, the lead underwriter, and other underwriters for the public to consult. 4.105

After the application document is accepted but before the application is approved by the CSRC and the prospectus is published according to law, neither the issuer nor other parties related to the issuance may give publicity to the public offering of stocks by means of advertisement or conference, etc. 4.106

4.5. Sponsorship

4.5.1. Overview

The use of sponsorship as a regulatory device by the CSRC is an example of extended institutional borrowing. The practice originated in the Alternative Investment Market of the London Stock Exchange, where regulatory oversight of listed companies is delegated to private bodies, known as 'nominated advisors' or 'Nomads', which are typically investment banks. Hong Kong borrowed this practice from the UK and China, in turn, modelled its practice on Hong Kong. 4.107

Essentially, the sponsor (also translated as 'recommender') is a gatekeeper, because a company cannot get listed on the stock exchange without the support of a 4.108

sponsor.²⁹ The sponsor performs a dual role in relation to an IPO. On the one hand, it acts as an adviser to the IPO applicant: for instance, it advises the company as to the commercial aspects of being listed, including the pricing and marketing of the company's shares. If the securities offering is underwritten, the sponsor assumes this role alone or leads a underwriting syndicate. It also guides the company through the listing process in accordance with applicable laws, regulations, and listing rules. On the other hand, the sponsor acts as a watchdog in the securities market. It is required to ensure that all relevant information disclosed regarding the IPO is truthful, accurate, and complete. The sponsor also needs to provide continuous supervision for a certain period of time after the company is listed. In performing its regulatory function, it must meet the standard of due diligence as required by law.

4.109 Article 11 of the Securities Law requires the use of sponsorship in securities offerings, stating that:

> (1) An issuer that applies for the public issuance of stocks or convertible corporate bonds by means of underwriting according to law or for the public issuance of any other securities, which is subject to recommendation as is prescribed by any law or administrative regulation, shall hire an institution with the qualification of recommendation as its recommender.
> (2) A recommender shall observe the operational rules and industrial norms and, based on the principles of being honesty, creditworthy, diligent and accountable, carry out a prudent examination of the application documents and information disclosure materials of its issuers as well as supervise and urge its issuers to operate in a regulative manner.
> (3) The qualification requirements of the recommender as well as the relevant measures for administration shall be formulated by the securities regulatory authority under the State Council.

4.110 Further, Article 49 of the Securities Law requires the use of sponsorship in securities listings, stating:

> For an application for the listing of any stocks, convertible corporate bonds or any other securities, which are subject to recommendation as is prescribed by any law or administrative regulation, an institution with the qualification of recommendation shall be hired as the recommender.. . . The provisions of paragraphs 2 and 3 of Article 11 of the present Law shall apply to the recommender of stock listing.

4.111 The CSRC has promulgated the Administrative Measures for the Sponsorship Business of the Issuance and Listing of Securities (Measures on Sponsorship) to provide more guidance on the operation of the sponsor regime.³⁰

---

²⁹ For detailed discussion of gatekeepers, see John C Coffee Jr, *Gatekeepers: The Professions and Corporate Governance* (New York: Oxford University Press, 2006).
³⁰ Zhengquan Faxing Shangshi Baojian Yewu Guanli Banfa (Administrative Measures for the Sponsorship Business of the Issuance and Listing of Securities) (promulgated by the CSRC in 2008, amended in 2009).

4.5.2. Qualifications of sponsors and sponsor representatives

Sponsorship business is normally carried on by securities companies. Under Article 9 of the Measures on Sponsorship, to apply for qualification as a sponsor, a securities company shall meet the following conditions: **4.112**

(1) It shall have registered capital of no less than RMB 100 million, and net capital of no less than RMB 50 million.
(2) It shall have effective systems of corporate governance and internal control, and the risk control indicator shall conform to the relevant provisions.
(3) The sponsorship business department shall have sound business procedures, an internal risk assessment and control system, reasonably set-up internal organizations, relevant background support for the research and sales capacity, etc.
(4) It shall have a good sponsorship business team, which shall have a reasonable professional structure and shall have no less than 35 employees, at least 20 of whom shall have been engaged in the sponsorship-related businesses in the last three years.
(5) It shall have less than four employees satisfying the qualification requirements for sponsor representatives.
(6) It shall be free of any administrative punishment due to serious violation of any law or regulation in the past three years.
(7) Any other conditions as prescribed by the CSRC.

To apply for qualification as a sponsor representative, an individual shall: **4.113**

(1) Have more than three years' experience in sponsorship-related businesses.
(2) Have experience of working as a project assistant in a domestic project of securities issuance as prescribed in Article 2 of these Measures during the preceding three years.
(3) Have attended the sponsor representatives' competence examination as acknowledged by the CSRC, where the grade is eligible and valid.
(4) Be honest and in good faith, of good character, have no record indicating bad integrity, and not have been subject to any administrative punishment by the CSRC in the preceding three years.
(5) Have no large sum of unpaid due debt.
(6) Meet any other conditions as prescribed by the CSRC.[31]

4.5.3. Sponsor responsibilities

Under Article 23 of the Measures on Sponsorship, a sponsor shall recommend with due diligence the issuance and listing of an issuer's securities. After the listing of the **4.114**

---

[31] Measures on Sponsorship, Art 11.

issuer's securities, the sponsor shall continuously supervise and guide the issuer to fulfil its obligations such as operating normatively, keeping its commitments, and disclosing information.

4.115 In recommending the issuance and listing of an issuer's securities, a sponsor shall abide by the principles of keeping good faith and performing duties with due diligence, and shall, according to CSRC requirements on the due diligence investigation work of the sponsor, conduct a comprehensive investigation about the issuer so as to fully understand the operation of the issuer and the risks and problems it faces.[32]

4.116 Before a sponsor recommends the IPO and listing of an issuer's stock, it shall give guidance to the issuer and provide systematic training on the knowledge of laws, regulations, and the securities market to directors, supervisors and senior managers, shareholders holding 5 per cent or more of the shares, and the actual controller (or legal representative) of the issuer, so as to ensure that the aforesaid personnel have good and comprehensive understanding of the laws, regulations, and rules relating to issuance, listing, and normative operation, etc. and are aware of responsibilities and obligations such as information disclosure and committed performance. The sponsor must also foster awareness of good faith, self-discipline, and rule of law for entry into the securities market.[33]

4.117 A sponsor shall conclude a sponsorship agreement with an issuer to clarify the rights and obligations of both parties and determine through negotiations the relevant fees for the performance of sponsorial obligations according to industry norms. After the conclusion of the sponsorship agreement, the sponsor shall file it with the CSRC representative office at the locality of the issuer for archival purposes within five working days.[34]

4.118 Among the application documents made by an issuer and the securities issuance-financing documents, those containing the professional opinions issued by a securities service institution and its signatories shall be prudently checked by a sponsor in consideration of the information obtained from the due diligence investigation; the sponsor shall independently make a judgement on the materials provided by the issuer and the information it has disclosed. Where there is any major discrepancy between the judgements made by the sponsor and the professional opinions of the securities service institution, the related items shall be investigated and reviewed, and another securities service institution may be invited to provide professional services.[35]

4.119 With regard to contents of an issuer's application documents and securities issuance-financing documents that are not supported by the professional opinion

---

[32] Measures on Sponsorship, Art 24.
[33] Measures on Sponsorship, Art 25.
[34] Measures on Sponsorship, Art 27.
[35] Measures on Sponsorship, Art 29.

of a securities service institution and its signatory, a sponsor shall obtain sufficient evidence of due diligence investigation and independently make a judgement on the materials provided by the issuer and the information disclosed by it on the basis of a comprehensive analysis of all kinds of evidence, and shall have adequate reason to affirm that there is no material discrepancy between the judgement made by it and the issuer's application documents and securities issuance-financing documents.[36]

A sponsor shall make commitments on the following items in the issuance sponsor letter and the listing sponsor letter: **4.120**

(1) It has adequate reason to believe that the issuer conforms to the relevant provisions on issuance and listing of securities as prescribed by laws, regulations and the CSRC.
(2) It has good reason to believe that there is no false record, misleading statement, or major omission in the issuer's application documents and the materials on information disclosure.
(3) It has good reason to believe that the grounds on which the opinions of the issuer and its directors expressed in the application documents and the materials on information disclosure are sufficient and reasonable.
(4) It has good reason to believe that there is no material discrepancy between the application documents, the materials on information disclosure, and the opinions expressed by the securities service institution.
(5) It shall guarantee that the sponsor representatives it designated and the relevant personnel of this sponsor have fulfilled their duties diligently, and have conducted due diligence investigation into and prudent examination of the application documents of the issuer and the materials on information disclosure.
(6) It shall guarantee that there is no false record, misleading statement or major omission in the sponsor letter and other documents related to the fulfilment of the sponsorial obligations.
(7) It shall guarantee that the professional services and the professional opinions provided to the issuer are in line with the provisions of laws, administrative regulations, and the CSRC and the industrial norm.
(8) It shall voluntarily accept the supervisory measures taken by the CSRC in accordance with the present Measures.
(9) Other items as prescribed by the CSRC.[37]

After a sponsor has submitted the issuance sponsor letter, it shall assist the examination conducted by the CSRC and shall undertake the following tasks: **4.121**

(1) Organizing the issuer and the securities service institution to reply to the opinions of the CSRC.

---

[36] Measures on Sponsorship, Art 30.
[37] Measures on Sponsorship, Art 33.

(2) Conducting a due diligence investigation into or making examination of the special matters concerning the current issuance and listing of securities in pursuance to the requirements of the CSRC.
(3) Designating the sponsor representatives to conduct professional communications with the functional department of the CSRC; the sponsor representatives shall accept the commissioners' inquiry in the meeting of the Issuance Review Committee.
(4) Other tasks as prescribed by the CSRC.[38]

4.122 A sponsor shall determine the content of the continuous supervision and guidance after the issuance and listing of securities in light of the actual situation of the issuer, supervise and guide the issuer to perform the obligations related to the listed company's normative operation, observance of its commitments, information disclosure, etc.; check and approve the documents on information disclosure and other documents submitted to the CSRC and the stock exchange; and undertake the following tasks:

(1) Supervise and guide the issuer to effectively implement and perfect a system which prevents the controlling shareholders, actual controllers, and other affiliated parties from encroaching upon the issuer's resources in violation of regulations.
(2) Supervise and guide the issuer to effectively implement and perfect an internal control system which prevents the directors, supervisors, and senior managers from damaging the interests of the issuer by taking advantage of their position.
(3) Supervise and guide the issuer to effectively implement and perfect a system which ensures the fairness and compliance of the affiliated transactions, and provide its opinions on the affiliated transactions.
(4) Continuously pay attention to such commitments as the issuer's deposit in the special account of funds raised and the implementation of the investment projects.
(5) Pay continuous attention to such matters as the provision of a security by the issuer for others, and express its opinions on such.
(6) Other tasks as prescribed by the CSRC and the stock exchange and stipulated in the sponsorship agreement.[39]

4.123 Under Article 36 of the Measures on Sponsorship, the period of continuous supervision and guidance varies depending on whether the securities are listed on the main board or the second board.

(1) With regard to the IPO and listing on the main board, the period of continuous supervision and guidance shall be the remaining time in the current

---

[38] Measures on Sponsorship, Art 34.
[39] Measures on Sponsorship, Art 35.

year of the listing of securities and the following two full fiscal years. As to a main board-listed company which issues new stocks or convertible corporate bonds, the period of continuous supervision and guidance shall be the remaining time of the current year of the listing of securities and the following one full fiscal year.
(2) With regard to the IPO and listing on the second board, the period of continuous supervision and guidance shall be the remaining time of the current year of the listing of securities and the following three full fiscal years. For a second board-listed company which issues new stocks or convertible corporate bonds, the period of continuous supervision and guidance shall be the remaining time of the current year of the listing of securities and the following two full fiscal years.
(3) With regard to the IPO and listing on the second board, in the period of continuous supervision and guidance, a sponsor shall disclose the follow-up report on the website designated by the CSRC within 15 working days from the disclosure of the annual report or mid-term report made by the issuer, analysing and giving independent opinions on the matters involved in Article 35 of these Measures. Where the information disclosed in the temporary report of the issuer involves raising of funds, affiliated transactions, authorized financial management, provision of guarantee for others, and any other major matter, the sponsor shall conduct analysis and give independent opinions on the website designated by the CSRC within ten working days from the disclosure of the temporary report.

4.124 The period of continuous supervision and guidance shall start from the day when the securities are listed.[40]

4.125 Importantly, the sponsor has duties to monitor the behaviours of the issuer and report to the CSRC in certain circumstances. Prior to the issuance of securities, if an issuer fails to co-operate with the sponsor in performing the sponsorial obligations, the sponsor shall express its reservations, and shall give an explanation in the issuance sponsor letter; if the circumstance is serious, it shall refuse to make recommendation or shall withdraw the recommendation it has made.[41]

4.126 After the issuance of securities, if a sponsor has good reason to hold that the issuer may have committed any illegal act or other improper acts, it shall supervise and urge the issuer to make explanations and to make a correction within a prescribed time limit; if the circumstance is serious, it shall report the circumstance to the CSRC and the stock exchange.[42]

---

[40] Measures on Sponsorship, Art 36.
[41] Measures on Sponsorship, Art 56.
[42] Measures on Sponsorship, Art 57.

4.127 The sponsor has similar monitoring and reporting duties when dealing with the behaviours of other professionals hired by the issuer for the issuance and listing of securities, such as accounting firms, law firms, asset appraisal institutions, and other securities service institutions.[43]

4.5.4. Procedures for the sponsorship business

4.128 A sponsor shall establish and improve the internal control system of the sponsorship work; practically guarantee that the person in charge of the sponsorship business, the person in charge of the internal examination, the person in charge of the sponsorship business department, sponsor representatives, project assistants, and other personnel relating to the sponsorship business perform their duties with due diligence; strictly control risks; and improve the overall quality of the sponsorship business.[44]

4.129 If the total shares of a sponsor, its controlling shareholder, its actual controller, and important affiliated parties exceed 7 per cent of the shares of an issuer or the shares held or controlled by an issuer exceed 7 per cent of the shares of a sponsor, the sponsor shall jointly fulfil the sponsorial obligations with a non-affiliated sponsor when it recommends the issuance and listing of the issuer's securities, and the non-affiliated sponsor shall be the primary sponsor.[45]

4.130 From the publication of the securities issuance-financing documents to the completion of the continuous supervision and guidance work, the sponsor and the issuer shall not terminate the sponsorship agreement, except in circumstances with appropriate reasons. If the issuer hires another sponsor due to its re-application for the issuance of securities or the qualification of the sponsor is cancelled by the CSRC, the sponsorship agreement shall be terminated. Where a sponsorship agreement is terminated, the sponsor and the issuer shall report it to the CSRC and the stock exchange and give them explanations within five working days from the day of termination.[46]

4.131 A sponsor shall designate two sponsor representatives to take charge of the specific sponsorship work of an issuer, issue a special authorization signed by the legal representative, and ensure that the relevant departments and personnel of the sponsor efficiently co-operate with each other based on division of work. The sponsor may assign a project assistant.[47]

4.132 After the issuance of the securities, a sponsor shall not change the sponsor representatives unless the sponsor representatives have left their posts or their sponsor

---

[43] Measures on Sponsorship, Arts 58–60.
[44] Measures on Sponsorship, Art 38.
[45] Measures on Sponsorship, Art 43.
[46] Measures on Sponsorship, Art 45.
[47] Measures on Sponsorship, Art 48.

representative qualifications are revoked. If the sponsor changes any sponsor representative, it shall notify the issuer and shall report it to the CSRC and the stock exchange and give them an explanation within five working days. If the former sponsor representatives fail to perform their duties during the period when they take charge of the specific sponsorship work, they shall not be exempted from liabilities or their liabilities shall not be terminated due to the change in the sponsor representatives.[48]

After a sponsor has completed the continuous supervision and guidance work, it shall submit a sponsorship summary report to the CSRC and the stock exchange within ten working days from the announcement of the annual report made by the issuer. The legal representative of the sponsor and the sponsor representatives shall affix their signatures to the sponsorship summary report. The sponsorship summary report shall cover the following: **4.133**

(1) Basic information about the issuer.
(2) A summary of the sponsorship work.
(3) Major matters which occurred in the performance of the sponsorial obligations and the disposal thereof.
(4) A statement and assessment of the issuer's co-operation in the sponsorship work.
(5) A statement and assessment on the participation of the securities service institution in the work relating to the issuance and listing of securities.
(6) Other items as required by the CSRC.[49]

4.5.5. Supervisory measures and legal liabilities[50]

The CSRC shall establish a sponsorship credit supervision system to conduct continuous and dynamic registration management of the sponsors and sponsor representatives and to record their practising information, illegal acts, other bad acts, supervisory measures taken against them, etc, and it may announce details of such records when necessary. **4.134**

Where any application document for the sponsor qualification contains any false record, misleading statement, or major omission, the CSRC shall not approve the application, or shall revoke the qualification of the sponsor if the application has been approved. Where the application document for the sponsor representative qualification contains any false record, misleading statement, or major omission, the CSRC shall not approve the application, or shall revoke the qualification of the sponsor representative if the application has been approved. The CSRC shall **4.135**

---

[48] Measures on Sponsorship, Art 49.
[49] Measures on Sponsorship, Art 52.
[50] Measures on Sponsorship, Arts 62–79.

refuse to accept any application for the sponsor representative qualification recommended by this sponsor within six months from the day of revocation.

4.136 Where any of the sponsors, the sponsor representatives, the person in charge of the sponsorship business, or the person in charge of the internal examination fail to perform the relevant obligations faithfully and diligently as in violation of these Measures, the CSRC shall order it or him to make a correction and take such supervisory measures against it or him as arranging a supervisory talk, paying great attention, ordering it or him to receive continuing education, issuing a letter of warning, ordering it or him to make an open explanation, and determining it or him to be inappropriate for the post. Those subject to administrative punishments shall be punished according to the relevant provisions. If the circumstance is serious and it or he is suspected of committing any crime, it or he shall be transferred to a judicial organ and subject to criminal liabilities.

4.137 Where any sponsor is under any of the following circumstances, the CSRC shall suspend the sponsor's qualification for three months from the day of confirmation. If the circumstance is serious, the CSRC shall suspend the sponsor's qualification for six months and may order the sponsor to change the person in charge of the sponsorship business or the person in charge of the internal examination; if the circumstance is especially serious, its sponsor's qualification shall be cancelled:

(1) The documents relating to the sponsorship work submitted to the CSRC and the stock exchange contain any false record, misleading statement, or major omission.
(2) Failure to effectively implement the internal control system.
(3) Failure to effectively implement the due diligence investigation system, internal examination system, continuous supervision and guidance system, or sponsorship working paper system.
(4) The sponsorship working paper contains any false record, misleading statement, or major omission.
(5) Instigation, assistance, or attendance to the issuer's and securities service institution's provision of documents that involve any false record, misleading statement, or major omission.
(6) Instigation, assistance, or attendance to the issuer's interfering in the examination and verification conducted by the CSRC and its Issuance Review Committee.
(7) Seeking any improper benefit from being engaged in the sponsorship business.
(8) Any other circumstance seriously violating the obligations of keeping good faith and performing duties with due diligence.

4.138 Where any sponsor representative falls into any of the following circumstances, the CSRC may refuse to accept the specific recommendation for which the relevant sponsor representatives are responsible, depending on the severity of circumstances, for 3–12 months from the day of confirmation; if the circumstance is especially serious, it may cancel the sponsor representative's qualification:

(1) The work log of due diligence investigation is lost, or has omitted or concealed important issues.
(2) Failure to complete or to participate in the guidance work.
(3) Failure to attend to continuous supervision and guidance work, or to perform duties diligently in the continuous supervision and guidance work.
(4) Having been decried by the stock exchange or the Securities Association of China during the sponsorship period due to the sponsorship business or the issuer for whom he is responsible for the specific sponsorship work.
(5) Instigation, assistance, or attendance to the issuer's interfering in the examination and verification conducted by the CSRC and its Issuance Review Committee.
(6) Any other circumstance seriously violating the obligations of keeping good faith and performing duties with due diligence.

4.139 Where a sponsor representative falls into any of the following circumstances, the CSRC shall cancel his sponsor representative qualification; if the circumstance is serious, it shall take the measure of prohibiting him from accessing the securities market:

(1) Recommending the issuance and listing of the issuer's securities by affixing his signature to the documents relating to the sponsorship work, but failing to make due diligence investigations; or the due diligence investigation made is incomplete or inadequate or is evidently inconsistent with business rules and industry norms.
(2) Seeking any improper benefit by taking advantage of the sponsorship business in which he is involved.
(3) Holding the issuer's shares himself, or his spouse doing so.
(4) Instigation, assistance, or attendance to the issuer's or securities service institution's provision of documents that involve any false record, misleading statement, or major omission.
(5) Documents relating to the sponsorship work which the sponsor representative has participated in the organization and preparation of contain false records, misleading statements, or major omissions.

4.140 Where an issuer is subject to any of the following circumstances, the CSRC shall suspend the qualification of the sponsor for three months from the day of confirmation, and cancel the sponsor representative qualification of the relevant person:

(1) There is any false record, misleading statement, or major omission in the securities issuance-financing document or any other application document.
(2) A business loss occurs in the current year of the listing of the publicly offered securities.

(3) During the period of continuous supervision and guidance, there is any false record, misleading statement, or major omission in the documents on information disclosure.

4.141 Where an issuer is under any of the following circumstances during the period of continuous supervision and guidance, the CSRC shall refuse to accept the specific recommendation for which the relevant sponsor representatives are responsible, depending on the severity of circumstances, for 3–12 months from the day of confirmation; if the circumstance is especially serious, the sponsor representative qualification of the relevant person shall be cancelled:

(1) More than 50 per cent of the cumulative amount of the funds raised in the current year of the securities listing is used for purposes inconsistent with the commitments made.
(2) The business profit in the current year of public offering of securities and listing on the main board falls by more than 50 per cent of that of the previous year.
(3) There is any change in the controlling shareholder or the actual controller within 12 months from the day of the IPO and listing of stocks.
(4) More than 50 per cent of the assets or main businesses accumulated have been restructured within 12 months from the day of the IPO and listing of stocks.
(5) More than 50 per cent of the assets or main businesses accumulated have been restructured within 12 months from the day when a listed company issues new stocks or exchangeable corporate bonds, and no disclosure was made in the securities issuance-financing documents.
(6) Actual profits are more than 20 per cent lower than expected profits.
(7) The affiliated transaction is not made under the arm's-length principle or the procedures are in violation of the regulations, and the amount of money involved is comparatively large.
(8) The controlling shareholder or actual controller or any other affiliated party encroaches upon the issuer's resources in violation of regulations, and the amount of money involved is comparatively large.
(9) Security is provided for others in violation of the regulations, and the amount of money involved is comparatively large.
(10) Purchasing or selling assets, lending, or entrusting the assets management in violation of regulations, and the amount of money involved is comparatively large.
(11) Any of the directors, supervisors, or senior managers has been subject to administrative punishment or criminal liabilities due to encroachment upon the issuer's interests.
(12) Violation of the relevant laws and regulations on normative operation of listed companies and information disclosure, etc, and the circumstance is serious.
(13) Any other circumstance as prescribed by the CSRC.

4.6. Pricing and Underwriting

In carrying out IPOs or subsequent offerings, there are two important issues, namely pricing and underwriting. The CSRC has promulgated the Measures for the Administration of Securities Offering and Underwriting (Measures on Offering and Underwriting) to provide detailed rules on issues including, but not limited to, pricing and underwriting.[51]

4.142

4.6.1. Pricing

Under Article 5 of the Measures on Offering and Underwriting, in an IPO of shares, the issue price of shares may be determined by the mechanism of price inquiry where market participants are asked about the opinions on the issue price, or by any other legal and feasible means such as direct determination of price through negotiation between the issuer and the managing underwriter, but the issuer shall specify the means of pricing for the current share issue in the share issuance announcement.[52]

4.143

4.6.1.1. Price inquiry participants

Inquiry participants[53] are securities investment fund management companies, securities companies, trust and investment companies, finance companies, insurance institution investors, qualified foreign institutional investors, and institutional and individual investors independently recommended by the managing underwriter which meet the conditions prescribed in these Measures, and other investors recognized by the CSRC.

4.144

To independently recommend inquiry participants, a managing underwriter shall, according to the provisions of these Measures and the self-disciplinary rules of the Securities Association of China, develop clear recommendation principles and criteria, establish a transparent recommendation decision-making mechanism, and file them with the Securities Association of China. Independently recommended inquiry participants include institutional investors that have relatively strong pricing abilities and long-term investment intentions and individual investors that have relatively abundant investment experience.

4.145

Inquiry participants and the securities investment products under its management (hereinafter referred to as placees) shall be registered at the Securities Association

4.146

---

[51] Zhengquan Faxing yu Chengxiao Guanli Banfa [Measures for the Administration of Securities Offering and Underwriting] (promulgated by the CSRC in 2006, amended in 2010, 2012).

[52] The securities issued by a listed company shall be priced in accordance with the relevant CSRC provisions regarding the issuance of securities by listed companies.

[53] Measures on Offering and Underwriting, Arts 5–8.

of China for record and be subject to the self-discipline management of Securities Association of China.

4.147 As an inquiry participant, an institutional investor shall meet all of the following conditions:

(1) It is legally established and has not received any administrative punishment or regulatory department or any criminal punishment for any gross violation of laws and regulations in the past 12 months.
(2) It is legally qualified to make stock investments.
(3) It has a good credit history and has the institutions and personnel necessary for independent engagement in securities investment.
(4) It has a sound internal risk evaluation and control system which is able to operate effectively, and its risk control indicators are in compliance with the relevant provisions.
(5) It has been 12 months since it was removed from any list of inquiry participants by the Securities Association of China under these Measures.

4.148 As an inquiry participant, an individual investor shall have five or more years of investment experience, relatively strong analysis abilities, and relatively strong risk tolerance. A managing underwriter shall strictly adhere to the predetermined recommendation principles, criteria, and procedures.

4.149 The following institutional investors, as inquiry participants, shall also satisfy the following conditions in addition to those prescribed in Article 7:

(1) A securities company, it may conduct securities self-operated business and securities assets management business upon approval.
(2) A trust and investment company shall have been registered at the relevant supervising department for two or more years, its registered capital shall not be lower than 400 million yuan, and there is an active record of securities market investments in the preceding 12 months.
(3) A financial company shall have been established more than two years previous, its registered capital shall not be lower than 300 million yuan, and there is an active record of securities market investments in the latest 12 months.

4.6.1.2. The procedure for price inquiry

4.150 The procedure for price inquiry[54] has two stages: preliminary inquiry and accumulated bidding inquiry.

4.151 After the prior disclosure of the (draft) prospectus, the issuer and the managing underwriter may preliminarily communicate with specific inquiry participants in

---

[54] Measures on Offering and Underwriting, Arts 9–22.

a non-public form to solicit their price intentions and estimate the issue price range, and may also estimate the issue price range in other reasonable manners.

Preliminary communications may not be publicly conducted, directly or indirectly, and inquiry participants may not be provided with any issuer information other than the open information such as the information in the (draft) prospectus disclosed in advance.

4.152 Where price is determined in the manner of price inquiry, the issuer and the managing underwriter may directly determine the issue price according to the preliminary inquiry results or determine an issue price range through preliminary inquiry and then determine the issue price within the range through accumulated bidding inquiry.

4.153 After the preliminary prospectus of an IPO is published, the issuer and its managing underwriter may conduct promotion and price inquiry to selected market participants and conduct promotion to public investors on the Internet and in other manners. When the issuer and its managing underwriter conduct promotion to public investors, the issuer information provided to public investors shall be consistent with the information provided to inquiry participants in terms of content and integrity.

4.154 Where the issue price is determined in the manner of price inquiry, an inquiry participant may, at its sole discretion, decide whether to participate in the initial inquiry; the managing underwriter may not, without justifiable reason, refuse an inquiry participant's application to participate in the initial inquiry. Inquiry participants that have not participated in the initial inquiry or have participated in the initial inquiry but have not submitted a valid quotation may not participate in the accumulated biding inquiry and offline placement.

4.155 An inquiry participant shall make reasonable quotation in accordance with the principles of independence, objectiveness, and sincerity, and may not negotiate on the quotation or lower or raise prices on purpose.

4.156 The managing underwriter's proprietary securities account may not participate in price inquiry, offline placement, and online issuance in the current share issue. The proprietary account of an inquiry participant that has an actual control relationship with the issuer or its managing underwriter may not participate in the price inquiry and offline placement but may participate in the online issuance in the current share issue.

4.157 An issuer and its managing underwriter shall, after determining the issue price range and the issue price, respectively report them to the CSRC for record and make public announcements accordingly.

4.158 Where an issuer and its managing underwriter determine the issue price by independent negotiations between them or in any other legal and feasible manner other than price inquiry, they shall specify the pricing manner in the issue plan and publish a preliminary prospectus after filing the issue plan with the CSRC.

4.6.1.3. Strategic investors

4.159 Where the number of the IPO of shares is more than 400 million,[55] shares may be rationed to strategic investors. The issuer shall conclude a ration agreement with strategic investors in advance and shall report to the CSRC for record. An issuer and its managing underwriter shall disclose the standards for selecting strategic investors, the total amount of shares rationed to strategic investors, the proportion in the current share issue, restrictions on holding periods, etc.

4.160 The strategic investor may not participate in the IPO's initial inquiry and its subsequent inquiry which is an accumulated bidding inquiry, and shall make a promise that the holding period of the shares rationed to it this time shall not be less than 12 months. The holding period shall be calculated as of the date when the share publicly offered this time is listed.

4.6.2. Underwriting

4.6.2.1. Overview

4.161 Underwriting has two important functions in relation to an issue of securities: insurance and marketing. It is an important mechanism in the securities market in guaranteeing the capital sought to be raised against the vagaries of the market.

4.162 From a comparative perspective, there are three different types of underwriting. The first is the so-called 'classic' underwriting, which is known as *yu e bao xiao* in China. This involves a contract whereby the underwriter, for a fee or commission, agrees to sell the securities on an agency basis and to subscribe itself for any not taken up. In China this is the dominant form of underwriting. Other examples of such underwriting are seen in Australia and Hong Kong.

4.163 A second type is the so-called 'firm-commitment' underwriting, known as *quan e bao xiao* in China, whereby the underwriter is allotted the whole issue, usually at a discount price, and then sells the securities to investors. This is the most common type of underwriting arrangement in the UK and the US.

4.164 A third type of underwriting is the so-called 'best-effort' underwriting, known as *dai xiao* in China, where the underwriter agrees to use its best efforts to sell the securities. This is essentially a selling agreement and involves no obligation to take up the shortfall. In other words, there is no insurance element to this type of underwriting. As the underwriting risk is lower, the fee is proportionately reduced. Thus, it is a good option when the securities to be offered are expected to be in high

---

[55] Measures on Offering and Underwriting, Arts 23–24.

demand and the risk of offering failure is minimal. A common example is a rights issue.

4.6.2.2. Specific rules

4.165 Article 28 of the Securities Law provides for all three types of underwriting arrangements discussed. Where a securities company underwrites securities, it shall conclude an underwriting agreement with the relevant issuer, which shall indicate the following items:

(1) The name, domicile, and name of the legal representative of the parties concerned.
(2) The classes, quantity, amount, and issuing prices of the securities under sale by proxy or exclusive sale.
(3) The term of sale by proxy or exclusive sale as well as the start–stop date.
(4) The ways and date of payment for sale by proxy or exclusive sale.
(5) The expenses for and settlement methods of sale by proxy or exclusive sale.
(6) The liabilities for breach.
(7) Any other matter as prescribed by the securities regulatory authority under the State Council.[56]

4.166 Where the total face value of securities as issued to non-specified objects exceed RMB 50 million yuan, the said securities shall be underwritten by an underwriting syndicate. An underwriting syndicate shall be composed of a securities company acting as the principal underwriter and other participant underwriters.[57]

4.167 The term for sale by proxy or exclusive sale shall not exceed than 90 days at the most. A securities company shall, within the term of sale by proxy or exclusive sale, guarantee the priority of the relevant subscribers in purchasing securities under sale by proxy or exclusive sale. A securities company shall not reserve in advance any securities under sale by proxy thereby or purchase in advance and sustain any securities under exclusive sale thereby.[58]

4.168 As for a public offer of stocks through sale by proxy, when the term of sale by proxy expires and if the number of stocks fails to reach 70 per cent of the planned number in the public offer, it shall be deemed as a failure. The relevant issuer shall refund the issuing price plus interest as calculated at the bank deposit rate for the contemporary period of time to the subscribers of stocks.[59]

4.169 The Measures on Offering and Underwriting provide more details on the regulation of underwriting. Before underwriting securities, a securities company shall

---

[56] Securities Law, Art 30.
[57] Securities Law, Art 32.
[58] Securities Law, art 33.
[59] Securities Law, Art 35.

report the issuing plan and the underwriting plan to the CSRC.[60] A listed company that issues shares non-publicly and does not adopt the mode of distribution by itself, or that is rationed with shares, shall adopt the mode of sales by proxy.[61]

4.170 Where more than 400 million IPO shares are issued, the issuer and its managing underwriter may adopt greenshoe; the exercise of this option shall abide by the relevant provisions of the CSRC, securities exchanges, and securities registration and clearing institutions.[62]

4.171 In the public offering of securities, the managing underwriter shall, within ten days of the securities entering public trading, file a summary underwriting report with the CSRC, summarizing and explaining the basic condition during the issuance period and the performance of the securities after they enter public trading, and shall provide the following documents:

(1) A separate edition of the prospectus.
(2) The underwriting agreement and the underwriting syndicate agreement.
(3) A witness opinion of a lawyer.
(4) A capital verification report issued by an accounting firm.
(5) Other documents required by the CSRC.[63]

4.172 Where a listed company makes a non-public issuance of a share, the issuer and its managing underwriter shall file the following documents with the CSRC upon the accomplishment of the issuance:

(1) Statement on issuance situation.
(2) Report prepared by the managing underwriter on compliance with this issuing process and participant of subscription.
(3) Opinions of witness on compliance with this issuing process and participant of subscription presented by the lawyer of the issuer.
(4) Report on the verification of capital produced by the accounting firm.
(5) Other documents as required by the CSRC.[64]

---

[60] Measures on Offering and Underwriting, Art 39.
[61] Measures on Offering and Underwriting, Art 40.
[62] Measures on Offering and Underwriting, Art 49.
[63] Measures on Offering and Underwriting, Art 50.
[64] Measures on Offering and Underwriting, Art 51.

5

POST-LISTING ISSUES

5.1. Introduction	5.01	5.3.1. Overview	5.19
5.2. Information Disclosure	5.04	5.3.2. Independent directors	5.22
5.2.1. Periodic reports	5.04	5.3.3. Substantial asset transactions	5.38
5.2.2. Interim reports	5.08	5.3.4. Related party transactions	5.60
5.2.3. Comments	5.14	**5.4. Listing Suspension and Delisting**	5.74
5.3. Corporate Governance of Listed Companies	5.19	5.4.1. Criteria	5.74
		5.4.2. Special treatment measures	5.77
		5.4.3. Comments	5.80

5.1. Introduction

After the initial public offering (IPO) and listing, the listed company will be subject to a raft of regulatory requirements, in several important aspects. First, it is required to make information disclosure. This includes periodic disclosure by the company of its financial performance and position, and timely disclosure of major new developments or changes in its financial condition, performance, or outlook which are not publicly available and which would be likely to affect its stock price if disclosed to the market. The term 'continuous disclosure', in a narrow sense, refers only to the latter type of disclosure, but in a broad sense it encompasses both types of disclosure. To avoid confusion, the term 'continuous disclosure' is used in the narrow sense in this book. In China, periodic disclosure takes the form of periodic reports while continuous disclosure takes the form of interim reports. **5.01**

Second, the listed company needs to comply with more stringent regulation of conduct through higher governance standards and trading restraints. In China, for instance, the listed company is required to have independent directors. Restraints are imposed on certain types of transactions, such as related party transactions and substantial asset transactions. **5.02**

Finally, in certain circumstances, trading of the securities may be suspended, or the company may even be delisted. In China, delisting has long been a difficult issue, and so far very few delistings have actually occurred. It is thus important to **5.03**

5.2. Information Disclosure

5.2.1. Periodic reports

5.04 Under the Securities Law, the listed company is required to prepare annual and half-yearly reports. The requirements with respect to annual reports are contained in Article 66 of the Securities Law, which states:

> A listed company whose shares or bonds have been listed for trading shall, within four months as of the end of each accounting year, submit to the securities regulatory authority under the State Council and the stock exchange an annual report indicating the following contents, and make a public announcement for it:
> (1) A brief account of the company's general situation;
> (2) The financial statement and business situation of the company;
> (3) A brief introduction to the directors, supervisors, and senior managers of the company well as the information regarding their shareholdings;
> (4) The information on the shares and corporate bonds it has already issued, including a name list of the top 10 shareholders who hold the largest number of shares in the company as well as the amount of shares each of them holds; and
> (5) The actual controller of the company; and
> (6) Any other matter as prescribed by the securities regulatory authority under the State Council.

5.05 Article 65 of the Securities Law provides for half-yearly reports, stating:

> A company whose shares or bonds have been listed for trading shall, within two months as of the end of the first half of each accounting year, submit to the securities regulatory authority under the State Council and the stock exchange a midterm report indicating the following contents and mak[ing] a public announcement for it:
> (1) The financial statements and business situation of the company;
> (2) The major litigation the company is involved in;
> (3) The particulars of any change concerning the shares or corporate bonds thereof it has already issued;
> (4) The important matters as submitted to the general assembly of shareholders for deliberation; and
> (5) Any other matter as prescribed by the securities regulatory authority under the State Council.

5.06 Under Article 68 of the Securities Law, the directors and senior managers of a listed company shall produce written opinions to confirm the periodic reports of the company. The board of supervisors of a listed company shall carry out examination of the periodic reports of its company as formulated by the board of directors and produce the relevant examination opinions in written form. The directors, supervisors, and senior managers of a listed company shall guarantee the authenticity, accuracy, and integrity of the information as disclosed by the listed company.

To facilitate listed companies' preparation of annual reports and half-yearly reports, the CSRC has promulgated a series of detailed rules to provide practical guidance on the content and format of those reports. It should be noted that in practice the CSRC has further required the preparation of quarterly reports, even though there is no such explicit requirement in the Securities Law.[1] **5.07**

5.2.2. Interim reports

Article 67 of the Securities Law sets out the requirements with respect to interim reports, under which, in the case of a major event that may considerably affect the trading price of a listed company's shares and that is not yet known to the investors, the listed company shall immediately submit a temporary report regarding the said major event to the CSRC and the stock exchange, as well as making an announcement to the general public, in which the cause, present situation, and possible legal consequence of the event shall be indicated. **5.08**

To facilitate enforcement, further guidance is provided on the term 'major event' mentioned in the preceding paragraph by enumerating a list of examples, including: **5.09**

(1) A major change in the business guidelines or business scope of the company.
(2) A decision of the company on any major investment or major asset purchase.
(3) An important contract as concluded by the company, which may have an important effect on the assets, liabilities, rights, interests, or business achievements of the company.
(4) The incurrence of any major debt in the company or default on any major debt that is due.
(5) The incurrence of any major deficit or a major loss in the company.
(6) A major change in the external conditions for the business operation of the company.
(7) A change concerning directors, no less than one third of supervisors, or managers of the company.
(8) A considerable change in the holdings of shareholders or actual controllers each of whom holds or controls no less than 5 per cent of the company's shares.
(9) A decision of the company on capital decrease, merger, division, dissolution, or application for bankruptcy.

---

[1] Gongkai Faxing Zhengquan de Gongsi Xinxi Pilu Bianbao Guize Di 13 Hao—Jidu Baogao Neirong yu Geshi Tebie Guiding [No 13 of the Rule for Preparing Information Disclosure Documents by Companies Conducting Public Offerings of Securities—Special Rules for the Content and Format of Quarterly Reports] (issued by the CSRC in 2003, revised in 2007, 2008).

(10) Any major litigation in which the company is involved, or where the resolution of the general assembly of shareholders or the board of directors has been cancelled or announced invalid.

(11) Where the company is involved in any crime, which has been filed as a case as well as investigated by the judicial organ or where any director, supervisor, or senior manager of the company is subject to compulsory measures as rendered by the judicial organ.

(12) Any other matter as prescribed by the securities regulatory authority under the State Council.

5.10 The CSRC has set out further items of information which are considered 'major events', including:

(1) Any newly promulgated law, regulation, rules, or industrial policy that may considerably affect the company.

(2) A resolution of the board of directors on the new stock offering plan or any other financing plan or equity incentive plan.

(3) A court ruling which prohibits the controlling shareholder from transferring its shares; or 5 per cent or more of the shares held by any shareholder is pledged, frozen, judicially auctioned, kept in custody or in trust; or the voting rights of such shareholder are limited.

(4) The main assets have been sealed up, detained, frozen, mortgaged, or pledged.

(5) The main or all businesses have stopped.

(6) Providing any important external guaranty.

(7) Obtaining a large sum of government subsidy or any other extra proceeds which are likely to produce important effects on the assets, liabilities, rights, and interests or business achievements of the company.

(8) Changes in accounting policies or accounting estimates.

(9) Any error in the information disclosed previously, or the company fails to disclose information as required, or the information disclosed contains any false record so that the company is ordered to make a correction by the relevant organ or the board of directors of the company decides to make a correction.

(10) Other circumstances as prescribed by the CSRC.[2]

5.11 As interim reports should be made on a timely basis, it is critical to determine when the disclosure obligation arises. This is no easy task, particularly when the events concerned are still developing. If the information is disclosed too late, then it defeats the purpose of continuous disclosure; if the information is disclosed too

---

[2] Shangshi Gongsi Xinxi Pilu Guanli Banfa [Administrative Measures for the Disclosure of Information of Listed Companies] (issued by the CSRC in 2007), Art 30.

early, it may cause unnecessary confusion in the market. The CSRC has provided some crude guidance on the timing for interim reports:

> A listed company shall timely perform the obligation to disclose the information about a major event when any of the following circumstances is the first to occur:
> (1) The board of directors or board of supervisors makes a resolution about the major event;
> (2) The parties concerned enter into a letter of intent or agreement on the major event; or
> (3) The directors, supervisors or senior managers know the major event and report it.
>
> Where any of the following circumstances occurs before the occurrence of the circumstances as mentioned in the preceding paragraph, the listed company shall timely disclose the present situation and the risk factors which may affect the progress of the major event:
> (1) It is difficult to keep this major event confidential;
> (2) This major event has been divulged or there is already any hearsay in the market; or
> (3) There is any abnormal transaction of the corporate securities or their derivatives.[3]

5.12 Stock exchange listing rules allow the postponement of or even exemption from interim reports in certain circumstances. For instance, Article 2.17 of the Shanghai Stock Exchange Listing Rules provides that

> the listed company can apply to the Exchange for postponing information disclosure, if the information to be disclosed is uncertain, or belongs to temporary business secrets, or falls within other circumstances as recognized by the Exchange, and the immediate disclosure may harm the interests of the disclosing company or mislead the investors, and the following conditions are satisfied: (1) the information to be disclosed has not been leaked out; (2) relevant insiders have promised in writing to keep the Information confidential; (3) there is no anomaly in the trading of the company's shares and derivatives.

5.13 Under Article 2.18 of the Shanghai Stock Exchange Listing Rules, the listed company can apply for exemption from disclosure if the information to be disclosed belongs to the category of state secrets or business secrets, or falls within other circumstances recognized by the Exchange, and disclosure of the information may be a breach of relevant laws on confidentiality or may harm the interests of the company.

5.2.3. Comments

5.14 The requirement of continuous disclosure (prompt disclosure) has not been a universal practice in the international arena. Perhaps to the surprise of many, continuous disclosure is not generally required in the US, a jurisdiction with one of

---

[3] Shangshi Gongsi Xinxi Pilu Guanli Banfa [Administrative Measures for the Disclosure of Information of Listed Companies] (issued by the CSRC in 2007), Art 31.

the most advanced securities markets in the world. Indeed, although continuous disclosure is espoused by stock exchanges rules there, US securities law does not generally require listed companies to disclose material non-public information during the interval between the filing of Securities and Exchange Commission (SEC) periodic reports.[4] To be sure, there are some affirmative disclosure obligations in certain circumstances—for example, a duty to disclose when the company is issuing or trading its securities in the markets;[5] a duty to update previous disclosures if they have become materially misleading in light of subsequent events;[6] a duty to correct or verify rumours if they are prevalent and can be attributed to the company;[7] and a duty to file a Form 8-K which requires specific disclosure items such as major transactions.[8]

5.15 Thus, unless subject to specified affirmative disclosure obligations, listed companies in the US are not legally required to promptly disclose material non-public information in the interval between SEC mandated periodic reports. The timing of disclosure during this period normally is a matter of business judgement on the part of the company management. In theory, the company generally may delay making disclosure under the US securities laws until the filing of the next SEC periodic report.

5.16 In contrast, under the laws of many other jurisdictions, absent sufficient business justification, material non-public information must be promptly disclosed without delay. In 1994, Australia introduced statutory backing for stock exchange listing rules requiring continuous disclosure. After several rounds of public consultation, Hong Kong finally followed the Australian practice in 2013. So far, the continuous disclosure regime has been adopted in almost all jurisdictions outside the US with developed securities markets, such as the UK, Canada, Germany, France, and Italy.

5.17 There are many reasons behind the US approach. For instance, it is hard to judge the timing for making continuous disclosure. Further, continuous disclosure may stifle management's ability to overcome setbacks. Finally, the US periodic reporting regime is considered stringent as it mandates comprehensive disclosure in periodic reports which are required on a quarterly basis, rather than on a half-yearly basis as is the case in many other jurisdictions. In 1991, when Australia tried to strengthen its corporate disclosure regime, it had two options, namely mandatory

---

[4] In practice, due to various reasons such as lack of regulatory powers and conflicts of interest, stock exchanges have rarely enforced continuous disclosure rules they make against listed companies. Marc I Steinberg, 'Insider Trading, Selective Disclosure, and Prompt Disclosure' (2001) 22(3) *University of Pennsylvania Journal of International Economic Law* 635.
[5] See eg Greenfield v Heublein, Inc., 742 F.2d 751, 756 (3d Cir 1984).
[6] See eg Rubinstein v Collins, 20 F.3d 160, 170 (5th Cir 1994).
[7] See eg State Teachers Retirement Board v. Fluor Corp, 654 F.2d 843, 850 (2d Cir 1981).
[8] 17 C.F.R. §249.308 (2000).

quarterly reporting and continuous disclosure, and after careful consideration, it chose the latter in 1994.

However, Chinese listed companies are subject to both a stringent periodic disclosure regime—including mandatory quarterly reporting obligations—and a statutory requirement for continuous disclosure. Considering the international experiences previously discussed, it seems that China has introduced both the disclosure requirements from the US approach and the continuous disclosure approach adopted in other jurisdictions. Hence, there could be either over-regulation of the market, if the law was rigorously enforced, or under-enforcement of the law to mitigate the draconian regulatory requirements. **5.18**

5.3. Corporate Governance of Listed Companies

5.3.1. Overview

Despite the fact that listed companies account for a very small percentage of all companies in China, this small group generally contains the countries' largest and most significant companies. Also, due to the public nature of listed companies, they have a direct impact on millions of investors, including individual, small investors. Thus, listed companies in China, as is the case elsewhere, are subject to more stringent corporate governance standards. **5.19**

As discussed in previous chapters, Chinese listed companies generally have a highly concentrated share ownership pattern, and in most cases the controlling shareholder is the state.[9] Therefore, unlike the situation in many common law jurisdictions—particularly the US, where the shareholding pattern of listed companies is widely dispersed—the main corporate governance problem in China is not the conflicts of interest between corporate management and shareholders, but rather the conflicts of interest between majority shareholders and minority shareholders. **5.20**

No doubt, corporate governance of listed companies is a huge topic that deserves a book-length discussion in its own right; thus, this section will single out three more significant corporate governance measures which apply specifically to listed companies in China, including the institution of independent directors, the regime for substantial asset transactions, and the regime for related party transactions. **5.21**

5.3.2. Independent directors

In August 2001, the CSRC issued its 'Guidance Opinion on the Establishment of an Independent Director System in Listed Companies' (Independent Director Opinion),[10] **5.22**

---

[9] See Chapter 1.
[10] Guanyu zai Shangshi Gongsi Jianli Duli Dongshi Zhidu de Zhidao Yijian [Guidance Opinion on the Establishment of an Independent Director System in Listed Companies] (issued by the CSRC in August 2001).

despite the fact that the then Company Law did not provide for the institution of independent directors. Later in 2005, when the Chinese Company Law was revised, the institution of independent directors was formally recognized in the national law. Article 123 of the 2005 Company Law states that a listed company shall have independent directors and the detailed measures shall be formulated by the State Council. However, to date the State Council has not yet issued any such regulation, and thus the 2001 Independent Director Opinion still applies. In addition, the stock exchanges have issued relevant guidelines on the institution of independent directors. As the 2001 Independent Director Opinion is issued by the CSRC and constitutes the most comprehensive measure taken so far in this area, it is the focus of the discussion below, and reference is to this instrument unless otherwise specified.

5.3.2.1. General requirements

5.23 Article 1(1) defines 'independent director' as a director who does not have posts other than the directorship in the company, and who does not have any relationship with the company they work for or its major shareholders which may hamper them making an independent and objective judgement.

5.24 The independent directors owe a duty of good faith (*chengxin*) and diligence (*qinmian*) to the company and to the entire body of shareholders, particularly small and medium shareholders. In discharging their duties, the independent directors are not to be influenced by major shareholders, controlling persons, or others who have a relationship of interest with the company. Further, in principle, one person is allowed to serve as an independent director in up to five companies, though they must ensure that they have sufficient time and energy to effectively discharge their duties.[11]

5.25 Listed companies were required to have at least two independent directors by 30 June 2002, and such directors were to constitute at least one third of the board by 30 June 2003. Under the Company Law, listed companies should have 5–13 directors. Thus, if, as is often the case in practice, the company has more than six directors, the percentage requirement is more stringent than the absolute number threshold. Moreover, it is required that at least one independent director should be an accounting professional.[12]

5.26 Independent directors are required to undergo a training course organized by the CSRC.[13] In practice, the CSRC has organized such training courses in conjunction with Tsinghua University, a top Chinese university in Beijing.

---

[11] Independent Director Opinion, Art 1(2).
[12] Independent Director Opinion, Art 1(3).
[13] Independent Director Opinion, Art 1(5).

5.3.2.2. Qualifications of independent directors

5.27 Under Article 2 of the Independent Director Opinion, an independent director must (1) be qualified to serve as a director pursuant to the Company Law and other regulations; (2) possess the independence required by the Opinion itself; (3) possess basic knowledge relevant to the operations of the listed company, and be familiar with relevant laws and administrative rules and regulations; (4) possess at least five years' work experience in law, economics, or other fields necessary for the proper exercise of his functions as independent director; and (5) possess other qualifications stipulated in the company's articles of association.

5.28 No doubt, the independence requirement noted is the distinctive feature of independent directors, and thus further guidance is provided on the circumstances where the independence requirement is not met. Article 3 states that the following persons may not serve as independent directors: (1) a person who holds a position in the listed company or its subordinate affiliates, as well as the direct relatives of, and those with important social connections to, the former;[14] (2) a person, or the direct relative of a person, who directly or indirectly holds at least 1 per cent of the company's stock or is among the top ten shareholders of the company; (3) a person, or the direct relative of a person, who is employed by an entity that directly or indirectly holds at least 5 per cent of the company's stock or is among the top five non-natural person shareholders of the company; (4) a person with regard to whom any of the above conditions have been met within the last year; (5) a person who supplies accounting, legal, consulting, or other similar services to the company or its subordinate affiliates; (6) any other person specified in the company's articles of association; and (7) any other person specified by the CSRC.

5.3.2.3. Selection process and tenure

5.29 Article 4 provides for the process by which independent directors are selected. In general, the board of directors, the board of supervisors, and individuals or groups representing at least 1 per cent of the shares could nominate independent director candidates, which will then be voted on the shareholder meeting. The Article is silent however on how the voting should be carried out. The general voting requirement under the Company Law may thus come into play here: any director must be elected to office by a vote of the majority of shares at a shareholders' meeting.

5.30 It should be noted that before the company holds a shareholder meeting to elect independent directors, it should send the relevant materials about the nominees to the CSRC and the stock exchange where it is listed. The CSRC will assess whether

---

[14] 'Direct relatives' are defined as a 'spouse, mother, father, son, daughter, etc' while 'important social connections' covers 'brother, sister, father-in-law, mother-in-law, son-in-law, daughter-in-law, spouse of a brother or sister, brother or sister of a spouse, etc': Independent Director Opinion, Art 3(1).

the nominee meets the qualification and independence requirements. If the CSRC disapproves, the candidate can still be elected as an ordinary director, but not as an independent director.

5.31 The tenure of independent directors is the same as that of ordinary directors, and re-election is allowed; however, the longest continuous period of service cannot exceed six years. If the independent director fails to attend three consecutive board meetings in person, the board of directors can request the shareholder meeting to remove the independent director.

5.3.2.4. Powers and responsibilities

5.32 The Independent Director Opinion gives special powers to independent directors as follows: (1) to pass on important transactions with affiliates, defined as transactions with affiliates (*guanlian ren*) where the amount at stake is more than 3 million yuan or more than 5 per cent of the net asset value of the company according to its most recent audit report; (2) to recommend engagement or dismissal of the company's accounting firm; (3) to recommend the holding of interim shareholders' meetings; (4) to recommend the holding of board meetings; (5) to hire outside auditors and consultants (at the company's expense); and (6) to solicit proxies prior to a shareholders' meeting.[15]

5.33 Several points need to be noted about the powers listed above. First, most of the powers are advisory rather than decision-making in nature, but the company needs to make public disclosure if the recommendations made by independent directors are not actually adopted. Second, the powers cannot be exercised by individual independent directors; their exercise must receive the consent of at least half of the independent directors as a body. Third, the board of directors can set up special committees, such as audit, nomination, and remuneration committees, but there is no such requirement. If the board of directors chooses to do so, then at least half of the committee members must be independent directors. Fourth, in addition to the above powers, independent directors can express independent opinions in relation to certain major matters of the listed company.[16]

5.34 In order for independent directors to properly perform their duties, the Independent Director Opinion requires the listed company to provide necessary conditions. For instance, the listed company should ensure that independent directors have the same access to relevant information as ordinary directors; the company should cover the costs which independent directors incur in their work; independent directors should receive an appropriate amount of stipend, which should be proposed by the board of directors and approved by the shareholder meeting; and the listed company may buy liability insurance for independent directors.[17]

---

[15] Independent Director Opinion, Art 5(1).
[16] Independent Director Opinion, Art 6.
[17] Independent Director Opinion, Art 7.

5.3.2.5. Comments

Originally, China introduced the institution of independent directors for the purpose of facilitating Chinese companies' listing in overseas markets. In 1993, when Tsingtao Beer was listed in Hong Kong, it appointed two independent directors, in accordance with the listing rules there. Later, the institution of independent directors gradually came to be seen as a possible way to strengthen corporate governance in China. **5.35**

Due to its civil law background, China traditionally adopts a two-tiered corporate governance model, in which the company has both a board of directors and a board of supervisors. The board of supervisors has responsibility for monitoring the performance of the board of directors, but for many reasons, the institution of supervisory boards is not effective in practice. Hence, the institution of independent directors from common law jurisdictions is introduced as a potential solution to Chinese corporate governance problems. It has been argued, however, that proponents of the institution of independent directors misconceive the nature of the corporate governance problem in China, and have not taken into account specific features of the Chinese institutional environment.[18] **5.36**

A recent empirical study conducted by the Shanghai Listed Companies Association and the CSRC Shanghai Office produces some interesting findings on the institution of independent directors in China:[19] **5.37**

(1) The role of the independent director was widely seen as that of adviser rather than monitor.
(2) Most independent directors have good qualifications or experiences. Nearly 80 per cent of the companies had academics serve as their independent directors, and about half of the companies had independent directors who were directors, supervisors, and management of other companies.
(3) Up to 79.87 per cent of independent directors were nominated by major shareholders, the actual controller, and corporate management. This is seen as the primary factor adversely affecting the independence of independent directors.

---

[18] See eg Donald C Clarke, 'The Independent Director in Chinese Corporate Governance' (2006) 31 *Delaware Journal of Corporate Law* 125.
[19] Shanghai Listed Companies Association and the CSRC Shanghai Office, *Duli Dongshi, Jianshihui, Dongshihui Mishu Zhidu Yanjiu yu Shijian Tansuo* [Independent Directors, Supervisory Boards and Secretaries of the Board of Directors: Institutional Research and Empirical Investigation] (2013). This study uses a combination of empirical methods, including questionnaires, case studies and seminars; it covers 203 listed companies located in Shanghai, out of which 154 listed companies completed the questionnaire, representing a high response rate of 76 per cent.

(4) Independent directors attended more than 87.14 per cent of the meetings they needed to attend, but they had never cast 'no' votes.
(5) The stipend for independent directors varied significantly, with the highest being 350,000 yuan and the lowest 20,000; in most cases, the amount was about 60,000 yuan.
(6) Independent directors were rarely punished by the company or the regulator.
(7) Only 6.49 per cent of companies bought liability insurance for independent directors.

5.3.3. Substantial asset transactions

5.38 Substantial asset transactions, also known as material asset reorganizations in China, are assets transactions conducted by listed companies and companies held or controlled by them beyond their daily operating activities, such as the purchase and sales of assets which reach a prescribed proportion and cause major changes in the principal business, assets, and income of listed companies. In many cases, substantial asset transactions may lead to the transfer of corporate control, and thus this can be used as an alternative way to get listed. This is called 'reverse takeover' or 'backdoor' listing, and is particularly common in China due to its local institutional environment.[20]

5.39 The current regulatory regime for substantial asset transactions is mainly contained in the Administrative Measures for the Material Asset Reorganizations of Listed Companies (Measures for Material Asset Reorganizations), which was issued by the CSRC in 2008.[21] Similar to the Issuance Examination Committee, the CSRC has established a specialist committee, entitled the 'Takeovers and Reorganizations Committee' (*binggou chongzu weiyuanhui*), to help examine and approve applications for substantial asset transactions.

5.3.3.1. Principles and standards

5.40 To execute a material asset reorganization, a listed company shall meet the following requirements:

(1) It conforms to the state industrial policies and the state laws and administrative regulations on environmental protection, land management, anti-monopoly, etc.
(2) The reorganization will not cause the company to fail to meet the listing conditions.
(3) The price of the assets involved in the reorganization is fair, and there are no circumstances which damage the legitimate rights and interests of the company and its shareholders.

---

[20] For more discussion of this, see Chapter 10.
[21] Shangshi Gongsi Zhongda Zichan Chongzu Guanli Banfa [Administrative Measures for the Material Asset Reorganizations of Listed Companies (Measures for Material Asset Reorganizations)] (issued by the CSRC in 2008, revised later).

(4) The ownership of the assets involved in the reorganization is clear, there are no legal obstacles in the transfer of such assets, and the related creditor's rights and debts have been disposed of according to law.
(5) The reorganization is good for strengthening the company's sustained operation capacity, and no circumstances arise such as that the major assets of the company after reorganization are cash or the company has no specific business after reorganization.
(6) The reorganization is good for the company to maintain independence from its actual controller in terms of business, assets, finance, personnel, and organizational setting, and the reorganization conforms to the relevant CSRC provisions on independence of listed companies.
(7) The reorganization is good for the company to form or maintain a healthy and efficient corporate governance structure.[22]

5.41 Where a listed company or any company controlled by it purchases or sells assets to the following extent, it forms a material asset reorganization:

(1) The total assets purchased or sold account for 50 per cent or more of the end-of-period total assets in the audited consolidated financial statement of the last accounting year of the listed company.
(2) The business income from the purchased or sold assets in the last accounting year account for 50 per cent or more of the business income in the audited consolidated financial statement of the same period; or
(3) The net assets purchased or sold account for 50 per cent or more of the end-of-period net assets in the audited consolidated financial statement of the last accounting year, and are over 50 million yuan.

Even if the asset transaction does not fall within the above circumstances, if the CSRC finds that there exist major problems that may damage the legitimate rights and interests of the listed company or investors, it may, on the principle of prudent supervision, order the listed company to disclose information which should have been disclosed, suspend the transaction, and file the application documents in accordance with the Measures for Material Asset Reorganizations.[23]

5.42 When calculating the proportions mentioned in the preceding paragraph, four important points should be noted.[24] First, if the purchased assets are stock rights, the total assets shall be the total assets of the invested enterprise multiplied by the proportion of shares held from the investment, or the value of the transaction, whichever is higher; the business income shall be the business Income of the invested enterprise multiply the proportion of shares held from the investment; and the net assets shall be the net assets of the invested enterprise multiply the proportion of

---

[22] Measures for Material Asset Reorganizations, Art 10.
[23] Measures for Material Asset Reorganizations, Art 11.
[24] Measures for Material Asset Reorganizations, Art 12.

shares held from the investment, or the value of the transaction, whichever is higher. If the sold assets are stock rights, the total assets, business income, and net assets shall be those of the invested enterprise multiply the proportion of shares held from the investment, respectively. If the purchase of stock rights means the listed company gets holding rights to the invested enterprise, the total assets shall be the total assets of the invested enterprise or the value of the transaction, whichever is higher; the business income shall be the business income of the invested enterprise; and the net assets shall be the net assets of the invested enterprise or the value of the transaction, whichever is higher. If the sale of stock rights means the listed company loses holding rights to the invested enterprise, the total assets, business income and net assets shall be those of the invested company, respectively.

5.43 Second, if the purchased assets are non-equity assets, the total assets shall be the book value of the purchased assets or the value of the transaction, whichever is higher, and the net assets shall be the difference between the book value of assets and that of debts, or the value of the transaction, whichever is higher. If the sold assets are non-equity assets, the total assets shall be the book value of the sold assets, and the net assets shall be the difference between the book value of assets and that of debts. If the non-equity assets do not involve debts, the requirement on net assets as specified in Article 11(3) shall not apply.

5.44 Third, if the listed company purchases and sells assets simultaneously, the relevant proportions shall be calculated separately, and whichever is higher shall be taken as the proportion needed.

5.45 Fourth, if the listed company consecutively purchases and sells the same or relevant assets in 12 months, the corresponding amount shall be calculated on a cumulative basis, except for the asset trading behaviours which have already been filed with and approved by the CSRC in accordance with the Measures for Material Asset Reorganizations. Further, if the traded assets are owned or controlled by the same trading party, in the same or similar business scope, or under other circumstances recognized by the CSRC, such assets can be regarded as the same or relevant assets.

5.46 The final element of the definition of substantial asset transactions is that transactions may be effected not only through the common method of purchase and sale, but also in other forms. This includes: (1) establishing new enterprises with other parties, or increasing or reducing the capital of established enterprises; (2) being entrusted to operate or lease the assets of other enterprises, or entrusting the operating assets to other parties to operate or lease; (3) accepting conditional asset donations, or donating assets to other parties; and (4) other circumstances recognized by the CSRC on the principle of prudent supervision. If the above-mentioned forms of asset transfer constitute the purchase and sale of assets in nature, and the relevant proportion calculated in accordance with the Measures for Material Asset Reorganizations reaches 50 per cent or above, the listed company concerned shall fulfil obligations including information disclosure and file the application documents in accordance with the Measures for Material Asset Reorganizations.[25]

5.3.3.2. Approval by directors and shareholders

5.47 In general, the material asset reorganization of the listed company shall be decided by the board of directors through resolution and be submitted to the general meeting of shareholders for approval.

5.48 The board of directors of the listed company shall make an explicit judgement on whether the material asset reorganization constitutes an affiliated transaction and disclose the judgement as one of the issues subject to the resolution of the board of directors.

5.49 Independent directors of the listed company shall express independent opinions on the material asset reorganization on the basis of full knowledge of the relevant information. If the material asset reorganization constitutes an affiliated transaction, independent directors may hire an independent financial advisor in another initiative to express opinions on the impact of the transaction on the non-affiliated shareholders of the listed company. The listed company shall actively assist independent directors to transfer and look up the relevant material and, by arranging field investigation, organizing securities service agencies to report the relevant information, or in another way, provide necessary support and advantage for independent directors to perform duties.

5.50 The resolution of the general meeting of shareholders of the listed company on the material asset reorganization issues must be voted for by two thirds of present shareholders with voting power. If the material asset reorganization issues are affiliated to a group of shareholders of the company or their affiliated parties, such shareholders shall withdraw when the general meeting of shareholders puts such issues to the vote. If the counterpart of the transaction has reached an agreement or tacit understanding with the controlling shareholder of the listed company on accepting the transfer of the equity of the listed company or recommending directors to the listed company, and such a move may cause changes in the actual control of power of the listed company, the controlling shareholder and the affiliated parties thereof shall withdraw from voting.

5.51 The general meeting of shareholders convened to discuss the material asset reorganization issues shall be a spot meeting, and the listed company shall, by online voting or in another way, make it more convenient for shareholders to attend the general meeting of shareholders.

---

[25] Measures for Material Asset Reorganizations, Art 13.

5.3.3.3. Approval by the China Securities Regulatory Commission (CSRC)

5.52 The listed company shall, on the next working day after the board of directors makes the resolution on material asset reorganization, disclose at least the following documents, and file a copy thereof with the dispatched office of the CSRC of the place where the listed company is located (hereinafter referred to as dispatched office): (1) the resolution of the board of directors and the opinions of independent directors; and (2) the material asset reorganization plan of the listed company.[26]

5.53 Again, the listed company shall announce the resolution of the general meeting of shareholders on material asset reorganization on the next working day after the resolution is made, prepare the application documents in accordance with the relevant CSRC provisions, entrust the independent financial advisor to submit the documents to the CSRC within three working days, and send a copy thereof to the dispatched office.[27]

5.54 The CSRC shall make a decision of approval or disapproval on the application for material asset reorganization in accordance with the statutory conditions and procedures. For more significant transactions, particularly those to the effect of backdoor listings, the listed company shall submit its material asset reorganization plan to the Takeovers and Reorganizations Committee for examination and approval. Such circumstances include: (1) the total assets sold and purchased by the listed company account for 70 per cent or more of the end-of-period total assets in the consolidated financial statement of the last accounting year; (2) the listed company intends to sell all its operating assets and purchase other assets at the same time; and (3) any other circumstances which the CSRC determines necessary to submit the reorganization plan to the Takeovers and Reorganizations Committee for examination and approval.

5.55 If, instead of the above-mentioned circumstances, the reorganization falls under any of the following, the listed company may apply to the CSRC to submit the reorganization plan to the Sub-committee for examination and approval: (1) the asset purchased by the listed company is an integrated business entity under Article 48 of the Measures for Material Asset Reorganizations, and the performance thereof needs to be evaluated through simulated computation; or (2) the listed company has objections to the feedback opinion of the relevant functional department of the CSRC.[28]

5.3.3.4. Information management

5.56 In China, substantial asset transactions of listed companies are among the circumstances in which market misconduct, particularly insider trading, is most

---

[26] Measures for Material Asset Reorganizations, Art 20.
[27] Measures for Material Asset Reorganizations, Art 23.
[28] Measures for Material Asset Reorganizations, Art 27.

frequently committed.²⁹ Thus, relevant rules are provided for information management during the process of substantial asset transactions.

Under Article 37 of the Measures for Material Asset Reorganizations, where the listed company plans or executes the material asset reorganization, the related obligors of information disclosure shall impartially disclose to all investors all information that may greatly affect the trading price of the shares of the listed company (hereinafter referred to as share price-related sensitive information), and may not disclose such information to certain selected parties in advance. 5.57

The shareholders and the actual controller of the listed company, as well as other related institutions and personnel that have participated in the planning, argumentation, and decision-making of the material asset reorganization, shall inform the listed company of the relevant information in a timely and accurate manner, and co-operate with the listed company to disclose information in a timely, accurate, and integrated manner. After being informed of the share price-related sensitive information, the listed company shall apply to the stock exchange for suspension of licence and shall disclose such information.³⁰ 5.58

The following parties shall have the obligation of keeping confidential the share price-related sensitive information concerned in the material asset reorganization before it is disclosed according to law, and are prohibited from using such information for insider trading: the directors, supervisors, and senior managers of the listed company; the counterpart of the material asset reorganization and its affiliated parties; the directors, supervisors, and senior managers, or the chief persons in charge of the counterpart and its affiliated parties; the securities service agencies hired by the parties concerned in the transaction and the staff of such agencies; institutions and personnel involved in the planning, argumentation, decision-making, and examination and approval of the material asset reorganization; and other institutions and personnel that have been or may be informed of the share price-related sensitive information due to linear relative relationships, service provision, business contacts, etc.³¹ 5.59

5.3.4. Related party transactions

Related party transactions are the most common way by which controlling shareholders and company management transfer interest and exploit the listed company. This is particularly so in China, where most listed companies have been spun off from state-owned enterprises, and thus have parent and sibling companies. 5.60

---

[29] Hui Huang, 'Insider Trading and the Regulation on China's Securities Market: Where Are We Now and Where Do We Go From Here?' (2012) 5 *Journal of Business Law* 379. For more discussion of insider trading, see Chapter 8.
[30] Measures for Material Asset Reorganizations, Art 38.
[31] Measures for Material Asset Reorganizations, Art 39.

5.61 The rules governing related party transactions in China are scattered across national law, CSRC regulation, and stock exchange listing rules. Article 21 of the Company Law provides that neither the controlling shareholder, nor the actual controller, nor any of the directors, supervisors, or senior management of the company may injure the interests of the company by taking advantage of its connection relationship (see the next section). This is a very general provision, and more specifically, the law governing related party transactions includes the following important elements.

5.3.4.1. The definition of related party transactions

5.62 Article 217 of the Company Law defines 'connection relationship' (*guanlian guanxi*) as the relationship between the controlling shareholders, actual controllers, directors, supervisors, or senior management persons of a company and the enterprise directly or indirectly controlled thereby, and any other relationship that may lead to the transfer of any interest of the company. However, the enterprises controlled by the state do not incur a connection relationship simply because their shares are controlled by the state.

5.63 Stock exchange listing rules provide further guidance on the definition of related party transactions. For instance, Section 1 of Chapter 10 of the Shanghai Stock Exchange Listing Rules contains detailed rules regarding who are related parties of the listed company, and what are transactions.[32]

5.64 In general, the related party of a listed company includes related legal persons and related natural persons. A legal person shall be a related legal person of a listed company if it is under any of the following circumstances:

(1) It directly or indirectly controls the listed company.
(2) It is a legal person other than the listed company and the controlled subsidiary of the listed company that is controlled either directly or indirectly by the legal person specified in the preceding subparagraph.
(3) It is a legal person other than the listed company and the controlled subsidiary of the listed company that is controlled either directly or indirectly by a related natural person of the listed company as set out in Section 10.1.5, or such related natural person serves either as its director or senior officer.
(4) It is a legal person holding more than 5 per cent of the listed company.
(5) It is a legal person as recognized by the CSRC, the Exchange, or the listed company in accordance with the principle of essence counting more than form, who has a special relation with the listed company, and such special relation may help it obtain more than justifiable interest from the listed company.

---

[32] Shanghai Stock Exchange Listing Rules, Ch 10, S1.

Further, where a listed company forms a related party relationship with the legal person set out in (2) of Section 10.1.3, the only reason being that they are both controlled by the same state asset management institution, the listed company may apply to the Exchange for exemption from performance of relevant obligations as required for a related party transaction, except in cases where the chairman, president, or more than half of the directors of the legal person fall within (2) of Section 10.1.5.

5.65 A natural person shall be a related natural person of a listed company if he is under any of the following circumstances:

(1) He holds more than 5 per cent interest either directly or indirectly in the listed company.
(2) He is a director, supervisor, or senior officer of the listed company.
(3) He is a director, supervisor, or senior officer of the legal person set out in (1) of Section 10.1.3.
(4) He is a close family member of a person referred to in (1) and (2) of this sub-section, including spouse, parent or parent-in-law, brother or brother's spouse, sister or sister's spouse, child aged 18 or above or such child's spouse, spouse's brother or sister, or child's spouse's parent.
(5) As recognized by the CSRC, the Exchange, or the listed company in accordance with the principle of essence counting more than form, he has another special relationship with the listed company and might accordingly obtain more than justifiable interest from the listed company.

5.66 Finally, a legal person or natural person shall be deemed as a related party of a listed company if it or he meets any of the following conditions: (1) as a result of its or his signing an agreement or making another arrangement with the listed company, and after such agreement or arrangement takes effect or within the next 12 months, it or he falls under any of the circumstances set out in Section 10.1.3 or Section 10.1.5; (2) it or he has ever been under any of the circumstances set out in Section 10.1.3 or Section 10.1.5 in the preceding 12 months.

5.67 As well as the term 'related parties', the term 'transactions' is defined. A related party transaction of a listed company, which means transfer of resources or obligations between a listed company or its controlled subsidiary and a related party of the listed company, includes the following: (1) transactions set out in Section 9.1; (2) purchasing raw materials, fuel, and power; (3) selling products and commodities; (4) providing or accepting labour; (5) selling by consignment or selling on commission; (6) co-investing with a related party; (7) other agreed matters that may result in transfer of resources or obligations.

5.68 The term 'transactions' under Article 9.1 of Shanghai Stock Exchange Listing Rules includes the following: (1) acquiring or disposing of assets; (2) external investment (including trustee investment and entrusted loan); (3) providing financial assistance; (4) granting guarantee (excluding counter-guarantee); (5) leasing in or out assets; (6) signing management-related contracts (including operation by commission and operation on commission); (7) donating assets or accepting asset donation; (8) restructuring debts or creditor's rights; (9) transferring R&D programmes; (10) signing licensing contracts; (11) other transactions as recognized by the Exchange. The aforesaid asset acquisition or disposal excludes acquisitions of raw materials, fuel, and power and sales of products and commodities related to the day-to-day operation. But if acquisition or sale of such assets is involved in asset swaps, it shall be treated as 'a transaction' as previously defined.

5.3.4.2. Approval requirement

5.69 Related party transactions require the approval of the board of directors and the shareholder meeting. In general, where any of the directors has any relationship with the enterprise involved in the matter to be decided at the meeting of the board of directors, he shall not vote on this resolution, nor may he vote on behalf of any other person. The meeting of the board of directors shall not be held unless more than half of the unrelated directors are present at the meeting. A resolution of the board of directors shall be adopted by more than half of the unrelated directors. If the number of unrelated directors in presence is less than three persons, the matter shall be submitted to the shareholders' assembly of the listed company for deliberation.[33]

5.70 The concept of related directors is further defined in stock exchange listing rules. Under Article 10.2.1 of Shanghai Stock Exchange Listing Rules, 'related directors' include the following directors or any director falling within any of the following circumstances:

(1) Counterparty to the transaction.
(2) A director holding a post in the counterparty to the transaction, or holding a post in any legal person unit that directly or indirectly controls the counterparty to the transaction.
(3) A director holding direct or indirect controlling power over the counterparty to the transaction.
(4) A close family member (as defined in (4) of Section 10.1.5) of the counterparty to the transaction or a close family member of the direct or indirect controller of the counterparty to the transaction.
(5) A close family member (as defined in (4) of Section 10.1.5) of the director, supervisor or senior officer of the counterparty to the transaction or a close family member of a director, supervisor, or senior officer of the direct or indirect controller of the counterparty to the transaction.

---

[33] Company Law, Art 125.

(6) A person whose independent business judgement may be affected for other reasons as recognized by the CSRC, the Exchange, or the listed company.

5.71 The CSRC has provided guidance on the procedure for the shareholder meeting reviewing related party transactions. When the shareholders' assembly is deliberating the related transactions, the related shareholders shall not participate in the vote, and their represented stock shall not be calculated in the total number of valid votes; the announcement of the shareholders' conference shall fully reveal the votes of the non-related shareholders.[34]

5.72 Again, Shanghai Stock Exchange Listing Rules set out a definition of related shareholders, which includes:

(1) A counterparty to the transaction.
(2) A legal or natural person holding direct or indirect controlling power over the counterparty to the transaction.
(3) A legal or natural person directly or indirectly controlled by the counterparty to the transaction.
(4) A legal or natural person directly or indirectly controlled both with the counterparty to the transaction by the same legal person or natural person.
(5) A legal or natural person whose voting power is restricted or affected as a result of incomplete implementation of any agreement on transfer of equity interest or other agreements.
(6) Another legal person or natural person, as recognized by the CSRC or the Exchange, who might obtain more than justifiable interest from the listed company.[35]

5.3.4.3. Information disclosure

5.73 Related party transactions are subject to the continuous disclosure regime. More specifically, where a related party transaction between a listed company and its related natural person is worth more than RMB 300,000, the listed company shall make disclosure in a timely manner. Also, where a related party transaction between a listed company and its related legal person is worth more than RMB 3 million and accounts for more than 0.5 per cent of the listed company's latest audited net assets, the listed company shall make timely disclosure.[36]

---

[34] Shangshi Gongsi Zhangcheng Zhiyin [Guidance for the Articles of Listed Company] (issued by the CSRC) (2006 revision).
[35] Shanghai Stock Exchange Listing Rules, Art 10.2.2.
[36] Shanghai Stock Exchange Listing Rules, Arts 10.2.3–4.

5.4. Listing Suspension and Delisting

5.4.1. Criteria

5.74 Under Article 55 of the Securities Law, where a listed company is under any of the following circumstances, the stock exchange shall decide to suspend the listing of its stocks:

(1) Where the total amount of capital stock or share distribution of the company changes and thus fails to meet the requirements for listing.
(2) Where the company fails to publicize its financial status according to the relevant provisions or has any false record in its financial statements which may mislead the investors.
(3) Where the company has any major irregularity.
(4) Where the company has been operating at a loss for the preceding three consecutive years.
(5) Under any other circumstance as prescribed in the listing rules of the stock exchange.

5.75 Article 56 of the Securities Law sets out the criteria for delisting, stating that where a listed company is under any of the following circumstances, the stock exchange shall decide to terminate the listing of its stocks:

(1) Where the total amount of capital stock or share distribution of the company changes and thus fails to meet the requirements of listing, and where the company fails again to meet the requirements of listing within the period prescribed by the stock exchange.
(2) Where the company fails to publicize its financial status according to the relevant provisions or has any false record in its financial statements, and refuses to make any correction.
(3) Where the company has been operating at a loss for the preceding three consecutive years and failed to increase its profits in the past year.
(4) Where the company is dissolved or is declared bankrupt.
(5) Under any other circumstance as prescribed in the listing rules of the stock exchange.

5.76 As suspension and delisting are major events, information disclosure is required to keep the market informed. Thus, where a stock exchange decides to suspend or terminate the listing of any securities, it shall announce the decision in a timely manner and report it to the CSRC for archival filing.[37] Also, the company concerned has a duty to make the relevant information disclosure. The stock exchange listing rules have provided further guidance on the criteria and procedure of suspension and delisting.

---

[37] Securities Law, Art 72.

5.4.2. Special treatment measures

In order to warn investors of the risks associated with certain listed companies, stock exchanges have adopted the so-called 'special treatment system'. The risk here is divided into two categories—delisting risk and other major risk—which are subject to their respective special treatment measures. **5.77**

In the case of other major risks, the trading code of the listed company will have a prefix of 'ST', which stands for special treatment. Further, the range of daily price fluctuation will be reduced to 5 per cent, as opposed to the 10 per cent applicable in normal situations. Stock exchange listing rules set out the circumstances in which the special treatment measure will be taken. For instance, Article 13.3.1 of the Shanghai Stock Exchange Listing Rules lists the following circumstances: **5.78**

(1) The company has restored its listing status from suspension or delisting, but has not yet published its first annual report.
(2) The business activities of the listed company have been severely affected and are not likely to return to normal within three months.
(3) The main banking account of the listed company has been frozen.
(4) The board of directors cannot hold normal meetings and reach resolutions.
(5) The controlling shareholder or related parties have misappropriated the funds of the listed company for non-productive purposes or caused the listed company to provide security in breach of law and regulation, and the above problem is very serious.
(6) Other circumstances recognized by the CSRC or the Exchange.

In a similar vein, if the listed company is at the risk of delisting, its trading code will be prefixed with '*ST', and the permitted daily price fluctuation will be within the reduced range of 5 per cent. Article 13.2.1 of the Shanghai Stock Exchange Listing Rules lists the following circumstances in which the listed company will be subject to the above special treatment measure for delisting risk: **5.79**

(1) The audited net profit of the listed company is in the negative for the preceding two consecutive accounting years, or, after retrospective restatement, is in the negative consecutively.
(2) The audited net assets of the listed company are in the negative for the latest accounting year, or, after retrospective restatement, are in the negative.
(3) The audited business revenue of the listed company is lower than 10 million yuan for the latest accounting year, or, after retrospective restatement, is in the negative.
(4) The accounting firm has issued an audit report in which it cannot express its opinion, or has negative opinions, on the financial statement of the listed company in the latest accounting year.
(5) Because the financial statement of the listed company contains major accounting errors or false information, it has been asked by the CSRC to

rectify the problem but has not done so within the specified period, and the trading of its shares has been suspended for two months.

(6) The listed company has failed to produce its annual report or half-yearly report within the legally specified period, and the trading of its shares has been suspended for two months.

(7) The listed company is likely to be dissolved.

(8) The court has accepted applications to restructure and liquidate the listed company.

(9) The shareholding structure of the listed company does not meet the listing requirements due to Article 12.14, and it has submitted a solution to the problem to the Exchange within the specified period of one month, and the solution has been agreed by the Exchange.

(10) Other circumstances recognized by the Exchange.

5.4.3. Comments

5.80 Despite the delisting mechanism discussed, a very small number of listed companies have been delisted in practice. The first delisting case arose as late as 2001, more than ten years after the two stock exchanges were established in Shanghai and Shenzhen. In many cases, the listed companies were not delisted even though they committed serious market misconduct and thus clearly met the delisting requirements.

5.81 This gap between the law in the book and the law in practice can only be understood by reference to the peculiar context in which the law operates. First, as a general matter, delisting is not an apt response to infringement of a listing rule or law, since it may deny holders a market for their securities and thereby compound the harm they have suffered. Second, the off-exchange market in China is currently underdeveloped, making it a particularly hard decision to delist a company. Finally and most importantly, listed status is a scarce commodity on the Chinese securities market due to the merits review regulation of securities offerings. Hence, listed companies try to keep their listed status by all means, notably through material asset reorganizations, often with the support of local governments.

5.82 The under-enforcement of the delisting regime has led to many problems. It fuels speculative activities in the market and distorts the functioning of the market mechanism. The CSRC has recently indicated that it will strengthen the enforcement of the delisting regime, using the Growth Enterprise Market (GEM) board of the Shenzhen Stock Exchange as a testing ground. It remains to be seen whether and how the CSRC will achieve its purpose.

6

LIABILITY FOR MISREPRESENTATION

6.1. Overview	6.01	6.2.5. Causation	6.25
6.1.1. Types of legal liabilities	6.01	6.2.6. Calculation of compensation	6.34
6.1.2. The development of securities civil liability	6.07	**6.3. Procedural Rules of Civil Litigation**	6.39
6.2. Substantive Rules of Civil Litigation	6.13	6.3.1. Prerequisite procedure	6.39
6.2.1. Scope of application	6.13	6.3.2. Statute of limitation	6.50
6.2.2. Definition of misrepresentation	6.17	6.3.3. Jurisdiction of the court	6.54
6.2.3. Scope of defendants	6.20	6.3.4. Forms of litigation	6.59
6.2.4. Defences to liability	6.22	**6.4. Comments**	6.78

6.1. Overview

6.1.1. Types of legal liabilities

In China, there are generally three types of legal liability, namely administrative liability, civil liability, and criminal liability. The administrative liability is imposed by the regulator, namely the China Securities Regulatory Commission (CSRC). According to Article 193 of the Securities Law, in the case of securities misrepresentation, **6.01**

> Where an issuer, a listed company or any other obligor of information disclosure fails to disclose information according to the relevant provisions or where there is any false record, misleading or major omission in the information it has disclosed, it shall be ordered to correct, given a warning and imposed a fine of 300,000 yuan up to 600,000 yuan. The person-in-charge and any other person as held to be directly responsible shall be given a warning and be imposed a fine of 30,000 yuan up to 300,000 yuan.
>
> Where an issuer, a listed company or any other obligor of information disclosure fails to submit relevant reports or where there is any false record, misleading or major omission in any report it has submitted, it shall be ordered to correct, given a warning and imposed a fine of 300,000 yuan up to 600,000 yuan. The person-in-charge and any other person-in-charge as held to be directly responsible shall be given a warning and be imposed a fine of 30,000 yuan up to 300,000 yuan.
>
> The controlling shareholder or actual controller of any issuer, listed company or any other obligor of information disclosure [who] instigates any irregularity as

prescribed in the preceding 2 paragraphs herein shall be subject to the punishments as prescribed in the preceding 2 paragraphs.[1]

6.02 Article 231 provides that if the contravention of the Securities Law is serious enough to constitute a crime, criminal liability shall be pursued.[2] This, of course, applies to the provisions governing market misconduct, including securities representation. Criminal liability for securities misrepresentation is set out in detail in Articles 160 and 161, which apply to securities misrepresentation at the time of issuance and after issuance, respectively. The count of securities misrepresentation under Article 160 is called the crime of fraudulent issuance of shares and debentures:

> Concealment of material facts or fabrication of major fraudulent contents in share-soliciting prospectuses, share-subscription applications, and bond solicitation by companies and enterprises for the purpose of issuing shares or company or enterprise bonds shall, in cases involving large amounts, with serious consequences, or of a serious nature, be punished with imprisonment or criminal detention of less than five years, with a fine or a separately imposed fine of over 1 percent and less than 5 percent of the illegally raised capital.
>
> Units committing offenses under the preceding paragraph shall be punished with a fine, with personnel directly in charge and other personnel directly responsible being punished with imprisonment or criminal detention of less than five years.

6.03 In contrast, Article 161 provides for the crime of provision of false accounting reports on the secondary market, stating that

> Personnel directly in charge and other directly responsible personnel of a company that presents false financial accounts or financial accounts with concealment of material facts to its shareholders and members of the public, that seriously hurt their interests, shall be punished with imprisonment or criminal detention of less than three years, with a fine or a separately imposed fine of over 20,000 yuan and less than 200,000 yuan.

6.04 As seen above, there are two notable differences between the criminal liability for securities misrepresentation at the time of issuance under Article 160 and its counterpart after issuance under Article 161. First, the penalty under Article 160 is heavier than that under Article 161; second, while Article 160 imposes liability for both individuals and entities, Article 161 only penalizes individuals. It is unclear why a dual regime is adopted for criminal liability for securities misrepresentation, while at the same time administrative liability for securities misrepresentation is subject to a uniform regime prescribed under Article 193.

---

[1] Zhonghua Renming Gongheguo Zhenquan Fa [Securities Law of the People's Republic of China] (promulgated on 29 December 1998 and effective from 1 July 1999, amended in 2004, 2005 and 2013) (2005 Securities Law), Arts 193. Unless indicated otherwise, reference to Securities Law is to the 2005 Securities Law.
[2] Securities Law, Art 231.

Finally, the person committing misrepresentation will also be subject to civil liability in private civil suits, which are brought by aggrieved investors seeking compensation. Private securities litigation is commonly known as private enforcement, as opposed to public enforcement carried out by the regulator. There has been an ongoing debate as to the relative importance of private enforcement versus public enforcement of investor protection laws.[3] What is clear though is that the two forms of law enforcement have their own strengths and weaknesses. For instance, public enforcement has advantages vis-à-vis private enforcement in terms of the power to investigate and impose severe penalties. Private enforcement, however, has its own strengths. To begin with, while the function of deterring misconduct is common to both public and private enforcement, private enforcement also has the important function of compensating investors which public enforcement usually cannot perform. Further, the regulator is subject to resource constraints and incentive issues in dealing with securities fraud, whereas investors—often driven by lawyers who are dubbed 'private attorney-generals'—are relatively well-resourced and well-incentivized in pursuing relevant cases. In sum, public enforcement and private enforcement are both important, and they complement each other in setting up a comprehensive and effective system of legal liability for securities fraud. **6.05**

As with other civil law countries, China has traditionally relied on public enforcement of securities law. Only in recent years has China started utilizing private enforcement of securities law in the form of civil suits brought by investors. As private enforcement is gaining momentum in China, and involves more difficult issues such as the scope of plaintiffs, the scope of defendants, and calculation of damages, this chapter will be focused on civil liability for securities misrepresentation. **6.06**

6.1.2. The development of securities civil liability

Under the 1998 Securities Law, while civil liability for market misconduct such as misrepresentation was provided for in principle,[4] there were no detailed provisions to implement the remedy. Indeed, the law was silent on relevant issues concerning civil liability, such as questions of who the eligible plaintiff is, how to calculate the damages, and how to bring the suit, thus rendering the private civil liability provision virtually a dead letter. To be sure, the statutory remedies in the Securities Law are not exhaustive, and those committing misrepresentation could be theoretically **6.07**

---

[3] See eg LLSV, 'What Works in Securities Laws?' (2006) 61 *Journal of Finance* 20 (arguing that compared with private enforcement, the important of public enforcement is at best modest); cf Howell E Jackson and Mark J Roe, 'Public and Private Enforcement of Securities Laws: Resources-Based Evidence' (2009) 93 *Journal of Financial Economics* 207 (finding that public enforcement is more important than private liability rules in explaining financial market outcomes around the world).

[4] Zhonghua Renming Gongheguo Zhenquan Fa [Securities Law of the People's Republic of China] (promulgated on 29 December 1998 and effective from 1 July 1999) (1998 Securities Law), Art 207 (simply stated that 'Civil compensation liability shall be imposed if the law is violated...'). The 1998 Securities Law was later revised several times, with the most significant one conducted in 2005.

based on the general contract law or on the tort regime. However, due to the special nature of on-market securities transactions, for example, being impersonal and anonymous, it is extremely difficult, if not impossible—particularly in terms of the causation and reliance requirement—to bring private civil suits on those conventional grounds.

6.08 The above problem was well illustrated in the 1998 case of *Liu Zhongmin vs Bohai Group*, which is widely regarded as the first ever securities civil case in China. There, the court rejected the plaintiff's claim to compensation on the grounds that the plaintiff failed to prove the causal link between his trading loss and the defendant's misrepresentation. Although the case was not successful, its significance should not be underestimated. For the very first time, Chinese investors tried to vindicate their rights in the courtroom, showing the potential utility of this legal mechanism as well as the problems with the then prevailing Chinese law in this area. The case marked the beginning of the history of private securities litigation in China, serving as a wake-up call for China to consider the value of private enforcement of securities law.

6.09 The simmering development of China's legal regime for private securities litigation finally reached boiling point in 2001. As was the case in many overseas markets, such as the US, at that time, there was a sudden outbreak of corporate scandals on the Chinese securities market. As a result, many Chinese investors suffered large losses and a spate of civil cases for compensation were filed across the nation. It was against this backdrop that the Supreme People's Court (SPC) issued three important circulars on private securities litigation in 2001, 2002, and 2003, respectively.

6.10 On 21 September 2001, the SPC issued the first circular (hereinafter the SPC First Circular) instructing China's courts not to accept civil compensation claims over securities market misconduct, on the grounds that the courts were not ready to hear such cases due to 'legislative and judicial limitations at the moment'.[5] This circular was vehemently criticized by many, and public pressure forced the SPC to change its position less than four months later. On 15 January 2002, the SPC issued its second circular (hereinafter the SPC Second Circular), lifting the restriction on civil cases arising from misrepresentation, but not those arising from other forms of market misconduct such as insider trading and market manipulation.[6] The SPC Second Circular has only five brief provisions and leaves unaddressed many issues concerning the bringing and hearing of civil compensation suits. Hence, although some cases were accepted according to this second circular, they

---

[5] Zuigao Renmin Fayuan Guanyu she Zhengquan Minshi Peichang Anjian Zan Buyu Shouli de Tongzhi [The Notice of the Supreme People's Court on Temporary Refusal of Filings of Securities-Related Civil Compensation Cases] (21 September 2001).

[6] Zuigao Renmin Fayuan Guanyu Shouli Zhengquan Shichang Yin Xujiachengshu Yinfa de Minshi Qinquan Jiufen Anjian Youguan Wenti de Tongzhi [The Notice of the Supreme People's Court on Relevant Issues of Filing of Civil Tort Dispute Cases Arsing from Misrepresentation on the Securities Market] (15 January 2012).

were all stayed pending further guidance from the SPC. On 9 January 2003, the SPC circulated the eagerly awaited third instrument (hereinafter the SPC Third Circular), which, while not without problems, contains 37 detailed provisions to set up a relatively complete legal framework for private securities litigation arising from misrepresentation in China.[7]

In the 2005 overhaul of the Securities Law, the legal basis for civil suits on securities misrepresentation was written into the statute, with all detailed aspects left in the SPC Third Circular.[8] Under the Securities Law, there are two provisions governing private civil liability for securities misrepresentation, according to who the defendant is. Article 69 provides for civil liability for the following persons: (1) the issuer company; (2) the issuer company's director, supervisor, senior manager, or any other person directly responsible for misrepresentation; (3) the issuer company's controlling shareholder and actual controller; and (4) the sponsor and underwriter.[9] Article 173 extends private civil liability to securities trading service institutions which formulate and issue any auditing report, asset appraisal report, financial advising report, credit rating report, or legal opinions for the issuance, listing, and trading of securities.[10] Common examples are accounting firms and law firms that are typically involved in the issuance, listing, and trading of securities.   6.11

The above is a significant development, because in the hierarchy of the Chinese legislative system, the Securities Law as a national law enjoys a much higher level of legal force than the rules issued by the CSRC, thereby providing a more solid foundation for private securities litigation over misrepresentation in China. Since detailed rules are still to be found in the SPC Third Circular, it remains the centrepiece of China's legal regime for private securities litigation, and therefore the focus of analysis in this chapter.   6.12

6.2. Substantive Rules of Civil Litigation

6.2.1. Scope of application

The SPC Third Circular clearly stipulates its scope of application and thus not all instances of securities misrepresentation will give rise to the civil liability therein. Article 1 defines the subject of the circular, namely the case of civil compensation arising from misrepresentation in securities market, as a case of civil compensation   6.13

---

[7] Zuigao Renmin Fayuan Guanyu Shenli Zhengquan Shichang Yin Xujia Chenshu Yinfa De Minshi Peichang Anjian De Ruogan Guiding [Provisions of the Supreme People's Court Concerning the Acceptance and Trial of Civil Compensation Securities Suits Involving Misrepresentation] (effective from 1 February 2003).
[8] Securities Law, Arts 69, 173.
[9] Securities Law, Art 69.
[10] Securities Law, Art 173.

for which an investor in securities market brings a lawsuit to the people's court against the obligor for information disclosure who violates legal provisions by making misrepresentation, thus causing losses to him.[11]

6.14 The terms 'investor' and 'securities markets' mentioned above are further clarified under Article 2. The term 'investor' refers to a natural person, legal person, or any other organization that engages in securities subscription or transaction in the securities market; the term 'securities market' encompasses a number of different markets, including (1) the issuance market for the issuer to raise shares publicly, (2) the market for securities transaction made through the price quotation system in the securities exchange, (3) the market for securities companies to handle the transfer of shares on behalf of others, and (4) any other securities market established upon approval by the state. In practice, the second type of market above refers to the two national stock exchanges in Shanghai and Shenzhen; the third refers to the various third-board markets.

6.15 Article 3 makes clear that the SPC Third Circular does not apply to civil litigation arising from any of the following transactions: (a) transactions made outside the securities market established upon approval by the state; (b) transactions made by means of agreed transfer in the securities market established upon the approval by the state. According to the drafters of the SPC Third Circular, the first type of excluded transaction refers to illegal securities transactions on the off-exchange markets; the second refers to block trading of tradable shares and transfer of non-tradable shares by way of private agreement.[12]

6.16 From the above discussion, it is clear that the SPC Third Circular makes no distinction between misrepresentation on the primary market and on the secondary market. There is however a significant difference between misrepresentation at the time of securities issuance and after securities have been listed: with regard to misrepresentation at the time of issuance, investors enter into subscription contracts with the misrepresenting issuance company, while on the secondary market investors do not have similar contractual relationships with the misrepresenting listed company, but rather trade with other investors. Hence, the civil liability regime for misrepresentation on the primary market may need to be different from that for misrepresentation on the secondary market. Indeed, in overseas jurisdictions, notably the US, there is a specific prospectus civil liability regime in addition to a general regime against securities fraud.

---

[11] SPC Third Circular, Art 1.
[12] Guoguang Li and Wei Jia, *Zhengquan Shichang Xujia Chenshu Minshi Peichang Zhidu [Civil Compensation Regime for Misrepresentation on the Securities Markets]* (2003, Law Press) 46; Guoguang Li (ed), *Zuigao Renmin Fayuan Guanyu Shenli Zhengquan Shichang Xujia Chenshu Anjian Sifa Jieshi de Lijie yu Shiyong [The Understanding and Application of the Judicial Interpretation of the Supreme People's Court on Hearing Cases arising from Misrepresentation on the Securities Markets]* (2003, People's Court Press), 114.

6.2.2. Definition of misrepresentation

6.17 Securities misrepresentation may take different forms. Under Article 17, misrepresentation in securities market is defined as: (1) false recording (*xujia jizai*); (2) misleading statement (*wudaoxing chenshu*); (3) material omission (*zhongda yilou*); or (4) improper disclosure (*buzhengdang pilu*), all of which are made against the true fact of major events by the obligor for information disclosure (*xinxi pilu yiwuren*), namely those who have a duty to disclose information on the securities market. As to the meaning of 'major events', reference is made to the predecessor to Article 67 of the 2005 Securities Law.

6.18 Article 17 further defines these four types of misrepresentation: (1) a false recording occurs when the obligor for information disclosure presents non-existing facts in disclosure documents; (2) a misleading statement refers to a statement made in the disclosure document or through the media which causes the investors to have an incorrect estimation of their investments and also has major influence; (3) a material omission means the failure of the obligor for information disclosure to wholly or partially record in the disclosure document the particulars that should be recorded; (4) improper disclosure occurs when the obligor for information disclosure fails to disclose information within an appropriate time frame or in the appropriate manner prescribed by law.

6.19 In theory, misrepresentation can be in the form of either good news or bad news, and thus has the effect of inducing investors to either purchase or sell the securities concerned (*youduo* or *youkong*). Interestingly enough, the SPC Third Circular only covers the instance of misrepresentation inducing investors to purchase. According to the drafters of the SPC Third Circular, there are several reasons for this. First, it is harder for the court to determine on misrepresentation inducing investors to sell than on misrepresentation inducing investors to purchase. Second, and more important, when the SPC Third Circular was issued, China did not allow short sale, and thus in practice, misrepresentation inducing investors to sell was rarely seen.[13] However, as the CSRC introduced the facility of short sale in 2009 on an experimental basis,[14] it will be interesting to see whether this will bring about more misrepresentation inducing investors to sell in the future; if this is the case, the civil liability regime would need to be expanded to cover that type of misrepresentation as well.

6.2.3. Scope of defendants

6.20 Article 7 of the SPC Third Circular provides a specific list of possible defendants in private securities litigation against misrepresentation, including: (1) promoters,

---

[13] Li and Jia, *Civil Compensation Regime for Misrepresentation*, 148.
[14] Hui Huang, 'China's Legal Responses to the Global Financial Crisis: From Domestic Reform to International Engagement' (2010) 12(2) *Australian Journal of Asian Law* 157.

controlling shareholders and the like who exercise actual control; (2) issuers or listed companies; (3) securities underwriters; (4) securities listing sponsors; (5) professional intermediaries including accountant firms, law firms, and asset valuation firms; (6) responsible directors, supervisors, managers, and other senior management personnel of the issuers, listed companies, securities underwriters, or securities listing sponsors, or directly responsible persons of professional intermediaries; and (7) other organizations or individual persons who make misrepresentation.

6.21 In general, the above defendants bear joint and several liability for misrepresentation and the plaintiff can choose to claim compensation from any or all of them. However, proportional liability applies to some defendants—notably professional intermediaries, including accountant firms, law firms, and asset valuation firms—in the sense that they are liable for misstatements only in the limited portion of the disclosure document they supply.[15] Further, as discussed below, the persons named in the list will escape liability if they establish the elements of one or more of the defences applicable to the particular disclosure document.

6.2.4. Defences to liability

6.22 The civil liability can be strict liability, ordinary fault-based liability, or presumed fault-based liability, depending on the type of defendant. To start with, strict liability applies to promoters, issuers, and listed companies.[16] This means that these defendants are liable for civil compensation for the losses caused by their false statement to the investors, regardless of whether they are at fault in making misrepresentation.

6.23 Second, ordinary fault-based liability applies to controlling shareholders or those who have actual control over issuers or listed companies. Under Article 22, where an actual controller rigs the issuer or listed company to violate the securities laws by making a false statement in the name of the issuer or listed company and thus causing losses to the investors, the liability for compensation may be borne by the issuer or listed company. The issuer or listed company may, after bearing the liability for compensation, recover the compensation from the actual controller. Further, where an actual controller makes misrepresentation in their own name in violation of relevant provisions of the Securities Law, thus causing losses to the investors, he shall bear the liability for compensation.[17] Since no fault requirement is explicitly mentioned in the above provision, it seems that the liability is strict liability. Later, however, Article 69 of the 2005 Securities Law makes it clear that if the plaintiff can show there is fault on the part of the actual controller, the actual controller can

---

[15] SPC Third Circular, Art 24.
[16] SPC Third Circular, Art 21(1).
[17] SPC Third Circular, Art 22.

be directly asked to bear joint and several liability with the issuer or listed company. Hence, the joint and several liability of the actual controller is fault-based and the plaintiff has the burden to prove the existence of fault.

Third, the liability of other defendants is also fault-based, but they are subject to a rebuttable presumption of fault in that they can escape liability only if they can show that there is no fault on their part.[18] This effectively shifts the burden of proof from the plaintiff to the defendant, thereby facilitating the pursuing of private securities litigation. It is unclear however what would be required to rebut the presumption of fault. In overseas jurisdictions, there are more specific defences such as due diligence, reliance, and withdrawal of consent. These overseas experiences are worthy of serious consideration in China's future efforts to improve its civil liability regime for securities misrepresentation. **6.24**

6.2.5. Causation

In private securities litigation, a key issue is establishing the causal link between the securities misconduct and the losses suffered by investors. Empirical studies have shown that a high proportion of investors, particularly retail investors, do not actually read prospectuses; even if they do occasionally read them, they may not be able to understand the highly technical information included in the disclosure documents.[19] Hence, it would be very difficult, if not impossible, for the investor to affirmatively prove that the misrepresentation causes him to trade and thus suffer a loss. **6.25**

To solve the above problem, China has borrowed from the US the fraud-on-the-market theory to presume reliance or causality (*yinguo guanxi*). Under Article 18 of the SPC Third Circular, causality is to be presumed if all of the following conditions are met: (1) the investments were securities directly connected with the misrepresentation; (2) the purchase date of the securities was between the date on which the misrepresentation is made (misrepresentation date) and the date on which the misrepresentation is exposed (exposure date) or corrected (correction date); and (3) investors suffered losses as a result of selling securities on or after the date on which the misrepresentation was exposed or corrected, or as a result of continued ownership of the securities after the misrepresentation was exposed or corrected.[20] Hence, if the investor can show that they purchased relevant securities after the misrepresentation date and sold or continued to hold them after the exposure date or correction date, they will be presumed to have traded the securities in reliance on the misrepresentation. **6.26**

---

[18] SPC Third Circular, Arts 21(2), 23, 24.
[19] Lauren E Willis, 'Against Financial Literacy Education' (2008) 94 *Iowa Law Review* 197; John R Nofsinger, *The Psychology of Investing* (Prentice Hall, 2005).
[20] SPC Third Circular, Art 18.

6.27 The presumption of reliance can be rebutted if the defendant proves one of the following: (1) the plaintiff sold the relevant securities before the exposure date or correction date; (2) the plaintiff purchased the relevant securities on or after the exposure date or correction date; (3) the plaintiff knew the existence of the misrepresentation but nevertheless made the investment; (4) the losses suffered by the plaintiff were, in whole or in part, caused by other factors, such as the systemic risk of the market;[21] or (5) the plaintiff made the investment in bad faith or in order to manipulate the market.

6.28 As can be seen above, the Chinese law has provided quite clear rules on the rebuttable presumption of causation. This greatly facilitates the making of securities civil claims, because in the typical setting of on-market securities transactions it is usually very hard, if not impossible, to affirmatively establish causation between the impugned misrepresentation and the harm suffered by the investor plaintiff. Now, under the rebuttable presumption of causation, all that the civil court needs to decide is usually the three important dates: namely, the misrepresentation date, the exposure date, or the correction date.

6.29 The SPC Third Circular has set out more detailed rules to assist the court to decide on the three important dates: (1) the misrepresentation date refers to the date the misrepresentation is made. This should be quite straightforward in cases of false or misleading statements. As to material omission or improper disclosure, the misrepresentation date is the last day of the time period in which the disclosure is required to be made in accordance with law; (2) the exposure date refers to the date the misrepresentation is publicly exposed for the first time by relevant media that is circulated or broadcasted nationwide, such as newspapers, radio, or television; and (3) the correction date refers to the date when the person who made the misrepresentation voluntarily announces to correct it in the CSRC-designated media and also goes through the relevant procedure to suspend the trading of the securities concerned.[22] The exposure date and correction date are conceptually clear, but in practice they may sometimes be difficult to determine. The guiding principle is that the exposure or correction of misrepresentation essentially acts to send a warning message to the market, with the effect of alerting the investors and affecting the price of the securities concerned.

6.30 Relevant cases have shed further light on the determination of the three important dates, particularly the exposure date. For instance, a recent case concerned Datang Telecommunications Technology Ltd Co (Datang Telecommunications), a Shanghai-listed company.[23] On 6 April 2005 Datang Telecommunications

---

[21] This item is broadly similar to the 'negative causation' defence under section 11(e) of the 1933 Securities Act in the US. See John C Coffee Jr and Joel Seligman, *Securities Regulation: Cases and Materials* (Foundation Press, 9th edn, 2003) 916–20.

[22] SPC Third Circular, Art 20.

[23] Chen Zhuling vs Datang Telecommunications Technology Ltd Co (Securities Misrepresentation Compensation Dispute case), (2009) First Hearing Civil Judgement by the First Intermediate People's Court of Beijing City, No 8216.

issued its 2004 annual report, and on 8 November 2005 the company announced in the *China Securities News*, a CSRC-designated newspaper with nationwide circulation, that it was under investigation by the CSRC for misrepresentation. Almost two years later, on 20 August 2007, the CSRC issued to Datang Telecommunications a preliminary notice about its administrative penalty decision, and Datang Telecommunications announced it the following day. Finally, on 26 May 2008, the CSRC handed down the formal administrative penalty decision. The plaintiff, Mr Chen, bought shares in Datang Telecommunications after 27 February 2007. The key issue here is which day is the exposure day. The plaintiff argued that the preliminary notice on 20 August 2007 (announced by Datang Telecommunications the following day) should be the exposure day, while the defendant, Datang Telecommunications, contended that the exposure date should be 8 November 2005, the date on which it announced the CSRC's investigation.

6.31 The court accepted the defendant's argument for three reasons. First, the announcement about the CSRC's investigation on 8 November 2005 was first made in a newspaper that is circulated nationwide. Second, although the announcement was about the launch of the investigation rather than final conclusion, it amounted to exposure of the misrepresentation because the investigation was conducted by the official regulatory body, namely the CSRC. In other words, the investors should consider the announcement significant in deciding their trading behaviour. This is supported by the fact that after the announcement on 8 November 2005, the share price of Datang Telecommunications immediately plummeted, even though the index of the market as a whole actually went up slightly. Finally, the CSRC's preliminary notice is just a follow-up disclosure and not the initial exposure of misrepresentation. As the plaintiff traded after the exposure date as decided above, the court rejected the plaintiff's claim.

6.32 Another case shows how the presumption of causation can be rebutted. In this, the defendant Nantong Technology Investment Group Ltd Co (Nantong Technology) issued its 2000 annual report on 30 March 2001; just over one year later, on 30 May 2002, it publicly announced that it was under investigation by CSRC for misrepresentation.[24] On 21 August 2004, Nantong Technology announced that it had received an administrative penalty decision from the CSRC for misrepresentation. The plaintiff, Mr Su, bought shares in Nantong Technology between 5 July 2001 and 24 October 2001; he sold part of the shares on 27 August 2001, and continued to hold the rest of them at the time of the civil suit.

6.33 At trial, the Intermediate People's Court of Nanjing City held that the plaintiff bought shares between the misrepresentation date (30 March 2001) and

---

[24] Su Wanfu vs Nantong Technology Investment Group Ltd Co (Securities Misrepresentation Compensation Dispute case), (2006) First Hearing Civil Judgment by the Intermediate People's Court of Nanjing City, No 250; appealed as (2007) Second Hearing Civil Judgment by the High People's Court of Jiangsu Province, No 112.

the exposure date (30 May 2002), and thus the presumption of causation was established. The defendant appealed the case, arguing that the trial court did not take into account the systemic risk of the market. The appellate court, the High People's Court of Jiangsu Province, made the following points. First, between the time Mr Su bought shares (5 May 2001) and the exposure date (30 May 2002), the Shanghai Composite Index and the Index of the sector to which Nantong Technology belongs dropped by 30.17 per cent and 26.26 per cent, respectively. This means that the share price of Nantong Technology should have dropped even without the misrepresentation. In other words, at least part of the losses suffered by Mr Su was not caused by misrepresentation, but by the systemic risk of the market. Second, in calculating the portion of losses attributable to the market risk, attention should be paid to all relevant indicators, such as the Shanghai Composite Index and the relevant industry index. In the end, the court held that 26 per cent of the price drop was attributable to the market systemic risk and thus should be excluded from the compensation.

6.2.6. Calculation of compensation

6.34 In principle, the compensation is limited to the actual loss suffered by the investors as a result of misrepresentation.[25] The actual loss may be composed of three parts: (1) investment loss (*Touzi Cha'e Sunshi*), namely the difference of the investment of the investors. This is the main component of actual loss; (2) transaction costs, such as brokerage, stamp duty, and other fees, in connection with their lost investment; and (3) interest loss, namely the interest lost on their investment as calculated according to bank deposit rates for the relevant period.[26]

6.35 Further details are provided on the calculation of the investment loss. This is based on a so-called benchmark day (*Jizhun Ri*), which is usually set to be the date on which aggregated trading volumes of the security affected by the misrepresentation reach 100 per cent of its tradable volumes after the exposure or correction day.[27] On the basis of this benchmark day, two formulas are provided to calculate the actual loss: if the investors sold the relevant securities on or before the benchmark day, the actual loss is determined by multiplying the number of securities they held by the difference between the average purchase price and the actual price at which they sold the securities;[28] if the investors sold their securities after the benchmark day or continued to hold them at the time of litigation, the actual loss is calculated by multiplying the number of securities they hold by the difference between their average purchase price and the average closing prices of every trading day from the date when the misrepresentation was exposed or corrected to the benchmark day.[29]

---

[25] SPC Third Circular, Art 30.
[26] SPC Third Circular, Art 30.
[27] SPC Third Circular, Art 33.
[28] SPC Third Circular, Art 31.
[29] SPC Third Circular, Art 32.

Cases have illustrated the application of the measure of damages. For instance, a **6.36**
point of dispute in the high-profile case of Yin Guangxia is what the term 'average price' means. Yin Guangxia, a Shenzhen-listed company, was once called the 'number one blue chip company in China'. In August 2001, its misrepresentation problem came to light, as a result of which its share price plummeted from 75.88 yuan to less than 6 yuan, and thus the company earned itself another title: 'China's Enron'. After many ups and downs, civil suits against Yin Guangxia were accepted by the Intermediate People's Court of Yinchuan City. Since there was little doubt over the facts of the case, including the existence of misrepresentation and the relevant days, the major issue was how to calculate damages. As shown above, the measure of damages under the SPC Third Circular uses the term 'average price', but it is not clear whether this refers to arithmetic average price, weighted average price, or something else. Despite opposition from the plaintiffs, the court finally held the term to mean arithmetic average price.

Although the measure of damages as set out in the SPC Third Circular has been **6.37**
criticized by some commentators,[30] it provides a clear and uniform method of calculation, so that parties to the dispute are able to predict the amount of compensation with a reasonable degree of certainty. It is worth noting that there is no universally accepted measure of damages for securities civil cases anywhere in the world. In the US, for instance, a multiplicity of methods have been used to measure damages in securities fraud cases. These measures are broadly classified as the 'out-of-pocket' measure, the modified 'out-of-pocket' measure, the 'benefit-of-bargain' measure, the measure of consequential damages, the cover measure, the measure of rescission or rescissory damages, and the windfall-profits measure.[31]

Despite the clarity of the rules, there are still technical difficulties in their appli- **6.38**
cation. In practice, expert witnesses have been retained in some cases to provide opinions as to how to calculate compensation. In the case of Nantong Technology

---

[30] See eg Feng Guo, Xujia Chenshu Qingquan de Rending ji Peichang [Determination of Tort of Misrepresentation and Compensation] (2003) 2 *Zhongguo Faxue* [*China Legal Science*] 96 (stating that the calculation method may not necessarily reflect the reality of market demand and supply when the market as a whole improves); Yixing Song, Xujia Chenshu Minshi Peichang Susong Zhidu Ruogan Wenti de Sikao [Thoughts on Several Issues of the Litigation System for Civil Compensation Arising from Misrepresentation], (2003) 4 *Falv Shiyong* [*Application of Law*] 10 (arguing that the method is prone to abuse, because those committing misrepresentation may try to manipulate the trading volumes by all means).

[31] A detailed discussion of these measures of damages is well beyond the scope of this article. The issue has been examined extensively elsewhere—see eg Robert B Thompson, 'The Measure of Recovery Under Rule 10b-5: A Restitution Alternative to Tort Damages' (1984) 37 *Vanderbilt Law Review* 349; Robert B Thompson, '"Simplicity and Certainty" in the Measure of Recovery Under Rule 10b-5' (1996) 51 *Business Lawyer* 1177; Comment, 'The Measure of Damages Under Section 10(b) and Rule 10b-5' (1987) 46 *Maryland Law Review* 1266; Recent Development, 'Damages For Insider Trading in the Open Market: A New Limitation on Recovery Under Rule 10b-5' (1981) 34 *Vanderbilt Law Review* 797. For a useful summary of these measures of damages, see Hui Huang, *International Securities Markets: Insider Trading Law in China* (London: Kluwer Law International, 2006), Chapter 7.

discussed earlier, two professors of the College of Economics and Management of Shanghai Jiaotong University appeared as expert witnesses before the court to provide assistance with the calculation of damages.

6.3. Procedural Rules of Civil Litigation

6.3.1. Prerequisite procedure

6.39 A unique feature of the SPC Third Circular is the procedural prerequisite that in order to bring a securities civil suit, there must be a prior criminal judgment or administrative sanction by the relevant bodies.[32] In practice, the administrative bodies mainly include the CSRC, as the securities market watchdog, and the Ministry of Finance, which has power to regulate the accounting profession in China. A recent empirical study shows that most civil cases are based on the CSRC's administrative sanctions.[33]

6.40 The prerequisite has both procedural and evidential effects. Procedurally, investors can bring civil suit only if there is already an administrative or criminal sanction against securities misrepresentation. It has been argued that administrative or criminal sanction should be treated only as a basis for the civil court to accept cases, and not as a basis for determining defendants in the civil suit.[34] In other words, the plaintiff should be allowed to sue those who are not included in the prerequisite sanctions. Nevertheless, this argument has not been well received by the courts. In the case of ST Jiuzhou, for instance, the CSRC punished only the listed company, ST Jiuzhou, in its administrative penalty decision. There is no doubt that civil action can be brought against ST Jiuzhou, but it is less clear whether the sponsor and underwriter for ST Jiuzhou, albeit not mentioned in the CSRC decision, can also be sued in civil proceedings. At the first instance, the court rejected the claims against the sponsor and underwriter on the basis that they were not punished by the CSRC—therefore the prerequisite was not met. This decision was affirmed on appeal.

6.41 Evidentially, the fact finding of misrepresentation in the administrative or criminal proceedings can be admissible in the civil suit. As a result, the civil court does not need to deal with otherwise difficult issues such as whether there is misrepresentation and whether the defendant is liable, and the major issue to be addressed is how to calculate the compensation.

---

[32] SPC Third Circular, Art 6.
[33] Hui Huang, 'Private Enforcement of Securities Law in China: A Ten-year Retrospective and Empirical Assessment' (2013) 61(4) *American Journal of Comparative Law* 757.
[34] Sanzhu Zhu, 'Civil Litigation Arising from False Statements on China's Securities Market' (2005) 31 *North Carolina Journal of International Law and Commercial Regulation* 377, 390; Guoguang Li (ed), *Zuigao Renmin Fayuan Guanyu Shenli Zhengquan Shichang Xujia Chenshu Anjian Sifa Jieshi de Lijie yu Shiyong [The Understanding and Application of the Judicial Interpretation of the Supreme People's Court on Hearing Cases arising from Misrepresentation on the Securities Markets]*, (Beijing: People's Court Press, 2003), 138.

Liability for Misrepresentation

In overseas jurisdictions such as the US, it is generally difficult for the civil court to decide on the commitment of misrepresentation and other fraud, due to tricky issues such as materiality, due diligence, and subject elements.[35] However, for securities civil cases brought in China, the above otherwise difficult issues are not a problem at all. This is simply because, thanks to the prerequisite procedure, those issues would have already been dealt with in the administrative or criminal proceedings which are required to be taken before the civil proceedings. This piggy-back effect is well illustrated in the widely publicized case of Daqin Lianyi Petro-Chemical Ltd Co (Daqin Lianyi),[36] the first adjudicated securities civil case in China. **6.42**

There, Daqin Lianyi did an initial public offering (IPO) and was listed in the Shanghai Stock Exchange in 1997, with Shenyin Wanguo Securities Ltd Co (Shenyin Wanguo) acting as the sponsor and underwriter for the listing. On 31 March 2000, the CSRC issued an administrative penalty decision finding Daqin Lianyi and Shenyin Wanguo liable for misrepresentation made in various disclosure documents, including the prospectus, the listing announcement, and the 1997 annual report of Daqing Lianyi. Based on the administrative penalty decision, Chen Lihua and 22 other investors filed a securities civil suit against Daqing Lianyi and Shenyin Wanguo before the Intermediate People's Court of Harbin City, Heilongjiang Province. **6.43**

In defence, Shenyin Wanguo argued, among other things, that the misrepresentation was made by Daqing Lianyi and, as the sponsor and underwriter, it did not know about the making of misrepresentation; further, it said, it was beyond the duty and capacity of Shenyin Wanguo to successfully detect and stop the misrepresentation. This actually raised two issues: first, whether Shenyin Wanguo had actual knowledge about the misrepresentation—an issue similar to the US scienter requirement; second, whether Shenyin Wanguo should have known about the misrepresentation by way of due diligence investigation. However, the court did not address the first issue at all; as to the second issue, it held that Shenyin Wanguo did not qualify for the due diligence defence, because as a matter of fact it had failed to detect and stop misrepresentation. **6.44**

The case was appealed, and the appellate court, the High People's Court of Heilongjiang Province, found no need to conduct it own investigation into the above two issues in dispute. Rather, the court simply piggy-backed on the CSRC administrative penalty decision, which had already confirmed the wrongdoing of Shenyin Wanguo. Hence, without the benefit of the prerequisite procedure, it **6.45**

---

[35] Richard C Sauer, 'The Changing Dimensions of Director Liability Under the Federal Securities Laws' (2005) 37 *Sec Reg & L Rep.* 413, 414; David I Michaels, 'An Empirical Study of Securities Litigation After Worldcom' (2009) 40(2) *Rutgers Law Journal* 319, 331.

[36] Lihua Chen et al vs Daqing Lianyi Ltd Co and Shenyin Wanguo Securities Ltd Co, Second Hearing Civil Judgement, The High People's Court of Helongjiang Province, 21 December 2004.

would have been very difficult, as is the case in the US, for the court to decide on those issues.

6.46 This prerequisite rule has been a subject of heated debate ever since the SPC Third Circular was issued. It has been severely criticized as unduly limiting the scope of securities civil litigation in China. First, the prerequisite, it is argued, can leave investors without remedy if the criminal court or relevant administrative bodies, for whatever reason, fail to address the underlying misrepresentation.[37] Indeed, both the courts and regulators in China may be prevented from effectively responding to securities frauds for a variety of reasons, such as lack of independence, bureaucratic inefficiency, inadequate enforcement resources, and regulatory capture or outright corruption. A second line of attack upon the prerequisite is directed to the difference in standards of proof between civil proceedings and criminal/administrative proceedings. For instance, the criminal standard of proof, being 'beyond reasonable doubt',[38] is significantly higher than that for civil proceedings, which is the balance of probabilities—that is, the evidence needed for the party to win is 'more forceful'.[39] Yet the prerequisite essentially requires the criminal standard of proof for civil cases, and thus may deprive investors of civil claims arising from securities frauds which fall short of constituting a crime.[40]

6.47 On the other hand, proponents of the prerequisite argue that it is necessary for the time being, for the following reasons. First, without the prerequisite, there could be a flood of private securities litigation which would disturb the stable development of the securities markets and overstretch the limited resources of China's judicial system. Second, compared to the Chinese judiciary, the specialist regulatory bodies—notably the CSRC—are more competent to handle complicated securities cases, particularly with regard to determining whether there is misrepresentation and who should be held liable. Finally, as discussed above, the prerequisite rule has beneficial evidentiary effects for investors, allowing them to piggy-back on the efforts of the regulator or prosecutor in the prerequisite proceedings.

6.48 Which side of the debate has greater merit? Does the prerequisite unduly limit the number of private securities litigation? Is it needed in China's current institutional

---

[37] Guiping Lu, 'Private Enforcement of Securities Fraud Law in China: A Critique of the Supreme People's Court 2003 Provisions Concerning Private Securities Litigation' (2003) *Pacific Rim Law and Policy Journal* 795; Sanzhu Zhu, *Securities Dispute Resolution in China* (Ashgate Publishing, 2007) 167.

[38] Zhonghua Renmin Gongheguo Xingshi Susong Fa [Criminal Procedural Law of the PRC (Criminal Procedure Law)] (promulgated on 1 July 1979, amended in 1996 and 2012) Art 53.

[39] Zhonghua Renmin Gongheguo Minshi Susongfa [Civil Procedure Law of the People's Republic of China (Civil Procedure Law)] (passed on 9 April 1991, amended on 28 October 2007 and on 31 August 2012) art 64.

[40] The standard of proof for administrative proceedings in China seems to be flexible, and it can range from the civil standard to criminal standard, depending on the nature of the administrative case. See Xiangjun Kong, *Administrative Litigation Evidence Rules and Legal Applications* (Beijing: Law Press, 2005), 226–7.

environment? A recent empirical study found that during the first decade of the introduction of private securities litigation in China, civil cases actually brought represent only about one quarter of the eligible criminal judgment/administrative sanctions which may lead to securities civil suits.[41] This suggests that even within the bounds set by the procedural prerequisite, many more securities civil suits could have been brought. Further, usage of the piggy-back benefits of regulatory actions is also seen elsewhere: in the US, for example, up to 55 per cent of enforcement actions by the Securities and Exchange Commission (SEC) have had parallel securities class actions.[42] Hence, at present, the prerequisite does not seem to be a 'devastating weakness' as asserted by some commentators,[43] and there is no pressing need to abolish the prerequisite—at least for now—as there is still much scope for more securities civil cases to be brought even within the confines of the prerequisite.

6.49 To be sure, the above view is not to deny the problems with the prerequisite. The main weakness of the prerequisite as a screening mechanism is that it makes civil litigation simply a copycat effort, thereby reducing the utility of 'private attorneys general' as a supplement to the regulators to enforce securities law. In order to harness the power of 'private attorneys general' while maintaining some level of control over private litigation, it is necessary to gradually relax the prerequisite so as to expand the scope of securities civil action. For instance, it has been argued that the procedural prerequisite should be extended beyond the administrative penalty decision by the governmental regulators to cover enforcement activities by other relevant entities such as the stock exchanges.[44]

6.3.2. Statute of limitation

6.50 In China, the limitation period for civil suits is generally two years, starting from the day when the plaintiff knows or ought reasonably to have known that his or her rights have been infringed.[45] According to Article 5 of the SPC Third Circular, the above rule applies to securities civil cases too.

6.51 More guidance is provided on the counting of the limitation period. First, in the case of administrative penalty decisions meeting the prerequisite rule, the limitation period starts from the date when the CSRC or its branches, the Ministry of Finance, or other administrative bodies and institutions announce the decision against the defendant. Second, if the defendant is not subject to administrative penalty but has been found criminally liable, the limitation period starts from the date that the

---

[41] Hui Huang, 'Private Enforcement of Securities Law in China'.
[42] Verity Winship, 'Fair Funds and the SEC's Compensation of Injured Investors' (2008) 60 *Florida Law Review* 1103, 1134.
[43] Walter Hutches, 'Private Securities Litigation in China: Material Disclosure about China's Legal System?' (2003) 24 *University of Pennsylvania Journal of International Economic Law* 599, 634.
[44] Hui Huang, 'Private Enforcement of Securities Law in China'.
[45] Zhonghua Renmin Gongheguo Minfa Tongze (General Principles of the Civil Law of the PRC) (promulgated 12 April 1986, effective 1 January 1987), Art 135.

criminal judgment comes into effect. Third, if there are more than two administrative penalty decisions concerning the same misrepresentation but different misrepresentation makers, the limitation period is calculated from the date when the first administrative decision is announced. Fourth, if both an administrative penalty decision and a criminal judgment have been announced, the limitation period starts from the date when the criminal judgment becomes effective.

6.52 The application of the above rules is straightforward when the administrative penalty decision and the criminal judgment in question are final. The situation may become complicated if they are not final—that is, if the administrative penalty decision is subject to administrative review or administrative litigation, or the criminal judgment is subject to a supervision procedure. With respect to administrative penalties, it is made clear that after the civil court begins to hear a case it may suspend the hearing if the defendant applies for an administrative review or brings administrative litigation against the administrative penalty decision he received, and if the penalty decision is cancelled in the end, the civil court should terminate the hearing.[46] However, the SPC Third Circular does not provide any guidance regarding criminal judgments. A possible reason is that in practice it is quite rare to see criminal judgments go through the supervision procedure.

6.53 The case of Guangdong Meiya sheds further light on the counting of the limitation period. There, the defendant company, Guangdong Meiya, issued its 2003 annual report on 19 March 2004; just over one year later, on 30 April 2005, it announced that it was under investigation by CSRC for alleged misrepresentation in the 2003 annual report. On 29 May 2007, the CSRC issued to Guangdong Meiya an administrative penalty decision in relation to the misrepresentation, but Guangdong Meiya did not announce this until 21 June 2007. The plaintiff bought shares in Guangdong Meiya in February 2004 and suffered a loss. The plaintiff brought civil action against Guangdong Meiya on 1 June 2009. One of the issues under dispute is whether the suit is within the limitation period. This turns on the question of whether the limitation period should start from 29 May 2007, when the CSRC issued the administrative penalty decision, or 21 June 2007, when Guangdong Meiya announced the CSRC penalty decision. The court held that the limitation period started from 21 June 2007, because although the decision was issued on 29 May 2007, investors did not know about it until it was announced by Guangdong Meiya on 21 June 2007.

6.3.3. Jurisdiction of the court

6.54 Under Chinese law, the jurisdiction issue has two components, namely hierarchical jurisdiction (*jibie guanxia*) and geographical jurisdiction (*diyu guanxia*).

---

[46] SPC Third Circular, Art 11.

Hierarchical jurisdiction concerns what level of the court system has jurisdiction over relevant cases. In China, there are four levels of court, including—in order of authority—the basic court, the intermediate court, the high court, and the People's Supreme Court. As securities cases are usually complicated and technical, the SPC Third Circular designates the intermediate court as the court of first instance to hear such cases.[47]

6.55 As to geographical jurisdiction, the SPC Third Circular makes a distinction between issuer or listed company defendants and other defendants.[48] Where the defendants are issuers or listed companies, jurisdiction over the civil case rests with the intermediate court at the location of the issuers or listed companies. Where the civil case is brought against people other than the issuer or listed company, the intermediate court located at the residence of the defendants shall have jurisdiction over the case. Thus, if, as is often the case in practice, there are multiple defendants, two or more than two courts may have jurisdiction over the same case. In general, the plaintiffs can choose to bring action at any of them, and the court that first accepts the case shall have jurisdiction, subject to the following special rules.

6.56 Where the defendants are not issuers or listed companies, the intermediate court that has accepted the case may, upon application by the parties involved or consent by all the plaintiffs, add relevant issues or listed companies as defendants to the case.[49] In such circumstances, however, the court must transfer the case to the intermediate court located at the residence of the issuer or listed company. In the case that the parties to the litigation do not apply for or the plaintiffs do not consent to the adding of issuers or listed companies as defendants, the court can still do so if it deems it necessary, but cannot transfer the case to the local court of issues or listed companies.

6.57 In practice, the courts have been unsympathetic towards securities civil suits, as evidenced by the difficulty in getting the case accepted, the long delays in accepting and hearing cases, and the enforcement problem.[50] To be sure, there are many factors contributing to this. For instance, most listed companies are former state-owned enterprises (SOE), and thus the courts are naturally cautious about hearing securities civil cases. Further, securities civil cases usually involve a large number of litigants and, if not handled properly, may pose a threat to social stability. The court would hence shy away from this minefield as far as possible, given that social stability is currently the top priority of the Chinese government.

6.58 Finally, there is a serious problem of judicial local protectionism in the handling of securities civil cases. Local protectionism means that in dealing with litigation, courts are often biased in favour of parties from the local regions. This problem

---

[47] SPC Third Circular, Art 8.
[48] SPC Third Circular, Art 9.
[49] SPC Third Circular, Art 10.
[50] Hui Huang, 'Private Enforcement of Securities Law in China'.

is well-known and deep-rooted in China due to the lack of the courts' independence—the local courts are dependent on the local government in terms of funding, and personnel decisions relating to the local judiciary are also in the hands of the local government.[51] The problem is particularly severe in the area of securities civil cases, because listed companies are usually the mainstay of the local economy and thus the main source of revenues for the local government. Hence, it is argued that plaintiffs should be given the option to bring securities civil action in the courts in the locality where the issuer company is listed.[52]

6.3.4. Forms of litigation

6.3.4.1. Chinese law from a comparative perspective

6.59 China does not allow investors to bring private securities suits in the form of class action (*jituan susong*); rather, investors can sue either in the form of individual action (*dandu susong*) or joint action (*gongtong susong*).[53] The court can, depending on the circumstances, decide whether the civil suit should be filed as individual action or joint action: if one or both parties to individual actions consist of two or more persons and the object of action is the same or in the same category—as is often the case in a securities civil suit—the court can, with the consent of the parties, combine the individual actions into a joint action.

6.60 In order to better understand the ways in which securities civil action can be brought in China, it is necessary first to look at the broader picture of various litigation forms available in China. The SPC Third Circular was issued in 2003 within the framework of the now-repealed 1991 Civil Procedure Law.[54] The SPC Second Circular makes it clear that 'the litigation form for securities civil action can be individual action or joint action, and it is not appropriate to use the form of *class action*'.[55] However, as the term 'class action' has never been legally defined in China, there is some confusion over what it actually refers to in the SPC Second Circular.[56]

6.61 Apart from individual action, the 1991 Civil Procedure Law also provided for joint action. Under Article 53 of the 1991 Civil Procedure Law, if one or both parties to individual actions consist of two or more persons and the object of action is the same or in the same category, the court can, with the consent of the parties,

---

[51] Albert Chan, *An Introduction to the Legal System of the People's Republic of China* (4th edn, LexisNexis, 2011), 203.
[52] Hui Huang, 'Private Enforcement of Securities Law in China'.
[53] SPC Third Circular, Art 12.
[54] Civil Procedure Law.
[55] SPC Second Circular, Art 4 (emphasis added).
[56] Wallace Wen-Yeu Wang and Jian-Lin Chen, 'Reforming China's Securities Civil Actions: Lessons from PSLRA Reform in the US and Government-Sanctioned Non-Profit Enforcement in Taiwan' (2008) 21(2) *Columbia Journal of Asian Law* 115, 130 (stating that '[t]his prohibition [over class action] is perplexing, because there were no provisions in China's law allowing such class actions in the first place').

combine the individual actions into a joint action. Joint action was further divided into two categories—first, under Article 54, cases in which the number of parties is fixed at the time of filing; second, under Article 55, cases in which the number of parties is not known at the time the case is filed. These provisions have been carried over to the 2007 Civil Procedure Law, with both the content and numbering remaining exactly the same.[57]

6.62 The SPC Third Circular essentially limits securities civil suits to the first category of joint action, namely action in which the number of parties is fixed at the time of filing. Article 12 of the SPC Third Circular states that a securities civil suit may be brought either as individual action or joint action. Importantly, it is made clear that the number of plaintiffs in a joint action should be finalized before the hearing.[58] Further, where possible, preference is given to joint action over individual action. Under Article 13 of the SPC Third Circular, in the event that multiple plaintiffs sue the same defendants for the same misrepresentation and that some of the plaintiffs sue individually while others sue jointly, the court may ask the plaintiffs in individual action to join the joint action.

6.63 Thus, it seems that the term 'class action' used in the SPC Second Circular actually refers to the second category of joint action—namely, action in which the number of parties is not known at the time when it is filed. For ease of reference, this will be termed 'Chinese-style class action' here. The propriety of using this term, of course, depends on how one understands 'class action' from a comparative perspective. Indeed, there are similarities as well as differences between the US-style class action and the Chinese-style class action. In both situations, a multiplicity of litigants is involved, and the judgment of the action applies to members of the plaintiff class who have not participated in the lawsuit. On the other hand, however, there are some important differences. For instance, while the US-style class action adopts the so-called 'opt-out' rule, the Chinese-style class action adopts the 'opt-in' rule under which the plaintiff class covers those who have not registered with the court at the time the case is filed but who later actually bring suits within the prescribed time period.[59] Hence, there is no consensus as to the usage of the term 'class action' in the context of Chinese law.[60] Since the second category of joint action has already been

---

[57] The Supreme People's Court has provided guidance on the application of the provisions. See Zuigao Renmin Fayuan Guanyu Shiyong 'Zhonghua Renmin Gongheguo Minshi Susong Fa' Ruogan Wenti de Yijian [Opinion of the Supreme People's Court on the Several Questions Concerning the Application of the 'Civil Procedure Law of the PRC'] (issued on 14 July 1992, amended in December 2008). Although the Civil Procedure Law has recently been amended again in August 2012 with effect from 1 June 2013, the content of the above provisions remains unchanged.

[58] SPC Third Circular, Art 14.

[59] See Binhua Tu, 'Zhengquan Xujia Chenshu Minshi Peichang Zheren Jizhi Ren [On the Mechanism for Civil Compensation Liabilities for Securities-related Misrepresentation]' (2003) 6 *Faxue [Legal Science]* 97.

[60] See eg Donald C Clarke, 'The Private Attorney-General in China: Potential and Pitfalls' (2009) 8 *Washington University Global Studies Law Review* 241, 248 (using the term 'group litigation' rather than 'class action' because 'China does not have true class actions in the American sense. . .').

referred to by many commentators as 'class action',[61] this paper follows suit, but, in order to distinguish it from US-style class action, refers to it as Chinese-style class action.

6.3.4.2. Criticisms and responses

6.64 The current rule over the forms of litigation for securities civil action has drawn a considerable body of criticism.

6.65 First and foremost, it is argued that because the court does not consolidate multiple suits into one class suit, the current litigation form for securities civil action causes inefficient use of limited judicial resources.[62] On the face of it, this argument seems to make sense, but in reality the force of the argument has proven widely exaggerated. In some cases, the misrepresentation gives rise to quite a small number of suits, in which case the litigation form would have little impact on judicial resources. Further, even when there are a large number of suits arising from the same misrepresentation, the consumption of judicial resources may not be significantly greater than if there was just one class action.

6.66 In practice, the Chinese court has tried to achieve judicial economy through a procedural innovation called 'test suits', under which the court will choose a representative suit, from the multiple suits arising from the same misrepresentation, to be fully adjudicated, and then apply the judgment to other suits.[63] This works because all the cases arising from the same misrepresentation involve similar legal issues, such as the presumption of causation and measure of damages, and they only differ in relation to the number of shares for which each of the plaintiffs can get compensation. In fact, even if the multiple cases were consolidated into one class action, the court would still need to separately calculate the damages for each plaintiff. Interviews with judges having heard such cases suggest that there is no significant difference in terms of the substantive issues that the court needs to address.

---

[61] See eg Benjamin L Liebman, 'Class Action Litigation in China' (1998) 111 *Harvard Law Review* 1523 (using the term 'class action' to describe suits brought under Articles 54 and 55 of the Civil Procedure Law); Guiping Lu, 'Private Enforcement of Securities Fraud Law in China: A Critique of the Supreme People's Court 2003 Provisions Concerning Private Securities Litigation' (2003) *Pacific Rim Law and Policy Journal* 795, 799 (stating that 'Article 55 of the Civil Procedure Law governs *class actions* where the number of litigants is not fixed') (emphasis added); Bin Luo, 'Theoretical Analysis about the Practical Mode for Class Action Over Securities in China' (2010) 5 *Faxue Zazhi [Legal Magazine]* 116.

[62] Wallace Wen-Yeu Wang and Jian-Lin Chen, 'Reforming China's Securities Civil Actions: Lessons from PSLRA Reform in the US and Government-Sanctioned Non-Profit Enforcement in Taiwan' (2008) 21(2) *Columbia Journal of Asian Law* 115, 130; Guo Li and Allen VY Ong, 'The Fledging Securities Fraud Litigation in China' (2009) 39(3) *Hong Kong Law Journal* 697, 710–11; Guiping Lu, 'Private Enforcement of Securities Fraud Law in China: A Critique of the Supreme People's Court 2003 Provisions Concerning Private Securities Litigation' (2003) *Pacific Rim Law and Policy Journal* 795, 800–1.

[63] Donald C Clarke, 'The Private Attorney-General in China: Potential and Pitfalls' (2009) 8 *Washington University Global Studies Law Review* 241, 250.

6.67 The only difference thus lies in the number of judgments, or settlements, as the case is more likely to be (for brevity, collectively referred to as judgments in this part)—in the current system, the court will need to issue a judgment for each case, but if it was a class action there would be only one super-judgment covering all plaintiffs. Compared with the one super-judgment, however, the making of multiple judgments involves minimum extra work, because once the first judgment for the model case is written it can serve as a template for other judgments, with just a couple of items changed, such as the case number, the plaintiff's name, and the compensation amount.[64]

6.68 The above point is well exemplified in the case of Dongfang Electronics, which has been the largest securities civil action so far in terms of the number of plaintiffs (6,989) and cases (2,716). The cases were filed either as individual action or joint action. Faced with the large number of cases arising from the same statement, the court chose to hear one exemplary case first on 24 August 2004, dealing with relevant issues such as the presumption of causation, the determination of the relevant dates (eg the misrepresentation day, the exposure day, and the benchmark day), the measure of damages, and other relevant issues which apply to all other cases. Thereafter, the court could simply use the exemplary case as a model to hear other cases, and the issues already addressed in the exemplary case would not be examined again. Hence, this practice also dispels concern over the inconsistency of judgments for a series of cases arising from the same misrepresentation.

6.69 Another criticism of the current regime is that it does not promote investor protection, as it is financially burdensome for plaintiffs to bring action. It is asserted that 'litigation costs would prevent most investors from making separate claims'.[65] Since litigation costs in China are composed mainly of an attorney fee and court fee, these will be discussed in turn.

6.70 First, let us take a look at the attorney fee. A distinctive feature of securities civil suits is 'large scale, small claim'—that is, overall a large number of investors are injured by the misrepresentation, but individually the injury to each of the investors is small. Hence, most investor plaintiffs would not take the initiative to bring action as the litigation costs may well exceed the benefits derived from the litigation. It is in this situation that entrepreneurial lawyers can play a significant role.

6.71 The US experience well illustrates the role of entrepreneurial lawyers in driving securities civil suits. In the US, there are many securities civil cases in the form of class action, and entrepreneurial lawyers are believed to be one of the main

---

[64] In fact, the judge is incentivized to break up multiple-plaintiff litigation arising from the same misrepresentation into multiple separate cases, because one of the performance indicators for the judge is the number of cases they have handled.

[65] Wallace Wen-Yeu Wang and Jian-Lin Chen, 'Reforming China's Securities Civil Actions: Lessons from PSLRA Reform in the US and Government-Sanctioned Non-Profit Enforcement in Taiwan' (2008) 21(2) *Columbia Journal of Asian Law* 115, 130–1.

reasons for this.[66] Indeed, due to the free-rider and other collective action problems that make it ineffective to bring individual suits, entrepreneurial lawyers are actually the driving force behind securities class actions. A key galvanizing element in this process is the contingency fee system, under which lawyer fees are contingent on the case being successfully litigated or on settlement of the case—that is, the entrepreneurial lawyer usually bears the costs of litigation, and charges fees as a percentage of the amount recovered, whether by judgment or settlement. This can effectively address the litigation incentive issue on the part of the investor plaintiffs, because they would not incur any costs, no matter how the case ends, and could gain something—however small—in the event that the case successfully generates proceeds.

6.72 The contingency fee system is more commonly known as the 'risk agency fee' (*fengxian daili Shoufei*) in China, and has long been used in practice. Under the now-repealed 1997 Provisional Measures for the Administration of Lawyers' Service Charges, lawyers can charge fees as a percentage of the value of the subject matter in cases involving monetary disputes.[67] The successor to the above regulation, namely the 2006 Measures for the Administration of Lawyers' Service Charges,[68] has provided more detail on the application of the contingency fee system in China.

6.73 It requires that the lawyer must first inform their client of the government-guided legal fee standard and then allow the latter to choose whether to apply the risk agency fee.[69] To charge fees on the basis of risk agency, a law firm must enter into a fee-charging agreement with the client to stipulate such matters as the division of risks and liabilities between the two parties, the methods of payment, and the charging amount or proportion.[70] The maximum amount charged on the basis of risk agency shall not be higher than 30 per cent of the value of the subject matter of the case as stipulated in the fee-charging agreement.

6.74 It is important to note that the risk agency fee cannot be used in all cases. In principle, the risk agency fee can only be used in civil cases involving property disputes. Further, the 2006 Measures for the Administration of Lawyers' Service Charges

---

[66] See eg John C Coffee Jr, 'Rescuing the Private Attorney General: Why the Model of the Lawyer as Bounty Hunter Is Not Working' (1983) 42 *Maryland Law Review* 215; Jonathan R Macey and Geoffrey P Miller, 'The Plaintiffs' Attorney's Role in Class Action and Derivative Litigation: Economic Analysis and Recommendations for Reform' (1991) 58(1) *The University of Chicago Law Review* 1.
[67] Lvshi Fuwu Shoufei Guanli Zanxing Banfa [Provisional Measures for the Administration of Lawyers' Service Charges] (promulgated by the Ministry of Justice on 3 March 1007, repealed), Art 7.
[68] Lvshi Fuwu Shoufei Guanli Banfa [Measures for the Administration of Lawyers' Service Charges] (promulgated by the National Development and Reform Commission and the Ministry of Justice on 13 April 2006, effective 1 December 2006).
[69] Measures for the Administration of Lawyers' Service Charges, Art 11.
[70] Measures for the Administration of Lawyers' Service Charges, Art 13.

specifically carve out certain types of cases from the scope of application of the risk agency fee.

6.75 Of particular relevance to this paper is the exclusion of cases of mass litigation from using the risk agency fee. The term 'mass litigation' (*Qunti Susong*) is not clearly defined in Chinese law, even though it generally refers to cases where a multiplicity of litigants is involved. Significantly, in the literature on this issue, the term is often used to refer to class action (*Jituan Susong*).[71] Under the Civil Procedure Law in China, as well as the usual individual action, there are two more forms of action available: joint action and class action.[72] As noted, securities civil action in China presently can only take the form of either individual action or joint action, not class action; therefore it appears that the prohibition on the use of the risk agency fee in mass litigation does not apply to securities civil action.[73]

6.76 Now let us turn to the issue of the court fee. When a case is filed before the court, the plaintiff needs to pre-pay a filing fee, which is calculated as a percentage of the value of the claim.[74] The requirement to advance the filing fee, some commentators argue, may 'make it impossible for small plaintiffs to assert large claims'.[75]

6.77 Again, while there is some merit in the above argument about the court fee, the problem is not as serious as is suggested by critics. In the first place, the filing fee does not usually come as a major financial problem for most investors. The filing fee is calculated on a sliding scale, and the percentages are reasonable. Second, even in those cases where the potential plaintiffs are unable or unwilling to pay the filing fee, the entrepreneurial lawyer may choose to pay the fee for their clients—with a higher rate of risk agency fee in return. Further, in China, the filing fee is subject to the so-called 'loser pays' rule, under which the losing party to the litigation needs to bear the fee. In practice, the success rate of securities civil action is found to be very high in China, which means that in the end, the filing fee prepaid by the plaintiffs or their lawyers will be returned to them.[76] Hence, the court fee does not seem to pose an insurmountable hurdle for the bringing of securities civil action.

---

[71] See eg Lihang Geng, 'Mass Litigation and Judicial Constraints' (2006) 3 *Faxue Yanjiu [Chinese Journal of Law]* 63; Wusheng Zhang, 'Resolution Mechanism for Collective Disputes: Analysis and Transplantation of the US Class Action' (2007) 3 *Zhongguo Faxue [China Legal Science]* 20.
[72] Civil Procedure Law Arts 53, 55.
[73] For more discussion of this, see Hui Huang, 'Private Enforcement of Securities Law in China'.
[74] Susong Feiyong Jiaona Banfa [Measures of Charging Litigation Fees] (Promulgated by the State Council on 29 December 2006, effective from 1 April 2007), Art 13. The court fee consists of the filing fee (Anjian Shouli fei) and other litigation fees (Qita Susong feiyong) such as the costs of travel, accommodation, living allowances and subsidies paid to expert witnesses, accountants, translators, etc. As other litigation fees are contingent on actual needs, the focus of discussion is on the filing fee.
[75] See eg Sanzhu Zhu, 'Civil Litigation Arising from False Statements on China's Securities Market' (2005) 31 *North Carolina Journal of International Law and Commercial Regulation* 377; Feng Guo, 'Xujia Chenshu Qingquan de Rending ji Peichang [Determination of Tort of Misrepresentation and Compensation]', (2003) 2 *Zhongguo Faxue [China Legal Science]* 96.
[76] Hui Huang, 'Private Enforcement of Securities Law in China'.

6.4. Comments

6.78 The SPC Third Circular contains a fairly complete set of rules to cover both substantive and procedural issues in relation to private securities litigation. As discussed earlier, it stipulates the types of misrepresentation activities, the scope of eligible plaintiffs, a list of potential defendants, the availability of defences, the rebuttable presumption of causation and reliance, the calculation of damages, and the territorial jurisdiction rule under which jurisdiction goes to the place where the issuer is established. This set of rules provides very useful guidance on the bringing and hearing of private securities action in China.

6.79 It is worth noting that the main purpose of private securities litigation in China is explicitly stated to be compensatory. The official Chinese term used in the SPC Third Circular to refer to private securities litigation literally means 'civil *compensation* cases' (*Minshi Peichang Anjian*), and the rules contained in the SPC Third Circular all serve to clarify how investors get compensation. Hence, when evaluating the efficacy of the law governing private securities litigation in China, it is important to examine the extent to which the SPC Third Circular has achieved its stated mission of generating meaningful compensation to aggrieved investors.

6.80 A recent empirical study found that the number of securities civil suits brought during the first decade of the introduction of private securities litigation in China have been much lower than expected.[77] It refutes the conventional wisdom that the procedural prerequisite built in the Chinese private securities litigation regime is the main factor to blame and argues that the main obstacle to the bringing of securities civil action in China actually rests with the court, which has caused significant difficulties and delays in the pursuit of securities civil claims.

6.81 On the other hand, it is found that the rate of recovery generated by securities civil suits in China is significantly higher than that in the US. The study argues that this is due to several possible factors, including the piggy-back effect of the procedural prerequisite, the clarity of the relevant rules governing securities civil action, and the defendants' weak incentive to defend.

---

[77] Hui Huang, 'Private Enforcement of Securities Law in China'.

Part III

REGULATION OF TRADING IN SECURITIES

7

MARKET MISCONDUCT (OTHER THAN INSIDER TRADING)

7.1. Introduction	7.01	7.3. Market Manipulation		7.13
7.2. Types of Misconduct	7.02	7.3.1. Overview		7.13
7.2.1. Fabricating or disseminating false information	7.02	7.3.2. What constitutes market manipulation?		7.19
7.2.2. Fraud by a securities firm and its employees	7.05	7.3.3. What are the legal liabilities for market manipulation?		7.37
7.2.3. Prohibited trading acts	7.07	7.3.4. Comments		7.48

7.1. Introduction

The Securities Law dedicates a whole section to setting out a list of prohibited trading acts.[1] Among these acts, some have counterparts in overseas jurisdictions, such as insider trading and market manipulation, while others are unique to China, such as the prohibition on misappropriating public money to trade securities. This chapter will focus on market misconduct other than insider trading, which will be dealt with in the next chapter. **7.01**

7.2. Types of Misconduct

7.2.1. Fabricating or disseminating false information

Apart from insider trading and market manipulation, the first item on the list of prohibited trading acts is Article 78, under which it is prohibited for certain people to fabricate or disseminate false information. First, it is prohibited for state functionaries, practitioners of the news media, and other relevant personnel **7.02**

---

[1] Zhonghua Renming Gongheguo Zhenquan Fa [Securities Law of the People's Republic of China] (promulgated on 29 December 1998 and effective from 1 July 1999, amended in 2004, 2005 and 2013) (2005 Securities Law), Part 4 of Chapter 3. Unless indicated otherwise, reference to Securities Law is to the 2005 Securities Law.

concerned to disturb the securities market by fabricating or disseminating any false information. Second, it is prohibited for stock exchanges, securities companies, securities registration and clearing institutions, securities trading service institutions, and practitioners thereof, as well as securities industry associations, securities regulatory bodies, and their functionaries, to make any false statement or give any misleading information in the activities of securities trading. Finally, media should disseminate the securities market information in an authentic and objective way, and any dissemination of misleading information on their part is prohibited.[2]

7.03 The above provision complements the legal regime against misrepresentation in information disclosure documents that was discussed in the preceding chapters. Under the information disclosure regime, certain people, such as the issuer, the listed company and their senior employees, and market professionals, have an affirmative duty to disclose information and will face liability if the disclosure is not made in accordance with law. In contrast, the people listed under Article 78 do not have similar duties and are thus not covered under the information disclosure regime. However, those people, during the course of their work, may make misleading or false statements, and Article 78 is a legislative response to this problem.

7.04 Two points are noted here about Article 78. First, it is interesting that Article 78 only lists certain people and entities. In theory, it should be prohibited for *anybody* to fabricate or disseminate false information to disturb the securities market. A possible explanation may be that due to their positions, those listed people and entities are more likely to commit misrepresentation, or their misrepresentations are likely to have a larger social impact. Second, it is unclear whether the liability of those listed people and entities is fault-based or not. The act of fabricating false information implies that there is an element of intention, but in terms of the act of disseminating false information, it may well be the case that the person, after reasonable due diligence, failed to discover the false nature of the information.

7.2.2. Fraud by a securities firm and its employees

7.05 Article 79 prohibits various fraudulent acts by a securities company as well as the practitioners thereof in the process of securities trading, which may injure the interests of their clients. These include:

(1) Violating the entrustment from its client in the course of purchasing or selling any securities on its behalf.
(2) Failing to provide any client with written confirmation of any transaction within the prescribed period of time.
(3) Misappropriating the securities as entrusted by any client for purchase or sale, or misappropriating the funds in any client's account.

---

[2] Securities Law, Art 78.

(4) Unlawfully purchasing or selling securities for its client without authorization, or unlawfully purchasing or selling any securities in the name of any client.
(5) Inveigling any client into making any unnecessary purchase or sale of securities in order to obtain commissions.
(6) Making use of mass media or any other means to provide or disseminate any false or misleading information to investors.
(7) Any other act that goes against the true intention as expressed by a client and damages the interests thereof.[3]

Further, where the above fraudulent act incurs any loss to the clients, the actor shall make compensation according to law.

7.06 In overseas jurisdictions, securities firms which serve as a broker for investors are subject to fiduciary duties. Although the Chinese law does not explicitly state the broker–client relationship to be fiduciary, the specific acts prohibited under Article 79 reflect the idea. The third subsection refers to a form of misconduct which is particularly serious in China: securities firms misappropriating the securities as entrusted by any client for purchase or sale, or misappropriating the funds in any client's account. The act under the fifth subsection is called 'churning'. This was once a very serious issue, but now with the advent of online trading investors no longer not usually get trading advice from the broker, and thus securities firm have far less opportunity for churning.

7.2.3. Prohibited trading acts

7.07 Below is a group of prohibitions with Chinese characteristics. They may seem strange to the eyes of foreigners, and cannot be properly understood without looking at the broad context in which the Chinese securities market operates.

7.08 Under Article 80, it is prohibited for any legal person to unlawfully make use of any other person's account to undertake any securities trading and it is prohibited for any legal person to lend out its own or any other person's securities account.[4] The acts mentioned here would rarely happen in overseas jurisdictions in the first place, but they are quite widespread in China due to the Chinese culture. In China, the boundary of interpersonal relationships is typically blurred and there is a long tradition of collectivism. As a result, it is commonplace for people to share things and lend things to each other, including money.

7.09 Using other people's accounts or multiple accounts to trade is a typical way to camouflage problematic transactions. Even if the transaction is detected, the perpetrator may still get away, because regulators may only know of the accounts used to commit misconduct and have no idea who actually used the accounts. China requires

---

[3] Securities Law, Art 79.
[4] Securities Law, Art 80.

real names in order to open securities trading accounts, and thus if one person wants to have more than one account, they must borrow or buy accounts from others. This trading trick is widely used in China. For example, there is a dramatic anecdotal story about an instance of market manipulation that was found to be connected with a deceased peasant in a remote rural region, whose ID card was previously lent to someone to open securities trading accounts in exchange for money.

7.10 Under Article 81, the channel for capital to enter into the stock market shall be broadened according to law. It is prohibited for any unqualified capital to go into the stock market.[5] This provision reflects China's policy to follow the international trend of financial modernization, under which the traditional boundaries between financial sectors, namely banking, insurance, and securities, have become increasingly blurred. As discussed in other chapters, the Chinese financial markets are generally segregated along the traditional lines of financial services.[6] Before the 2005 Securities Law revision, funds in the banking and insurance sectors were strictly prohibited from entering the stock market. The 2005 Securities Law relaxes this blanket prohibition, allowing banks and insurance companies to invest in the stock market in certain circumstances and only restricting 'unqualified capital' from the stock market.

7.11 Under Article 82, it is prohibited for any person to misappropriate any public fund to trade securities.[7] This prohibition is so straightforward that it may not need to be specifically set out in other jurisdictions. It is however needed in China, simply because the problem is widespread there. In practice, many people misappropriate public funds to trade and make money fast in the stock market. The provision may have important educational and deterrent effects in relation to such behaviour.

7.12 Finally, under Article 83, the state-owned enterprises and state-controlled enterprises that engage in any trading of listed stocks shall observe the relevant provisions of the state.[8] State-owned/controlled enterprises are seen as the basis and symbol of the socialist economy in China, and their performance has significant political–economic consequences. As securities trading is inherently risky, it is important to restrict the exposure of state-owned/controlled enterprises to the securities markets.

7.3. Market Manipulation

7.3.1. Overview

7.13 Market manipulation has long been regulated because of the damaging effect that it has upon market efficiency and investor confidence. Despite this, an examination

---

[5] Securities Law, Art 81.
[6] See Chapter 2.
[7] Securities Law, Art 82.
[8] Securities Law, Art 83.

of the regulatory regimes in various jurisdictions shows that it has been very difficult to satisfactorily produce a precise definition of market manipulation. Market manipulation is better understood by looking at its essential characteristics, including interference with the natural forces of supply and demand in a market for securities, inducement of persons to trade in a particular security, or attempts to force a security's price to an artificial level.

The regulation of market manipulation in common law jurisdictions traces its lineage to the English case of *R v de Berenger*, decided by the King's Bench in 1814.[9] There, on the morning of 21 February 1814, a man—named de Berenger, and dressed in a military uniform—arrived in Winchester from Dover, scattering French coins along the road, to spread information about the defeat of Napoleon and the capture of Paris by English forces. As the stock market rose on this good news, the man and his friends sold their holdings at substantial profit. The news later proved to be unfounded and, of course, the stock market fell as a result. De Berenger and his friends were charged and convicted. **7.14**

It should be noted however that there has been debate on whether the above case really created the crime of market manipulation. Indeed, the charge brought in the case was conspiracy to defraud, not market manipulation. As one commentator pointed out, the case is simply 'a demonstration of how English common law of crimes fashioned the law of criminal conspiracy to address *an instance* of market manipulation'.[10] This common law approach may be inadequate: for instance, as the essence of criminal conspiracy is an agreement to enact a fraud on somebody, an individual acting alone to manipulate the market would arguably fall outside the ambit of the case. Nevertheless, the case can be regarded as the origin of present-day market manipulation regulation, because it proclaims, for the first time, that a natural market should not be tampered with—this is the essence of market manipulation prohibition. **7.15**

The *R v de Berenger* case involves the use of false rumours to effect the purpose of raising the price of public securities. By the end of the nineteenth century, the concept of market manipulation was extended to manipulation by trading alone, without accompanying rumours and misinformation. In reality, market manipulation may take many forms, but they can be broadly grouped into two categories—namely, information-based market manipulation and trade-based market manipulation. Nowadays, it appears that most cases of market manipulation are **7.16**

---

[9] (1814) 3 Maule & S 67; 105 ER 536. For a detailed discussion of this case, see eg Louis Loss and Joel Seligman, *Securities Regulation* (Aspen Publishers, 2004) Vol XIII, § 3986.11; Robert Baxt, Ashley Black, and Pamela Hanrahan, *Securities and Financial Services Law* (LexisNexis, 2003), 471–2.

[10] Alexander FH Loke, 'The Investors' Protected Interest against Market Manipulation in the UK, Australia and Singapore' (2007) 21 *Australian Journal of Corporate Law* 22.

trade-based, presumably because it is much more difficult to detect trade-based market manipulation than information-based market manipulation.

7.17 It is interesting to note the argument that an attempt to commit trade-based market manipulation is likely to be self-defeating, and there is no need to legally prohibit it.[11] According to this argument, profitable manipulation requires the satisfaction of two conditions: first, trading must cause the security price to rise; second, the manipulator must be able to sell at a price higher than the price at which the manipulator purchased (plus transactions costs incurred). The first condition is not easy to meet, the argument goes, because in a liquid market such as NYSE, share price is unlikely to be affected by individual sales or purchases unless the trades are in very large volumes. Further, it is almost impossible to satisfy the second condition because price-pressure effects are symmetrical, which means that any gains made on the way up would be lost on the way down. At first glance, this argument seems to be plausible, but it is clearly inconsistent with the reality that many trade-based manipulations do occur. This argument has been met with criticism, particularly from the perspective of behavioural economics, which usefully leads us to deeper understanding of market manipulation and securities regulation more generally. The continuing debate itself, however, shows that the complexity of market manipulation is yet to be fully understood.

7.18 In practice, there are different motivations for committing market manipulation. For instance, a person has a substantial holding of shares in its investment portfolio; a person wishes to dispose of his/her shares in a company; in a contested takeover, the directors of a target company have an interest in seeing that the price of its securities is higher than the bid price; an issuer or underwriter might seek to prevent a decline in the trading price of its securities, since investors will not take up shares if the trading price is less than the issue price (a practice called price stabilization); manipulation of share prices might allow an investor to derive profits on the futures market, or affect the exercise price of options, or the number of shares issued on the conversion of preference shares.

7.3.2. What constitutes market manipulation?

7.3.2.1. Overview

7.19 Article 77 provides the principal prohibition of market manipulation in China. Under Article 77(1), anyone is prohibited from manipulating the securities market by any of the following means:

a) Where anyone, independently or in collusion with others, manipulates the trading price of securities or trading quantity of securities by centralizing

---

[11] Daniel R Fischel and David J Ross, 'Should the Law Prohibit Manipulation in Financial Markets?' (1991) 105 *Harvard Law Review* 503.

their advantages in funds, their shareholding advantages or taking their information advantage to trade jointly or continuously.
b) Where anyone collaborates with any other person to trade securities pursuant to the time, price, and method as agreed upon in advance, thereby affecting the price or quantity of the securities traded.
c) Where anyone trades securities between accounts under his own control, thereby affecting the price or quantity of the securities traded.
d) Where anyone manipulates the securities market by any other means.[12]

Subsection 77(1)(a) is intended to provide a general definition of market manipulation, while subsections 77(1)(b) and 77(1)(c) set out two specific forms of market manipulation, known as 'matched orders' and 'wash sales' respectively. The last subsection 77(1)(d) is a catch-all provision to make the law flexible enough to cover any other possible forms of market manipulation. **7.20**

Hence, it seems that Article 77 is broad enough to cover all forms of market manipulation, whether trade-based or information-based. But information-based market manipulation may also trigger other relevant provisions, such as Article 78, where false or misleading statements are used as a vehicle for market manipulation. **7.21**

7.3.2.2. Article 77(1)(a)

In China, market manipulators are colloquially called *Zhuangjia*, a term used to refer to the banker in a gamble, who usually has the advantage in terms of fund and information. Indeed, Article 77(1)(a) basically defines market manipulation by reference to the means of trading. It lists 'funds advantages', 'shareholding advantages', and 'information advantages' as the means of market manipulation. It is unclear however what these terms mean. The China Securities Regulatory Committee (CSRC) has issued internal guidance for its staff to better understand these terms.[13] **7.22**

According to the CSRC, the term 'funds advantages' means that, compared to ordinary investors, the trader has a quantitative advantage in relation to the funds he can amass for the purpose of trading securities. In deciding whether there are funds advantages, attention must be paid to a totality of relevant factors, including the absolute amount of the funds, the ratio of the securities traded with the funds to the total trading volume of the securities, and the overall level of activeness of the trading of the securities.[14] In a similar vein, the term 'shareholding advantages' is defined to mean the trader having a quantitative advantage in terms of his holding of the securities.[15] **7.23**

---

[12] Securities Law, Art 77.
[13] *Zhengquan Shichang Caozong Xingwei Rending Zhiyin (Shixing)* (Provisional Guidance on Identification of Market Manipulation on Securities Markets) (issued by the CSRC on 27 March 2007).
[14] Provisional Guidance, Art 17.
[15] Provisional Guidance, Art 18.

7.24 The term 'information advantages' refers to circumstances where, compared to ordinary investors, the trader is advantaged in obtaining major information about relevant securities or is able to obtain information more easily, earlier, more accurately, or more completely. The term 'major information' means information which may influence the investment decisions of reasonable investors, including inside information.[16]

7.25 The above three means of market manipulation are objectively defined and there are problems with this approach. Manipulators may have fund advantages, shareholding advantages, or information advantages, but not vice versa: that is, one should not be treated as a manipulator simply because one is in an advantageous position in relation to funds, shareholding or information. Further, anyone who gains advantages in terms of inside information could be caught under the insider trading regime.

7.26 Indeed, it is difficult to distinguish manipulative from non-manipulative trading by reference only to the objective factors, such as the means or effect of the particular trade in the market. The central feature of manipulative trading is the intention of the trader. This issue will be discussed in more detail later.

7.27 There is another problem with Article 77(1)(a), under which market manipulation can be carried out by one person or more than one person, and the securities trades must be joint or continuous. This means that in the case of joint transactions involving more than one person, one single trade can constitute manipulation, while in the case of non-joint transactions involving only one person, trades must be continuous and one single trade may not constitute manipulation. In fact, one single trade by one single person can be manipulative and is no less objectionable than multiple trades.

7.28 Perhaps due to the above problems, Article 77(1)(a) has not been frequently used by the CSRC to combat market manipulation in practice.

7.3.2.3. Article 77(1)(b) and (c)

7.29 Article 77(1)(b) and (c) in effect provide for two specific forms of market manipulation, namely 'matched orders' and 'wash sales'. The term 'matched orders', known as *Yueding Jiaoyi* or *Duiqiao* in Chinese, refers to the situation where anyone collaborates with any other person to trade securities pursuant to the time, price and method as agreed upon in advance, thereby affecting the price or quantity of the securities traded. According to the CSRC, 'matched orders' involve at least two traders,[17] and the buy and sell orders are matched if they are placed at close times, similar prices and in similar numbers.[18]

---

[16] Provisional Guidance, Art 19.
[17] Provisional Guidance, Art 24.
[18] Provisional Guidance, Art 25.

7.30 The practice of 'wash sales', translated as *Xishou* in Chinese, occurs when anyone trades securities between the accounts under his own control, thereby affecting the price or quantity of the securities traded. Unlike matched orders, wash sales are conducted by one trader only, but this single trader uses multiple accounts he controls to manipulate. The accounts can be registered under the trader's own name or under other people's names.[19]

7.31 As these two forms of market manipulation are relatively easy to recognize, the CSRC has used Article 77(1)(b) and (c), or sometimes in conjunction with Article 77(1)(a), in a majority of its enforcement actions. But as will be discussed later, although 'matched orders' and 'wash sales' are usually indicative of market manipulation, there may be circumstances where these two forms of transactions are not conducted for the purpose of manipulating the market. In other words, it is not appropriate to objectively determine 'matched orders' and 'wash sales' without examining the intent of the trader.

7.3.2.4. Article 77(1)(d)

7.32 Article 77(1)(d) is a catch-all provision, which can be used by the CSRC to catch other forms of market manipulation. It was not until 2007 that the CSRC started using this provision.

7.33 The 2007 case of Zhou Jianming is the first case in which a person was found to have violated Article 77(1)(d).[20] In this case, Mr Zhou Jianming influenced the price of a stock in the following way: he first placed a large number of orders to buy the stock in question, and then before the transaction was completed, he cancelled the orders. In doing so, he created a false appearance that the stock was sought after and actively traded, leading to an increase in the price of the stock. This means of manipulation does not fall under any of the three subsections of Article 71(1), and thus the CSRC used Article 77(1)(d) to punish Mr Zhou. This practice is called 'false orders'.[21]

7.34 In the case of Zhou Jianming, the CSRC found Article 77(1)(d) a convenient regulatory tool to wield, and thereafter continued to make use of this provision to catch other innovative manipulative transactions. In 2008, the case of Wang Jianzhong was handled on the basis of the catch-all provision.[22] In this case, Mr Wang Jianzhong was the large shareholder, executive director, and manager of Beijing Shoufang Investment Consulting Ltd. Between 1 January 2007 and 29 May 2008, Beijing Shoufang published a series of investment reports recommending 'buy' stocks, and the reports proved influential among general investors. Mr Wang bought relevant stocks before the investment report was published, and sold

---

[19] Provisional Guidance, Art 28.
[20] CSRC Administrative Sanction Decision (on Zhou Jianming) [2007] No 35.
[21] CSRC Decision on Zhou Jianming, Art 30.
[22] CSRC Administrative Sanction Decision (on Wang Jianzhong) [2008] No 42.

them at a higher price after the release of the investment report. Mr Wang made a net profit of up to 125 million yuan through the above scheme. Again, the CSRC found it hard to catch Mr Wang under the first three subsections of Article 77(1), and finally decided to invoke the catch-all provision.

7.35 The above trading practice of Mr Wang is commonly called 'scalping' in overseas markets, and is translated as *Qiang Maozi Jiaoyi* in China.[23] There has been some ongoing academic debate on the nature of this transaction, and different jurisdictions have chosen to regulate it in different ways. The CSRC staff members had different opinions as to how to treat the case of Mr Zhang, and in the end chose to punish Mr Wang under Article 77(1)(d). Since this case, the CSRC has used the catch-all provision to deal with more cases of scalping.

7.36 Apart from false orders and scalping, the CSRC explicitly states that the catch-all provision may also cover the following means of manipulation: (1) the practice of *Guhuo Jiaoyi*, which means manipulation with false or misleading statements;[24] (2) the practice of *Weishi Jiaoyi*, namely transactions at or near the close of trading with the effect of increasing, decreasing, or maintaining securities prices;[25] (3) other manipulative practices as identified by the CSRC.[26]

7.3.3. What are the legal liabilities for market manipulation?

7.37 There are generally three types of legal liabilities for market manipulation: criminal liability, administrative liability, and civil liability.

7.3.3.1 Administrative liability

7.38 Article 203 of the Securities Law sets out administrative liability for market manipulation, including: (1) the manipulator shall be ordered to dispose the securities as illegally held in the course of market manipulation; (2) the illegal proceeds shall be confiscated and a fine of 1–5 times the illegal proceeds shall be imposed; (3) where there are no illegal proceeds or the illegal proceeds amount to less than 30,000 yuan, a fine of between 30,000 yuan and 300,000 yuan shall be imposed; (4) where an entity manipulates the securities market, the person in charge and any other person as held directly responsible shall be given a warning and a fine of between 100,000 yuan and 600,000 yuan shall also be imposed.

7.39 The CSRC has power to impose administrative liabilities without the need to go to court. In practice, a vast majority of the cases against market manipulation are cases handled by the CSRC where administrative liabilities are imposed. Apart from the sanctions above—namely warning, confiscation of illegal gains, and

---

[23] CSRC Decision on Wang Jianzhong.
[24] CSRC Decision on Wang Jianzhong, Art 31.
[25] CSRC Decision on Wang Jianzhong, Art 45.
[26] CSRC Decision on Wang Jianzhong, Art 30.

fines—the CSRC has used its general power to bar responsible persons from the market.

7.3.3.2. *Criminal liability*

Criminal liability for market manipulation is provided for under the Criminal Law rather than the Securities Law. Article 182 of the Criminal Law states that: **7.40**

> Where any of the following circumstances arises, and if the circumstances are serious, the person who manipulates the securities or futures market shall be sentenced to fixed-term imprisonment of not more than five years or detention, and/or shall be fined. If the circumstances are extremely serious, he shall be sentenced to fixed-term imprisonment of not less than five years but not more than 10 years, and shall be fined:
> (1) Manipulating the trading prices of securities or futures or the trading volume of securities or futures by concentrating independently or by collusion the advantages in capital or the advantages in shareholding or positions or the advantage in information so as to carry out colluded or continuous transactions;
> (2) Colluding with any other person to carry out securities or futures transactions with each other according to the time, price or ways as agreed to in advance so that the trading prices or volumes of securities or futures are affected;
> (3) Making securities transactions among the accounts under the actual control of his own or taking himself as the object of trading of futures agreements so that the trading prices or volumes of securities or securities are affected;
> (4) Manipulating the securities or futures markets by any other means.
>
> Where any entity commits a crime as described in the preceding paragraph, a fine shall be imposed upon the entity, and the persons in charge who are held to be directly responsible or any other liable persons shall be penalized according to the preceding paragraph.[27]

It can be seen that the description of market manipulation in the above provision is essentially identical to Article 77 of the Securities Law, as discussed earlier. Hence, the same impugned manipulative transaction may attract either administrative or criminal liability, depending on the degree of its seriousness. **7.41**

The Ministry of Public Security and the Supreme People's Procuratorate have provided guidance on when criminal liability may arise for market manipulation: **7.42**

> Where anyone manipulates the securities or futures market, a case shall be filed for investigation and prosecution under any of the following circumstances:
>
> 1. The number of tradable shares of the same securities held or actually controlled individually or in collusion reaches more than thirty percent of the total actually tradable securities, and the accumulative number of such shares jointly or successively traded for 20 consecutive trading days reaches more

---

[27] Criminal Law (Amendment in 2006), Art 182.

than thirty percent of the total trading volume of such shares of the securities over the same period;
2. The number of the same futures contract held or actually controlled individually or in collusion reaches more than fifty percent of the position as prescribed in the business rules of the futures exchange, and the accumulative number of such a futures contract jointly or successively traded for 20 consecutive trading days reaches more than thirty percent of the total trading volume of such a futures contract over the same period;
3. In collusion with any other person, securities or futures contracts are traded mutually according to the pre-determined time, price or method, and the accumulative trading volume of such a securities or futures contract for 20 consecutive trading days reaches more than 20 percent of the total trading volume of such a securities or futures contract over the same period;
4. Securities are traded between the accounts actually controlled by oneself or futures contracts are traded with oneself, and the accumulative trading volume of such securities or such a futures contract during 20 consecutive trading days reaches more than 20 per cent of the total trading volume of such securities or such a futures contract over the same period;
5. Buy or sell orders are placed successively for the same securities or futures contract and are cancelled before deal on the same day individually or in collusion, and the amount in such cancelled orders accounts for more than fifty percent of the total amount in the orders placed for such securities or such a futures contract on the same day;
6. A listed company, any of its directors, supervisors or senior managers, its actual controller or controlling shareholder or any other affiliate of it manipulates the trading price or trading volume of any securities of the company individually or in collusion by using any information advantage;
7. A securities company, securities investment consulting institution or professional intermediary institution or any employee thereof buys, sells or holds the relevant securities to seek benefits from the trading of the securities by offering any public evaluation, forecast or investment advice on the securities, issuer of the securities or the listed company in violation of the relevant provisions on occupational prohibitions, which is serious; or
8. There is any other serious circumstance.[28]

---

[28] Zuigao Renmin Jianchayuan, GongAnBu Guanyu Yinfa 'Zuigao Renmin Jianchayuan, GongAnBu Guanyu GongAn Jiguan Guanxia de Xingshi Anjian LiAn Zuisu Biaozhun de Guiding (2) de Tongzhi (Notice of the Supreme People's Procuratorate and the Ministry of Public Security on Issuing the Provisions (II) of the Supreme People's Procuratorate and the Ministry of Public Security on the Standards for Filing Criminal Cases under the Jurisdiction of the Public Security Organs for Investigation and Prosecution) (issued on 05 July 2010 by the Ministry of Public Security and the Supreme People's Procuratorate), Art 39.

7.43 Hence, if the CSRC, after investigation, finds a case of market manipulation is serious enough to warrant criminal liability, it will transfer the case to the prosecutor. In recent years there has been an increase in the number of criminal cases against market manipulation, but compared to administrative cases, criminal cases are still quite small in number.

7.3.3.3. Civil liability

7.44 Article 77(2) of the Securities Law stipulates that where anyone incurs any loss to investors by manipulating the securities market, the actor shall be subject to the liabilities of compensation according to law. This simple provision is not, however, supported by more detailed rules on how civil cases can be brought for the purpose of seeking compensation. As a result, it is very difficult to successfully pursue civil liability against market manipulation in China, at least for the time being.

7.45 To begin with, many courts simply refused to accept civil cases against market manipulation. Even if the court accepts civil cases, the prospect of success is remote. As of November 2013, there were only two reported civil cases brought to seek compensation for the loss suffered as a result of market manipulating, and both failed.

7.46 In the first case, 18 individual investors brought a joint civil action against two manipulators, namely Cheng Wenshui and Liu Yanze, after they had been sanctioned by the CSRC in 2009 for manipulating the share price of a listed company named Taibai. The difficulty in this case is that the law is silent on the issue of causation and calculation of damages. The plaintiffs submitted that the two issues could be dealt with by reference to the Supreme People's Court (SPC)'s judicial interpretation on the hearing of civil cases against misrepresentation. However, the court rejected this submission, stating that market manipulation is different from misrepresentation in terms of the nature of the act, the lasting period of the event, and the scope of the influence, and that it would be a mistake to simply apply the rules for civil cases against misrepresentation to deal with civil cases against market manipulation.

7.47 The other civil case arose from the case of Wang Jianzhong discussed earlier. There, Wang Jianzhong and Beijing Shoufang Ltd were civil-sued to pay compensation after they were found guilty of market manipulation by the CSRC. In this case, the plaintiff claimed that he made his securities investment relying on the report produced by Wang Jianzhong and Shoufang, and suffered a loss as a result. Similarly, the court rejected the plaintiff's submission that the case could be adjudicated by reference to the SPC rules on civil cases against misrepresentation, particularly in relation to issues such as causation. The court held that apart from the report produced by the defendants, there were many other reports making similar recommendations, and that the plaintiff needed to affirmatively prove his reliance on the report produced by the defendants.

7.3.4. Comments

7.3.4.1. A critique of the definition of market manipulation

7.48 Under Article 77(1)(a), market manipulation may occur if 'anyone, independently or in collusion with others, *manipulates* the trading price of securities or trading quantity of securities by centralizing their advantages in funds, their shareholding advantages or taking their information advantage to trade jointly or continuously'. This is clearly a circular definition, as it uses the word 'manipulate' to define what constitutes market manipulation.

7.49 Further, as discussed earlier, Article 77(1) does not explicitly contain the element of intent in defining market manipulation. The three means of manipulation as stipulated under Article 77(1)(a), 'matched orders' under 77(1)(b) and 'wash sales' under 77(1)(c), are all stated in objective terms, without requiring the presence of intent on the part of the trader. As will be discussed in detail, this would lead to regulatory overreach, as socially desirable trading activities could be caught under the current regulatory regime.

7.3.4.2. Artificiality-based definition

7.50 In general, intent is difficult to prove, and this may impede successful market manipulation prosecutions. Hence, in some jurisdictions like Australia, efforts have been made to solve this problem by defining market manipulation in terms of price artificiality.[29] Debates have arisen, however, as to how artificiality is be determined and, at a more fundamental level, whether it is possible at all to objectively define market manipulation.

7.51 Indeed, artificiality of securities prices is indicative of manipulation, but it appears to be a particularly elusive concept. Economic studies have been resorted to in the hope that they may ascertain the content of artificiality, but none have proven satisfactory. There are traditionally two main economic methods used to produce evidence of price artificiality, and within each method, some variations exist.

7.52 Under one method, a price will be considered artificial if it deviates in its relationship to other prices from a set of expected price relationships.[30] Put another way, an artificial price is one that is historically unusual, either because of its absolute level or because of its relationship to other prices. In determining whether a price is unusual, courts have considered, among other things, the historical price movement.

---

[29] Hui Huang, 'Redefining Market Manipulation in Australia: The Role of an Implied Intent Element' (2009) 27 *Company and Securities Law Journal* 8.

[30] This method has been used to determine manipulation with respect to commodities and securities. See Wendy Collins Perdue, 'Manipulation of Futures Markets: Redefining the Offence' (1987) 56 *Fordham Law Review* 345, 367 (discussing the usage of the method in the commodities market); Emilios E. Avgouleas, *The Mechanics and Regulation of Market Abuse—A Legal and Economic Analysis* (New York: Oxford University Press, 2005), 110 (examining the method in the context of securities trading).

An artificial price will then be identified as severance of the normal pricing mechanisms with no apparent reason.

7.53 It is acknowledged that the above 'historically unusual price' method has a number of weaknesses. The first problem results from the fact that its assumption about comparability of historical data is frequently unwarranted. Plainly, in order to conduct a meaningful comparison, the prices with which the comparison is drawn must be historically comparable and not themselves 'artificial' or manipulated. In comparing a current price with a prior price, there is often no basis to believe that the current price, rather than the prior one, is artificial. In fact, it is quite possible that the historical prices might themselves have been influenced by manipulation, which in turn forced them to artificial levels. Second, and more importantly, it is inconsistent with the commercial reality that new circumstances constantly arise and prices respond accordingly in an ever-changing market. A total reliance on historical comparisons incorrectly assumes that the commercial world always develops along a preset trajectory, and thus runs the risk of labelling as artificial any price which deviates from historical patterns, even when that price is justified by unusual circumstances.

7.54 The other method of defining artificiality does not look directly at the price, but rather at the forces of supply and demand behind the price. Under this approach, artificial price is defined as 'a price that does not reflect the "basic" or "legitimate" forces of supply and demand'.[31] In economic language, it is a non-equilibrium price. This method involves quantifying the divergence between two equilibria derived from historical data: the equilibrium arising as a result of abuse and the equilibrium forecast to have arisen in the absence of the abusive interference.

7.55 As with the first method discussed above, this 'legitimate supply and demand' approach is also fraught with difficulties. Determining 'supply and demand' is not a simple mechanical process. This is because neither supply schedules nor demand schedules have tangible manifestations in a marketplace, and it is necessary to take into account a wide spectrum of unquantifiable factors. As such, it is very difficult to determine supply and demand. This problem is further exacerbated by the fact that the historical data do not incorporate new buyers' demand and new suppliers' supply, and thus do not provide an accurate measure of the current size of supply and demand.[38] Indeed, in assessing whether a past price is adequately reflective of supply and demand, one must look not at whether that price reflects conditions as we now know them with hindsight, but at whether it reflects conditions as they were then understood.

---

[31] Wendy C Perdue, 'Manipulation of Futures Markets' 370; Thomas Hieronymus, 'Manipulation in Commodity Futures Trading: Towards a Definition' (1977) 6 *Hofstra Law Review* 41, 45; Linda N. Edwards and Franklin R. Edwards, 'A Legal and Economic Analysis of Manipulation in Futures Markets' (1984) 4 *Journal of Futures Markets* 333.

7.56 In sum, there is significant difficulty in establishing an artificial price for the purpose of market manipulation. All the existing economic methods used to define an artificial price have proven conceptually problematic and practically unreliable. Experts may arrive at different conclusions depending on the methods used and the assumptions made. This makes the concept of 'artificiality' either inappropriate to, or unhelpful in, the determination of what constitutes manipulation. Therefore, defining manipulation on the basis of artificiality simply substitutes one unhelpful term for another.

7.3.4.3. The role of 'intent'

7.57 The preceding discussion has shown the difficulty of objectively determining the artificiality of a price, and therefore market manipulation, from an economic perspective. In fact, as well as those technical problems, there is one more fatal weakness inherent in any attempt to find an objective test of market manipulation.

7.58 As some leading commentators have stated, 'there is no objective definition of manipulation – manipulation trade must be defined with respect to the intent of the trade',[32] because manipulative trades do not result in an 'objectively harmful act or bad outcome' and they 'are indistinguishable from all other trades'.[33] Indeed, every transaction will naturally have an impact on the price of the security traded. A manipulative transaction may look exactly the same as a non-manipulative one in terms of its price impact and other economic indicators; the only differentiating factor is the intention of the trader. Where alleged manipulative transactions are examined in isolation without regard to the underlying intent, it would be very difficult, if not impossible, to state conclusively whether the transaction is of a manipulative nature.

7.59 The Australian case of *Fame Decorator Agencies Pty Ltd v Jeffries Industries Ltd* (1998) 28 ACSR 58 provides a good example of the relevance of intent in determining market manipulation. This case concerned an attempt of the appellant to push down the relevant share price to increase its entitlement on conversion of preference shares. The appellant sold a large amount of relevant stock within about three minutes of the close of trading, not at the highest possible price but at the lowest possible price. Since the shares were then thinly traded, this transaction easily resulted in the share price dropping rapidly from 35 cents to 13 cents. Although this transaction appeared relatively abnormal, this evidence alone was insufficient to prove that the transactions were manipulative. It was the intent behind the transactions, namely lowering the price so as to obtain more shares from the conversion, which persuaded the court of the manipulative nature of the transaction. The court disbelieved the appellant's explanation that the shares were sold due to a pressing need for cash to pay debts. Clearly, had the transaction been carried out

---

[32] Daniel R Fischel and David J Ross, 'Should the Law Prohibit Manipulation in Financial Markets?' (1991) 105 *Harvard Law Review* 503, 510.
[33] Fischel and Ross, 'Should the Law Prohibit Manipulation', 519.

for the purposes stated by the appellant or due to other legitimate reasons such as complying with margin calls, the conclusion would have been different.

7.60 Therefore, the trader's intention is pivotal in distinguishing legitimate and illegitimate transactions. Objectively similar transactions can be treated differently depending on the subjective motivations of the trader which inform the issue of determining artificiality. When deciding the artificiality of a price, it will still be necessary to have regard to the individual circumstances and the intention of the trader. In short, the artificiality-based definition of market manipulation does not obviate the need to inquire into the mind of the trader.

7.61 Conversely, if the intent element was to be completely removed from the new provisions, bona fide traders carrying out socially desirable transactions could be caught as manipulative. Indeed, even transactions such as 'wash sales' and 'matched orders', which generally smack of manipulation and thus are deemed to be manipulative, perform legitimate functions in some instances. For instance, it is not uncommon for fund managers to decide that a security no longer suits the profile of one of its funds but does suit the profile of another fund, and hence instruct their stockbroker to transfer the securities from one fund to another. In order to ensure the same purchase/sale price, the transaction often goes through the market as a crossing transaction, based on the knowledge that the buying and selling funds are different. However, since the order comes from and the securities are held in the name of a single responsible entity (albeit with different designations), the transactions could technically constitute wash sales.

7.62 In addition to portfolio switching for fund managers, further examples include crossing between proprietary trading accounts and crossing stock between family members or members of a corporate group or in/out of superannuation funds for tax or other reasons. In these circumstances, the beneficial ownership of financial products is moved from one person to another in the same group for a commercially justifiable reorganization of the holding in ownership of assets. However, under a purely objective test for manipulation, they could be caught even if there were no intention to manipulate the market, as long as the action was likely to effectuate an appearance of false or misleading trading. Plainly enough, these would be questionable consequences, which highlight the importance of 'intent' in separating legitimate trading from illegitimate trading.

7.63 Some may be concerned that intent is too difficult to prove and this may impede successful market manipulation prosecutions. There is some merit in this argument, but the difficulty of proving intention is not as serious as suggested by some commentators. Market manipulation often leaves a trace and can be proved by direct evidence from sources such as letters, emails, or telephone communication. For instance, in the Australian case of *Donald v Australian Securities and Investments Commission* (2001) 38 ACSR 10; [2001] AATA 366, the accused was found to have actually said that he 'want(ed) to give [the share price] a bit of a nudge upwards'. This directly showed the intent to manipulate the share price and thus was relied on for the final judgment.

7.64 Further, even where direct evidence is not available, proof of intention can rest upon inferences deduced from circumstantial evidence. In practice, circumstantial indicators include, among other things, consistent increases in a trader's bid to acquire shares from the previous sale price ('upticking'); the making of purchases and sales at successively higher prices ('ramping'); purchases of a significant volume of shares, allowing a trader to dominate the market and artificially set market prices; and placing actual bids at or near the close of trading, causing the stock to close at a higher price than the previous sale price. It should be noted that circumstantial evidence is just indicative and not conclusive.

7.65 Hence, as the intent element can be inferred from the circumstances surrounding the impugned act of market manipulation, the absence of the defendant's admission may not be an insurmountable barrier for the prosecution to establish its case.

7.3.4.4. International experience

7.66 When assessing the Chinese law on market manipulation, it is instructive to look at international experience. The Australian law was discussed earlier; the laws in the United States and the United Kingdom are now examined.

7.67 In the United States, Section 9 of the *Securities Exchange Act 1934* (US) deals specifically with manipulative practices. On the one hand, Section 9(a)(1) prohibits a person from carrying out transactions such as 'wash sales' and 'matched orders' *for the purpose of* creating a false or misleading appearance of active trading in any security registered on a national securities exchange, or a false or misleading appearance with respect to the market for any such security. On the other hand, Section 9(a)(2) makes it unlawful for any person, alone or with others, to effect a series of transactions in any security registered on a national securities exchange creating actual or apparent active trading in the security, or raising or lowering its price, *for the purpose of* inducing others to purchase or sell the security. It is thus clear that the above provisions contain the element of intent in defining market manipulation.

7.68 It should be noted that market manipulation cases in the United States are often brought under the general anti-fraud rule 10b-5, rather than the specific provisions of Section 9, but the calculus of choice has nothing to do with the intent issue. Although rule 10b-5 is very broad in coverage, it requires the element of 'scienter', a peculiarly US concept encompassing intention and recklessness.[34] Consequently, no matter whether

---

[34] In *Ernst & Ernst v Hochfelder* 425 US 185 at 193–4 (1976), the court declined to decide whether recklessness is sufficient for the purposes of imposing liability under s 10(b) and rule 10b-5. In subsequent cases, almost all of the Courts of Appeal have concluded that recklessness could be enough to meet the scienter requirement in non-criminal cases, though these courts have set forth different versions of the definition of 'recklessness'. It seems clear, however, that recklessness may not suffice in criminal cases. For more discussion of this issue, see Hui Huang, *International Securities Markets: Insider Trading Law in China* (The Hague: Kluwer Law International, 2006), 221–3.

Section 9 or rule 10b-5 is used to bring action, there is an essential requirement for fault elements in the United States market manipulation regime.

In the United Kingdom, although there appears to be an attempt towards formulating an objective test of manipulation, intent still remains irreducibly relevant. To begin with, Section 397(3) of the Financial Services and Market Act 2000 (UK) applies to a criminal prosecution against manipulative conduct, providing that there will be a contravention if the accused created 'a false or misleading impression as to the market in or the price or the value of any investments... *for the purpose of* creating that impression and of thereby inducing another person to [trade in those investments]'. 7.69

Clearly, intention is required for criminal liability under Section 397(3) of the Act. For civil liability under Section 118(2)(b) of the Financial Services and Market Act 2000 (UK), it may appear at first glance that intention is not necessary. This section prohibits 'behaviour that is likely to give a regular user of the market a false or misleading impression as the supply of, or demand for, or as to the price or value of, investment of the kind in question'. However, the above attempt to dispense with the subjective elements in the United Kingdom legislation has been found to be inconsistent with the European Union Market Abuse Directive (EU Directive). In 2005, the United Kingdom extensively revised its market abuse provisions to bring them into line with the EU Directive. As a result, manipulative conduct now refers to: 7.70

> behaviour [that] consists of effecting transactions or orders to trade (otherwise than for *legitimate reasons* and in conformity with accepted market practices on the relevant market) which
> (a) give or are likely to give, a false or misleading impression as to the supply of, or demand for, or as to the price of, one or more qualifying investments, or
> (b) secure the price of one or more such investments at an abnormal or artificial price.[35]

Further, the Code of Market Conduct (the Code) promulgated by the Financial Services Authority under Section 119 of the Financial Services and Market Act 2000 (UK) is relevant in the determination of behaviour that would amount to market abuse. The Code expressly mentions the requisite fault elements and what are considered 'legitimate reasons'. For example, it makes explicit reference to 'purpose' both in the prohibition on creating 'false or misleading impressions' and in the 'price positioning' prohibition. In those sections that do not feature a 'purpose' qualifier, acts with 'legitimate reasons' are expressly permitted. Further guidance is provided on the relevant factors to be taken into account when deciding what would be 'legitimate reasons'. This shows that intent remains a key element in the United Kingdom market manipulation law. 7.71

---

[35] Financial Services and Markets Act 2000 (UK), s 118(5) (inserted by the Financial Services and Markets Act 2001 (Market Abuse) Regulations 2005, SI 381/2005) (emphasis added).

7.3.4.5. Summary

7.72 The element of intent plays an indispensable role in differentiating between manipulative and non-manipulative transactions. The idea of formulating a purely objective test of manipulation is not feasible; it has serious conceptual and practical defects. It is the common position of major jurisdictions that when deciding market manipulation, regard must be had not only to the objective elements of the impugned conduct but also to the fault elements of the trader. This should inform the application and reform of the Chinese market manipulation law.

8

INSIDER TRADING

8.1. Introduction	8.01	8.3.4. Comments: theoretical basis of China's insider trading law	8.33
8.2. Background	8.05		
8.2.1. The regulatory framework	8.05	8.4. How Is the Law Enforced?	8.43
8.2.2. The extent of insider trading	8.08	8.4.1. Overview of enforcement mechanisms	8.43
8.3. What Constitutes Insider Trading in China?	8.10	8.4.2. Empirical data: cases from 1991 to 2011	8.48
8.3.1. Who is an insider?	8.10	8.4.3. Analysis and policy implications	8.61
8.3.2. What is inside information?	8.16	8.5. Conclusion	8.76
8.3.3. Subjective elements	8.22		

8.1. Introduction

8.01 Insider trading is a fundamental concern of securities regulation. It is the most widely known and, perhaps, practised form of market abuse. 'Insider trading' is a term of art that generally refers to unlawful trading in securities by persons in possession of relevant material non-public information. This term is a misnomer, however, to the extent that the insider trading prohibition is not confined to corporate insiders like directors and other senior officers; rather, the term often means trading by anyone, whether an insider in the company or not, on the basis of any type of material non-public information about the company whose securities are traded or the market for its security. The difficult question is how the term 'insider trading' should be defined—or, put another way, what should be the appropriate scope of a proscription on trading while in possession of material non-public information.

8.02 There has been a long-standing debate on the economic effects of insider trading—that is, whether insider trading is economically beneficial or harmful. One of the most powerful arguments about the beneficial effects of insider trading is that profits from insider trading are appropriate compensation for corporate insiders.[1] Further, it has been argued that market price actually departs from the true value before inside information is disseminated to the market and that insider

---

[1] Henry G Manne, *Insider Trading and the Stock Market* (Free Press, 1966), 132–41.

trading will move prices in the correct direction, because the trading volume and price movement itself may send a message to outside investors that something is happening.[2] On the other hand, many argue that insider trading has harmful effects in several aspects, such as harm to the market; harm to corporations, including those particular corporations whose securities are traded and all corporations as a class in the market; and harm to investors, including those individual investors involved in specific insider trading cases and all investors as a group in the market.[3]

8.03 Although the theoretical debate on the effects of insider trading has not yet been settled, almost half a century after it began, the case for its detrimental effects seems to have grown stronger. As a matter of fact, insider trading has been increasingly disfavoured by legislators on the global level. The 1990s witnessed an explosion in the number of nations adopting laws prohibiting insider trading. Before 1990, just 34 countries had insider trading laws; by 2000, this number had surged to 87.[4] Thus, the world has evolved from a situation, at the start of the 1990s, in which the majority of countries with stock markets did not prohibit insider trading, to a situation in which the overwhelming majority of countries with stock markets had adopted such a prohibition by the year 2000.

8.04 China is one of the countries which prohibits insider trading. This chapter attempts to examine both the rules and the enforcement of insider trading regulation in China. This is because the formal legal rules can be very different from the reality of actual practice, particularly in developing countries such as China. Indeed, research into the efficacy of insider trading regulation shows the key issue to be not whether a country has a formal regime of insider trading regulation, but whether it actually enforces the regulation.[5] Hence, this chapter will go beyond the formal rules to look at various enforcement mechanisms of insider trading regulation, including public and private enforcement.

8.2. Background

8.2.1. The regulatory framework

8.05 The history of the regulation of insider trading in China can be traced back to as early as 1990, when the stock market was in its very early stage.[6] Drawing upon overseas experience—particularly of the US, which is the pioneer in the field—China has established a relatively complete regulatory regime regarding insider

---

[2] Henry G Manne, *Insider Trading and the Stock Market*, 99; Dennis W Carlton and Daniel R Fischel, 'The Regulation of Insider Trading' (1983) 35 *Stanford Law Review* 857, 866–8.
[3] For a summary of the debate, see Hui Huang, *International Securities Markets: Insider Trading Law in China* (London: Kluwer Law International, 2006), ch 4.
[4] See eg Utpal Bhattacharya and Hazem Daouk, 'The World Price of Insider Trading' 57 *Journal of Finance* 75 (2002).
[5] Bhattacharya and Daouk, 'The World Price of Insider Trading'.
[6] For a discussion on the historical development of China's insider trading regulatory regime, see Hui Huang, *International Securities Markets*, 19–22.

trading, even though, as shall be discussed later, it is not without problems.⁷ The key provisions in Chinese insider trading regulation that give technical effect to the regulatory goals, are now enshrined in the Securities Law of the People's Republic of China ('Securities Law').⁸ The Securities Law pays a fair amount of attention to insider trading, devoting as many as five articles to issues such as the definition of an insider, the scope of insider information, and the types of prohibited activities. On 29 March 2012, the Supreme People's Court and the Supreme People's Procuratorate jointly issued a judicial interpretation to provide guidance on the handling of criminal insider trading cases ('Judicial Interpretation on Insider Trading Law in Criminal Cases').⁹

Apart from the key insider trading provisions noted, there are also other sources of law regulating insider trading indirectly, as preventative measures. For instance, Article 142 of the Company Law of the People's Republic of China stipulates that traditional insiders such as directors, supervisors, and senior management cannot sell shares they hold in their company within one year from the time of listing and within six months of their resignation from the company.¹⁰ Further, Article 13 of the Rules on Administrating the Shares Held by Directors, Supervisors and Senior Management in Their Company and Changes to Their Shareholdings provides for black-out periods during which directors, supervisors, and senior management are not allowed to trade shares in their company.¹¹ Another preventative measure is contained in Article 3 of the Notice on Regulating the Information Disclosure Issue of Listed Companies and the Behaviour of Relevant Parties Concerned, requiring that, at the stage of planning major events which may affect the share price of a listed company, parties who may be privy to the planning exercise, such as the directors, supervisors, and senior management of the company; parties directly involved in the event; and market intermediaries retained for the exercise have a duty of confidentiality before public disclosure of the event.¹²

8.06

---

⁷ See Part III.
⁸ Zhonghua Renming Gongheguo Zhenquan Fa [Securities Law of the People's Republic of China (Securities Law)] (promulgated by the Standing Commission of the National People's Congress, 29 December 1998, effective 1 July 1999, amended in 2004, 2005, and 2013).
⁹ Zuigao Renmin Fayuan and Zuigao Renmin Jianchayuan Guanyu Banli Neimu Jiaoyi and Xielu Neimu Xinxi Xingshi Anjian Juti Yingyong Falv Ruogan Wenti de Jieshi [Judicial Interpretation on Several Issues concerning the Application of Insider Trading Law in Criminal Cases] (promulgated on 29 March 2012, effective 1 June 2012).
¹⁰ Zhonghua Renming Gongheguo Gongsi Fa [Company Law of the People's Republic of China (Company Law)] (promulgated by the Standing Commission of the National People's Congress, 29 December 1993, effective 1 July 1994, amended in 1999, 2004, 2005, and 2013), Art 142.
¹¹ Shangshi Gongsi Dongshi, Jianshi he Gaoji Guanli Renyuan Suochi Bengongsi Gufen jiqi Biandong Guanli Guize [Rules on Administrating the Shares Held by Directors, Supervisors and Senior Management in Their Company and Changes to Their Shareholdings] (promulgated by the China Securities Regulatory Commission, 5 April 2007), Art 13.
¹² Guanyu Guifan Shangshi Gongsi Xinxi Pilu ji Xiangguan Gefang Xingwei de Tongzhi [Notice on Regulating the Information Disclosure Issue of Listed Companies and the Behaviour of Relevant Parties Concerned] (promulgated by the China Securities Regulatory Commission, 29 January 2008), Art 3.

8.07 Finally, Article 47 of the Securities Law, modelled after Section 16(b) of the US Securities and Exchange Act of 1934,[13] prohibits so-called short-swing trading. Specifically, it requires directors, supervisors, senior managers, and substantial shareholders of a listed company (counted as a shareholder holding 5 per cent or more of the outstanding shares) to divulge to the company any short-swing profits, namely profits made from any purchase and sale (or sale and purchase) of the company's equity securities in any six-month period.[14]

8.2.2. The extent of insider trading

8.08 Insider trading appears to be a very serious problem in China. In 2003, this author carried out the first fieldwork of its kind on insider trading in China, using semi-structured and in-depth interviews to obtain empirical data on issues such as the incidence of insider trading in China.[15] Despite some concerns, this methodology has proved to be of particular value in collecting useful first-hand information in the area of insider trading, due to the fact that insider trading is by nature a hidden form of misconduct and thus there is no readily observable data. One can, of course, compile a list of reported cases, but this by no means paints a complete picture of the extent of insider trading, simply because many insider trading activities have gone undetected and the reported cases may just be the tip of the iceberg.

8.09 My 2003 study found that insider trading was widespread in China; nine years on, the insider trading problem is likely to remain the same and, in fact, may be more severe than before as a result of the new developments in the markets. For instance, a growth enterprise market (GEM) was established in the second half of 2009; the systems of short sale and margin lending were implemented on a trial basis from 31 March 2010; and index futures were introduced on 16 April 2010. These market developments pose new challenges for China in its battle against insider trading, because they increase both the opportunity for and the scope of insider trading. In the face of this, on 16 November 2010 the China Securities Regulatory Commission (CSRC), together with several other government agencies such as the Ministry of Public Security, the Ministry of Supervision, and the National Bureau of Corruption Prevention, issued a joint circular on the need to strengthen efforts to crack down on insider trading in China.[16] It states:

---

[13] 15 U.S.C. § 78p(b) (1994).
[14] Securities Law, Art 47.
[15] Huang, *International Securities Markets*, 37–46.
[16] Guanyu Yifa Daji he Fangkong Ziben Shichang Neimu Jiaoyi de Yijian [Opinion on Preventing and Combating Insider Trading in the Capital Markets in accordance with the Law (Opinion on Preventing and Combating Insider Trading)] (promulgated by the China Securities Regulatory Commission, the Ministry of Public Security, the Ministry of Supervision, the State-owned Assets Supervision and Administration Commission, and the National Bureau of Corruption Prevention, 16 November 2010).

At present, the situation we face in preventing and fighting insider trading in the capital markets is very dire. The identities of insiders are very complicated, the trading methods very elusive, the operating forms very secretive, and the detection work very difficult. With the introduction of index futures, insider trading has become more complicated and more secretive.[17]

8.3. What Constitutes Insider Trading in China?

8.3.1. Who is an insider?

As discussed above, the Chinese insider trading law is heavily influenced by the US experience. In general, China's insider trading law centres on primary insider trading situations, and extends liability to those who trade on the basis of misappropriated information. Aside from trading, tipping and procuring are also prohibited.[18] **8.10**

Article 73 of the Securities Law generally prohibits persons with knowledge of inside information on securities trading from using such inside information to trade securities.[19] Other articles, however, restrict this wide net. Article 74 lists some specific types of persons considered to be 'persons with knowledge of inside information', including: **8.11**

(1) Directors, supervisors, managers, deputy managers, and other senior management persons of companies that issue shares or corporate bonds.
(2) Shareholders who hold not less than 5 per cent of the shares in a company.
(3) The senior management persons of the holding company of a company that issues shares.
(4) Persons who are able to obtain material company information concerning the trading of its securities by virtue of the position they hold in the company.
(5) Staff members of the securities regulatory authority, and other persons who administer securities trading pursuant to their statutory duties.
(6) The relevant staff members of public intermediary organizations who participate in securities trading pursuant to their statutory duties and the relevant staff members of securities registration and clearing institutions and securities trading service organizations.
(7) Other persons specified by the securities regulatory authority under the State Council.[20]

According to this list, statutory insiders can be categorized into several groups. The first group is corporate directors and officers, including directors, supervisors, managers, deputy mangers, and other persons in senior management roles of the

---

[17] Opinion on Preventing and Combating Insider Trading, para 1.
[18] Securities Law, Art 76.
[19] Securities Law, Art 73.
[20] Securities Law, Art 74.

corporation[21] and its holding corporation.[22] Second, in addition to members of senior management, lower-level employees are also deemed insiders if they have obtained inside information in connection with their employment.[23] This category may represent the largest number of insiders. Third, substantial shareholders are also deemed insiders for the purpose of insider trading law.[24]

8.12 The above three groups are all traditional corporate insiders, but the insider trading prohibition is not limited to them. There are two more groups of persons who are nominal outsiders but nevertheless subject to the prohibition. One group corresponds to what are called temporary or constructive insiders in the USA, namely a variety of nominal outsiders who participate in securities trading pursuant to their statutory duties or private contracts, such as underwriters, accountants, lawyers, consultants, and staff members of securities registration and clearing institutions.[25] The other group are regulatory officials, namely persons who have regulatory authority over securities trading.[26]

8.13 While defining insiders by means of enumeration has the benefit of providing specific guidance, it could potentially be narrowing, thereby inviting loopholes in an unintended manner. Elsewhere this author has discussed in detail some groups of people who may possess material, non-public information and yet could circumvent the prohibition to trade affected securities with impunity, such as retired corporate officers and tippees.[27] Potentially, the last subsection of Article 74 may plug these loopholes, as it is a catch-all provision referring to 'other persons' specified by the CSRC. To date, the CSRC has not issued any formal regulation to provide further details on the scope of the provision.[28]

8.14 A recent high-profile case sheds some light on the persons who may potentially fall within this category. In the *Li Qihong case*, Mrs Li was then the mayor of the city of Zhongshan of Guangdong Province. She was in charge of the asset restructuring exercise of a listed company which was majority-owned by the Zhongshan government.

---

[21] Securities Law, Art 74(1).
[22] Securities Law, Art 74(3).
[23] Securities Law, Art 74(4).
[24] Securities Law, Art 74(2). In China, a shareholder with 5 per cent or more of the shares issued by a listed company is considered to be a substantial shareholder.
[25] Securities Law, Art 74(6).
[26] Securities Law, Art 74(5).
[27] Hui Huang, 'The Regulation of Insider Trading in China: A Critical Review and Proposals for Reform' 17 (2005) *Australian Journal of Corporate Law* 281, 294–6.
[28] The CSRC has issued an internal guidance document, listing several other types of people as insiders under the last subsection of Article 74. See Zhongguo Zhengquan Jiandu Guanli Weiyuanhui Guanyu 'Zhenquan Shichang Caozong Xingwei Rending Zhiyin (Shixing)' ji 'Zhengquan Shichang Neimu Jiaoyi Xingwei Rending Zhiyin (Shixing)' de Tongzhi [Notice of the CSRC Regarding the Printing and Distribution of the '(Provisional) Guide for the Recognition and Confirmation of Manipulative Behaviour in the Securities Markets' and the '(Provisional) Guide for the Recognition and Confirmation of Insider Trading Behaviour in the Securities Markets' (2007 CSRC Guide on Insider Trading)] (promulgated by the China Securities Regulatory Commission

Mrs Li divulged the confidential information on the restructuring matter to her husband and sister-in-law, who subsequently traded shares of the said company at a huge profit. The CSRC later conducted an investigation into the matter, and Mrs Li was accused of insider trading before the Intermediate People's Court of Guangzhou City on 6 April 2011. This case shows that government officials other than those in the regulatory body, namely the CSRC, are included in the category of 'other persons'.

Apart from the above primary insider trading instances, China has also introduced the misappropriation theory from the US to expand the scope of its insider trading regulation.[29] Under Article 76, a person who has illegally obtained material non-public information has an insider's duty and thus is prohibited from trading on the basis of the information.[30] As noted before, the Judicial Interpretation on Insider Trading Law in Criminal Cases was recently issued to provide further guidance on the application of insider trading law in China. Under Article 2 of the above instrument, a person may be found to have illegally obtained inside information if the inside information is obtained in the following three circumstances: (1) through such ways as theft, cheating, tapping, spy, extraction, bribery, and private trading; (2) from close relatives of primary insiders, or people with other types of close relationships with primary insiders; (3) from people who have contact with primary insiders during the sensitive period of the inside information.[31] This provision casts a very wide net and provides a clear legal basis for pursuing tippee liability. **8.15**

8.3.2. What is inside information?

Article 75(1) of the Securities Law generally defines what constitutes 'inside information' in China, providing that '[i]nside information is information that is not made public because, in the course of securities trading, it concerns the company's business or financial affairs or may have a major effect on the market price of the company's securities'.[32] **8.16**

However, this broad standard may be too vague and indeterminate, making it potentially very difficult to resolve litigation and for insiders to decide whether **8.17**

---

on 27 March 2007). Article 6(2) of the above document elaborates on the category of 'other people' within the meaning of Article 74 of the 2005 Securities Law. It should be noted however that the 2007 CSRC Guide on Insider Trading is strictly for the CSRC's internal use only. The 2007 CSRC Guide on Insider Trading serves the purpose of helping CSRC staff to better understand the insider trading law and ensuring consistency of enforcement standard. To date, it has never been publicly referred to as a legal basis in any administrative penalty decisions on insider trading. For a more detailed discussion of the 2007 CSRC Guide on Insider Trading, see Nicholas Calcina Howson, 'Enforcement Without Foundation?—Insider Trading and China's Administrative Law Crisis', (2012) 60(4) *American Journal of Comparative Law* 955 arguing that the 2007 CSRC Guide on Insider Trading is void and unenforceable).

[29] For discussion of the misappropriation theory, see Part 8.3.4.
[30] Securities Law, Art 76.
[31] Judicial Interpretation on Insider Trading Law in Criminal Cases, Art 2.
[32] Securities Law, Art 75(1).

they must disclose information before trading. In order to give some guidance and facilitate its application, Article 75(2) itemizes some specific types of facts that are regarded as inside information,[33] including:

(1) The major events listed in the second paragraph of Article 67 of this law.
(2) Company plans concerning distribution of dividends or increase of registered capital.
(3) Major changes in the company's equity structure.
(4) Major changes in security for the company's debts.
(5) Any single mortgage, sale, or write-off of a major asset used in the business of the company that exceeds 30 per cent of the asset concerned.
(6) Potential liability for major damages to be assumed in accordance with law as a result of an act committed by a company's director(s), supervisor(s), manager(s), deputy manager(s), or other senior management person(s).
(7) Plans concerning the takeover of listed companies.
(8) Other important information determined by the securities regulatory authority under the State Council to have a significant effect on the trading prices of securities.

8.18 A listed company is obligated to disclose major events by submitting an ad hoc report on the 'major events' to the CSRC and to the stock exchange where it is listed. Under Article 67, types of 'major events' include:[34]

(1) A major change in the company's business guidelines or scope of business.
(2) A decision made by the company concerning a major investment or major asset purchase.
(3) Conclusion by the company of an important contract which may have an important effect on the company's assets, liabilities, rights, interests, or business results.
(4) Incurrence by the company of a major debt or default on an overdue major debt.
(5) Incurrence by the company of a major deficit or incurrence of a major loss exceeding 10 per cent of the company's net assets.
(6) A major change in the external production or business conditions of the company.
(7) A change in the chairman of the board of directors, or not less than one-third of the directors or the manager of the company.
(8) A considerable change in the holdings of shareholders who each hold not less than 5 per cent of the company's shares.
(9) A decision made by the company to reduce its registered capital, to merge, to divide, to dissolve, or to file for bankruptcy.

---

[33] Securities Law, Art 75(2).
[34] Securities Law, Art 67.

(10) Major litigation involving the company, or lawful cancellation by a court of a resolution adopted by the shareholders' general meeting or the board of directors.
(11) Other events specified in laws or administrative regulations.

Several points are noteworthy about the above provisions on inside information. First, inside information is defined to encompass any material, non-public information, no matter whether or not it is derived from within the company whose securities are traded. Put another way, inside information includes both 'corporate information', which is internally generated by the issuer of the subject security, and 'market information', which is externally generated but nevertheless has a major effect on the stock price of the issuer.

Second, it appears that the definition of inside information is not confined to information that specifically relates to one or more companies or securities. A literal reading of Article 75 implies that any confidential price-sensitive information would be deemed inside information, regardless of whether it is related to securities specifically or generally. This should be immediately relevant to the status of government policies, which always have a general market application, affecting all or at least a whole sector of companies or securities in the market. If one such government policy—for example, a change in the interest rate—has a major effect on the price of the affected securities, it would constitute inside information in China. This treatment is very important in China, where government policies are fast-changing and frequently abused by those with privileged access to make money in the market.

Finally, as with the scope of insiders, there is also an open-ended category of inside information, referring to 'other information' as determined by the CSRC. Recent cases have provided some insights into what information might be included under this category. In the *Pan Haishen* case, the alleged insider trading was based on non-public earning forecasts. Looking into the words of the provisions, neither Article 67 nor Article 75 explicitly covers this type of inside information, and thus the CSRC held that it fell into the catch-all category.[35]

8.3.3. Subjective elements

8.3.3.1. Is negligence enough?
The insider trading provisions in the Securities Law do not directly address the issue of subjective elements. For criminal liability, the Criminal Law generally requires actual intent or recklessness as to the existence of the facts and intentionality to

---

[35] Zhongguo Zhengjianhui Xingzheng Chufa Juedingshu 2008 No. 12 [Administrative Penalty Decision of the CSRC, 2008, No 12] (promulgated by the China Securities Regulatory Commission, 16 March 2008).

engage in illegal behaviour, stipulating that 'the crime is constituted as a result of clear knowledge that one's own act will cause socially harmful consequences, and of hope for or indifference to the occurrence of those consequences'.[36] Insider trading liability is no exception, and thus for criminal liability to attach to insider trading, there should be the presence of either intention or recklessness.[37]

8.23 In non-criminal settings, however, the CSRC has recently held that negligence may be sufficient to sustain administrative penalties for insider trading. In the *Kuang Yong* case, Mr Kuang Yong was involved in the negotiation of a backdoor listing deal. He often took telephone calls at home, discussing the progress of the deal. His wife overhead some of the calls and, after figuring out what it was about, traded relevant shares at a profit. In August 2010, the CSRC found that Mr Kuang had negligently divulged inside information, and imposed a fine of RMB 30,000 on Mr Kuang for his negligent behaviour.

8.24 Although the above case shows the intensified effort of the CSRC to combat insider trading, it has arguably gone too far in allowing mere negligence to be the basis of insider trading liability. First, at the conceptual level, the term 'tipping' connotes a conscious transfer of inside information and thus blameworthiness. In the USA, tipping liability even further requires a 'personal benefit' test, namely 'whether the insider receives a direct or indirect personal benefit from the disclosure, such as a pecuniary gain or a reputational benefit that will translate into future earnings'.[38] Second, for the practical purpose, it would be simply too easy to attract insider trading liability on the basis of negligence, as overhearing or even eavesdropping is very hard to avoid in the real world. In contrast, for insider trading liability to arise under Rule10b-5 in the USA, there is a requirement of scienter. Although the term 'scienter' has never been clearly defined, it generally refers to intent and in some cases, recklessness, but certainly not mere negligence.[39]

8.3.3.2. *The 'use or possession' debate*

8.25 It is hardly surprising that for the purpose of insider trading liability, the precondition for those to be considered as insiders is that they actually possess inside information. In China, the statutory phrase 'persons with knowledge of inside information' (*Zhixi Neimu Xinxi de Zhiqing Renyuan*) under the Securities Law suggests that possession of inside information is required for insider trading liability to attach.[40] Further, for insider trading liability to occur, a necessary element is the defendant's knowledge of the nature of the information—more accurately, the

---

[36] Criminal Law, Art 14. The Criminal Law distinguishes between intentional crimes and negligent crimes. Criminal liability is to be imposed for negligent crimes only when the law explicitly stipulates: Criminal Law, Art 15.
[37] Criminal Law, Art 180.
[38] *Dirks v SEC*, 463 U.S. 646, 663 (1983).
[39] William KS Wang and Marc I Steinberg, *Insider Trading* 171 (Little, Brown, 1996).
[40] Securities Law, Art 74.

knowledge that the possessed information is material and non-public. In China, there are two tests for proving the defendant's knowledge that the information is inside information; namely, the subjective knowledge test to prove the insider 'knew', and the objective knowledge test to prove that the insider 'ought to have reasonably known'.[41]

8.26 While the possession requirement is conceptually straightforward, the crux of the issue lies in proving it. Indeed, the evidentiary problem has been regarded as the biggest difficulty facing Chinese regulators in fighting against insider trading. The CSRC has long tried to solve the issue by exploring the possibility of reversing the burden of proof.

8.27 The CSRC has gained strong support from the Supreme Court in this aspect. On 13 July 2011, the Supreme Court held a symposium on issues associated with conducting judicial review of the CSRC's administrative penalties for insider trading, and clearly supported the idea of reversing the burden of proof in such cases.[42] Further, on 1 June 2012, the newly issued Judicial Interpretation on Insider Trading Law in Criminal Cases made formal provision for reversal of burden of proof in the criminal prosecution of insider trading cases. Under Article 1 of this instrument, the types of insiders as enumerated in Article 74 of the Securities Law, such as directors and senior managers, will be presumed to possess relevant inside information; under Article 2, the same presumption of possession of inside information applies to close relatives of primary insiders, or people with other types of close relationships with primary insiders, or people who have contact with primary insiders during the sensitive period of the inside information, if their relevant transactions are 'obviously abnormal'.

8.28 Article 3 provides guidance on when transactions may be considered 'obviously abnormal'. In making such determination, one needs to take into account the totality of the circumstances, including the degree of time matching, the degree of trading deviation, and the degree of interest connectedness:

(1) The time at which an account is opened, an account is closed, a fund account is activated, or trading (custody) is designated or designated trading (custody transfer) is revoked is basically consistent with the time when the insider information is formed, changed, or disclosed.
(2) The time of funds change is basically consistent with the time when the insider information is formed, changed, or disclosed.
(3) The time at which the securities or futures contract related to insider information is purchased or sold is basically consistent with the time at which the insider information is formed, changed, or disclosed.

---

[41] Securities Law, Art 74.
[42] Zuigao Renmin Fayuan Guanyu Shenli Zhengquan Xingzheng Chufa Anjian Zhengju Ruogan Wenti de Zuotanhui Jiyao [Minutes of the Symposium Held by the Supreme Court on Various Issues Associated with Conducting Judicial Review of the Evidence in Securities Administrative Penalty Cases) (issued by the Supreme Court on 13 July 2011).

Regulation of Trading in Securities

(4) The time at which the securities or futures contract related to insider information is purchased or sold is basically consistent with the time at which the insider information is obtained.
(5) The purchase or sale of a securities or futures contract is clearly different from the normal trading habit.
(6) The purchase or sale of a securities or futures contract, or the intensive holding of a securities or futures contract, clearly deviates from the fundamentals reflected by the disclosed securities or futures information.
(7) The withdrawal from and deposit in the account are relevant to or have interest relations with the person who has access to or illegally obtains such insider information.
(8) Any other obviously abnormal transactions.

8.29 The above presumption of possession of inside information can be rebutted if the defendant can show that they have justifiable reasons or justified information sources for the seemingly abnormal transactions.

8.30 The next logical question is whether *mere possession* of inside information at the time of trading is sufficient for one to attract liability, or, more specifically, whether the imposition of liability requires a further showing that the insider actually *used* the information. In other words, is it required to prove a causal connection between the inside information possessed and the defendant's trading? This issue is well known as the 'possession versus use' debate in the US, and at the international level there are four different approaches to the issue: namely, the strict possession, strict use, modified use, and modified possession tests.[43]

8.31 It was not until a recent case in 2008 that the CSRC had the chance to decide on the above issue. In the case of *Deng Jun & Qu Li*,[44] Mr Deng and Mrs Qu were senior management of a company which was the target of a takeover. At the initial stage of the takeover negotiation, the bidder company sent two officers to the target company to do preliminary due diligence, and for confidentiality reasons the two officers did not disclose their identities. But Mr Deng and Mrs Qu managed to figure out who the two visitors were, and traded relevant shares at a profit. During the CSRC investigation, Mr Deng and Mrs Qu argued that they did not have knowledge of the takeover and, more importantly, that they traded shares not because of the alleged inside information but instead due to their independent research on the price movement of the relevant stock.[45] In response, the CSRC essentially

---

[43] See Hui Huang, 'The Insider Trading 'Possession versus Use' Debate: An International Analysis' 33 (2006) *Securities Regulation Law Journal* 130.
[44] Zhongguo Zhengjianhui Xingzheng Chufa Juedingshu (2008) No 46 [The Administrative Penalty Decision of the CSRC, 2008, No 46] (promulgated by the China Securities Regulatory Commission, November 10, 2008).
[45] The Administrative Penalty Commission of the CSRC, Explanations on Securities Administrative Penalty Cases 4 (2009).

adopted the modified use test, under which the actual use of inside information is a requisite element of liability but, in order to alleviate the evidentiary problem, a rebuttable inference of use applies to people in possession of inside information. As Mr Deng and Mrs Qu did not successfully adduce evidence to rebut the inference, they were held to have used the information to trade.

8.32 The CSRC's position has been supported by the judiciary in the recently issued Judicial Interpretation on Insider Trading Law in Criminal Cases. Article 4 of this instrument provides that a transaction conducted by a person in possession of inside information would not be treated as insider trading if the transaction was conducted according to a pre-existing written contract, plan, or instruction, or based on another legal source of information or other legal grounds.[46]

8.3.4. Comments: theoretical basis of China's insider trading law

8.33 The preceding discussion has provided an updated examination of the core elements of China's insider trading law in light of recent cases and, from a comparative perspective, pointed out some problems therein with respect to the scope of insiders, inside information, and subjective elements. At the fundamental level, those problems actually have their roots in confusion around the theory of insider trading liability in China.

8.34 As previously discussed, China's insider trading law has benefited greatly from overseas experiences, notably that of the USA. Unfortunately, however, China's legislators appear to have simply put all of them together without paying adequate attention to how they relate to each other and how they will function as a whole. Indeed, over time, under the general anti-fraud provision of Rule 10b-5, US courts have developed several different and even conflicting theories of insider trading liability, as will be seen.[47]

8.35 Initially, the equality-of-access theory was adopted in the *SEC v Texas Gulf Sulphur Co* case by the Second Circuit in 1968.[48] Under this theory, anyone with unequal access to inside information, whether they are corporate insiders or outsiders, has a duty of disclosure before trading; if they fail to disclose, they will breach the duty and thus Rule 10b-5. In 1980, however, the US Supreme Court replaced the quality of access theory with the classical theory in *Chiarella v United States*, under which insider trading liability under Rule 10b-5 occurs only when one party owes a fiduciary duty to the other party with whom he is trading.[49] The scope of the classical theory was further expanded to the tipping situation in *Dirks v SEC*, under which tippees can be held liable on the grounds that they have violated their

---

[46] Judicial Interpretation on Insider Trading Law in Criminal Cases, Art 4.
[47] For a detailed discussion of the evolution of USA insider trading jurisprudence from a comparative perspective, see Hui Huang, *International Securities Markets*, 297–303.
[48] 401 F.2d 833 (2d Cir. 1968), cert denied, 394 U.S. 976 (1969).
[49] 445 U.S. 222 (1980).

fiduciary duty, inherited from tippers/insiders who breached their fiduciary duty to disclose confidential information in the first place.[50] Finally, the US Supreme Court endorsed the misappropriation theory to complement the classical theory in *United States v O'Hagan*.[51] Under this theory, insider trading liability arises when insiders breach their fiduciary duty owed to the source of the inside information, as distinct from the party with whom they trade.

8.36 As discussed before, Article 73 generally provides that 'persons with knowledge of inside information on securities trading are prohibited from taking advantage of such inside information to engage in securities trading'. A literal reading of this article suggests that China adopts the equality-of-access theory. This implies that anyone with unequal access to inside information would be generally subject to the prohibition.

8.37 However, this above situation does not sit comfortably with Article 74 and Article 76. As discussed above, Article 74 curbs the broad nature of Article 73 by enumerating specific types of persons who are regarded as insiders. The list seems to be wholly based on the *Chiarella-Dirks* classical insider trading theory. First, it covers traditional insiders, such as directors, officers, and substantial shareholders. Second, constructive or temporary insiders—staff members of intermediaries, including underwriters, accountants, consultants, and lawyers—are also listed. Moreover, Article 76 essentially introduces the misappropriation theory by reference to 'other persons who have illegally obtained such insider information'.[52] Thus, it appears that Articles 74 and 76 have jointly imported the classical theory and the misappropriation theory, which are collectively called 'fiduciary-duty-based theories' by this author elsewhere.[53] It is thus not unfair to say that when enacting the Securities Law, China's legislators appear to have failed to fully understand the nature and function of the USA insider trading regime.

8.38 This is well illustrated in the recent controversy over the issue of front-running—a practice dubbed 'rat-trading' in China—where fund managers trade for their own accounts prior to placing an order for the fund, in order to take advantage of any change in the market price of financial instruments resulting from the order for the fund. The first such case reported in China was the *Tang Jian* case.[54] In March 2006, Mr Tang Jian, then the assistant fund manager of an influential fund management company in China, allegedly traded a stock ahead of the execution of his fund's order to purchase the same stock. As the fund's order involved a large quantity of the stock, the price of the stock rose significantly after completion of

---

[50] 463 U.S. 646 (1983).
[51] 521 U.S. 642 (1997).
[52] 521 U.S. 642 (1997).
[53] Hui Huang, *International Securities Markets*, 281.
[54] Zhongguo Zhengjianhui Xingzheng Chufa Juedingshu 2008 No 22 [The Administrative Penalty Decision of the CSRC, 2008, No 22] (promulgated by the China Securities Regulatory Commission, 8 April 2008).

the fund's order. Mr Tang then sold his stock in April 2006, reaping a big profit. He repeated this pattern of trading in May 2006.

This case generated considerable debate in China as to the nature of front-running. There is little doubt that Mr Tang, as a fund manager, stood in a fiduciary relationship with the unit holders of the fund, and therefore his behaviour in front-running the fund's order constituted a breach of fiduciary duty. Indeed, Mr Tang profited at the expense of the unit holders, because his personal trading may have increased the price at which the fund's order was executed. This problem also has a broad negative impact on investor confidence, as it undermines the integrity of the market. It is thus clear that front-running has harmful effects and should be regulated;[55] the more difficult question, however, is how to regulate it and, in particular, whether front-running is actually a form of insider trading and hence should be subject to insider trading law. **8.39**

In April 2008, the CSRC held that front-running was not insider trading (without providing any reasons in its ruling), and punished Mr Tang merely on the basis of his breach of fiduciary duty. At that time, breach of fiduciary duty only attracted administrative and civil liabilities, so Mr Tang did not receive criminal sanctions. This result was widely criticized as unsatisfactory, prompting the legislature, namely the National People's Congress (NPC), to hastily add a provision to the Criminal Law of the People's Republic of China to make front-running a criminal offence, on 28 February 2009.[56] **8.40**

The chaos surrounding the regulation of front-running could have been avoided if the CSRC had a better understanding of the underlying theories, and thus the functioning of, the overseas insider trading laws on which China's law is modelled. In the early 1990s, US commentators were already arguing that front-running could constitute insider trading under Rule 10b-5 based on the misappropriation theory, as the fund manager owes a fiduciary duty to the fund which is the source of the information about imminent orders.[57] This view was essentially adopted in a case decided in 2004, where a broker, knowing of a large imminent order from a client, put through a transaction on another client's behalf, thus benefiting from the pre-warning.[58] Similarly, in Australia, which adopts the insider trading theory of equality of access, front-running has long been seen as a form of insider trading, **8.41**

---

[55] For a detailed discussion of the theoretical bases for regulating front-running, see eg Jason Carley, 'The Future of Front-running' (1995) 13 *Company and Securities Law Journal* 434.
[56] Zhonghua Renmin Gongheguo Xingfa Xiuzhengan (7) [The Seventh Amendment to the Criminal Law of the PRC (Criminal Law)] (promulgated by the Standing Committee of the NPC, 28 February 2009).
[57] Mark S Howard, 'Front-running in the Marketplace: A Regulatory Dilemma' (1991) 19(263) *Securities Regulation Law Journal* 278.
[58] *United States v Martha Stewart and Peter Bacanovic*, 305 F. Supp. 2d 368 (S.D.N.Y. 2004). For a critique of this case, see Ray J Grzebielski, 'Why Martha Stewart Did Not Violate Rule 10b-5: On Tipping, Piggybacking, Front-running and the Fiduciary Duties of Securities Brokers' (2007) 40 *Akron Law Review* 55.

the rationale being that the front-runner enjoys unequal and privileged access to the information about large or market-sensitive orders.

8.42 As previously discussed, China's insider trading law appears to have transplanted both the equality-of-access theory and the fiduciary duty-based theories consisting of the classical theory and the misappropriation theory. However, the CSRC has failed to use either of them to deal with the issue of front-running, which has resulted in problems with the scope of China's insider trading regulation. In order for Chinese insider trading to be more effective, it is imperative that its theoretical basis be clarified and streamlined. This author has previously suggested that the equality-of-access theory is preferable to fiduciary duty-based theories, especially in the context of China.[59]

8.4. How Is the Law Enforced?

8.4.1. Overview of enforcement mechanisms

8.43 In China, there are generally three types of legal liability: administrative liability, civil liability, and criminal liability. However, in action against insider trading, only administrative and criminal liability are currently available. According to Article 202 of the Securities Law, administrative liability could be imposed in the case of insider trading:

> [The inside trader] shall be ordered to dispose of the illegally obtained securities according to law, his illegal gains shall be confiscated and, in addition, he shall be imposed a fine of not less than the amount of but not more than five times the illegal gains, or a fine of not more than the value of the securities illegally purchased or sold.[60]

8.44 Article 202 also provides that if an insider trading case is serious enough to constitute a crime, criminal liability shall be pursued.[61] Criminal liability is set out in detail in Article 180 of the Criminal Law, which states:

> [Inside traders] shall be sentenced to not more than five years in prison or criminal detention, provided the circumstances are serious. They shall be fined, additionally or exclusively, a sum not less than 100 percent and not more than 500 percent as high as their illegal proceeds. If the circumstances are especially serious, they shall be sentenced to not less than five years and not more than 10 years in prison. In addition, they shall be fined a sum not less than 100 percent and not more than 500 percent as high as their illegal proceeds.[62]

8.45 The newly issued Judicial Interpretation on Insider Trading Law in Criminal Cases provides further guidance as to what constitutes 'serious circumstances' and 'very serious circumstances' within the meaning of the above-mentioned Article 180 of

---

[59] Hui Huang, *International Securities Markets*, 281.
[60] Securities Law, Art 202.
[61] Securities Law, Art 202.
[62] Criminal Law, Art 180.

the Criminal Law. Circumstances that would be considered 'serious' include: (1) the cumulative trading amount of securities is more than 500,000 yuan; (2) the cumulative amount of used margin for futures trading is more than 300,000 yuan; (3) the cumulative amount of profits gained or losses avoided is more than 150,000 yuan; (4) insider trading is conducted or insider information is leaked more than three times; or (5) any other serious circumstance.[63] 'Very serious circumstances' include: (1) the cumulative trading amount of securities is more than 2,500,000 yuan; (2) the accumulative amount of used margin for futures trading is more than 1,500,000 yuan; (3) the cumulative amount of profits gained or losses avoided is more than 750,000 yuan; (4) any other very serious circumstance.[64]

8.46 Under the Securities Law, nothing has been said about private civil liability for insider trading, except for a simple provision that generally prioritizes private civil liabilities for all securities violations. Article 232 of the Securities Law reads: 'If the property of a person, who violates the provisions of this Law and who therefore bears civil liability for damages and is required to pay a fine, is insufficient to pay both the damages and the fine, such person shall first bear the civil liability for damages.'[65]

8.47 However, the Securities Law does not devote any specific provisions to civil damages payable to the aggrieved party by a person who has engaged in insider trading. No provisions in the Securities Law expressly address the issues concerning civil remedies, such as the standing of the plaintiff and measure of damages, rendering private civil liabilities virtually unavailable in practice and thus making Article 232 illusory.[66] To be sure, a private right of action could be theoretically based on the existing general contract law or on the tort regime. However, due to the special nature of insider trading—for example, the impersonality and anonymity of exchange transactions—it is extremely difficult, if not impossible, in terms of causation and reliance to assert insiders' liability on those conventional grounds.

8.4.2. Empirical data: cases from 1991 to 2011

8.4.2.1. Methodology

8.48 This Part endeavours to provide insights into the ways in which China's insider trading law has been enforced in practice. To this end, I examine all insider trading cases reported nationwide until the end of May 2011, covering a period of about 20 years since the birth of Chinese securities markets, as marked by the establishment

---

[63] Judicial Interpretation on Insider Trading Law in Criminal Cases, Art 6.
[64] Judicial Interpretation on Insider Trading Law in Criminal Cases, Art 7.
[65] Securities Law, Art 232.
[66] For an in-depth analysis of the issues concerning private civil liability for insider trading, see Hui Huang, 'Compensation for Insider Trading: Who should be Eligible Claimants?' (2006) 20 *Australian Journal of Corporate Law* 84.

of the two national stock exchanges in Shanghai and Shenzhen. I conducted an exhaustive search of relevant cases, using the following means.

8.49 To begin with, I accessed all reported decisions on administrative enforcement on the official website of the CSRC. According to Article 184 of the Securities Law, 'all the decisions reached by the [CSRC], on the basis of the results of its investigations, to impose penalties on illegal acts in relation to securities, shall be made public'.[67] The CSRC publicizes all of the cases it handles on its official website, which is freely accessible to all. The website provides a comprehensive source of information regarding enforcement action by the CSRC.

8.50 As the official website of the CSRC only contains administrative penalty decisions made by the CSRC, I then searched all reported insider trading cases adjudicated by the court in a widely used electronic database of Chinese law,[68] with search terms based on the relevant legislative provisions. This produced a very small number of criminal cases regarding insider trading. I discovered that this database is incomplete, for it omitted even some of the well-known cases. I therefore also searched media reports on the internet; this returned good results, which provided useful information about both closed and pending cases.

8.4.2.2. Empirical findings

8.51 The above search efforts produced a total of 39 cases, a number which is believed to be adequate to conduct statistical analysis. Each case in the data set was read and analysed according to the relevant research questions: (1) the year in which the case was heard; (2) the identity of the insider; (3) the nature of the inside information; (4) the use of criminal enforcement.

8.52 Table 1 divides the study period into several five-year windows in an effort to show temporal changes in the intensity of insider trading enforcement in China.[69] As the table shows, there are two peaks in the record of cases: during the 1996–2000 period and the 2006–2010 period, respectively.[70] This is evidence that insider trading is highly likely to happen in a bull market. The Chinese securities market experienced rapid development during these two periods. For instance, in 1996, the market went bullish and was so overheated that the government had to cool it down through a series of measures. China had another round of feverish bull

---

[67] Securities Law, Art 184.
[68] See http://Chinalawinfo.com.
[69] Note that each of the cases listed here involves either enforcement action by the CSRC or criminal prosecution in the court. There is a pattern that the CSRC does not bring enforcement action against insider trading once criminal enforcement is pursued. Thus, there is no duplication of cases in the data set, for no cases attracted both administrative penalty and criminal penalty. Further, there are a very small number of cases where private civil suits followed the public enforcement. These private civil suits are not included in order to avoid double-counting. For more discussion on private enforcement, see Part IV.C.
[70] Within the period from 2006 to 2010, the total number of 25 insider-trading cases shows a steady increase across the five years: one in 2007; four in 2008; six in 2009 and 14 in 2010.

Table 1 When was the case heard?

Time range	Number of cases	Percentage
1991–1995	2	5
1996–2000	7	18
2001–2005	3	8
2006–2010	25	64
2011–	2	5
Total	39	100

market from 2006 thanks to the state share reform, with the Shanghai Stock Exchange Composite Index surging from a low of 998 points on 6 June 2005 all the way up to a record high of 6,124 points on 16 October 2007.[71]

8.53 Two reasons can be advanced to explain the phenomena that insider trading is more likely to occur during periods of heightened market activities in a bull market. On the one hand, a bull market provides more opportunities for insider trading. In a bull market, share prices are highly volatile and there is a lot of investment activity. The volatility of the market offers more opportunity for profitable speculation such as insider trading. On the other hand, a bull market may make it safer to commit insider trading because the chance of detection becomes lower. Thus, the volatility in share prices encourages insider trading to a significant degree.

8.54 The surge in insider trading cases after 2006 is also evidence of the heightened enforcement effort by the CSRC to crack down on inside trading. In the past few years, the CSRC has made insider trading an emphasis of its enforcement action. For instance, the CSRC has improved its communication with the stock exchanges, so that the referral of suspected insider trading clues from the latter is more efficiently followed up by the former, and it prioritizes insider trading cases in allocating investigation resources. According to the CSRC's statistics, in the first half of 2011 the CSRC initiated a total of 83 investigations, 45 of which were related to insider trading. It is therefore likely that the number of reported insider trading cases after 2011 will grow significantly.

8.55 Table 2 examines the identity of the person(s) committing insider trading either by directly trading or by tipping others to trade. There are 51 cases listed, more than the overall number of cases, as some cases featured more than one insider defendant.[72] The table shows that traditional insiders, such as company directors, senior management, and officers, account for most of the insiders involved in the cases. However, there are also other types of insiders. In particular, up to five insiders in the cases

---

[71] See Shanghai Stock Exchange, http://www.sse.com.cn/sseportal/ps/zhs/home.html.
[72] Note that the number does not include secondary insiders, namely tippees. This is because the tippee is normally a spouse, relative, or friend of the primary insider/tipper, and usually has no relationship with the company whose shares were traded. Including tippees in the table would thus distort the picture of the persons likely to commit insider trading.

Table 2 Who was the insider?

Types of insiders	Number of cases	Percentage
Traditional insiders	36	70
Constructive insiders	5	10
Government officials	3	6
Listed companies themselves	3	6
Others	4	8
Total	51	100

Table 3 What was the inside information about?

Content of inside information	Number of cases	Percentage
Mergers and acquisitions	22	57
Major contracts or investments	6	15
Earnings	5	13
Dividend distribution plan	2	5
Capital increase	2	5
Others	2	5
Total	39	100

were investment bankers (so-called 'constructive insiders') who were retained to provide professional services and thus gained access to inside information.

8.56 It is also worth noting that in three cases, the listed companies themselves committed insider trading in relation to their own shares, but these cases are all before 2000. There is a discernible trend for more and more insider trading cases to involve individual insiders. Indeed, it is easier to detect insider trading committed by entities than by natural persons, because more people are involved in the former situation. This development suggests that insider trading is increasingly concealed and thus more difficult to detect.

8.57 Table 3 reveals that a majority of insider trading cases are based on inside information concerning mergers and acquisitions (M&A). This may be explained by at least three factors. The first is that takeovers always result in major price movements and thus create a favourable environment for committing insider trading. In the context of takeovers, insider trading is typically committed through buying shares ahead of information disclosure on takeovers and thereafter selling them at a profit. Second, the fact that many people are involved in preparing takeovers, and thus the relevant information may be easily leaked, increases the chances of insider trading. Finally, China's legal regime for M&A is far from effective, particularly in relation to information disclosure, providing a fertile breeding ground for insider trading.[73]

---

[73] For more discussion on China's takeover law, see Huang, 'The New Takeover Regulation in China: Evolution and Enhancement' (2008) 42 *The International Lawyer* 153.

Table 4 presents a significant finding about China's insider trading enforcement—namely, the aggressive use of criminal sanctions in recent years, particularly after 2008. Of the 39 insider trading cases examined in this study, criminal prosecutions were brought in up to ten cases, or about 26 per cent of all cases. **8.58**

It is fair to say that criminal prosecutions of insider trading have had a slow start in China—although criminal liability for insider trading has been available since 1997, it was not employed until 2003, in the *Shenshen Fang* case. In the ensuing five years there was only one other criminal insider trading case, namely the *Changjiang Konggu case*. This situation was criticized by many commentators—including this author—who called for greater use of criminal prosecutions to increase deterrent effects. Fortunately, since 2008, criminal prosecutions of insider trading have regained momentum. A spate of criminal cases has been reported and the penalties imposed therein are very severe, in some cases even by international standards. **8.59**

For instance, in the high-profile *Huang Guangyu* case, during the period from April to September 2007 Mr Huang bought RMB 1 billion worth of shares in a company called Beijing Zhongguancun, making use of inside information on the corporate restructuring of the said company. When the information was publicly disclosed and the share price rose accordingly, Mr Huang made a profit of RMB **8.60**

Table 4 How has criminal enforcement been used?

Case name	Year	Profit (Chinese yuan)	Penalty (Chinese yuan)	Decided or pending
Li Qihong case	2011	19,830,000		Pending
Tianshan Fangzhi case	2011	1,737,423.84	• Disgorgement of illegal profit; • fine of 3 million yuan • 3-year imprisonment	Decided
Huang Guangyu case	2010	306,000,000	• fine of 0.6 billion yuan • 9-year imprisonment	Decided
Guang Yawei case	2010	Not specified		Pending
Gao Yangcai case	2010	Not specified		Pending
Liu Baochun case	2010	About 7,000,000		Pending
Dong Zhengqing case	2009	22,846,712.42	• Disgorgement of illegal profit; • fine of 3 million yuan • 4-year imprisonment	Decided
Hangxiao Ganggou case	2008	40,370,000	• Disgorgement of illegal profit; • fine of 40,370,000 yuan • 2.5-year imprisonment	Decided
Changjiang Konggu case	2003	9,600,000	• Disgorgement of illegal profit; • fine of 100,000 yuan • 3-year imprisonment	Decided
Shenshen Fang case	2003	780,000	• Disgorgement of illegal profit; • fine of 800,000 yuan • 3-year imprisonment	Decided

0.3 billion on the book. However, he continued to hold the shares rather than sell them to realize the profit, and eventually suffered a huge loss of up to 65 per cent of the purchase value due to the share price plunge during the global financial crisis of 2008. In 2010, Mr Huang was sentenced to nine years in prison and fined RMB 0.6 billion (roughly US $93 million).[74] Two points are worth noting about this case. First, both the imprisonment term and the amount of monetary penalty are the highest so far in the history of China's insider trading enforcement. Second, this case suggests that insider trading liability may arise regardless of the actual result of the trading. This position has also been confirmed by the CSRC in its enforcement actions.[75]

8.4.3. Analysis and policy implications

8.61 The above empirical data shows that in recent years there has been a significant increase in the number of insider trading cases, with a growing tendency to use criminal sanctions. This comes as China has vowed to strengthen its enforcement efforts and launched a nationwide high-profile crackdown against insider trading. This is a very encouraging development in insider trading enforcement in China, but there is still more that needs to be done.

8.62 Indeed, although China's recent record of insider trading enforcement seems to compare favourably with that of the UK,[76] it clearly falls far behind that of the US, where, between 2001 and autumn 2006, over 300 insider trading enforcement actions were brought by the Securities and Exchange Commission (SEC) against over 600 individuals and entities.[77] Thus, the following text will discuss in more detail the issues of public and private enforcement, and set out policy recommendations to enhance the efficacy of China's insider trading law.

8.4.3.1. Public enforcement

8.63 In overseas jurisdictions, when examining the intensity of public enforcement, commentators often look at two aspects: enforcement outputs, namely enforcement actions brought and penalties imposed, and enforcement inputs, namely

---

[74] Note that Mr Huang was convicted of other crimes in addition to insider trading, and thus the overall imprisonment term is 14 years.

[75] See eg Zhongguo Zhengjianhui Xingzheng Chufa Juedingshu (Qu Xiang) 2008 No 49 [The Administrative Penalty Decision of the CSRC (Qu Xiang), 2008, No 49] (promulgated by the China Securities Regulatory Commission, 20 November 2008) (administrative penalty was imposed, even though the insider trading resulted in a loss rather than a profit).

[76] During the period from 2001 and 2007, the Financial Services Authority (FSA) in the UK reportedly brought only eight insider trading cases. See Grant Ringshaw, Hot on the Trail of the Insider Dealers, *Sunday Times* (London), 13 May 2007, Bus 8. Further, there had been few recorded criminal prosecutions of insider trading in the UK by 2007.

[77] Illegal Insider Trading: How Widespread Is the Problem and Is There Adequate Criminal Enforcement?: Hearing Before the S. Comm. on the Judiciary, 109th Cong 12 (2006) (statement of Linda Thompson, Director, Division of Enforcement, SEC).

the budget and staff size of the regulator.[78] These data are, of course, relevant in measuring enforcement intensity, but there is one more important dimension to the question, which is the institutional structure and governance framework of the regulator. Indeed, research focused exclusively on the inputs and outputs of enforcement implicitly treats the processor in the middle—ie the regulator—as a black box. This methodology may work only when the regulator can be sufficiently trusted in terms of its independence and accountability.

8.64 Where regulatory independence and accountability are in question, data on enforcement inputs and outputs may not tell the full story. There, even if the enforcement agency is seemingly strong both in terms of inputs (well-funded and well-staffed) and outputs (a good number of enforcement actions), one should not jump to any final conclusion, because the enforcement activity may be conducted in a dubious way. This unfortunately appears to be the case in China, as is illustrated in the following two examples.

8.65 The first example is the *Huang Guangyu case* discussed earlier. Mr Huang was once the richest self-made man in China, and even today is widely regarded as one of the most talented Chinese businessmen. In April 2009, having just turned 40, he was detained for market misconduct and attempted suicide in the detention centre. This was considered surprising, as Mr Huang reportedly had a very strong mind and had experienced many ups and downs in his life. Many believed that his suicide attempt was not due to the charge of market misconduct, but to political pressure. Indeed, soon after Mr Huang's detention, a number of high-ranking officials were detained and penalized, showing that Mr Huang was entangled in political corruption problems that were far more serious than mere commercial crimes. It was widely suspected that the background of the case had something to do with the severe penalty Mr Huang finally received for the commercial crimes.

8.66 The other case concerned Ms Li, who was then a regulatory official of the CSRC. It was reported that Ms Li and her husband divorced and had a bitter property dispute. In 2008, Ms Li's ex-husband and ex-mother-in-law reported to the CSRC that Ms Li had sent mobile messages containing inside information to her mother, and provided evidence such as call records and the trading account. Less than two days later, the CSRC responded that it had conducted an internal investigation and found no evidence of Ms Li committing insider trading. Despite strong calls from the public, the CSRC refused to comment on the evidence supplied by the informants, and no further investigation was carried out.

8.67 The above two cases provide some useful information which cannot be obtained from the data on enforcement inputs and outputs. To be sure, it is important to give more resources—such as funding and staff—to the regulator in order to enhance

---

[78] Howell Jackson and Mark J Roe, 'Public and Private Enforcement of Securities Laws: Resource-Based Evidence' (2009) 93 *Journal of Financial Economics* 207.

8.4.3.2. Private enforcement

8.68 The picture of securities law enforcement would not be complete without consideration of the issue of private enforcement. There has been international debate on the utility of private enforcement vis-à-vis public enforcement of securities law. Some have argued that private enforcement has played a more important role than public enforcement in the development of securities markets, while others found dominance of public enforcement over private enforcement. Regardless of the relative performance of public and private enforcement, it is generally accepted that private enforcement is a necessary and appropriate supplement to governmental enforcement to deter insider trading. If this is the case even in the US, where the SEC is relatively well-resourced and efficient, it should be more so in China where, as discussed, public enforcers may fail to act due to a lack of independence and accountability, in addition to the general issue of resource constraints.

8.69 As noted earlier, although the Securities Law in principle provides for private action against insider trading, the functioning of that system is hampered by the absence of detailed implementing rules. Indeed, in the open-market setting, private civil liability for insider trading has long raised some extremely difficult questions. In the US, this problem has been aptly captured by Professor Clark, who has pointed out:

> Once a private right of action under Rule 10b-5 was implied and recognized, there was bound to be a period of painful growth, as the courts struggled to give shape and meaning to the standard list of elements of a tort action as applied to the new context. Who was to have standing to bring private actions? Who could be sued? What exactly would constitute the duty imposed? What would be needed to show a violation of the duty and causation of injury? What would the measure of damages be?[79]

8.70 If western judges, who are usually chosen from among leading lawyers in relevant areas, find it difficult to handle the complex issues of private enforcement of insider trading law, then Chinese judges, who are ill-equipped in terms of education and experience, may only find it harder. This situation has been well illustrated in the three circulars issued by the Supreme People's Court of China (SPC) in relation to the hearing of civil cases arising from securities fraud. First, on 21 September 2001, the SPC issued a circular refusing to accept civil remedy cases over securities frauds such as misrepresentation, market manipulation, and insider trading, stating that

---

[79] Robert C Clark, *Corporate Law* 316 (Little, Brown & Company, 1986). For a detailed discussion of the technical issues of private litigation against insider trading, see Huang, 'Compensation for Insider Trading'.

the judiciary did not have the necessary expertise and resources to hear those difficult cases. Due to mounting public pressure, however, the SPC soon issued an additional circular on 15 January 2002 agreeing in principle to accept and hear civil cases arising from securities misrepresentation, and further, on 9 January 2003, issued a circular to provide detailed rules on the hearing of such cases.

Importantly, under the two SPC circulars issued in 2002 and 2003, it is clearly stipulated that securities civil cases can be brought against misrepresentation only, to the exclusion of other types of securities fraud such as insider trading. On 30 May 2007, however, Mr Xi Xiaoming, the vice-president of the SPC, stated at a national conference on the adjudication of civil and commercial cases that courts should also accept securities civil cases arising from insider trading and market manipulation. Mr Xi's statement was later distributed as an official SPC document to courts at all levels across the nation. Since then, there have been some attempts to bring civil cases in the context of insider trading. 8.71

On 4 September 2008, *Chen Ningfeng v Chen Jianliang*, the first civil compensation case over insider trading, was heard before the Intermediate People's Court of Nanjing. This civil case piggybacked on an administrative penalty decision by the CSRC previously imposed on Mr Chen Jianliang for insider trading.[80] Significantly, the hearing of the civil case was conducted and ended in an unusual way. First, only Mr Song Yixin, the attorney for the plaintiff, appeared at the hearing; the plaintiff, the defendant, and the attorney for the defendant were all absent. Second, an assistant to the attorney for the defendant delivered to the court a statement from the plaintiff requesting the withdrawal of the suit. Third, the plaintiff's statement was made without the knowledge of the plaintiff's own attorney. Finally, the court allowed the case to be withdrawn. 8.72

In comparison, the 2009 case of *Chen Zuling v Pan Haishen* produced the first judgment on a civil claim for insider trading in China.[81] Like the case just discussed, this case followed an administrative penalty decision by the CSRC against Mr Pan Haishen for insider trading. Since the CSRC had earlier found Mr Pan guilty of insider trading, the court went directly to examine the issues specific to civil claims—in particular, whether there was causation between the plaintiff's trading and the defendant's insider trading. In this case, the defendant's insider trading took place on 16 April 2007, more than two months before the plaintiff's trading on 18 June 2007. Further, the plaintiff did not suffer a loss but rather made a profit from his trading. In the end, the court rejected the case, on the grounds that no causal link existed between the plaintiff's trading and the defendant's insider trading. 8.73

---

[80] Zhongguo Zhengjianhui Xingzheng Chufa Juedingshu 2007 No 15 [Administrative Penalty Decision by the CSRC, 2007, No 15] (promulgated by the China Securities Regulatory Commission, 28 April 2007).
[81] Chen Zuling v Pan Haishen (2009) Yi Zhong Min Chu Zi No 8217 (Civil Judgment, The First Intermediate Court of Beijing, 2009).

8.74 Although those two cases did not succeed, their significance should not be understated. They have opened the door to civil action against insider trading, attracting considerable social attention to the new concept of private enforcement of insider trading regulation in China. Indeed, more cases have been filed recently for civil remedies against insider trading, including those based on the high-profile insider trading case of *Huang Guangyu* previously discussed. These cases are representative of the tendency for public and private enforcement to be used on a cumulative and overlapping basis. This is a welcome development in terms of increasing the deterrent threat for insider trading, as well as generating some compensation for aggrieved investors. For instance, in the case of *Chen Ningfeng v Chen Jianliang*, it is likely that the defendant had offered compensation to the plaintiff privately outside the court in return for the plaintiff's withdrawal of the case.

8.75 On the other hand, there is much left to be desired in relation to private enforcement of insider trading regulation in China. The bringing of civil cases against insider trading has a shaky legal basis: such cases are allowed only under a conference speech of a SPC vice-president, while the two formal circulars issued in 2002 and 2003 remain unchanged in their statement that only cases arising from misrepresentation can be accepted. Further, the conference speech previously noted simply calls for the courts to accept securities civil cases arising from insider trading, without providing detailed guidance on how such cases should be adjudicated. Indeed, civil suits against insider trading involve some different and more complicated issues than those in the context of misrepresentation. It is thus imperative that, like the circular issued in 2003 on civil cases arising from misrepresentation, a new circular be formally issued to clarify the rights of action and provide detailed rules with respect to civil cases arising from insider trading.

8.5. Conclusion

8.76 It is fair to say that, 20 years on, China has made great achievements in gradually setting up a regulatory regime for insider trading in line with international experiences. There are, however, remaining problems and uncertainties in relation to some of the key elements of insider trading regulation, such as the types of insiders, the scope of inside information, and the requisite state of mind. These problems arise essentially due to the confusion surrounding the theoretical basis of China's insider trading law, which borrows from various overseas experiences without paying adequate attention to their mutual relationships and compatibility with local conditions in China.

8.77 In recent years China's securities markets have experienced significant developments, such as the introduction of index futures, which provide new opportunities for committing insider trading and thus new challenges for the regulator. This has prompted Chinese authorities to strengthen their efforts to crack down on insider trading, making more use of criminal sanctions and increasing the level of penalties. As a result, there has been a surge in the number of insider trading cases since 2006. This body of cases provides insights into how the law has been interpreted and enforced in practice. It is found, for instance, that methods of committing insider trading have become increasingly concealed and sophisticated, making it more difficult for regulators to detect insider trading, and that a majority of insider trading cases have occurred in the context of M&A.

8.78 Despite recent progress on the enforcement front, more needs to be done. Apart from the obvious suggestion to give more resources to the regulator, the issues of regulatory independence and accountability must be properly addressed in order to ensure the integrity and efficacy of public enforcement. This is particularly important in a transitional and emerging market like China, where the rule of law is yet to be fully established. On the other hand, private enforcement is an integral part of the enforcement picture, no matter how important it is relative to public enforcement. It is particularly important in China, as it may help to mitigate the issues of regulatory independence and accountability. At present, however, private civil suits against insider trading are operating in a legal limbo due to the lack of implementing rules. Finally, as well as *ex post* enforcement, it is also important to have in place an effective system of *ex ante* prevention, such as improving the legal regime for information disclosure and strengthening internal control systems of relevant entities to prevent abuse of inside information.

9

SECURITIES INVESTMENT FUND

9.1. Introduction	9.01	9.3.4. Modification and termination of the fund contract and liquidation of fund assets	9.79
9.2. Organizational Structure of the SIF	9.07		
9.2.1. Overview	9.07	9.3.5. Exercise of rights by fund shareholders	9.83
9.2.2. The fund manager	9.15		
9.2.3. The fund custodian	9.39	9.4. Non-publicly Offered Fund	9.88
9.2.4. Fund unit-holders	9.47	9.4.1. The definition of a non-publicly offered fund	9.88
9.3. Publicly Offered Fund	9.55	9.4.2. The offering process	9.91
9.3.1. Public offering	9.55	9.4.3. Other issues	9.96
9.3.2. Fund share trading, subscription, and redemption	9.66	9.5. Fund Services Institutions	9.98
		9.5.1. Overview	9.98
9.3.3. Investment of a publicly offered fund and information disclosure	9.71	9.5.2. Types of fund services institutions	9.102
		9.6. Fund Association	9.115

9.1. Introduction

9.01 The term 'securities investment funds' (*zhengquan touzi jijin*, hereafter SIF) is used in China to refer to a type of collective investment arrangement under which money is pooled from public investors and then entrusted to professional managers to make investments in a variety of securities on behalf of the investors. China's SIF industry has quite a short history. The first two SIFs were formally established in 1991, in Shenzhen and Wuhan, respectively. The industry has since grown rapidly, and as of May 2013 there were 1,317 funds and 81 fund management companies.[1]

9.02 There are three important features of SIFs. First, SIFs are a form of indirect investment, in that public investors invest their money through market intermediaries. Second, they provide a service of expert management for public investors. Third, as the name suggests, the funds invest in publicly offered securities, including shares, debentures, and their derivatives, as well as money-market products such as treasury bills and commercial paper. This is to be contrasted with the so-called

---

[1] CSRC website http://www.csrc.gov.cn/pub/newsite.

industry investment fund (*chanye touzi jijin*), which channels money to productive enterprises in the real economy.

9.03 SIFs have several important economic functions. First, by pooling the assets of dispersed investors, SIFs allow investors to gain lower-cost access to the expertise of professional mangers. Clearly, it may not be cost-effective for an individual investor with a small investment to pay for the services of professional mangers. An SIF can achieve economies of scale in that it aggregates financial resources from investors and entrusts them to the professional manager to operate. As such, the cost of expert management is shared among many investors. Second, by way of the SIF, investors gain lower-cost access to the advantages of wide diversification of ownership in the securities market. Again, it is not cost-effective for most individual investors to achieve adequate diversification. Third, the SIF provides small investors with investment opportunities which would otherwise be unavailable. Some investment opportunities, for instance, may be open only to institutional investors or require a minimum amount of investment. Finally, the SIF reduces other transaction costs for securities investment, such as brokerage.

9.04 China's first national law on SIF, namely the Securities Investment Fund Law of the PRC (2003 SIF Law), was issued on 28 October 2003 to provide a relatively complete legal framework for the establishment and management of securities investment funds in China.[2] This law was recently revised on 28 December 2012 and was effective from 1 June 2013 (2012 SIF Law).[3] Judging by the number of provisions which have been amended, the 2012 reform is sweeping in scope. Specifically, the 2003 SIF Law had 103 provisions; of these, three were deleted, 74 amended, and 55 new provisions added.

9.05 As well as the 2012 SIF Law, which applies specifically to securities investment funds, other relevant laws apply in this field. To start with, the listing and trading of the units of SIFs is subject to the Securities Law, unless other laws or administrative regulations have special rules.[4] Further, as shall be discussed later, China's SIFs mostly adopt a trust structure, and as such the Trust Law of the PRC applies as a general law to the trust-based funds.

9.06 The China Securities Regulatory Committee (CSRC) is the securities regulatory authority in China and hence has power to regulate the activities of the SIF.[5] Responsibility for regulating the manager of the SIF is assigned to different regulators, however, depending on who the manager is. For publicly offered SIFs, the

---

[2] Zhonghua Renming Gongheguo Zhengquan Touzi Jijin Fa [Securities Investment Fund Law of the PRC] (promulgated on 28 October 2003) (2003 SIF Law).
[3] Zhonghua Renming Gongheguo Zhengquan Touzi Jijin Fa [Securities Investment Fund Law of the PRC] (promulgated on 28 October 2003, amended 28 December 2012) (2012 SIF Law).
[4] Zhonghua Renming Gongheguo Zhenquan Fa [Securities Law of the People's Republic of China (Securities Law)] (promulgated by the Standing Commission of the National People's Congress, 29 December 1998, effective 1 July 1999, amended in 2004, 2005 and 2013), Art 2.
[5] 2012 SIF Law, Art 11.

manager may be a fund management company or other entity approved by the CSRC, such as a securities company.[6] For privately offered SIFs, the role of manager can be played by an even wider variety of entities, such as a privately offered fund manager, insurance asset management company, or trust company. Consequently, the regulator for the SIF manager is not limited to the CSRC, but may be any financial regulator, including the China Banking Regulatory Committee (CBRC) or China Insurance Regulatory Commission (CIRC).[7] This is because, as discussed in preceding chapters, China's current financial regulatory framework is sector-based, with separate regulators responsible for banking, securities, and insurance.[8]

9.2. Organizational Structure of the SIF

9.2.1. Overview

9.07 From an organizational perspective, there are two different forms of SIFs operating in the global financial markets: the corporate form and the contractual/trust form.[9]

9.08 In the US, SIFs are more commonly known as mutual funds; the vast majority of these are organized as corporations and thus called corporate funds.[10] The corporate fund has the standard corporate structure with relevant corporate organs. Investors are shareholders of the corporate fund and can vote to elect a board of directors, whose function is to oversee the operations of the fund and review contractual arrangements with outside service providers, namely investment advisers. The assets of the corporate fund are typically managed by the investment adviser, who can be a person or company, pursuant to an advisory agreement between the fund and the adviser. In practice, it is usually the adviser that forms the fund and causes the initial directors to be elected. Then, as in an ordinary industrial corporation, the corporate fund's board of directors, including independent directors, has the power to decide to issue shares to the public and enter into an advisory agreement with the adviser.

9.09 Alternatively, the SIF can be established under contract or trust law, and thus referred to as a contractual/trust fund. This contractual/trust form is widely adopted in jurisdictions such as the UK, Germany, and Japan. Although there are some differences between the contractual/trust forms in different jurisdictions,

---

[6] 2012 SIF Law, Art 12.
[7] 2012 SIF Law, Art 32.
[8] See Chapter 2.
[9] Wallace Wen Yeu Wang, 'Corporate versus Contractual Mutual Funds: An Evaluation of Structure and Governance' (1994) 69 *Washington Law Review* 927; Feng Guo and Xia Chen et al, *Zhengquan Touzi Jijinfa Daolun [Introduction to the Securities Investment Fund Law]* (Beijing: Law Press, 2008), 86–90.
[10] Mutual funds can also take other forms such as partnership and trust. Investment Company Act of 1940 (US), 15 U.S.C. §80a.

they share a key common feature of being based on contractual arrangements rather than a centralized corporate hierarchy.

9.10 In Japan, the fund comprises three parties, including investors, a manager (usually a management company), and a trustee (usually a trust company or bank). The investors acquire fund shares publicly issued by the manager under a prospectus, and thus the money contributed forms the fund asset pool. The manager and the trustee enter into a trust agreement for the benefit of the investors, under which the manager is responsible for the management of the fund assets while the trustee has responsibility for safekeeping of the fund assets. It should be noted that as the investors are not a party to the trust agreement, they cannot sue the manager directly on the basis of the trust agreement. However, since the manager has a statutory fiduciary duty in relation to the fund assets, the investors can bring action against the manager for breach of fiduciary duties.

9.11 In Germany, however, there are usually two contracts involved in the structure of the fund. First, the investor and the manager enter into a contract under which the investor entrusts money to the manager for investment and the latter must keep the fund's assets separate from its own assets and those of other funds it controls. Second, the manager enters into a contract with a custodian bank whereby the latter agrees to administer and keep custody of the fund assets for the benefit of the fund unit-holders. Similarly, since the investors are not a party to this custody contract, they cannot claim rights directly against the custodian bank.

9.12 In the UK, SIFs are called unit trusts and are structured under trust law. There is typically a trust deed between a trustee and a manager: the money contributed by investors is held in trust, the manager manages the fund assets, and the trustee is responsible for monitoring the performance of the manager. Under this trust deed, the manager and the trustee work together for the benefit of the investors, who are both trustor and beneficiary.

9.13 From a comparative institutional perspective there are a number of structural differences between the corporate fund and the contractual fund, in terms of how the fund allocates decision-making power and control among its relevant stakeholders. For instance, in the case of the corporate fund the board of directors is the focus while in the case of the contractual fund, the focus is the manager; the corporate fund is characterized by broad delegation of discretionary authority to the board of directors, while the contractual fund relies more on rules than on discretion, with the fund contract containing standard and specific rules; compared to the corporate fund, the contractual fund depends much less on investor voting.

9.14 Naturally, each of the two fund forms has its respective advantages and disadvantages. For various reasons—particularly the influence of Hong Kong law, which follows UK law—China has adopted the contractual fund as the main structural form for SIFs, composed of a manager, a custodian, and unit-holders. Two points should be noted here. First, this trilateral contractual arrangement is mandated for publicly offered funds (*gongkai muji jijin*) but optional for non-publicly offered funds (*feigongkai muji jijin*), which are also called privately offered funds (*simu jijin*). For instance, privately offered funds can choose not to have a custodian. Second, aside from the contractual form, the 2012 SIF Law also allows a fund, whether publicly offered or not, to be set up as a company or a partnership.[11]

9.2.2. The fund manager

9.15 As noted above, the manager plays a central role in the establishment and operation of the contractual fund, and hence the 2012 SIF Law contains a total of 21 provisions on the manager, compared to 12 provisions on the custodian and four provisions on the unit-holder meeting.

9.16 The SIF manager should be a company or a partnership.[12] This means that an individual cannot act as the SIF manager. Further, the manager of a publicly offered SIF must be a fund management company or other institution approved by the CSRC. The latter group of 'other institutions' may include securities firms, insurance asset management companies, and even the institutions managing privately offered funds. The 2012 SIF Law contains provisions to regulate the manager of publicly offered funds, while managers for non-publicly offered funds are subject to the specific measures developed by the various financial regulatory authorities of the State Council, including the CBRC and CIRC, in accordance with the regulatory principles governing the manager for publicly offered funds.[13]

9.2.2.1 The formation of the fund management company

9.17 Under Article 13 of the 2012 SIF Law, if a fund management company is formed to manage publicly offered funds, it needs to meet certain conditions and be approved by the CSRC. The conditions include: (1) The fund management company's bylaws comply with the 2012 SIF Law and the Company Law of the People's Republic of China; (2) The registered capital of the fund management company must be paid-in monetary capital which is not less than 100 million yuan; (3) The major shareholder of the fund management company must have good business performance, financial conditions, and social reputation in conducting financial business or managing financial institutions, have assets reaching the standards prescribed by the State Council, and have no record of any violation of law in the past three years; (4) The number of employees qualified to engage in the fund business of the fund management company satisfies the statutory requirement; (5) The directors, supervisors, and senior executives of the fund management company meet the corresponding office conditions; (6) The fund management company has business

---

[11] 2012 SIF Law, Art 154.
[12] 2012 SIF Law, Art 12.
[13] 2012 SIF Law, Art 32.

premises and security protection facilities satisfying the relevant requirements and other facilities related to its fund management business; (7) The fund management company has a sound internal governance structure and adequate and effective internal auditing and monitoring rules and risk control rules; (8) Other conditions prescribed by laws and administrative regulations and by the CSRC with the approval of the State Council.

9.18 The application for establishing a fund investment company should be made to the CSRC. The CSRC shall, within six months after accepting an application for the formation of a fund management company, conduct examination according to the conditions set out in Article 13 of the 2012 SIF Law and under the principle of prudent supervision, make an approval or disapproval decision, and notify the applicant of the decision; in the case of disapproval, it shall explain the reasons for the disapproval.

9.19 Further, where a fund management company intends to modify a shareholder holding 5 per cent or more of the equity in the company, modify its actual controller, or modify any other major matter, the fund management company shall apply to the CSRC for approval. The CSRC shall, within 60 days after accepting the application, make an approval or disapproval decision and notify the applicant of the decision; in the case of disapproval, it shall explain the reasons for the disapproval.

9.2.2.2 *The qualifications of the employees of the fund management company*

9.20 The 2012 SIF Law takes both a positive and a negative approach to the qualifications of employees of the fund management company. On the positive side, the director, supervisor, or senior executive of a fund management institution for a publicly offered fund shall be familiar with securities investment laws and administrative regulations and have three or more years of work experience relevant to the position held, and a senior executive shall also be qualified for engaging in the fund business.[14]

9.21 On the negative side, under any of the following circumstances, a person shall not serve as a director, supervisor, senior executive, or any other employee of a fund management institution for a publicly offered fund:

(1) The person has received a criminal penalty for embezzlement, bribery, malfeasance, property encroachment, or disruption of the order of the socialist market economy.
(2) The person is personally liable for the bankruptcy liquidation of a company or enterprise due to poor business management or for the forfeiture of the business licence of a company or enterprise due to any violation of law, in which the person served as a director, supervisor, factory director, or senior

---

[14] 2012 SIF Law, Art 16.

executive, and it has not been five years since the date of completion of bankruptcy liquidation or the date of forfeiture of business licence.
(3) The person fails to repay a large amount of personal debt upon maturity.
(4) The person is an employee of a fund management institution, a fund custodian, a stock exchange, a securities company, a securities depository and clearing institution, a futures exchange, a futures company, or any other institution or an employee of a government agency from which the person has been dismissed for any violation of law.
(5) The person is a lawyer, a certified public accountant, an employee of an asset appraisal or verification institution, or an investment advisory employee who has forfeited his or her practising licence or who has been disqualified for any violation of law.
(6) The person is otherwise prohibited by any law or administrative regulation from engaging in the fund business.[15]

9.22 Further, the appointment or modification of the legal representative, chief executive officer, or chief compliance officer of a fund management institution for a publicly offered fund shall be subject to the approval of the CSRC in accordance with the office conditions prescribed by this Law and other relevant laws and administrative regulations.

9.2.2.3 The functions and duties of the fund management institution for a publicly offered fund

9.23 The fund management institution is the focus of the SIF, and in the case of a publicly offered fund it performs the following functions: (1) raising capital in accordance with law and handling the sale and registration of fund shares; (2) undergoing recording procedures for the fund; (3) applying separate management and separate accounts to the assets of different funds under management and making securities investments; (4) determining the income distribution of the fund according to the provisions of the fund contract and distributing income to the fund shareholders in a timely manner; (5) conducting fund accounting and preparing the fund's financial accounting reports; (6) preparing the fund's semi-annual and annual reports; (7) calculating and publishing the net asset value of the fund and determining the subscription and redemption prices for fund shares; (8) handling information disclosure regarding the management of fund assets; (9) convening the fund shareholders' meeting according to the relevant provisions; (10) preserving records, account books, statements and other materials regarding the management of fund assets; (11) exercising litigation rights or taking other legal actions in the name of the fund management institution for the benefit of the fund shareholders; (12) other functions prescribed by the CSRC.[16]

---

[15] 2012 SIF Law, Art 15.
[16] 2012 SIF Law, Art 20.

As the trustee of the SIF, the fund management institution is generally subject to **9.24** fiduciary duties in performing its functions. In the case of a publicly offered fund, the fund management institution and its directors, supervisors, senior executives, and other employees are prohibited from doing the following:

(1) Mixing the institution's or such a person's own assets or the assets of others with fund assets to engage in securities investment.
(2) Unfairly treating the assets of different funds under management.
(3) Seeking any benefit for any party other than the fundshare holders by using fund assets or taking advantage of his or her position.
(4) Illegally promising the fund shareholders any income or assumption of losses.
(5) Embezzling or misappropriating fund assets.
(6) Divulging any undisclosed information obtained by taking advantage of his or her position or using such information to engage or explicitly or implicitly advise any other person to engage in the relevant trading activities.
(7) Neglecting duties or failing to perform duties as required.
(8) Acting otherwise as prohibited by any law or administrative regulation or the provisions of the CSRC.[17]

Importantly, the sixth limb of the above provision is a direct response to the issue **9.25** of front-running, where fund managers trade for their own account prior to placing an order for the fund, to take advantage of any change in the market price of financial instruments resulting from the order for the fund. This problem is dubbed 'rat-trading' (*Laosu Cang*) in China, and has become increasingly serious in China's SIF industry. The first such case reported in China is the *Tang Jian* case,[18] which is discussed in detail in the previous chapter.[19]

In the end, the CSRC punished Mr Tang on the basis of the general provision against **9.26** breach of fiduciary duties in the 2003 SIF Law. At that time, however, breach of fiduciary duty only attracted relatively mild administrative and civil liabilities, and Mr Tang did not receive criminal sanctions. This result was widely criticized as unsatisfactory, prompting the legislature, namely the National People's Congress (NPC), to hastily add a provision to the Criminal Law of the People's Republic of China to make front-running a criminal offence on 28 February 2009.[20] However, this new addition to the Criminal Law cannot deal with all front-running problems, because it applies only when the front-running problem is serious enough to trigger the application of the Criminal Law. Hence, the 2012 SIF Law introduced the above Article 21(6) to specifically regulate the front-running problem.

---

[17] 2012 SIF Law, Art 21.
[18] The Administrative Penalty Decision of the CSRC (2008) No 22.
[19] Chapter 8, para 8.38.
[20] Zhonghua Renmin Gongheguo Xingfa Xiuzhengan (7) [The Seventh Amendment to the Criminal Law of the PRC] (issued by the Standing Committee of the NPC on 28 February 2009).

9.27 Further, relevant provisions are set out to require the avoidance of conflicts of interest for the directors, supervisors, senior executives, and other employees of a fund management institution for a publicly offered fund. First, they shall not hold any positions in a fund custodian or another fund management institution and shall not conduct any securities trading or other activities that cause damage to fund assets and the interests of the fund shareholders.[21]

9.28 Second, under Article 18 of the 2012 SIF Law, they shall declare to the fund management institution in advance any securities investment to be made by them, their spouses, or any interested parties, without any conflicts of interest with the fund shareholders.[22] There is no further guidance on what is meant by 'interested parties', but the term should include relatives, friends, and other people who are closely related to the directors, supervisors, senior executives, and other employees of a fund management institution and their spouses in terms of supplying money for securities trading or sharing profits of the trading.

9.29 In fact, the above provision represents a relaxation of the previous strict prohibition on employees of a fund management institution trading securities. Under Article 43 of the current 2005 Securities Law, practitioners in stock exchanges, securities companies, and securities registration and clearing institutions, functionaries of securities regulatory bodies, and any other personnel who have been prohibited by any law or administrative regulation from engaging in any stock trading shall not, within their tenures or the relevant statutory term, hold or purchase or sell any stock directly or in any assumed name or in the name of any other person; nor may they accept any stocks from any other person as a present. This broad prohibition however has never been rigorously enforced in practice, probably because it is too draconian and not well suited to the commercial reality. Hence, the 2012 SIF Law takes a more reasonable approach under which securities trading is no longer simply prohibited but is subject to a regime of disclosure and approval.

9.30 Finally, in the spirit of fiduciary duties, the shareholders, directors, supervisors, and senior executives of a fund management institution for a publicly offered fund shall exercise rights or perform duties under the principle of giving priority to the interests of the fund shareholders.[23]

9.31 The shareholders and actual controller of a fund management institution for a publicly offered fund shall perform their obligations to report major events in a timely manner in accordance with the provisions of the CSRC, and shall not: (1) make any false capital contribution or illegally withdraw any capital contribution; (2) intervene in the fund business of the fund management institution without

---

[21] 2012 SIF Law, Art 19.
[22] 2012 SIF Law, Art 18.
[23] 2012 SIF Law, Art 22.

Investment Fund

authorization by a resolution of the shareholders' meeting or board of directors of the fund management institution; (3) require the fund management institution to seek any benefits for them or any other person by using fund assets, damaging the interests of the fund shareholders; and (4) act otherwise as prohibited by the provisions of the CSRC.[24]

9.2.2.4 Sanctions and remedies

9.32 Where a fund management institution for a publicly offered fund violates any law or regulation or there is any noncompliance in its internal governance structure, auditing and monitoring, or risk control management, the CSRC shall order the fund management institution to make correction during a prescribed period; if the fund management institution fails to do so, or its conduct seriously endangers its robust operation or infringes upon the lawful rights and interests of the fund shareholders, the CSRC may, as the case may be, take the following measures against the fund management institution:

(1) Restricting its business activities and ordering suspension of a part or all of its business.
(2) Restricting its dividend distribution and restricting its payment of remuneration and provision of welfare to its directors, supervisors, and senior executives.
(3) Restricting it from transferring its own assets or creating any other right in its own assets.
(4) Ordering it to replace any of its directors, supervisors, and senior executives or restricting their rights.
(5) Ordering the relevant shareholder to transfer the equity held or restricting the relevant shareholder from exercising the shareholder's rights.

9.33 The fund management institution for a publicly offered fund shall, after making rectification, submit a report to the CSRC. The CSRC shall, after verifying that the fund management institution satisfies the relevant requirements, remove the relevant measures taken against the institution within three days from the date of completion of the verification.[25]

9.34 Where any director, supervisor, or senior executive of a fund management institution for a publicly offered fund fails to diligently perform his or her duties, thus causing the fund management institution to incur any material violation of any law or regulation or any material risk, the CSRC may order his or her replacement.

9.35 Further, where a fund management institution for a publicly offered fund engages in any illegal business operation or has incurred any material risk seriously disturbing the order of the securities market or infringing upon the interests of the fund

---

[24] 2012 SIF Law, Art 24.
[25] 2012 SIF Law, Art 25.

shareholders, the CSRC may take regulatory measures against the fund management institution, such as ordering it to cease business suspension for rectification, designating a custodial or receivership institution for it, disqualifying it for fund management, or administratively dissolving it.[26] During the period in which a fund management institution for a publicly offered fund is ordered to cease business operation for rectification, a custodial or receivership institution is legally designated for it or it is liquidated, or it incurs any material risk, the following measures may be taken against the directly responsible directors, supervisors, and senior executives and other directly liable persons of the fund management institution with the approval of the CSRC: (1) notifying the exit administrative authority to prevent them from exiting China in accordance with law; (2) requesting the judicial authority to prohibit them from displacing, transferring, or otherwise disposing of their respective assets or creating any other right in their respective assets.[27]

9.2.2.5 The termination of the manager role

9.36 Under any of the following circumstances, the functions of a fund management institution for a publicly offered fund shall terminate:

(1) Being disqualified for fund management in accordance with law.
(2) Being dismissed by the fund shareholders' meeting.
(3) Being dissolved, administratively dissolved, or declared bankrupt in accordance with law.
(4) Any other circumstances as agreed upon in the fund contract.[28]

9.37 Where the functions of a fund management institution for a publicly offered fund terminate, the fund shareholders' meeting shall appoint another fund management institution within six months, and before the appointment of the new fund management institution, the CSRC shall designate a temporary fund management institution. The fund management institution for a publicly offered fund shall, after its functions terminate, properly preserve all the fund management business data and undergo the handover formalities for the fund management business in a timely manner, and the new or temporary fund management institution shall receive the business in a timely manner.

9.38 A fund management institution for a publicly offered fund shall, after its functions terminate, employ an accounting firm to audit fund assets according to the relevant provisions, publish the auditing results, and, at the same time, file such results with the CSRC for recordation.

---

[26] 2012 SIF Law, Art 27.
[27] 2012 SIF Law, Art 28.
[28] 2012 SIF Law, Art 29.

9.2.3. The fund custodian

A custodian is required for publicly offered funds. Non-publicly offered funds can contract out of this requirement.[29]   **9.39**

A fund custodian shall be a commercial bank or any other financial institution legally formed. Here, the China Securities Depository and Clearing Corporation Limited and securities firms may fall into the category of 'other financial institution'. If a commercial bank wants to serve as a fund custodian, it shall obtain confirmation from both the CSRC and the CBRC; if any other financial institution wants to serve as a fund custodian, it shall obtain confirmation from the CSRC.[30]   **9.40**

To serve as a fund custodian, a commercial bank or any other financial institution shall meet the following conditions: **9.41**

(1) Its net assets and risk control indicators comply with the relevant provisions.
(2) It has especially set up a fund custody department.
(3) The number of its full-time personnel qualified for the fund business satisfies the statutory requirement.
(4) It meets the conditions for the safekeeping of fund assets.
(5) It has safe and efficient clearing and settlement systems.
(6) It has business premises and security protection facilities satisfying the relevant requirements and other facilities related to its fund custody business.
(7) It has adequate and effective internal auditing and monitoring rules and risk control rules.
(8) Other conditions prescribed by laws and administrative regulations and by the securities regulatory authority and the banking regulatory authorities of the State Council with the approval of the State Council.[31]

A fund custodian shall perform the following functions: **9.42**

(1) The safekeeping of fund assets.
(2) Opening the capital accounts and securities accounts for fund assets according to the relevant provisions.
(3) Maintaining separate accounts for the assets of different funds under custody and ensuring the integrity and independence of fund assets.
(4) Preserving records, account books, statements, and other relevant materials regarding the fund custody business.
(5) Handling clearing and settlement matters in a timely manner according to the investment orders of the fund management institution as agreed upon in the fund contract.
(6) Handling information disclosure matters related to the fund custody business.

---

[29] 2012 SIF Law, Art 89.
[30] 2012 SIF Law, Art 33.
[31] 2012 SIF Law, Art 34.

(7) Offering opinions on the fund's financial accounting reports and semi-annual and annual reports.
(8) Reviewing and examining the net asset value of the fund and the subscription and redemption prices for fund shares as calculated by the fund management institution.
(9) Convening the fund shareholders' meeting according to the relevant provisions.
(10) Overseeing the investment operations of the fund management institution according to the relevant provisions.
(11) Other functions prescribed by the securities regulatory authority of the State Council.[32]

9.43 Further, where a fund custodian discovers that any investment order of a fund management institution violates any law, administrative regulation, or other relevant provisions or the fund contract, it shall refuse to execute the order, immediately notify the fund management institution, and report to the CSRC in a timely manner. Where a fund custodian discovers that any investment order of a fund management institution which has been executed under the trading procedures violates any law, administrative regulation, or other relevant provisions or the fund contract, it shall immediately notify the fund management institution and report to the CSRC in a timely manner.[33]

9.44 As shown above, the fund custodian has responsibility for safekeeping of the fund assets and monitoring the behaviour of the fund manager. Hence, the fund custodian and the fund management institution for a fund shall not be the same institution and shall not make capital contribution to each other or hold shares in each other.

9.45 Similar to the case of the fund manager, the functions of a fund custodian shall terminate under any of the following circumstances: (1) being disqualified for fund custody in accordance with law; (2) being dismissed by the fund share holders' meeting; (3) being dissolved, administratively dissolved, or declared bankrupt in accordance with law; (4) ay other circumstances as agreed upon in the fund contract.[34]

9.46 The fund shareholders' meeting shall appoint a new fund custodian within six month after the functions of the fund custodian terminate, and before the appointment of the new fund custodian, the CSRC shall designate a temporary fund custodian. The fund custodian shall, after its functions terminate, properly preserve fund assets and fund custody business data and undergo the handover formalities for fund assets and the fund custody business in a timely manner,

---

[32] 2012 SIF Law, Art 37.
[33] 2012 SIF Law, Art 38.
[34] 2012 SIF Law, Art 42.

and the new or temporary fund custodian shall receive the same in a timely manner. Further, a fund custodian shall, after its functions terminate, employ an accounting firm to audit fund assets according to the relevant provisions, publish the auditing results, and at the same time file such results with the CSRC for recordation.

9.2.4. Fund unit-holders

9.47 The operating mode of a fund shall be agreed upon in the fund contract. A fund may be operated in a closed-end, open-end, or any other mode. A fund operated in a closed-end mode (hereinafter referred to as a 'closed-end fund') means a fund of which the fund shares remain unchanged in the total amount and may not be redeemed by the fund shareholders upon request during the term of the fund contract. A fund operated in an open-end mode (hereinafter referred to as an 'open-end fund') means a fund of which the fund shares are unfixed in the total amount and may be subscribed for or redeemed at the time and place agreed upon in the fund contract.

9.48 The 2012 SIF Law is focused on the fund share offering, trading, subscription and redemption of the funds operated in the closed-end and open-end modes. The measures for funds operated in other modes shall be separately developed by the CSRC.

9.49 Under the contractual/trust fund, the fund share holders are the beneficiary. More specifically, they enjoy the following rights:

(1) Sharing income from fund assets.
(2) Participating in the distribution of the residual fund assets upon liquidation.
(3) Transferring or requesting redemption of the fund shares respectively held by them in accordance with law.
(4) Requiring that the fund shareholders' meeting be convened or convening the fund shareholders' meeting according to the relevant provisions.
(5) Exercising their voting rights regarding matters deliberated at the fund shareholders' meeting.
(6) Instituting an action against the fund management institution, fund custodian, or fund service institution for its conduct that infringes upon their lawful rights and interests.
(7) Other rights as agreed upon in the fund contract.[35]

9.50 The fund shareholders of a publicly offered fund shall have the right to consult or copy the publicly disclosed information and data regarding the fund, and the fund shareholders of a non-publicly offered fund shall have the right to consult

---

[35] 2012 SIF Law, Art 47.

the financial accounting books and other financial data of the fund where their personal interests are involved.

9.51 The fund shareholders' meeting shall be composed of all fund shareholders and exercise the following powers: (1) deciding to offer new shares of the fund or renew the term of the fund contract; (2) deciding to amend the essential clauses of the fund contract or terminate the fund contract early; (3) deciding to replace the fund management institution or fund custodian; (4) deciding to adjust the remuneration standards for the fund management institution or fund custodian; (5) other powers as agreed upon in the fund contract.[36]

9.52 The fund shareholders' meeting may, as agreed upon in the fund contract, set up a general office to exercise the following powers:

(1) Convening the fund share holders' meeting.
(2) Proposing the replacement of the fund management institution or fund custodian.
(3) Overseeing the investment operations of the fund management institution and the custodial activities of the fund custodian.
(4) Proposing the adjustment of the remuneration standards for the fund management institution or fund custodian.
(5) Other powers as agreed upon in the fund contract.[37]

9.53 The general office, as mentioned in the preceding paragraph, shall be composed of members elected at the fund shareholders' meeting, and its rules of procedure shall be agreed upon in the fund contract. Two points need to be noted about the general office. First, it is not mandatory to set up the general office. The establishment of the general office is based on the fund contract. Second, the general office is important in improving the governance of the fund and protecting the interests of fund share holders. As will be discussed later, it is not easy for fund shareholders to convene or ask the manager or the custodian to convene the fund shareholders' meeting. The general office serves as the standing organization of the fund shareholders' meeting and the representative institution of fund shareholders, having power to convene the fund shareholders' meeting, make motions to replace the fund manager or custodian and adjust their fees, and generally monitor the performance of the fund manager and custodian.

9.54 In order to ensure the independent and efficient exercise of management powers by the fund management institution, it is stipulated that the fund shareholders' meeting and its general office shall not directly participate or intervene in the fund's investment management.

---

[36] 2012 SIF Law, Art 48.
[37] 2012 SIF Law, Art 49.

9.3. Publicly Offered Fund

9.3.1. Public offering

9.3.1.1. The definition of public offering and registration requirement

The definition of a public offering of a fund is modelled on the definition of securities public offering. An offering of fund units will be considered as a public offering if it falls into any of the following three circumstances: (1) raising capital from unspecific investors; (2) raising capital from more than 200 specific investors cumulatively; (3) other circumstances prescribed by laws and administrative regulations.[38]

The publicly offered fund is required to adopt the standard trilateral contractual fund structure. That is, it shall be under the management of the fund management institution and under the custody of the fund custodian.

The public offering of a fund shall be registered with the CSRC, and no fund may be offered publicly without such registration, whether explicitly or implicitly.[39] Whoever publicly offers a fund without the CSRC registration, whether explicitly or implicitly, in violation of the 2012 SIF Law shall be ordered to cease the offering and refund the capital raised plus the bank deposit interest over the same period, with any illegal income confiscated, and be fined 1–5% of the capital raised. Its directly responsible person in charge and other directly liable persons shall be warned and each fined 50,000–500,000 yuan.[40] If the matter is serious enough to constitute a crime, it will attract criminal liabilities.[41]

To register the public offering of a fund, the prospective fund management institution shall submit the following documents to the securities regulatory authority of the State Council: (1) The application report; (2) The draft fund contract; (3) The draft fund custody agreement; (4) The draft prospectus; (5) The legal opinions issued by a law firm; (6) Other documents required by the CSRC.[42]

The requirements of the contents of the fund contract and the prospectus are set out in detail in Articles 53 and 54 of the 2012 SIF Law. One important point to note here is that the fund contract should set out the methods for drawing and paying remuneration for the fund management institution and fund custodian, and the proportion. This allows flexibility and innovation in designing how to pay the manager and custodian. Traditionally, the fund manager and custodian are paid at a fixed rate of the value of the fund assets. This fixed rate model has been severely

---

[38] 2012 SIF Law, Art 152.
[39] 2012 SIF Law, Art 51.
[40] 2012 SIF Law, Art 128.
[41] 2012 SIF Law, Art 150.
[42] 2012 SIF Law, Art 52.

criticized because it is not effectively performance-based. Now, under the 2012 SIF Law, the fund can use other payment methods, such as floating rates and bonuses, to properly incentivize the manager and custodian.

9.60 The CSRC shall, within six months after accepting an application for the registration of the public offering of a fund, conduct examination in accordance with laws, administrative regulations, and the provisions of the CSRC; make a decision to approve or disapprove registration, and notify the applicant; and, in the case of disapproval, explain the reasons for the disapproval.

9.3.1.2. The offering process

9.61 The fund shares may be offered only after the application for registration of the fund offering is approved. The fund shares shall be offered by the fund management institution or a fund sales agency authorized by it.

9.62 The fund management institution shall conduct the fund offering within six months from the date of receiving the registration approval document. If the fund is offered after six months and there is no material change to the original registered matters, the fund management institution shall report to the CSRC for recordation; in the case of any material change, the fund management institution shall submit a new registration application to the CSRC. The fund offering shall not exceed the fund offering period approved by the securities regulatory authority of the State Council for registration. The fund offering period shall commence from the offer date of fund shares.[43]

9.63 Under Article 59 of the 2012 SIF Law, where, upon the expiration of the fund offering period, the total fund shares sold reach 80 per cent or more of the approved size for registration in the case of a closed-end fund or the total fund shares sold reach the approved minimum total shares offered for registration in the case of an open-end fund, and the number of fund shareholders complies with the provisions of the CSRC, the fund management institution shall, within ten days after the expiration of the fund offering period, employ a statutory capital verification institution to conduct capital verification and, within ten days after receiving the capital verification report, submit the report to the CSRC, undergo the fund recording formalities, and issue a public announcement.[44] The capital raised during the fund offering period shall be deposited in a specialized account, and no one may use such capital before the completion of fund offering.

9.64 A fund contract is formed when an investor pays for the fund shares for which the investor subscribes; the fund contract takes effect after the fund management institution undergoes the fund recordation formalities with the CSRC in accordance with Article 59 of the 2012 SIF Law. The capital raised during the fund offering

---

[43] 2012 SIF Law, Art 58.
[44] 2012 SIF Law, Art 59.

period shall be deposited in a specialized account, and no one may use such capital before the completion of fund offering.

9.65 Upon the expiration of the fund offering period, if the conditions prescribed in Article 59 of the 2012 SIF Law cannot be met, the fund management institution shall assume the following liabilities: (1) assuming the debts and expenses arising from the fund offering with its own assets; (2) refunding the payments already made by the investors plus the bank deposit interest over the same period, within 30 days after the expiration of the fund offering period.

9.3.2. Fund share trading, subscription, and redemption

9.66 To apply for the listing and trading of fund shares, the fund management institution shall file an application with a stock exchange; if the stock exchange approves it upon examination in accordance with law, both parties shall enter into a listing agreement.

9.67 Under Article 63 of the 2012 SIF Law, the following conditions shall be met for the listing and trading of fund shares: (1) the fund offering complies with the provisions of the 2012 SIF Law; (2) the term of the fund contract is five years or more; (3) the capital raised of the fund is not less than 200 million yuan; (4) there are not less than 1,000 fund share holders; (5) other conditions prescribed in the listing and trading rules for fund shares.[45] It should be noted that the listing and trading rules for fund shares are developed by a stock exchange and submitted to the CSRC for approval.

9.68 Under any of the following circumstances after the listing and trading of fund shares, the stock exchange shall terminate the listing and trading and report to the securities regulatory authority of the State Council for recordation: (1) the conditions for listing and trading prescribed in Article 63 of the 2012 SIF Law are no longer met; (2) the term of the fund contract expires; (3) The fund shareholders' meeting decides to terminate the listing and trading early; (4) other circumstances under which the listing and trading shall be terminated as agreed upon in the fund contract or prescribed in the listing and trading rules for fund shares.

9.69 The fund share subscription, redemption, and registration of an open-end fund shall be handled by the fund management institution or a fund service institution authorized by it. The fund management institution shall handle fund share subscription and redemption on each working day, except as otherwise agreed upon in the fund contract. Subscription is formed when an investor pays for the subscription; the subscription takes effect when the fund shares registration institution confirms the fund shares. Redemption is formed when a fund shareholder files a

---

[45] 2012 SIF Law, Art 63.

redemption request; the redemption takes effect when the fund shares registration institution confirms the redemption.[46]

9.70 The subscription and redemption prices for fund shares shall be calculated on the basis of the net asset value per share on the subscription or redemption date plus or minus relevant fees. Where any error occurs in the pricing based on the net asset value per share, the fund management institution shall immediately correct such an error and take reasonable measures to prevent further losses. If the pricing error reaches 0.5 per cent of the net asset value per share, the fund management institution shall issue a public announcement and report to the CSRC for recordation. Where any pricing error based on the net asset value per share causes any loss to the fund shareholders, the fund shareholders shall have the right to require the fund management institution and fund custodian to make compensation.[47]

9.3.3. Investment of a publicly offered fund and information disclosure

9.3.3.1. Investment rules

9.71 A fund management institution shall utilize fund assets for securities investment in the manner of a portfolio, except as otherwise required by the CSRC. The specific modes of portfolio and investment proportions shall be agreed upon in the fund contract in accordance with the 2012 SIF Law and the provisions of the CSRC.[48]

9.72 The 2012 SIF Law takes both a positive and a negative approach to the investment activities of the SIF. On the positive side, fund assets shall be invested in the following securities: (1) stocks and bonds listed and traded on a stock exchange; (2) other securities and their derivatives prescribed by the CSRC. The term 'derivatives' may include (1) the index futures which have been introduced since 2009, and (2) the treasury bond futures which are likely to be introduced in the future.

9.73 On the negative side, fund assets shall not be used for the following investment or activities:

(1) Underwriting of securities.
(2) Providing loans or collateral for others in violation of the relevant provisions.
(3) Engaging in any investment with unlimited liability.
(4) Trading the shares of any other fund, except as otherwise required by the securities regulatory authority of the State Council.
(5) Making capital contribution to the fund management institution or fund custodian.
(6) Engaging in insider trading, manipulating securities trading prices, or otherwise illicitly trading securities.

---

[46] 2012 SIF Law, Art 67.
[47] 2012 SIF Law, Art 71.
[48] 2012 SIF Law, Art 72.

Investment Fund

(7) Other activities prohibited by any law or administrative regulation or the provisions of the securities regulatory authority of the State Council.[49]

Where fund assets are used for the trading of securities issued or underwritten during the underwriting period by the fund management institution or fund custodian, the controlling shareholder or actual controller thereof or any other materially interested company, or for any other major affiliated transactions, the principle of giving priority to the interests of fund shareholders shall be adhered to, conflicts of interest shall be prevented, the provisions of the CSRC shall be complied with, and information disclosure obligations shall be fulfilled. **9.74**

The above rule on related party transactions is a major change made by the 2012 SIF Law. Previously, related party transactions were strictly prohibited as a prophylactic measure to prevent conflicts of interest and protect the interest of fund shareholders. This blanket prohibition however caused problems for the investment activities of the SIF. For instance, many commercial banks are blue chip stocks, but because such banks often serve as fund custodians, their shares could not be traded by the relevant fund. This problem is particularly acute for index funds, as some commercial banks are component stocks of important indexes. Hence, the 2012 SIF Law replaces the previous prohibition with a regime of disclosure to prevent the issue of conflicts of interest. **9.75**

9.3.3.2. *Information disclosure rules*

The fund management institution, fund custodian, and other parties with fund information disclosure obligations shall disclose fund information in accordance with law and ensure the veracity, accuracy, and integrity of the information disclosed. The parties with fund information disclosure obligations shall ensure that the information required to be disclosed is disclosed during the period prescribed by the CSRC and ensure that the investors are able to consult or copy the publicly disclosed information according to the time and method as agreed upon in the fund contract. **9.76**

The fund information to be publicly disclosed includes: (1) the prospectus of a fund, the fund contract, and the fund custody agreement; (2) the fund offering information; (3) announcements on the listing and trading of fund shares; (4) the net asset value of a fund and the net asset value per share; (5) the subscription and redemption prices for fund shares; (6) the quarterly portfolio reports on fund assets, financial accounting reports and semi annual and annual fund reports; (7) any ad hoc reports; (8) the resolutions of the fund shareholders' meeting; (9) any major personnel changes in the specialized fund custody department of the fund management institution or fund custodian; (10) any legal proceedings or arbitration **9.77**

---

[49] 2012 SIF Law, Art 73.

involving fund assets, the fund management business, or the fund custody business; and (11) other information to be disclosed as required by the CSRC.[50]

9.78 The following conduct shall be prohibited in the public disclosure of fund information: (1) making any false records, misleading statements, or major omissions; (2) predicting securities investment performance; (3) promising any income or assumption of losses in violation of the relevant provisions; (4) disparaging any other fund management institution, fund custodian, or fund sales agency; (5) acting otherwise as prohibited by any law or administrative regulation or the provisions of the CSRC.[51]

9.3.4. Modification and termination of the fund contract and liquidation of fund assets

9.79 A fund may change its operating mode or be merged with another fund as agreed upon in the fund contract or according to a resolution of the fund shareholders' meeting. No further guidance, however, is provided on the methods by which one fund merges with another fund, and to date there has been no such case in practice.

9.80 To offer new shares or renew the term of the fund contract, a closed-end fund shall meet the following conditions and report to the CSRC for recordation: (1) the fund has good operating performance; (2) the fund management institution has not received any administrative or criminal punishment for any violation of law or regulation in the past two years; (3) a relevant resolution has been adopted at the fund shareholders' meeting; (4) other conditions prescribed by the 2012 SIF Law.[52]

9.81 Under any of the following circumstances, a fund contract shall terminate: (1) the term of the fund contract expires without any renewal; (2) the fund shareholders' meeting decides to terminate the contract; (3) the functions of the fund management institution or fund custodian terminate and no new fund management institution or fund custodian undertakes the functions within six months after the termination; (4) other circumstances as agreed upon in the fund contract.[53]

9.82 Upon the termination of a fund contract, the fund management institution shall organize a liquidation group to conduct liquidation of fund assets. The liquidation group shall be composed of the fund management institution, fund custodian, and relevant intermediary service institutions. The liquidation report prepared by the liquidation group shall be filed with the CSRC for recordation after it is audited by an accounting firm and a law firm issues a legal opinion on it, and a relevant public

---

[50] 2012 SIF Law, Art 77.
[51] 2012 SIF Law, Art 78.
[52] 2012 SIF Law, Art 80.
[53] 2012 SIF Law, Art 81.

announcement shall be issued. The residual fund assets after liquidation shall be distributed proportionately according to the shares held by the fund shareholders.

9.3.5. Exercise of rights by fund shareholders

The fund shareholders' meeting shall be convened by the fund management institution. Where the fund shareholders' meeting has set up a general office, the fund shareholders' meeting shall be convened by the general office; if the general office fails to do so, the fund shareholders' meeting shall be convened by the fund management institution. If the fund management institution fails or is unable to convene the meeting according to the relevant provisions, the fund custodian shall convene the meeting. 9.83

Where the fund shareholders representing 10 per cent or more of fund shares require that the fund shareholders' meeting be convened regarding the same matters, but none of the general office of the fund shareholders' meeting, the fund management institution, or the fund custodian convenes the meeting, the fund shareholders representing 10 per cent or more of fund shares shall have the right to convene the meeting but shall report to the CSRC for recordation.[54] 9.84

To convene the fund shareholders' meeting, the convener shall issue a public announcement of the time and form of the meeting, the deliberation items, the rules of procedure, and the voting method, among others, 30 days in advance at a minimum. Matters not included in the public announcement shall not be voted on at the fund shareholders' meeting. The fund shareholders' meeting may be held at a meeting venue, by communication means, or otherwise. Each fund share represents one voting right, and the fund shareholders may exercise their voting rights at the fund shareholders' meeting by proxy. 9.85

The fund shareholders' meeting may be held only when fund shareholders representing more than half of fund shares attend the meeting. Where the fund shares held by the fund shareholders attending the fund shareholders' meeting are lower than the above proportion, the convener may reconvene the fund shareholders' meeting regarding the original deliberation items during the period of three months to six months after the announced time of the original fund shareholders' meeting. The reconvened fund shareholders' meeting may be held only when fund shareholders representing more than one third of fund shares attend the meeting. 9.86

Any decision on a deliberation item at the fund shareholders' meeting shall be made with more than half of the voting rights held by the fund shareholders attending the meeting; however, a decision on a change in the fund's operating mode, replacement of the fund management institution or fund custodian, the early termination 9.87

---

[54] 2012 SIF Law, Art 84.

of the fund contract, or a merger with another fund shall be made with more than two thirds of the voting rights held by the fund shareholders attending the meeting. The matters decided by the fund shareholders' meeting shall be reported to the CSRC for recordation, and a relevant public announcement shall be issued.[55]

9.4. Non-publicly Offered Fund

9.4.1. The definition of a non-publicly offered fund

9.88 An offering of fund shares will be considered non-public if the fund shares are offered to qualified investors, and the number of qualified investors shall not exceed 200 cumulatively. Further, the qualified investors are entities and individuals which meet each of the following three criteria: (1) reach the prescribed asset size or income level; (2) have corresponding risk identification ability and risk tolerance; and (3) subscribe for fund shares not lower than the prescribed limit. The specific standards for qualified investors shall be prescribed by the CSRC.[56]

9.89 From a comparative perspective, the above definitional rule on qualified investors is very stringent. In many overseas jurisdictions, including the US, UK, Australia, and Hong Kong, a qualified investor is not required to satisfy each of the three criteria. The stringent Chinese regulation on qualified investors may be justified on the grounds that non-publicly offered funds are still quite new to the relatively unsophisticated investors in China.

9.90 In terms of fund structure, non-publicly offered funds have some important differences from publicly offered funds. First, a non-publicly offered fund should have a custodian, although the fund contract can stipulate otherwise. Second, the fund management institution for a non-publicly offered fund needs only to register with the fund association, rather than obtain approval from the CSRC. Without registration, no entity or individual shall use the word 'fund' or words 'fund management' or any similar name to engage in securities investment, except as otherwise provided for by any law or administrative regulation.[57]

9.4.2. The offering process

9.91 Under Article 92 of the 2012 SIF Law, a non-publicly offered fund shall not raise capital from any entity or individual other than qualified investors and shall not be publicized or promoted to unspecific investors through public media such as newspapers and journals, radio stations, television stations, and internet, or in manners such as through lectures, seminars, and analysis meetings.[58]

---

[55] 2012 SIF Law, Art 87.
[56] 2012 SIF Law, Art 88.
[57] 2012 SIF Law, Art 91.
[58] 2012 SIF Law, Art 92.

For a non-publicly offered fund, a fund contract shall be prepared and signed. The fund contract shall include: 9.92

(1) The rights and obligations of the fund shareholders, fund management institution, and fund custodian.
(2) The operating mode of the fund.
(3) The manners and amounts of capital contribution for the fund and the time limit for payment.
(4) The fund's investment scope, investment strategies, and investment limits.
(5) The principles and execution methods for fund income distribution.
(6) The relevant expenses assumed by the fund.
(7) The content of fund information provided and methods of provision.
(8) The procedures and methods for fund share subscription, redemption, or transfer.
(9) The causes and procedures for the modification, rescission, and termination of the fund contract.
(10) The liquidation method for fund assets.
(11) Other matters as agreed upon by the parties.[59]

As shown in the above provision, the non-publicly offered fund is free to contract on many important issues. For instance, under the third subsection, as capital contribution may be made in different manners, it is possible to contribute not only in cash but also in other forms, such as securities. Also, the flexibility on payment time suggests that contributions can be made in instalments. Under the fifth subsection, methods of distributing fund profits are negotiable, and thus it is not necessarily the case that fund profits are to be distributed according to the holdings of fund shares. Further, although a non-publicly offered fund has no statutory duty to disclose fund information, the fund contract can impose duties on the manager and custodian to provide relevant fund information to fund shareholders. In practice, some non-publicly offered funds, nicknamed 'sunshine private funds' (*yangguang simu jijin*), publicly disclose the net value of their shares on a regular basis, in an effort to enhance their profile. 9.93

It is important to note that a non-publicly offered fund can be established using the form of limited partnership. Specifically, as agreed upon in the fund contract, some fund shareholders may serve in the capacity of a fund management institution responsible for the investment management of the fund and shall assume unlimited joint and several liability for the debts incurred by fund assets when fund assets are insufficient for repayment of such debts. In the case of such fund, the fund contract shall also state: (1) the names and domiciles of the fund shareholders assuming unlimited joint and several liability and other fund shareholders; (2) the conditions for removing and procedures for replacing the fund shareholders 9.94

---

[59] 2012 SIF Law, Art 93.

assuming unlimited joint and several liability; (3) the conditions and procedures for the increase and exit of fund shareholders and the relevant liability; and (4) the procedures for conversion between the fund shareholders assuming unlimited joint and several liability and other fund shareholders.[60]

9.95 After the fund offering of a non-publicly offered fund is completed, the fund management institution shall undergo recordation formalities at the fund association. Where the total amount of capital raised or the number of fund shareholders reaches the prescribed standard, the fund association shall report to the CSRC.[61] Hence, the offering process of the non-publicly offered fund is more flexible than that of the publicly offered fund. As discussed earlier, the latter needs *ex ante* registration and *ex post* recordation, but the former only needs *ex post* recordation.

9.4.3. Other issues

9.96 When the holder of fund shares transfers her shares, she should transfer only to qualified investors and after the transfer, and the number of qualified investors in the fund should not exceed 200 cumulatively. Further, when transferring fund shares, the prohibition on promoting the fund shares to unspecified investors, as contained in Article 92 of the 2012 SIF Law, should be complied with.

9.97 Compared to publicly offered funds, non-publicly offered funds can invest in a wider scope of securities, including publicly offered shares of joint-stock limited companies, bonds, fund shares, and other securities and their derivatives prescribed by the CSRC. First, while the shares in which the publicly offered fund invests must be listed, the non-publicly offered fund can invest in publicly offered shares whether listed or not. Second, the non-publicly offered fund can invest in shares of other funds, whereas the publicly offered fund is generally disallowed to do so, unless otherwise stipulated by the CSRC.

9.5. Fund Services Institutions

9.5.1. Overview

9.98 The 2012 SIF Law adds a new chapter to provide for various fund services institutions. The fund management institution may entrust fund service providers with share registration, accounting, valuation, investment advice, and other matters regarding the fund, and the fund custodian may entrust fund service providers with accounting, valuation, review, and other matters regarding the fund—which,

---

[60] 2012 SIF Law, Art 94.
[61] 2012 SIF Law, Art 95.

Investment Fund

however, shall not relieve the fund management institution or fund custodian from any liability assumed by it in accordance with law.[62]

Entities which provide the sale, trading payment, share registration, valuation, investment advice, rating, information technology system, and other fund services for publicly offered funds shall undergo registration or recordation formalities in accordance with the provisions of the CSRC.[63] Fund service institutions shall diligently perform their duties, establish emergency response and other risk management rules and a disaster backup system, and shall not divulge any undisclosed information regarding fund shareholders or fund investment operations. **9.99**

The new chapter on fund services institutions is of great significance. At the moment, China's fund services institutions are still in the early stage of development. As of the end of 2012, there were only 11 independent fund sale institutions; one independent fund share registration institution, namely the China Securities Depository and Clearing Corporation Limited; and no independent fund valuation institution at all. Due to the underdevelopment of fund services institutions, the fund management company in China adopts a comprehensive business model covering not only the core business of fund management but also the peripheral businesses such as the sale, registration, and valuation of fund shares. **9.100**

It is expected that the 2012 SIF Law will facilitate the development of fund services institutions in China. This will allow the fund management company to outsource the peripheral businesses to fund services institutions and thus concentrate on its core business of fund management. **9.101**

9.5.2. Types of fund services institutions

There are several different types of fund services institutions under the 2012 SIF Law. They will be discussed in turn. **9.102**

9.5.2.1. Fund sale institution

The fund sale institution shall fully disclose investment risks to the investors and sell fund products of different risk levels based on the investors' risk tolerance. This actually requires the fund sale institution to perform a suitability test when selling fund shares to investors.[64] **9.103**

9.5.2.2. Fund trading payment institution

A fund trading payment institution shall transfer fund sales settlement capital according to the relevant provisions and ensure the safe transfer of fund sales settlement capital in a timely manner.[65] Before 2011, only commercial banks could **9.104**

---

[62] 2012 SIF Law, Art 102.
[63] 2012 SIF Law, Art 98.
[64] 2012 SIF Law, Art 99.
[65] 2012 SIF Law, Art 100.

serve as the fund trading payment institution; since 2011, third party payment institutions have been allowed to enter this market. As of the end of 2012, there were a total of 223 third party payment institutions, but only seven of them provided payment services for the fund sale institution. Hence, there is great potential for the growth of fund trading payment institutions.

9.5.2.3. Fund shares registration institution

9.105 The data registered by a fund transfer agent in an electronic medium shall be the basis for determining the ownership of fund shareholders. Where a fund shareholder pledges fund shares, the pledge shall be formed when the fund transfer agent conducts pledge registration. A fund transfer agent shall properly preserve the registered data and submit a backup of such data, including but not limited to the name and identity information of fund shareholders and the detailed fund share information, to an institution accredited by the CSRC. Such data shall be preserved for not less than 20 years from the date of cancellation of the fund account. A fund transfer agent shall ensure the veracity, accuracy, and integrity of the registered data and shall not conceal, fabricate, tamper with, or destroy such data.[66]

9.106 The fund sales settlement capital and fund shares shall be independent from a fund distributor's, a fund trading payment agent's, or a fund transfer agent's own assets. When a fund distributor, a fund trading payment agent, or a fund transfer agent goes bankrupt or is liquidated, the fund sales settlement capital and fund shares are not bankruptcy property or liquidating property. The fund sales settlement capital and fund shares shall not be sealed, frozen, deducted, and transferred, or subject to enforcement, except for an investor's own debts or under other circumstances prescribed by law. Fund distributors, fund trading payment agents, and fund transfer agents shall ensure the safety and independence of fund sales settlement capital and fund shares, and no entity or individual shall, in any form, misappropriate fund sales settlement capital or fund shares.[67]

9.5.2.4. Fund valuation institution

9.107 In China, the current practice of fund valuation is that publicly offered funds are usually valued by the fund manager and verified by the custodian. This mechanism has two problems: on the one hand, the issue of conflicts of interest may arise because the fund manager has incentives to inflate investment profits and hide investment losses; on the other, due to the lack of specialized knowledge and information, the fund manager may not be able to make accurate judgements on the value of fund assets, particularly those financial products which have sophisticated structures without readily available market prices, such as illiquid bond derivatives.

---

[66] 2012 SIF Law, Art 103.
[67] 2012 SIF Law, Art 101.

One of the widely recognized causes of the global financial crisis of 2008 is that   9.108
financial assets were not properly valued. Hence, after the crisis, third party valuation institutions have developed rapidly, with some prominent players such as Interactive Data and Bloomberg in the US. Clearly, China needs to establish its own third party valuation institutions, and the 2012 SIF Law has now provided a solid legal foundation for this.

9.5.2.5. Fund investment advisory institution

A fund investment advisory institution and its employees shall provide fund investment advice services on a rational basis and make truthful statements on its service ability and business performance, and shall not promise or guarantee investment returns in any form or infringe upon the lawful rights and interests of the clients.[68] It should be noted that the fund investment advisory institution can only provide fund investment advice, and cannot make investment decisions in lieu of the fund manager.   9.109

9.5.2.6 Fund rating institution

A fund rating institution and its employees shall be objective and impartial and conduct the fund rating business in accordance with business rules developed in accordance with law, shall not mislead investors, and shall prevent potential conflicts of interest.[69]   9.110

The business of fund rating can be carried on by securities firms, securities investment advisory institutions, independent fund rating institutions, media, and other institutions approved by the CSRC. As of the end of 2012, there were a total of ten fund rating institutions, including four securities firms, three independent fund rating institutions, and three media.   9.111

9.5.2.7 Law firm and accounting firm

Where a law firm or an accounting firm issues legal opinions, audit reports, internal control evaluation reports, or other documents for the relevant fund business as authorized by a fund management institution or fund custodian, it shall diligently perform its duties and check and validate the veracity, accuracy, and integrity of the documents and data as the basis. Where the documents produced or issued by the law firm or accounting firm contain any false records, misleading statements, or major omissions causing any loss to the assets of others, the law firm or accounting firm shall assume compensatory liability jointly and severally with the client.   9.112

As shown above, a form of strict liability applies to law firms and accounting firms for misrepresentation in the documents they prepare in relation to relevant fund businesses. This stands in contrast with the fault-based liability applicable to law   9.113

---

[68] 2012 SIF Law, Art 104.
[69] 2012 SIF Law, Art 105.

firms and accounting firms under the Securities Law, where they can escape liability if they can 'prove they have no fault'.[70] In fact, the legislators stipulated the fault-based liability for law firms and accounting firms in the draft of the 2012 SIF Law, but in the end changed it to strict liability, probably in an effort to deter misrepresentation. It is, however, debatable whether this change is necessary and reasonable.

9.5.2.8 Other fund services institutions

9.114 In addition to the fund services institutions discussed above, the 2012 SIF Law allows the development of 'other funds services institutions'. One example is the third party e-commerce platform which can be used by a fund sale institution to sell fund shares to investors. Through this e-commerce platform, investors can buy fund shares in the same way that they buy ordinary goods on the internet. Against the background of rapid development in the e-commerce market in China, this new method of fund marketing has great potential.

9.6. Fund Association

9.115 The fund association is a self-regulatory organization of the SIF sector and has the status of legal person. Fund management institutions and fund custodians shall join the fund association, and fund service providers may join the fund association.[71] The supreme governing body of a fund association is the general assembly, consisting of all members. A fund association shall have a board of governors. The members of the board of governors shall be elected in accordance with the bylaws.[72] The bylaws of a fund association shall be adopted at the general assembly and filed with the CSRC.

9.116 A fund association shall perform the following functions:

(1) Educating and organizing members regarding compliance with laws and administrative regulations on securities investment and protecting the lawful rights and interests of investors.
(2) Protecting the lawful rights and interests of members in accordance with law and reflecting the suggestions and demands of members.
(3) Developing and implementing the self-regulatory rules of the sector, supervising and inspecting the practice of members and their employees, and taking disciplinary action according to the relevant provisions against those who violate the self-disciplinary rules or the bylaws of the association.

---

[70] For detailed discussion of liability for misrepresentation under the Securities Law, see Chapter 6.
[71] 2012 SIF Law, Art 109.
[72] 2012 SIF Law, Art 110.

(4) Developing the sector's practising standards and business rules and organizing practising examinations, qualification management, and business training for fund employees.
(5) Providing member services, organizing exchanges regarding the sector, promoting innovation in the sector, and conducting sector publicity and investor education.
(6) Conducting mediation for fund business disputes between members or between a member and its clients.
(7) Handling registration and recordation for non-publicly offered funds in accordance with law.
(8) Other functions prescribed by the bylaws of the association.[73]

9.117 In July 2012, the national fund association, named the Asset Management Association of China (*Zhongguo Zhengquan Touzi Jijinye Xiehui*), was established; Mr Sun Jie, the former Director of the Fund Department of the CSRC, was named president. As with other industrial associations in the financial sector, such as the Securities Association of China, it is doubtful that the Asset Management Association of China is truly a self-regulatory organization.

---

[73] 2012 SIF Law, Art 112.

Part IV

MERGERS AND ACQUISITIONS

10

TAKEOVERS OF LISTED COMPANIES (1)

10.1. Introduction	10.01	10.5.1. Overview	10.61
10.1.1. Terminology	10.03	10.5.2. Mitigating the harshness of the rule	10.70
10.1.2. Typology	10.09		
10.2. Shareholding Structure in Listed Companies	10.21	10.6. Tender Offer Rules	10.77
		10.6.1. Full/partial bids	10.77
10.2.1. Different types of shares	10.21	10.6.2. Payment methods and pricing rules	10.79
10.2.2. Reasons behind the structure	10.25		
10.2.3. Recent developments	10.31	10.6.3. Conducting the takeover bid	10.86
10.3. China's Takeover Law and Activities	10.39	10.7. Compulsory Buyout	10.89
		10.8. Indirect Takeovers and Management Buyouts	10.92
10.3.1. The legal framework	10.39		
10.3.2. The regulator	10.42	10.9. Disclosure of Substantial Shareholdings	10.95
10.3.3. Takeover activities	10.43		
10.4. The Guiding Principles for Takeover Regulation	10.47	10.10. Financial Consultants	10.101
10.4.1. Contestability of takeovers	10.49	10.11. Continuous Supervision	10.110
10.4.2. Shareholder protection	10.56	10.12. Comments	10.114
10.4.3. Two aspects of takeover law	10.60	10.12.1. Strengths	10.114
10.5. The Mandatory Bid Rule	10.61	10.12.2. Weaknesses	10.123
		10.12.3. Summary	10.132

10.1. Introduction

Takeovers are a significant feature of corporate life and as such have attracted enormous attention in securities law worldwide. Although there are other ways to effect corporate control transfer, takeovers are the main method of achieving that goal on the stock market. As their impact extends to the investing public, careful regulation has been developed to ensure fairness, efficiency, and investor protection from deception. Takeover rules have thus become an integral part of securities law. This chapter is intended to provide a detailed discussion of the rules governing takeovers of listed companies in China. **10.01**

Two points need to be noted here. First, the takeover law applies specifically to takeover activities on the securities markets. It operates essentially as a supplement to the general law of contract, which primarily governs the offers made by the acquirer to **10.02** buy stock or assets in the target company and the resulting obligations between the parties. These specific rules interfere with the acquirer's contractual freedom, as well as its freedom to make acquisitions generally. In both instances, they do so in the interests of securing the goals of corporate regulation. Second, the rules discussed in this chapter apply to both domestic and foreign acquirers. In the case of foreigners wishing to acquire listed companies in China, however, they need to comply further with rules on foreign investment, which will be examined in a later chapter.

10.1.1. Terminology

10.03 Before engaging in substantive discussion, it is important to clarify several closely related terms for the avoidance of confusion.

10.04 In common parlance, the term 'takeover' refers to the process of gaining control of a company (the target) by bidding under a formal process for sufficient shares to achieve that end. A takeover has two important features. First, it has the purpose and effect of changing corporate control. Second, it is carried out by means of share acquisition. In China, as only joint-stock companies can issue shares, takeover law applies to this type of company.

10.05 The next term is 'mergers and acquisitions', which is commonly abbreviated as 'M&A'. It is more commercially used jargon than a legally defined term. As the name suggests, any mergers and acquisitions may potentially fall within its scope. In practice, mergers and acquisitions can be done together or separately. In some cases, business integration may be needed after acquisitions; in others, mergers may be carried out without any acquisition transaction, or vice versa. Generally speaking, M&A is different from a takeover in two ways. First, it covers not only share acquisition, but also acquisition of other things such as assets, business, and undertaking. Second, the acquisition may or may not lead to a change in corporate control. Thus, in China, the application of M&A can extend beyond joint-stock companies to limited liability companies.

10.06 It should be noted, however, that the terms 'M&A' and 'takeover' are often used interchangeably in the context of acquiring control of listed companies. Accordingly, in China there is some confusion about using the term 'takeover', which has been translated as *Binggou* or *Shougou* in Chinese.[1] Strictly speaking, *Binggou* corresponds to M&A while *Shougou* refers to a takeover, but what they exactly mean depends on the particular circumstances in which they are used. For the purpose of this chapter, takeover or *Shougou* is defined as trading activities on the shares of listed companies with a view toward acquiring corporate control.

10.07 The last term is 'corporate control transaction', which is translated as *Gongsi Kongzhiquan Jiaoyi* in Chinese. This refers to any transaction involving corporate

---

[1] Hui Huang, 'China's Takeover Law: A Comparative Analysis and Proposals for Reform' (2005) 30(1) *Delaware Journal of Corporate Law* 145, 157.

control transfer, which, apart from acquisition in the traditional sense, may be effected by way of selective capital reduction, boardroom control, or restructuring.

In sum, a takeover through a formal offer for shares in the target company is but one way of acquiring control of a business and a variety of other means are available, particularly when the attempt is not contested or resisted. These include the purchase of assets, business, and undertakings of the company, reduction of capital to cancel shares not held by a particular shareholder, and restructuring processes involving the cancellation or transfer of shares not held by the person seeking control. In practice, however, takeover is the most common form of acquisition of control of listed companies, and thus is the focus of the discussion below. 10.08

10.1.2. Typology

Takeovers can be categorized according to different criteria. In China, the landscape of takeovers is quite interesting due to the country's unique political, economic, and cultural contexts. 10.09

10.1.2.1 Friendly and hostile takeovers

In terms of the attitude of the target company toward the takeover offer, a distinction can be made between friendly and hostile takeovers. Generally speaking, a hostile takeover is one that is resisted by the target company's board of directors. In contrast, a friendly takeover is welcomed and approved by the target company's board of directors. It is worth noting that the divide between friendly and hostile takeovers may not be easily drawn and sometimes may be misleading: many friendly takeovers would not occur without the threat of a hostile takeover,[2] and many takeovers that are initially hostile result in friendly negotiated settlements.[3] 10.10

The situation of takeovers and hostile takeovers is quite different in different jurisdictions. While takeovers have a history one century long in the US, hostile takeovers proliferated only during the 1980s, and did not achieve wide acceptance until the end of the 1990s. In contrast, takeovers in the UK and the continental Europe were not well documented until the early 1960s and the early 1980s, respectively. Like the US, the UK saw a boom of hostile takeovers during the 1980s; the same happened a decade later in continental Europe. After the new millennium, however, the number of hostile takeovers declined significantly across the Atlantic.[4] 10.11

In China, the takeover market began to develop in the early 1990s, but hostile takeovers have rarely been seen to date, with an estimation of about ten cases in the 10.12

---

[2] Michael C Jensen, 'Takeovers: Their Causes and Consequences' (1988) 2 *The Journal of Economic Perspectives* 22.
[3] William G Schwert, 'Hostility in Takeovers: In the Eyes of the Beholder?' (2000) 55 *The Journal of Finance* 2600.
[4] Marina Martynova and Luc Renneboog, 'A Century of Corporate Takeovers: What Have We Leaned and Where Do We Stand?' (2008) 32 *Journal of Banking & Finance* 2148, 2149–52.

Table 1 The shareholdings of the largest dominant shareholders of Chinese listed companies as of mid-2010

Percentage of the largest dominant shareholdings	Proportion of all companies listed in China
Less than 10% (inclusive)	1.83%
10 to 15% (inclusive)	4.89%
15 to 20% (inclusive)	8.76%
20 to 25% (inclusive)	12.9%
25 to 30% (inclusive)	13.22%
30 to 40% (inclusive)	19.72%
More than 40%	38.69%

past two decades. There are several possible reasons for this situation. To start with, the Chinese takeover law has an inhibiting effect on hostile takeovers. As will be discussed later, on the one hand, the Chinese takeover law contains a mandatory bid rule which increases the cost of takeovers; on the other, anti-takeover defences are widely used in China due to the ambiguity of the law. Apart from the law, a number of non-legal factors contribute to the dearth of hostile takeovers in China. First, the Chinese culture emphasizes harmony and friendship.

10.13 Second and more important, the ownership structure of Chinese listed companies is not conducive to hostile takeovers. In general, Chinese listed companies have a very high level of concentration in their shareholding, which makes it extremely difficult to launch hostile takeovers. Table 1 shows the shareholdings of the largest dominant shareholders of Chinese listed companies as of mid-2010.[5]

10.1.2.2. Horizontal, vertical, and conglomerate takeovers

10.14 Depending on the relationship between the acquirer and the target, takeovers can be grouped into three categories, namely horizontal takeovers/mergers, vertical takeovers/mergers, and conglomerate takeovers/mergers. Horizontal mergers occur when the acquirer and the target are competitors in the same industry; vertical mergers involve acquisition of a firm either upstream or downstream in the production process; and conglomerate mergers are usually a strategy for a company to diversify its business by moving into a range of other areas of business activity.

10.15 In China, all three types of takeovers are present; in recent years, conglomerate mergers have been on the rise as more Chinese companies develop into multi-business corporate groups to improve their risk-bearing capacity and market competitiveness.

10.1.2.3. Normal and reverse takeovers

10.16 Takeovers are categorized into normal/forward takeovers and reverse takeovers, according to the direction of the transaction. In normal/forward takeovers, the

---

[5] Wei Cai, 'The Mandatory Bid Rule in China' (2011) 4 *The European Business Organization Law Review* 653, 671.

acquirer purchases sufficient shares in the target company and as such gains the control of the latter. Reverse takeovers, also known as backdoor listing, run in the opposite direction. Under this model, a listed company acquires assets but such acquisition is in reality an attempt to achieve a listing of those assets. In practice, the listed company is usually a shell company and the target company wants to get listed. The listed company, as the acquirer, purchases the assets of the target company, and issues shares to the target company as consideration for the assets. The end result of this transaction is that the assets of the target company are transferred to the acquirer company and the target company becomes the shareholder of the acquirer company; if the shares issued to it are sufficient in number, it then becomes the controlling shareholder of the acquirer company. In this way, the target company in effect gets its assets listed through the acquirer company.

10.17 Backdoor listing is seen in many jurisdictions, including the US and Hong Kong, providing a useful alternative to the route of initial public offering (IPO). Compared to the IPO route, backdoor listing is usually quicker and less burdensome. But backdoor listing has disadvantages, too. For instance, it is not easy to find an appropriate and clean shell company, and if one is available, it will not be free. Backdoor listing is particularly popular in China due to its unique local circumstances. As discussed in other chapters, an IPO requires administrative approval from the China Securities Regulatory Committee (CSRC) and, in practice, the CSRC keeps tight control on this. This makes it very difficult for many companies to get listed via the IPO route, and they have to resort to backdoor listing.

10.18 Backdoor listing has recently become a subject of regulatory concern due to the fact that reverse takeovers are subject to different rules from those for IPO. In China, the CSRC has issued specific rules to regulate backdoor listings. First of all, guidance is provided on what would constitute backdoor listing.[6] Second, to purchase assets by stock issuance, the listed company shall satisfy the following requirements:

(1) Doing so is good for improving the asset quality of the listed company, improving its financial status and sustained profitability, reducing affiliated transactions, avoiding horizontal competition and increasing its independence.
(2) Certified public accountants have issued auditing reports with clean opinions on the company's financial statements for the past year and the preceding period; in the case of any auditing report with qualified opinions, negative opinions, or inexpressible opinions, certified public accountants must check to confirm that issues involved in the qualified opinions, negative opinions, or inexpressible opinions have been removed or are supposed to be removed by the reorganization.

---

[6] Shangshi Gongsi Zhongda Zichan Chongzu Guanli Banfa (Administrative Measures for the Material Asset Reorganizations of Listed Companies) (issued by the CSRC on 16 April 2008, effective 18 May 2008, and amended in 2011) (Measures for Material Asset Reorganizations), Art 12.

(3) The assets purchased by the listed company by stock issuance shall be operating assets with clear ownership, and the transfer formalities can be handled within the stipulated time limit.
(4) Other requirements as set forth by the CSRC.[7]

10.19 Further, shares of the listed company acquired by a specific subject with assets may not be transferred within 12 months from the date when the issuance is done, or within 36 months under any of the following circumstances:

(1) The specific subject is the controlling shareholder or actual controller of the listed company, or an affiliated party controlled by the controlling shareholder or actual controller.
(2) The specific subject acquires actual control over the listed company by purchasing the shares issued this time.
(3) By the time that the specific subject purchases the shares issued this time, it has been continually holding the assets used for purchase for less than 12 months.[8]

10.20 Finally, the listed company shall submit its application for purchasing assets by means of stock issuance to the CSRC for examination and approval.[9] The CSRC has indicated that it would strictly implement the regime at a standard comparable to that of IPO.[10]

10.2. Shareholding Structure in Listed Companies

10.2.1. Different types of shares

10.21 As ownership structure has a great impact on takeover activities, it is necessary first to understand the unique features of the shareholding structure of Chinese listed companies. Indeed, the equity structure of the Chinese stock market differs greatly from those in western nations. There are several different types of shares, distinguished by rules governing their ownership and trading. In addition to common and preference shares, which look familiar to westerners, there are other special classifications which seem to be peculiar to China.

10.22 First, depending on the nationality of eligible traders and the currencies in which the shares are traded, there are traditionally two broad types of shares in the

---
[7] Measures for Material Asset Reorganizations, Art 42.
[8] Measures for Material Asset Reorganizations, Art 45.
[9] Measures for Material Asset Reorganizations, Art 46
[10] Zhongguo Zhengquan Jiandu Guanli Weiyuanhui Guanyu zai Jieke Shangshi Shenhe zhong Yange Zhixing Shouci Gongkai Faxing Gupiao Shangshi Biaozhun de Tongzhi [Notice of the CSRC on the Rigorous Implementation of IPO Listing Standards in Approving Backdoor Listings] (issued by the CSRC in November 2013).

market: A-shares and B-shares. A-shares are basically limited to domestic investors, including individuals, legal persons, and the state, with both the principal and dividends denominated in the local currency, namely the Chinese Yuan (CNY). In contrast, B-shares are generally designed for foreign investors, including investors from Taiwan, Hong Kong, and Macao. While B-shares carry a face value denominated in CNY, they are traded in foreign currency on the basis of exchange rates at the time of transactions. No companies can issue B-shares unless they meet certain requirements prescribed by the government. Further, some Chinese companies are listed on overseas exchanges and their shares listed there are named after the exchanges. For instance, H-shares are stocks of Chinese companies listed on the Hong Kong Stock Exchange, while N-shares are those listed on the New York Stock Exchange. The trading of these shares is mainly subject to the laws of listing locations rather than Chinese laws.

Second, and more importantly, A-shares have been further subdivided into three subsets in light of the strictly defined groups of shareholders in China: state shares (*guojia gu*); legal person shares (*faren gu*); and public individual shares (*shehui geren gu*). Only public individual shares may be freely traded on the stock exchange (and therefore are called tradable shares); state shares and legal person shares are subject to severe trading restrictions (and therefore are collectively called non-tradable shares). **10.23**

This structure has important implications for takeovers of Chinese listed companies. First, while all the above types of shares carry the same voting and economic rights, their prices can be very different due to market segmentation. Normally, A-shares are materially more expensive than non-A-shares, such as B-shares and H-shares. Second, in terms of market capitalization, non-A-shares account for a fairly small proportion—usually less than 10 per cent of all shares in listed companies. Consequently, it is impractical to seek to gain control of Chinese listed companies through purchase of non-A-shares, save in very exceptional circumstances. Third, it is difficult to carry out a takeover, particularly a hostile takeover, by conducting a takeover bid for A-shares. As will be discussed later, there are two main methods of takeover in China: takeover by tender offer, which is used for tradable shares (mainly public individual shares), and takeover by private agreement, which is designed for non-tradable shares (consisting of state shares and legal person shares). Traditionally, non-tradable shares make up about two thirds of the shares in most listed companies. This makes it virtually impossible to take over a listed company without the support of the holder of non-tradable shares. **10.24**

10.2.2. Reasons behind the structure

The peculiar shareholding structure of Chinese listed companies is essentially a historical product of China's progressive economic reform. To start with, the severance of the A and B-share markets is largely due to the incomplete convertibility **10.25** of Chinese currency, namely Renminbi (RMB), and the so-called restricted foreign currency policy. For example, precluding domestic investors from B-shares is regarded as a measure to preserve the nation's foreign currency reserve. Once the RMB becomes fully convertible, the separation between A-shares and B-shares might disappear. As shall be discussed later, China's participation in economic globalization, as symbolized by its accession into the World Trade Organization (WTO), has actually resulted in the gradual mitigation of this problem.

10.26　Further, the rationale behind the dichotomy of tradable and non-tradable shares is both political and economic. The political reason is to prevent state assets from falling into the hands of individuals, while the economic reason is to protect state assets from depreciation and misappropriation (in a widely used Chinese term, *Fanzhi Guoyou Zichan Liushi*).

10.27　At the beginning of the establishment of the Chinese stock market, the political reason seemed more important. Most of the listed companies in China were previously large state-owned and managed enterprises, which are seen as the basis and symbol of a socialist economy. When these enterprises initially went public, their original state assets translated into state shares of the listed companies. Thus, those state shares are labelled as state assets, which, in turn, represent the state's ownership. State ownership is traditionally considered the highest form of ownership and the goal of socialism. Even after the 1999 amendment, the Chinese Constitution still provides that

> in the primary stage of socialism, [China] shall uphold the basic economic system in which *public ownership is dominant* and diverse forms of ownership develop side by side. It shall also uphold the distribution system with distribution according to work remaining dominant and with a variety of models of distribution coexisting.[11]

10.28　Individual ownership is still seen as inferior to public ownership, and is treated differently. The 1999 amendment to Article 11 of the Chinese Constitution reads as follows:

> the non-public sector, including self-employed and private businesses, *within the domain stipulated by law, is an important component of [China's] socialist market economy*. The state shall protect the legitimate rights and interests of the self-employed and private enterprises, and China should also exercise guidance, supervision and management over them according to the law.[12]

10.29　Prior to this amendment, private businesses enjoyed even lower status and were considered just a complement to the socialist public sector economy. Under this social and political framework, state shares, as the embodying form of state ownership, have been strictly protected from the threat of private ownership. It was feared

---

[11] ZhongHua Renmin Gongheguo Xianfa [The Constitution of the People's Republic of China (Chinese Constitution)] (promulgated by the National People's Congress), Art 6 (emphasis added).
[12] Chinese Constitution, Art 11 (1999 amendment) (emphasis added).

that if it was permitted to transfer state shares to private owners, then the socialist economy would be baseless. Thus, the prohibition of the free transfer of state shares serves to preserve the socialist nature of the Chinese economy, and thus China as a whole.

The economic reason to restrict the transfer of state shares is the fear that, if transferred, state shares could be mishandled or at least lose value. Because the Chinese stock market was deemed an experiment of economic reform at the outset, the government was understandably reluctant to risk state assets in this experiment. The original purpose of the establishment of the stock market was simply to raise funds for state-owned enterprises and to help those enterprises get out of financial distress: the so-called *Wei Guoyou Qiye Jiekun*. Other than for that purpose, the Chinese government had little interest in seeing its shares transferred. **10.30**

10.2.3. Recent developments

The segmentation of the Chinese securities market has given rise to a number of problems. The fact that the majority of the shares on the market are non-tradable has presented a serious impediment to further development of the market. Empirical research has suggested that corporate performance is negatively related to the proportion of state shares.[13] The tradable/non-tradable shares segregation has been widely seen as the fundamental problem with the Chinese stock market, and as largely responsible for serious corporate governance deficiencies. In particular, it inhibits the proper functioning of the market for corporate control, because in the face of non-tradable shares in listed companies running as high as about 60 per cent, takeover attempts by tender offer are practically impossible. **10.31**

More fundamentally, as the economic and political reform in China proceeds, the initial reasons for market segmentation have lost force. On the political front, the Chinese government has become more receptive to the non-public sectors of the economy. Most recently, the 2004 amendment to the Chinese Constitution has further elevated the political status of the non-public economic sectors, stating that 'the state *encourages and supports*. . . the development of the non-public sectors of the economy'.[14] Further, over time, the original experimental nature of the stock market has faded, and the market is seeming to function healthily and to play a more important role in the Chinese economy. The government has also realized that state shares could maintain their value, and perhaps even appreciate, through transfer on an open market. Finally, China has come under increasing pressure from western countries, notably the US, to further open up its financial markets. **10.32**

---

[13] See eg Jian Chen, 'Ownership Structure as Corporate Governance Mechanism: Evidence from Chinese Listed Companies' (2001) 34 *Econ of Planning* 53, 61.
[14] Chinese Constitution, Art 11 (2004 amendment) (emphasis added).

10.33 Thus, the government has been making great efforts to gradually solve the problem of market segmentation, with a view to bringing the market more in line with international norms.

10.2.3.1. Divide of A and B-shares

10.34 The A-share/B-share distinction has become blurred over time. On the one hand, the A-share market has gradually opened up to foreigners. First, in November 2002, the CSRC promulgated a rule to allow Qualified Foreign Institutional Investors (QFII) to invest in tradable A-shares.[15] To obtain QFII status, an application needs to be made to the CSRC and certain requirements must be met. It is usually impractical to acquire corporate control through QFII, as there are strict quotas of A-shares that QFII can purchase. For instance, investment by a QFII in any single listed company is capped at 10 per cent, and the total percentage of tradable A-shares in any single listed company held by all QFIIs may not exceed 20 per cent. Second, since December 2011, foreign investors have been able to invest their Chinese currency assets (RMB) in Chinese securities markets through the so-called Renminbi Qualified Foreign Institutional Investors (RQFII), which are Hong Kong subsidiaries of Chinese financial institutions, such as securities firms and fund management companies. Third, after 1 April 2013, people from Hong Kong, Macao, and Taiwan living in Mainland China have been able to invest directly in the A-shares market. In order to do so, they need to provide three documents: the identity card issued by their home government, their entry permit to the Mainland, and temporary residency registration in Mainland. This is a significant development in that it gives non-Mainland investors direct access to the A-share market, whereas the QFII and RQFII are vehicles for indirect investment.

10.35 On the other hand, since February 2001, B-shares have been made available for domestic investors to purchase with foreign currency. In another development, in July 2007, the CSRC issued a rule to set up the regime of Qualified Domestic Institutional Investors (QDII) through which Chinese investors can indirectly invest in securities markets overseas. Chinese financial institutions can apply to the CSRC for a QDII licence. In order to control investment risks, there are restrictions on the overseas markets in which the QDII can invest and the ways in which investments can be made.

10.36 Given the developments above, it is very likely that the A-share and B-share markets will be merged in future, and thus the distinction between A-shares and B-shares will become a matter of history.

---

[15] Hege Jingwai Jigou Touzizhe Jingnei Zhengquan Touzi Guanli Zanxing Banfa [Provisional Measures on Investing in Tradable Shares on China's Stock Market by Qualified Foreign Institutional Investors] (promulgated by the CSRC in November 2002, revised in 2006).

10.2.3.2. Divide of tradable and non-tradable shares

After several unsuccessful attempts, the government put forward a new plan for shareholding structure reform entitled *Guquan Fenzhi Gaige* in 2005, which has proven to be a great success.[16] The key to its success is that, unlike its predecessors, this 2005 plan adopts a market-based process rather than a government-imposed approach, under which the reform is carried out essentially through negotiation between the public shareholders who hold the tradable shares and the state holders of the non-tradable shares.[17]

10.37

Under this reform, the previously non-tradable shares will gradually become fully tradable in a period of time to which the parties autonomously agree in the negotiation process, subject to a statutorily specified minimum timeframe. As a result of the reform, the Chinese stock market has assumed a radically different landscape, which will have far-reaching implications for takeover activity.

10.38

10.3. China's Takeover Law and Activities

10.3.1. The legal framework

The legal regime regarding takeovers of listed companies in China consists of a number of laws and regulations. The first influential regulations containing takeover provisions were the Provisional Regulations for the Administration of Stock Insurance and Transaction ('Provisional Regulations'), promulgated in 1993 and still valid.[18] Since 1999, the Securities Law of the People's Republic of China ('Securities Law') has contained a whole chapter specifically regulating takeovers of listed companies.[19] These two sets of rules alone, however, established only a broadly sketched framework and appeared to be incapable of meeting the need to regulate takeovers.

10.39

In response to this, the CSRC promulgated two important regulations governing takeovers of listed companies in 2002, substantially improving the efficacy of the takeover law.[20] Still, on 31 July 2006, drawing upon these two

10.40

---

[16] For a more detailed discussion of this reform, see Hui Huang, 'The New Takeover Regulation in China: Evolution and Enhancement' (2008) 42(1) *The International Lawyer* 153, 156–7.
[17] See Shangshi Gongsi Guquan Fenzhi Gaige Guanli Banfa [Measures on the Shareholding Structure Reform of Listed Companies] (promulgated by the CSRC on 4 September 2005), Art 3.
[18] Gupiao Faxing Yu Jiaoyi Guanli Zanxing Tiaoli (Provisional Regulations for the Administration of Stock Issuance and Transaction] (promulgated by the State Council Securities Commission on 22 April 1993).
[19] Zhonghua Renming Gongheguo Zhenquan Fa [Securities Law of the People's Republic of China (Securities Law)] (promulgated by the Standing Commission of the National People's Congress, 29 December 1998, effective 1 July 1999, amended in 2004, 2005, and 2013), Chapter 4.
[20] The twin regulations were Shangshi Gongsi Shougou Guanli Banfa [Measures for Regulating Takeovers of Listed Companies (2002 Takeover Measures)] (promulgated 28 September 2002, effective 1 December 2002, repealed 1 September 2006) and Shangshi Gongsi Gudong Chigu Biandong Xinxi Pilu Guanli Banfa [Measures for Regulating Information Disclosure of the

regulations, the CSRC promulgated *Shangshi Gongsi Shougou Guanli Banfa* [Measures for Regulating Takeovers of Listed Companies] ('2006 Takeover Measures') to suit the new circumstances after the 2005 shareholding structure reform.[21] Along with other laws and regulations, this 2006 regulation has greatly enhanced China's takeover legal regime in terms of both form and substance. It consolidates into one single document the twin takeover regulations promulgated by the CSRC in 2002, rendering the legal framework more streamlined and easier to apply. More importantly, it makes a number of important substantive changes to fill the gaps in the previous regime. Although this regulation is not without defects, it now provides a sound basis for takeover activities in China.

10.41 It should be noted that there are also some other sources of law which may be relevant to takeover transactions. For example, the Company Law of the People's Republic of China contains some provisions about M&A.[22] In addition, the listing rules of the stock exchanges must also be consulted when conducting takeovers of listed companies.[23]

10.3.2. The regulator

10.42 As discussed earlier, the CSRC is the securities regulatory authority under the State Council and is charged with implementing centralized and unified regulation of China's securities market. It therefore has jurisdiction and power over takeovers of listed companies. Indeed, as a technocrat, it is assigned a virtually exclusive dispute resolution role with respect to takeovers. The 2006 Takeover Measures brought about a significant change whereby the CSRC established a special internal committee known as the M&A and Restructuring Examination Committee (*Binggou Chongzu Shenhe Weiyuanhui*). This committee is composed of professionals and relevant experts in the takeover area whose function is to provide opinions about takeover regulation at the request of a functional department of the CSRC.

Changes in Shareholdings of Listed Companies (2002 Information Disclosure Measures)] (promulgated 28 September 2002, effective 1 December 2002, repealed 1 September 2006). Both regulations were repealed as a result of the promulgation of the 2006 Takeover Measures, but their contents have been largely reproduced in its successor. For a detailed discussion of those two regulations, see Huang, 'China's Takeover Law'.

[21] Shangshi Gongsi Shougou Guanli Banfa [Measures for Regulating Takeovers of Listed Companies (2006 Takeover Measures)] (promulgated by CSRC on 31 July 2006 and effective from 1 September 2006, amended in 2008 and 2012).

[22] Zhonghua Renming Gongheguo Gongsi Fa [Company Law of the People's Republic of China (Company Law)] (promulgated by the Standing Commission of the National People's Congress, 29 December 1993, effective 1 July 1994, amended in 1999, 2004, 2005, and 2013).

[23] See eg Shanghai Zhengquan Jiaoyisuo Gupiao Shangshi Guize (Shanghai Stock Exchange, Share Listing Rules) (promulgated 1998, amended 2000, 2001, 2002, 2004, and 2006).

10.3.3. Takeover activities

10.43 In China, due to the short history of its securities market, takeovers are a recent phenomenon, but the number of takeovers has grown significantly since 1993. There are currently two main methods of takeover in China: one is takeover by tender offer; the other is takeover by private agreement.[24] As noted earlier, A-shares on China's stock market comprise tradable shares and non-tradable shares. Tradable shares—mainly public individual shares—can be purchased by tender offer, whereas non-tradable shares, consisting of state shares and legal person shares, can only be transferred by private agreement.

10.44 As previously shown, the predominant feature of China's stock market at present is that listed companies commonly have a highly concentrated ownership structure with the state as the controlling shareholder, and, more importantly, the majority of shares are non-tradable. In order to successfully acquire control of a listed company, one has to acquire the non-tradable shares by private agreement. Takeover by private agreement, therefore, has long been the main takeover method for acquiring control of a listed company in China.

10.45 For this reason, takeover by tender offer is presently not popular or feasible in China, given the traditional shareholding structure of most listed companies. To date, a very limited number of takeovers by tender offer in China have occurred, and almost all of the target companies had few non-tradable shares. For example, the *Shenzhen Baoan* case in 1993, sometimes regarded as the first takeover by tender offer in China, involved a small target company that was free of non-tradable shares.[25] This was a common feature shared by other cases.[26]

10.46 This situation is expected to change with the implementation of the 2005 shareholding structure reform, where non-tradable shares will be gradually transformed into tradable shares. Once all the previously non-tradable shares become tradable, there will be more takeovers by tender offer in China, including hostile takeovers. Against this background, the Chinese government has promulgated new regulations in recent years to keep up with market developments. Indeed, since then, there has been an increase in the number of takeovers by tender offer.[27]

---

[24] Securities Law, Art 85.
[25] See China Securities Regulatory Commission, Decision of the China Securities Regulatory Commission on the Punishment of the Shanghai Subsidiary Company of Shenzhen Baoan Group Company, the Baoan Huayang Health Care Production Company, and the Shenzhen Ronggang Baoling Electrical Lighting Company for Breaching the Securities Regulations, 4 Zhongguo Zhengquan Jiandu Guanli Weiyuanhui Gonggao (China Securities Regulatory Commission Official Bulletin) (25 October 1993).
[26] In another case, Shenzhen Vanke, a Shenzhen company, attempted to acquire control of Shanghai Shenhua Industrial, a Shanghai publicly traded company, which had a total of 27 million shares outstanding, of which there were no state shares. See Christine Chan, 'Shenhua Stake Cost Vanke 39M Yuan', *NanHua ZaoBao [Southern China Morning Post]* 15 November 1993, Business, 3.
[27] For instance, NanGan Gufen and Chengshang Group were the target companies, respectively, in two cases of takeover by tender offer. For a detailed discussion of the NanGan Gufen case, see Part IV.

10.4. The Guiding Principles for Takeover Regulation

10.47 The policy objective of China's securities regulation is that the securities transaction shall be conducted in line with the principles of openness (*Gong Kai*), fairness (*Gong Ping*), and equity (*Gong Zheng*), also known as the Three Gong Principles.[28] To that end, takeover regulation needs to be conducted in accordance with two guiding principles: (1) shareholder protection and (2) the contestability of takeovers. These two principles have been expressly endorsed by the CSRC in the 2006 Takeover Measures, which reads:

> According to Company Law, Securities Law and other laws and relevant administrative regulations, this measure is enacted in order to standardize the takeover activities of listed companies, stimulate the optimization of the resource allocation on the stock market, protect the lawful rights and interests of investors, safeguard the normal order of the stock market.[29]

10.48 These principles have had a profound shaping effect upon Chinese takeover law and are incorporated throughout the whole of the 2006 Takeover Measures. The two principles may be consistent in some instances, while in other situations they may be diametrically opposed. The issue of designing the best possible takeover law consists of nothing more than trying to strike a balance between the two guiding principles.

10.4.1. Contestability of takeovers

10.49 Takeover regulation appears to occupy a significant place in the corporate laws of various jurisdictions and the socio-economic effects of such regulations have been widely debated. Takeovers, especially hostile takeovers, have long been regarded as an effective mechanism of monitoring the management of corporations and, as such, are beneficial to the enhancement of corporate governance. Faced with the possibility of a hostile takeover, managers have an incentive to manage more efficiently, thus creating shareholder value.[30] This aids in aligning the interests of management with the interests of the shareholders and thus reduces the agency costs of management.[31]

10.50 The benefit of takeovers has been positively recognized by legislators. In debating the bill which would later become the Williams Act in the US, Senator Williams stated that '[i]n some instances, a change in management will prove a welcome

---

[28] Securities Law, Art 3.
[29] 2006 Takeover Measures, Art 1.
[30] Frank H Easterbrook and Daniel R Fischel, 'The Proper Role of a Target's Management in Responding to a Tender Offer' (1981) 94 *Harvard Law Review* 1161, 1169.
[31] Easterbrook and Fischel, 'The Proper Role', at 1173; see also Gregory R Andre, 'Tender Offers for Corporate Control: A Critical Analysis and Proposals for Reform' (1987) 12 *Delaware Journal of Corporate Law* 865; Ronald J Gilson, 'A Structural Approach to Corporations: The Case Against Defensive Tactics in Tender Offers' (1981) 33 *Stanford Law Review* 819; Henry G Manne, 'Mergers and the Market for Corporate Control' (1965) 73 *Journal of Political Economy* 110, 113.

boon for shareholder and employee, and in a few severe situations it may be necessary if the company is to survive'.[32] In addition, takeovers are also thought to improve the allocation efficiency of scarce social resources, to the benefit of society as a whole. Takeovers ensure that the resources are utilized by the most capable people and yield the maximum returns.[33] Further, takeovers could create value for shareholders by providing them with a substantial premium on the sale of their shares.[34]

10.51 This pro-takeover argument, however, is not without criticism. A powerful counterargument is that the threat of a hostile takeover forces managers to emphasize short-term gains and 'paper profits'. Under this view, management puts short-term concerns ahead of long-term concerns in making decisions. In other words, managers would be reluctant to devote corporate resources to research and development of new products and technologies; thus, shareholders would not receive long-term value for their investment.[35] Apart from this, hostile takeovers have also been regarded as leading to lost productivity from business disruption, creating dangerously leveraged capital structures, and causing inefficiency by diverting managers from *real* economic activity to financial reshuffling.[36] More severely, this might result in national industries losing their competitiveness in the international market.

10.52 The anti-takeover stance, however, has also been attacked. It has been opined that anti-takeover claims are 'impressionistic' and largely based 'on anecdotal evidence'.[37] Acknowledging that those claims appear to have gained some influence, other commentators have argued that such claims are untenable due to a lack of support from conclusive empirical evidence.[38] Others, notably Easterbrook and

---

[32] 113 CONG. REC. 854 (1967) (statement of Sen Williams).
[33] See eg John C Coffee Jr, 'Regulating the Market for Corporate Control: A Critical Assessment of the Tender Offer's Role in Corporate Governance' (1984) 84 *Columbia Law Review* 1145, 1221; Frank H Easterbrook and Daniel R Fischel, 'Corporate Control Transactions' (1982) 91 *Yale Law Journal* 698, 705; Michael C Jensen, 'Takeovers: Their Causes and Consequences' (1988) 2 *Journal of Economic Perspectives* 21, 23.
[34] Michael C Jensen, 'The Takeover Controversy: Analysis and Evidence', in John C Coffee Jr et al (eds), *Knights, Raiders, and Targets, The Impact Of The Hostile Takeover* 314 (Oxford: Oxford University Press, 1988) (stating that '[t]akeovers benefit target shareholders—premiums in hostile offers historically exceed 30%, on average, and in recent times have averaged about 50%'). See also Michael C Jensen and Richard S Ruback, 'The Market for Corporate Control, The Scientific Evidence' (1983) 11 *Journal of Financial Economics* 5, 9–16 (arguing that target shareholders can benefit from takeover premiums); Reinier Kraakman, 'Taking Discounts Seriously: The Implications of 'Discounted' Share Prices As An Acquisition Motive' (1988) 88 *Columbia Law Review* 891, 908 (observing that target shareholders can be better off selling shares at a premium).
[35] See eg Michael C Jensen, 'The Modern Industrial Revolution, Exit, and the Failure of Internal Control Systems' (1993) 48 *J Fin* 837.
[36] See eg Peter F Drucker, 'Drucker on Management: Taming the Corporate Takeover', *Wall Street Journal*, 30 October 1984, at 30, col 3.
[37] See eg John C Coffee Jr, 'Regulating the Market'.
[38] See Jeffrey N Gordon, 'Corporations, Markets, and Courts' (1991) 91 *Columbia Law Review* 1931, 1955.

Fischel, aggressively contend that management's fear of takeovers would not, as the anti-takeover claim posits, necessarily give rise to short-term strategies, on the grounds that '[i]f the market perceives that management has developed a successful long-term strategy, this will be reflected in higher share prices that discourage takeovers'.[39]

10.53 The debate over the economic value of takeovers remains largely inconclusive and, as such, will continue in the foreseeable future, as will the relevant empirical studies. As with most legal debates, the issue of takeovers cannot be sensibly examined without taking account of the specific context in which takeover activities operate. In the face of the contrasting effects associated with takeovers, we must prioritize them by analysing the needs of the specific situations in question.

10.54 In China, the problem of corporate governance is particularly serious, for various reasons. The lack of management supervision is generally thought to be at the heart of the issue. There are, in theory, several mechanisms for monitoring management in China. First, according to the Company Law, shareholders have the power to monitor managers.[40] State-owned shares, however, occupy a high percentage of all the outstanding shares in most listed companies. Due to the problems of agency costs and an omnipresent bureaucracy, the state as the majority shareholder has long seemed to be virtually non-existent with respect to the monitoring of management. This unique phenomenon is called *Guoyougu Suoyouzhe Quewei* (no functional proprietor of state-owned shares). Second, the two-tier corporate governance system in China has resulted in a specifically designed supervisory board to monitor directors and corporate officials. Unfortunately, in practice the supervisory board has proved to be ineffective in serving its purported function. Third, China has introduced the institution of independent directors, which was primarily modelled after the US system, with a focus on remedying the deficiency of management monitoring. So far, this practice has suffered many problems and has not solved the targeted management monitoring issue as originally expected.

10.55 Therefore, in the context of China, it appears that the monitoring mechanism at the heart of corporate governance is far more severe than in the US, and is the primary problem in need of a solution. Thus, the management monitoring value of takeovers should take precedence (at least at this stage of China's economic development). Furthermore, China is transitioning from a centrally planned economy to a market-oriented economy, and many problems exist regarding the inefficiency of the allocation of resources. Thus, whole industries urgently need to be restructured to optimally employ social resources. By reforming the takeover framework, China could improve the efficiency of management, optimize the allocation of

---

[39] Easterbrook and Fischel, 'The Proper Role of a Target's Management' (asserting that '[t]he threat of takeovers does not prevent managers from engaging in long-range planning').
[40] Company Law, Arts 38, 100 (listing the powers of the shareholders' general meeting).

social resources, enhance corporate governance, and boost the international competitiveness of its industries as a whole. After China's entry into the WTO, it has become crucially important to hasten the process of achieving these goals in order to survive in an increasingly competitive world economy. A vigorous corporate control market is central to the realization of this goal, and China needs to take a pro-takeover stance.

10.4.2. Shareholder protection

In addition to maintaining the contestability of takeovers to achieve the management monitoring value, another crucial principle with respect to takeovers is shareholder protection—more specifically, the protection of existing shareholders and their companies from unwanted takeovers and the protection of individual shareholders from unjust treatment during takeovers. In other words, the legal takeover framework must ensure fairness and justice in the course of takeover activities, while at the same time promoting economic efficiency. **10.56**

Hansmann and Kraakman, among others, have asserted that '[t]here is no longer any serious competitor to the view that corporate law should principally strive to increase long-term shareholder value'.[41] This shareholder protection principle is particularly prominent in circumstances where the takeovers are instituted by corporate raiders. In such a situation, there is a real possibility that some acquirers would expropriate the wealth of the existing shareholders, and thus the target company shareholders would be harmed by the takeover. This phenomenon has a long history[42] and eventually prompted the enactment of various takeover-oriented legislation, such as the Williams Act[43] in the US and similar laws in other jurisdictions, including China. The protection of investors is mainly achieved by requiring adequate information disclosure and specifying certain rules concerning tender offers. In Australia, for example, the Eggleston principle was introduced in 1969 with a view to the attainment of shareholder protection,[44] and has been viewed as 'the product of the application of. . . equity jurisprudence'.[45] **10.57**

---

[41] Henry Hansmann and Reinier Kraakman, 'The End of History for Corporate Law' (2001) 89 *Georgetown Law Journal* 439, 439.

[42] John Coffee has advanced the theory that investment bankers of the late nineteenth century performed the function of protecting 'the public shareholder from attempts by speculators to steal a firm's control premium'. See John C Coffee Jr, 'The Rise of Dispersed Ownership: The Roles of Law and the State in the Separation of Ownership and Control' (2001) 111 *Yale Law Journal* 1, 31.

[43] Pub L No 90-4393, 82 Stat 454 (1 968), codified as amended at 15 U.S.C. §§ 78m(d)–(f), 78n(d)–(f) (2000).

[44] The Eggleston Principle took its name from the Company Law Advisory Committee (the Eggleston Committee), which conducted a review of the situation of investor protection offered by the then existing takeover law. See Company Law Advisory Committee, Second Interim Report: Disclosure of Substantial Shareholdings and Takeover Bids 6 (Canberra: AGPS, 1969), available at http://www.takeovers.gov.au/display.acp?ContentID=494.

[45] Tony Greenwood, 'In Addition to Justin Mannolini' (2000) 11 *Australian Journal of Corporate Law* 308, 310.

10.58 The US provides another good example. A cash tender offeror could operate in virtual secrecy, like a corporate raider, in the pre-Williams Act era because the law did not require that '[a cash tender offeror] disclose his identity, the source of his funds, who his associate[s] were, or what he intended to do if he gained control of the corporation'.[46] The Williams Act was designed to protect investors by requiring sufficient information be provided to enable them to make an informed decision with respect to a tender offer. It is the purpose of the Williams Act that the target company management adopts appropriate defensive tactics to increase the value to target shareholders.

10.59 The objective of shareholder protection, however, may conflict with the economic objectives of efficiency in resource allocation, to the extent that the rule would render the hostile takeover more difficult and thus diminish the contestability of takeovers. The substantial costs associated with information disclosure and tender offer rules, which are designed to protect investors, may effectively deter many takeovers that otherwise would have been launched.[47] Furthermore, it is widely recognized that the target's management has the incentive to abuse defensive tactics with respect to hostile takeovers for the purpose of entrenchment.[48] Some takeover defences, which were originally designed as a means to protect target shareholders from raiders, have been found to be frequently misused by the target's management. For example, a target's management may use defensive measures to thwart a hostile takeover that would injure their interests, regardless of whether the takeover would be beneficial to the shareholders,[49] resulting in diminished contestability of takeovers. This problem has been at the heart of the discussion of takeover law and received a wide range of practical and academic attention.

10.4.3. Two aspects of takeover law

10.60 In general, a takeover transaction involves two-way traffic: one direction is the process under which the acquirer makes a takeover bid; the other is the way in which the target company, and in particular its management, respond to the bid. Correspondingly, takeover law has two main aspects to regulate the bid-making process and the use of takeover defences respectively. In assessing the takeover law of any given jurisdiction, one needs to examine both of the two aspects, as they comprise a complete legal regime for takeover transactions. Hence, these two aspects are to be discussed separately in this chapter and the next one.

---

[46] S. REP. NO. 90-550, at 2 (1967).
[47] See eg Justin Mannolini, 'Convergence or Divergence: Is there a Role for the Eggleston Principles in a Global M&A Environment?' (2002) 24 *Sydney Law Review* 336 (arguing that the protection of minority shareholders as advocated by Eggleston Principle is a 'luxury' of economically inefficient, albeit admirably egalitarian, rules).
[48] See eg Lucian A Bebchuk, 'The Case for Facilitating Competing Tender Offers' (1982) 95 *Harvard Law Review* 1028, 1029.
[49] See eg Lucian A Bebchuk and Allen Ferrel, 'Federalism and Corporate Law: The Race to Protect Managers from Takeovers' (1999) 99 *Columbia Law Review* 1168.

10.5. The Mandatory Bid Rule

10.5.1. Overview

In accordance with the equality-of-opportunity principle, a mandatory bid rule sits at the heart of China's takeover law. Under Article 88 of the Securities Law: **10.61**

> Where an investor holds or holds with any other person 30% of the stocks as issued by a listed company by means of agreement or any other arrangement through securities trading at a stock exchange and if the purchase is continued, he shall issue a tender offer to all the shareholders of the said listed company to purchase all of or part of the shares of the listed company.

The 2006 Takeover Measures set out more detailed provisions to implement this rule. Several points need to be noted here.

First, it is clear that an acquirer can become a controlling shareholder of a listed company by directly obtaining shares and can become an actual controller of a listed company by means of investment relationship, agreement, or any other arrangement.[50] This effectively recognizes that a listed company can be acquired by means of tender offer or private agreement as well as by any other legal means, such as inheritance, and that all of these acquisitions may trigger the mandatory bid rule.[51] **10.62**

Second, when calculating an investor's shareholding, the voting rights of its associates or parties acting in concert (so-called *Yizhi Xingdongren*) will also be counted. The associates are those with whom the primary person is acting in concert by way of private agreement or any other arrangement so as to increase their joint voting powers in a listed company.[52] To facilitate enforcement, the 2006 Takeover Measures provide a long list of situations where certain people are deemed to be associates of an investor in the absence of contrary evidence: **10.63**

(1) There is an equity control relationship between the investors.
(2) The investors are controlled by the same subject.
(3) Main members among directors, supervisors, or senior managers of one investor simultaneously act as the directors, supervisors, or senior managers of another investor.
(4) One investor purchases the shares of another investor, and can produce significant effects for major decisions of the purchased company.

---

[50] Securities Law, Art 88.
[51] Securities Law, Art 47 (providing that takeovers by private agreement are subject to the mandatory bid rule). In a recent case, Dikang Konggu Co was forced to make a tender offer because it acquired more than 30 per cent of the state shares of Chengshang Group by a private agreement. See Jun Li, 'The Transfer of State Shares of Chengshang Group Triggers Mandatory Bid', *Guoji Jingrong Bao [International Finance News]* 15 April 2003, at 7.
[52] 2006 Takeover Measures, Art 83.

(5) A legal person or any other organization other than the bank or a natural person provides the capital financing for the investor to obtain relevant shares.
(6) There is a partnership, co-operation, joint venture or any other relation of economic interests between the investors.
(7) A natural person holding 30 per cent or more of the shares of the investor holds the shares of the same listed company together with the investor.
(8) A director, supervisor, or senior manager of the investor holds the shares of the same listed company together with the investor.
(9) A natural person holding 30 per cent or more of the shares of the investor; a director, supervisor, or senior manager in the investor; or the above-mentioned person's parent, spouse, child and the child's spouse, the spouse's parent, the above-mentioned person's brother or sister and their spouses, brother or sister of the above-mentioned person's spouse and their spouses, etc, holds the shares of the same listed company as the investor.
(10) A director, supervisor, or senior manager of the listed company holds the shares of the said company together with any of his relatives as mentioned in the preceding Item, or together with any enterprise directly or indirectly controlled by himself or any of the aforesaid relatives.
(11) A director, supervisor, senior manager, or employee of the listed company holds the shares of the said company together with a legal person or any other organization under the control or authorization thereof.
(12) There is any other affiliated relationship between the investors.[53]

10.64 Compared with the already broad scope of associates in Australia,[54] the Chinese version appears to be even broader. For example, under Chinese law, the situations deemed relevant include those where there is an equity control relationship between the investors, where the investors are controlled by the same entity, and where one investor is capable of influencing the other person's affairs by virtue of private agreement or other business relationships. Moreover, other people, such as directors of the acquiring company and their family members, would also come within the definition, while they would not necessarily be counted as associates in Australia.

10.65 As the shares held by associates count toward the 30 per cent numerical threshold, transactions between associates do not seem to increase a person's overall shareholding under the formula. The CSRC has confirmed that share transfers between different entities under common control would not trigger the mandatory bid rule.[55] This is to be contrasted with the Australian takeover law, under

---

[53] 2006 Takeover Measures, Art 83.
[54] Corporations Act, 2001, § 12 (Austl.) [hereinafter 'Corporations Act'].
[55] Zhengquan Qihuo Falu Shiyong Yijian No 4 [The Fourth Opinion on the Application of the Law Governing Securities and Futures] (promulgated by the CSRC on 19 May 2009).

which associates are not necessarily at liberty to dispose of voting shares between each other.[56] The Australian position is based on the view that the criteria for defining associates do not necessarily give them a relevant interest in each other's shares.

10.66 In addition, the calculation of an investor's shareholding is not limited to shares but extended to those non-share securities that can be converted into shares in the future.[57] Examples may include options and warrants. There is a parallel provision in Australian takeover law.[58] One difference, however, is that convertible debentures appear to also be covered in the Chinese calculation, while in Australia they are not counted until the later time of conversion.

10.67 Third, the concept of control is clearly set out in Article 84 of the 2006 Takeover Measures. An investor controls a listed company if it has more than a 50 per cent shareholding, can exercise 30 per cent of voting rights, or otherwise has the capacity to determine the election of more than half of the directors or the outcome of decisions of shareholder meetings.[59] This concept seems similar to that in Australian takeover regulation, which is broad enough to embrace a factual control situation.[60]

10.68 From an international perspective, the mandatory bid rule has been an issue of contention. Australia and the UK have been among the proponents of such a mechanism: indeed, China's mandatory bid rule is almost identical to that in the UK as stated in the City Code on Takeovers and Mergers.[61] In Australia, acquiring more than 20 per cent of voting power in a company is prohibited, subject to a number of exceptions, including the making of a takeover bid.[62] In stark contrast, an acquirer under US law has greater flexibility—it is not required to make an offer if it becomes a 30 per cent shareholder, as it would under the Chinese regime.[63]

10.69 The mandatory bid rule could provide a great degree of shareholder protection by ensuring that the control premium is shared among all shareholders. This is seemingly in line with the Chinese 'Three Gong' principles. This is not the case in the United States, where 'it is possible for a bidder to purchase a control block from a private party without making an offer to other shareholders and probably without any sharing of a

---

[56] Corporations Act, Art 610(3).
[57] 2006 Takeover Measures, Art 85.
[58] See Corporations Act, § 608(8) (providing anticipatory relevant interests).
[59] 2006 Takeover Measures, Art 84.
[60] See Corporations Act, § 50AA.
[61] The Panel on Takeovers and Mergers, *The Takeover Code* (2006), Rule 9, F1. [hereinafter 'City Code on Takeovers and Mergers'].
[62] Corporations Act, §§ 606, 611, 616. It should be noted that the Australian takeover provisions are somewhat different from the mandatory bid rule. These provisions are in effect more stringent than the mandatory bid rule because the mandatory bid rule allows for control to pass prior to a general offer via 'pre-bid agreements or understandings between bidders and target shareholders', thus reducing the costs of takeovers. See Corporate Law Economic Reform Program, *Commonwealth of Australia Paper No 4, Takeovers—Corporate Control: A Better Environment for Productive Investment*, para 4.1 (1 April 1997).
[63] 15 U.S.C. §§ 78m(d)-(f), 78n(d) (2000).

control premium paid to the departing control group'.[64] Thus, China's takeover law seems more attractive than its American counterpart from the target shareholders' point of view.

10.5.2. Mitigating the harshness of the rule

10.70 The function of investor protection of the mandatory bid rule, however, comes at the expense of the contestability of takeovers, because it would increase the cost of takeovers and scare off some potential bidders at the margin. This concern could be better met by fine-tuning the mandatory bid rule rather than abandoning it, so as to keep a proper balance between the two conflicting goals of takeover law.

10.71 First, the height of the triggering barrier set in the rule could greatly influence the practical outcome of the rule. Even though it may be difficult to set the numbers to fit local situations, the inherent flexibility of the mandatory bid rule could be a valuable tool to meet the policy goals. For example, if the 30 per cent shareholding threshold proves to be too high in the context of China, it could be reduced to 20 per cent, as is the case in Australia. Similarly, the threshold could be raised to reduce the cost of takeovers.

10.72 Second, the mandatory bid rule can be relaxed by way of requiring a partial bid rather than a full bid. As will be discussed later, the 2006 Takeover Measures allows partial bids. This may reduce the cost of takeovers in two significant ways. On the one hand, the acquirer is not forced to acquire any more than is necessary to gain corporate control. For instance, the acquirer may only need to have relative control with a shareholding of less than 50 per cent; even if absolute control is the goal, the acquirer can purchase a bit over 50 per cent of shares in the target company. On the other hand, a partial bid can address concern over delisting of the target company. Under a full mandatory bid, it is indeed possible that shareholders of the target company tender sufficient shares so as to make the target company no longer meet the listing requirements. As discussed in previous chapters, due to the merits review mechanism for securities listings, listing status is highly valuable in China, and the acquirer would usually try to avoid the consequence of delisting the target company after the takeover.

10.73 Third, the harshness of the mandatory bid rule can be mitigated by providing a way out where appropriate. In China, the obligation to make mandatory bids can be exempted by the CSRC. As shall be discussed, since the exemption system had previously caused serious problems, the 2006 Takeover Measures paid considerable

---

[64] See Robert B Thompson, 'Takeover Regulation After the 'Convergence' of Corporate Law' (2002) 24 *Sydney Law Review* 323, 326. In the United States, the acquirer would most likely have to offer a large premium of about 50 per cent in its tender offer. See Michael C Jensen, 'The Takeover Controversy: Analysis and Evidence' (Summer 1986) *Midland Corporate Finance Journal* 1, 2 (stating that '[t]akeovers benefit target shareholders—premiums in hostile offers historically exceed 30 percent on average, and in recent times have averaged about 50 percent').

attention to this issue, clarifying the grounds upon which the CSRC may grant an exemption. Further, in order to improve the efficiency of the system, the CSRC sets out two application processes.

10.74 More specifically, in some cases where the matter is complicated, the application needs to go through a formal process, which takes no more than 20 days. Such cases include:[65]

(1) The purchaser and the transferor can prove that the transfer has not caused the alteration of the actual controller of the listed company.
(2) The listed company is confronted with serious financial difficulty, the purchaser has put forward a reorganization scheme for saving the company and received approval from of the general assembly of shareholders of the company, and the purchaser promises not to transfer the entitlements it holds in the company within the next three years.
(3) The purchaser obtains the new shares issued thereto to it by the listed company upon the approval of the non-related shareholders of the general assembly of shareholders of the listed company, and as a result, he holds more than 30 per cent of the shares in the company; he promises not to transfer his shares within three years and the general assembly of shareholders of the company agrees that the purchaser is exempted from making a tender offer.
(4) Any other circumstance as recognized by the CSRC for adapting to the development and alteration of the securities market or the requirements for protecting the lawful rights and interests of investors.

10.75 In other cases where crossing the 30 per cent threshold appears to be technically caused by non-takeover activities such as inheritance or underwriting arrangements, a simplified procedure is to be followed to allow quicker processing. These include:[66]

(1) The gratuitous transfer, alteration, and combination of state-owned assets upon the approval of the government or the state-owned assets administrative department results, so that the shares whose entitlements are held by the investor in a listed company are more than 30 per cent of the issued shares of the listed company.
(2) If the shares whose entitlements are held by the investor in a listed company reach or exceed 30 per cent of the issued shares of the company, the investor does not, after one year as of the occurrence of the aforesaid fact, increase his shareholding more than 2 per cent within any rolling period of twelve months.

---

[65] 2006 Takeover Measures, Art 62.
[66] 2006 Takeover Measures, Art 63. In 2008, the CSRC fine-tuned the simplified procedure to enhance its workability. Guanyu Xiugai Shangshi Gongsi Shougou Guanli Banfa Di 63 Tiao de Guiding (Decision on the Revision of Article 63 of the 2006 Takeover Measure) (promulgated by the CSRC on 27 August 2008).

(3) The shares whose entitlements are held by the investor in a listed company reach or exceed 50 per cent of the issued shares of the company, and the increased entitlements held by the investor in the company will not affect the listing of the company.
(4) The capital stock is reduced because the listed company repurchases shares from specific shareholders at a determined price as approved by the general assembly of shareholders, which causes the shares whose entitlements held by the party in the company to exceed 30 per cent of the issued shares of the company.
(5) The engagement in brokerage or loans, etc, of a securities company, bank, or any other financial institution within its business scope results in its holding more than 30 per cent of the issued shares of a listed company, but it does not have intent to or take actions to actually control the company and has put forward a solution to transfer the relevant shares to the non-affiliated party within a reasonable term.
(6) The shares whose entitlements are held by the investor exceed 30 per cent of the issued shares of a listed company due to inheritance.
(7) Any other circumstance as recognized by the CSRC for adapting to the development and alteration of the securities market or the requirements for protecting the lawful rights and interests of investors.

10.76 By way of comparison, the above exemptions appear much in line with those set out in Australian takeover law. For example, in addition to the CSRC powers, shareholders of the target company can pass a resolution to exempt the acquirer from the mandatory bid rule,[67] which is essentially the 'approval by resolution of target' exception in Australia.[68] There is also a newly introduced exemption under which an investor can increase its shareholding by less than 2 per cent in a rolling period of 12 months,[69] a counterpart of the Australian '3 per cent creep in six months' exception.[70]

10.6. Tender Offer Rules

10.6.1. Full/partial bids

10.77 As discussed earlier, whatever the method of acquiring more than 30 per cent of the shares in a target listed company, the mandatory bid rule will apply subject to exemptions granted by the CSRC. Under the 2002 Takeover Measures, the

---

[67] 2006 Takeover Measures, Art 62(2), (3).
[68] Corporations Act, §611(7).
[69] 2006 Takeover Measures, Art 63(2).
[70] Corporations Act, §611(9).

mandatory bid could only be a full bid. In 2005, the Securities Law was amended to permit the bid to be either full or partial.[71]

Partial takeover bids perform a useful economic function and may be beneficial to investors because they provide a cheaper way to conduct value-creating takeovers. But they are likely to be abused, and thus the CSRC retains strict control over them. For example, in the case of a partial bid, the percentage of shares the acquirer plans to acquire must not be less than 5 per cent of all outstanding shares in the target company.[72] This is intended to prevent the use of partial bids to commit market manipulation or insider trading. As shall be discussed later, however, the partial bid rule still suffers from other problems. **10.78**

10.6.2. Payment methods and pricing rules

Apart from the permission of partial bids, there are several other significant changes which the 2006 Takeover Measures have made to the previous regime. First, the method of payment in a takeover bid has become more flexible. Previously, an offer under a takeover bid had to be in cash only, which caused a lot of trouble for acquirers in terms of financing and post-takeover integration.[73] The 2006 Takeover Measures relaxed the stance on this issue, providing that an acquirer can pay the price of the takeover of a listed company by cash, securities, a combination of cash and securities, or any other lawful method.[74] This brings takeovers in China more in line with international practices, where a combination of cash and stock is commonly used in takeovers.[75] But in the case of a full bid, the acquirer must provide a cash alternative and target shareholders can choose which they prefer.[76] **10.79**

Second, the lower limit of the offer price has been substantially changed. According to the 2006 Takeover Measures, the price offered under a takeover bid must not be less than the maximum price that the bidder has paid for the bid security during the six months preceding the date of the bid.[77] Further, if the offer price is below the arithmetic average value of the daily weighted average prices during the 30 trading days prior to the date of the bid, a financial consultant must be hired by the bidder to produce a report on issues such as whether there has been any manipulation of stock prices, whether the bidder has failed to disclosed its concerned parties, **10.80**

---

[71] Baoshu Wang and Hui Huang (2006) 'China's New Company Law and Securities Law: An Overview and Assessment' (2006) 19(2) *Australian Journal of Corporate Law* 229, 237.
[72] 2006 Takeover Measures, Art 25.
[73] Shenggui Zhang, 'The Impact of the New Takeover Measures on the Market', available at http://www.9ask.cn (pointing out that the pure-cash rule had been a significant obstacle to takeovers in China).
[74] 2006 Takeover Measures, Art 36.
[75] See eg Richard Dobbs et al, 'Are Companies Getting Better at M&A?', *The McKinsey Quarterly* (December 2006), available at http://www.mckinseyquarterly.com; Corporations Act, § 621(1).
[76] 2006 Takeover Measures, Art 27.
[77] 2006 Takeover Measures, Art 35.

whether there has been any other arrangement for the bidder to obtain the shares of the target company during the previous six months, and finally whether the offer price is reasonable.[78]

10.81 This new price rule is a response to the problems arising from the 2002 Takeover Measures. Previously, the offer price had to be set differently between tradable and non-tradable shares. Specifically, the price for tradable shares was determined by reference to the market price, while the price for non-tradable shares was based on the net asset value per share.[79] In light of the 2005 shareholding structure reform, this dichotomous treatment has become obsolete, and a uniform rule for price setting was warranted. More importantly, under the 2002 Takeover Measures, one of the benchmarks for setting the offer price for tradable shares was 90 per cent of the arithmetic average value of the daily weighted average prices during the 30 trading days prior to the date of the bid.[80] As noted above, the 2006 Takeover Measures have removed the 90 per cent discount, which had caused perverse takeover activities, as illustrated in the following case.

10.82 The Nangang Gufen case has been widely seen as the first instance on the Chinese securities market of takeover by tender offer in the strict sense.[81] On 3 December 2003, Nangang Group, the parent company of Nangang Gufen, entered into an agreement with several business partners, including Fuxing Group, to form a new company called Nangang United. The Nangang Group agreed to transfer the state shares it held in Nangang Gufen to Nangang United as its contribution. Because the transferred state shares exceeded 30 per cent of all shares in Nangang Gufen, Nangang United, as the acquirer, had to face the mandatory bid rule. After failing to get an exemption from the CSRC, Nangang Untied was forced to make history in an offering that was the first ever takeover bid in China's stock market.

10.83 But the price-setting rule under the 2002 Takeover Measures made this first tender offer case an embarrassing farce. Clearly, Nangang United did not want the remaining shareholders to tender their shares. Therefore, the offer price was set at the minimum as required by the 2002 Takeover Measures. Specifically, the offer price for non-tradable shares was CNY 3.81 per share on the basis of the net asset value test, while the offer price for tradable shares was pitched at CNY 5.84 per share, equivalent to 90 per cent of the arithmetic average value of the daily weighted average prices during the 30 trading days prior to the date of the bid. Because the offer price for tradable shares was at a discount to the market price rather than at a premium, none of the shareholders of tradable shares accepted the offer, which was the expected and desired outcome for Nangang United.

---

[78] 2006 Takeover Measures.
[79] 2006 Takeover Measures, Art 34.
[80] 2006 Takeover Measures, Art 34(1).
[81] Wenzhi Luo and Hanbing Dong, *Shangshi Gongsi Binggou Falv Shiwu [Legal Practice for M&A of Listed Companies]* 145–52 (2005).

10.84 This case reflects two important problems with the 2002 Chinese takeover law. First, the segregated equity ownership structure has made the operation of the mandatory bid rule in China distinctly different from its overseas counterparts. It was precisely because of the tradable/non-tradable segregation that Nangang United was able to set a different price for the holders of tradable shares, shunning its duty to give shareholders of tradable shares an equal opportunity to share the premium granted to holders of non-tradable shares. As discussed before, this problem will disappear in the foreseeable future as a result of the shareholding structure reform.

10.85 The second problem, of course, can be found in the previous rule for setting the price for the holders of tradable shares. As illustrated in the above case, the 90 per cent discount rule could allow the bidder to deliberately set the offer price along the bottom line, where rejection of the offer would be almost a certainty and thus the bidder could lawfully avoid the financial costs imposed by the mandatory bid rule. In recognition of this, the CSRC has revised the price rule in the 2006 Takeover Measures, as has been discussed.

10.6.3. Conducting the takeover bid

10.86 In conformity with its underlying principles, the 2006 Takeover Measures set out detailed provisions on how to conduct a takeover bid. The principle of equal opportunity is expressed in Article 26, which provides that all target shareholders should be treated equally in takeovers.[82] This fundamental norm is reflected in a prohibition upon the giving of collateral benefits during the bid: a bidder may not purchase securities in the bid class outside the bid or give a benefit to induce acceptance of an offer which is beyond the terms as stipulated in the offer and is not provided to other offerees.[83] The principle of openness is embodied in the information disclosure regime with respect to takeovers and the principle of fairness, and sheds light on the procedures for conducting a takeover bid.[84]

10.87 These rules provide a safeguard for target shareholders to prevent coercive tender offers through adequate information disclosure about the tender offer and the right to have reasonable time to consider it. First, the bidder must inform the market of the terms of the offer and other relevant information, such as the purpose of the takeover, the offer price, and the payment arrangement.[85] Second, the offer should

---

[82] 2006 Takeover Measures, Art 26.
[83] 2006 Takeover Measures, Art 38. Apart from the prohibition on giving collateral benefits, Australia also prohibits escalation agreements made by a bidder under which a commitment is made to the seller of securities in the period up to six months before the bid is made or proposed that the consideration will increase retrospectively if a higher price is later offered under a takeover bid for the securities. Corporations Act, s 622. This prohibition on escalation agreements further reinforces the principle of equal treatment.
[84] 2006 Takeover Measures, pt III.
[85] 2006 Takeover Measures, Art 29.

be open for a minimum time to avoid shareholders making hasty decisions: the effective period of the offer must be no less than 30 days and no more than 60 days, except where there is a competing offer.[86] The bidder cannot withdraw the tender offer before the bid period expires.

10.88 There are also detailed rules on variation of the terms of offers. In practice, the bidder may vary the offers in two main respects: (1) improving the consideration or offering an alternative form of consideration; (2) extending the offer period before the end of the offer period. If the bidder wants to vary the terms of the offer, approval from the CSRC is required.[87] Variation cannot occur within 15 days prior to the expiration of the bid unless a competing bid is made.[88] In the case of a competing offer, if the initial bidder modifies its offer less than 15 days before the expiration of the initial offer, the offer period shall be extended so that the offer is open for at least another 15 days, but this shall not be extended to later than the expiry date of the last competing offer. The person who wants to make a competing offer must announce its intention to do so at least 15 days before the expiration of the initial offer. Finally, the target's shareholders can withdraw their acceptance within three days before the expiration of the bid.[89]

10.7. Compulsory Buyout

10.89 In order to ensure equal treatment of all target shareholders, China's takeover law pays particular attention to minority shareholders after takeovers. If the tender offer expires and the acquirer has enough shares (usually 75 per cent of all outstanding shares) to cause the de-listing of the target company, the remaining shareholders have the right to enforce the sale of their shares on the same terms as those in the offer.[90] In this way, the remaining minority shareholders can be protected from a freeze-out merger on terms less favourable than those of the offer. Previously, the compulsory buyout threshold in China was 90 per cent, but in 2005 it was changed by reference to the listing standard on the grounds that delisting is likely to expose the remaining target shareholders to exploitation on the part of the new controller.[91]

---

[86] 2006 Takeover Measures, Art 37.
[87] 2006 Takeover Measures, Art 39.
[88] 2006 Takeover Measures, Art 40.
[89] 2006 Takeover Measures, Art 42(2).
[90] Securities Law, Art 97; 2006 Takeover Measures, Art 44. According to the listing requirement, a listed company must meet a number of criteria, one of which is that the publicly held shares in a company must account for more than 25 per cent of all outstanding shares, and if the total amount of the issued capital of the company exceeds CNY 0.4 billion, then the publicly held shares must be more than 10 per cent. Securities Law, Art 50.
[91] See Baoshu Wang and Hui Huang, 'China's New Company Law and Securities Law: An Overview and Assessment' (2006) 19(2) *Australian J of Corp L* 229, 237 (2006).

Australian takeover regulations contain a similar regime regarding the compulsory buyout of bid class securities, providing that if the bidder has relevant interests in at least 90 per cent of the securities in the bid class at the end of the offer period, the bidder must offer to buy out the remaining holders of bid class securities.[92] The Australian law also provides for a scheme of compulsory acquisition under which a bidder can compulsorily acquire any remaining securities in the bid class if the bidder has successfully acquired at least 75 per cent of the securities in the bid and the total shareholding has increased to at least 90 per cent.[93]

10.90

In contrast, the US Williams Act provides less protection for remaining shareholders in a freeze-out merger. Thus, in the US, minority shareholders could be paid consideration with a value lower than the bid price in an immediate takeover.[94]

10.91

10.8. Indirect Takeovers and Management Buyouts

As takeover activity is becoming increasingly sophisticated on the Chinese market, new rules have accordingly been put in place. For example, in order to maintain a better informed market, the 2006 Takeover Measures add a new chapter to specifically regulate indirect takeovers.[95] The term 'indirect takeovers' refers to a situation where, although an investor does not itself take over a listed company by directly acquiring its shares, the investor gains the control of the listed company by other means such as private agreement, investment relationship, or any other arrangement.[96] This type of control over voting shares in a listed company is equivalent to the concept of relevant interests in securities in Australia,[97] or the notion of beneficial ownership of shares in the United States.[98]

10.92

In addition, the 2006 Takeover Measures contain rules with respect to management buyout (MBO) for the first time. The term MBO generally refers to the takeover of a company by its own management rather than outsiders. Since the vast majority of Chinese listed companies are actually reorganized state-owned enterprises, MBO has long raised serious political as well as ethical issues.[99] The *Yue Meidi* case, an influential MBO test case in China, occurred in January 2001, when the law was basically silent on MBO. Although this case was criticized with

10.93

---

[92] Corporations Act, §§ 662A–662C.
[93] Corporations Act, §§ 662A–662C.
[94] Lucian Arye Bebchuk, *The Pressure to Tender: An Analysis and a Proposed Remedy, in* John C Coffee Jr et al (eds), *Knights, Raiders, and Targets, The Impact Of The Hostile Takeover* (Oxford: Oxford University Press, 1988), 371, 374.
[95] 2006 Takeover Measures, pt V.
[96] 2006 Takeover Measures, Art 56.
[97] Corporations Act, Art 608.
[98] 17 C.F.R. § 240.13d-3 (2004).
[99] See On Kit Tam, 'Ethical Issues in the Evolution of Corporate Governance in China' (2002) 37 *Journal of Business Ethics* 303, 305.

regard to several issues, such as the price of the acquisition and information disclosure, it has provided valuable MBO experience for both practitioners and regulators in China.

10.94 Drawing upon this experience and overseas practice, the 2006 Takeover Measures regulate MBO for the very first time. Compared with ordinary takeovers, MBO is subject to much more stringent regulation.[100] For example, a resolution on MBO shall be made by disinterested directors, be consented to by two thirds or more of independent directors, be submitted to the general meeting of shareholders of the company for deliberation and be adopted by half or more of the voting rights held by disinterested shareholders who attend the general meeting of shareholders. Although the law is very restrictive in relation to MBO activity, at the very least MBO is now legitimized and has clear rules to follow. This certainly opens the door for more MBO cases in China.

10.9. Disclosure of Substantial Shareholdings

10.95 In the interest of ensuring an informed market for securities in the target and its control, the takeover laws of most jurisdictions generally require a bidder to make an adequate and timely disclosure of its interests in a listed target.[101] The so-called disclosure of 'substantial shareholdings' is intended to provide the market with an early warning of possible takeovers. In China, the promulgation of the 2006 Takeover Measures coupled with the Securities Law provides for broad disclosure with respect to substantial shareholders.[102] When an investor comes to hold 5 per cent of the shares issued by a listed company, the investor must disclose his or her position.[103] To do so, the investor must submit a written report to the CSRC and the stock exchange within three business days from the date when such shareholding occurs.[104] During this period, the investor may not continue to purchase or sell shares of the listed company.[105] Thus, the investor is prohibited from changing his or her ownership position until the market has been informed. In addition, if the shareholding of a substantial shareholder increases or decreases by 5 per cent each time, they should disclose this information in the same way and must not trade the relevant shares within the disclosure period or within two days thereafter.[106]

---

[100] 2006 Takeover Measures, Art 51.
[101] Hui Huang, 'China's Takeover Law' 145, 167.
[102] The 2002 Information Disclosure Measures were basically incorporated as a whole into the 2006 Takeover Measures as its second part, entitled 'Information Disclosure about Ownership of Listed Companies'.
[103] Securities Law, Art 86(1).
[104] Securities Law, Art 86(1).
[105] Securities Law, Art 86(1).
[106] Securities Law, Art 86(2).

10.96 The 2006 Takeover Measures set out more detailed provisions to implement the disclosure requirement. First, they clarify that when counting a person's interests in a listed company, the shareholdings of their associates or people acting in concert will be included.[107] Second, two different disclosure systems are established for use depending on the level of substantial shareholdings. Specifically, if an investor and its concerted parties are not the largest shareholder or actual controller of a listed company, and their joint shareholding is above 5 per cent but below 20 per cent, a simplified disclosure system applies.[108] If, however, their shareholding is more than 20 per cent up to 30 per cent, then a detailed report must be made.[109]

10.97 This requirement of disclosing substantial shareholdings can be found in the takeover laws of most jurisdictions. In the United States, Section 13(d) of the Securities Exchange Act imposes a similar disclosure requirement on persons within ten days of the date that they acquire beneficial ownership of more than 5 per cent of a public company.[110] Unlike in China, US law permits substantial shareholders to continue to purchase shares during this period before making the announcement.[111] If, however, there is a material change in the holdings, including an acquisition or disposition of 1 per cent of outstanding shares in the said company, the owner must promptly file an amendment.[112]

10.98 In Australia, if a shareholder begins to have or ceases to have a relevant interest in 5 per cent or more of all shares in a company or scheme, that shareholder is deemed to have acquired a substantial holding in that company or scheme.[113] This is relevant because once this occurs, that shareholder must disclose the information within two business days after he or she first becomes aware of this information.[114] Further, where there is a movement of at least 1 per cent in the substantial shareholders' holdings, such movement must be disclosed within two business days.[115] Thus, Australia requires disclosure in much the same fashion as both China and the United States.

10.99 Clearly, the threshold for substantial shareholdings and the time for disclosure would exert significant influence on the contestability of takeovers. The lower the threshold, the more protection the target shareholders will have; therefore, the resulting takeover would be more difficult. Generally, the bidder needs to accumulate a certain number of shares, called a 'toehold', before initiating a takeover. If the

---

[107] 2006 Takeover Measures, Art 13.
[108] 2006 Takeover Measures, Art 16.
[109] 2006 Takeover Measures, Art 17.
[110] 15 U.S.C. § 78m(d) (2000).
[111] 17 C.F.R. § 240.13d-1(e)(2)(ii) (2004).
[112] 17 C.F.R. § 240.13d-2(a).
[113] Corporations Act, § 9.
[114] Corporations Act, § 671B(6).
[115] Corporations Act, § 671B(1)(b).

bidder is required to disclose his or her holdings too early, the market will react to raise the share price, and the takeover will be more expensive.

10.100 Therefore, a trade-off must be made between the protection of shareholders and the contestability of corporate control by choosing the appropriate threshold and disclosure time. This balance should be determined on the basis of the local situation. Thus, it might concern adjustment of the threshold and disclosure time according to the changing commercial environment. In China, for example, the 1993 Provisional Regulations require a substantial shareholder to disclose a change in its holding of at least 2 per cent of the outstanding shares.[116] In order to encourage takeovers, this threshold has been raised to 5 per cent in the Securities Law, as previously discussed. The increase from 2 per cent to 5 per cent may be arbitrary and may seem to have an impressionistic flavour; however, in the absence of reliable empirical data, it is difficult to judge whether the figures are incapable of balancing shareholder protection with the contestability of takeovers.

10.10. Financial Consultants

10.101 One of the major initiatives introduced by the 2006 Takeover Measures is the requirement that in order to take over a listed company, the purchaser must hire a financial consultant. The financial consultant is a professional institution that is registered in China and has a financial consultancy qualification.[117] Further, the financial consultant must be independent.[118] In practice, financial consultants are often securities firms.

10.102 The financial consultant plays a dual role in the process of takeovers. On the one hand, it serves as a private adviser to the purchaser; on the other, it functions as a public watchdog to monitor the purchaser. More specifically, the financial consultant as hired by a purchaser shall perform the following duties:[119]

(1) Conducting diligent investigations of the relevant information on the purchaser.
(2) Providing professional services to the purchaser as required; comprehensively appraising the financial status and business situation of the target company; helping the purchaser analyse the legal, financial, and business risks involved in the takeover; putting forward countermeasures and suggestions about the takeover price, method, and payment arrangements, etc, involved in the

---

[116] Provisional Regulations, Art 47.
[117] 2006 Takeover Measures, Art 9.
[118] 2006 Takeover Measures, Art 9.
[119] 2006 Takeover Measures, Art 65.

takeover scheme; and guiding the purchaser to formulate declaration documents in light of the prescribed contents and format.
(3) Giving tutorship to the purchaser with respect to the normalized operation of the securities market, so that the directors, supervisors, and senior managers of the purchaser are familiar with have good knowledge of the relevant laws, administrative regulations, and provisions of the CSRC, and are fully aware of their obligations and liabilities, and urging them to perform the reporting, announcement, and other statutory obligations.
(4) Fully checking and verifying whether the purchaser meets the provisions in these Measures as well as the authenticity, accuracy, and integrity of the declaration documents, and delivering objective and fair professional opinions in connection to the takeover.
(5) Accepting the authorization of the purchaser to submit declaration materials to the CSRC, and organizing and co-ordinating the purchaser and other professional institutions to give a reply according to the examination opinions of the CSRC.
(6) Concluding a contract with the purchaser and, within 12 months upon the conclusion of the takeover, continuously supervising and guiding the purchaser to abide by laws, administrative regulations, provisions of the CSRC, rules of the stock exchange, and the articles of association of the listed company, to exercise the rights of the shareholders according to laws and practically fulfil commitments or relevant stipulations.

When the financial consultant submits declaration documents to the CSRC upon authorization, it shall make the following commitments in the financial consultancy report: **10.103**

(1) It has performed the obligation of diligent investigation according to the provisions as required, and has sufficient reason to firmly believe that there is no substantial difference between its professional opinions and the contents in the declaration documents of the purchaser.
(2) It has verified the declaration documents of the purchaser, and firmly believes that the contents and formats of the declaration documents meet the provisions.
(3) It has sufficient reason to firmly believe that the takeover in question meets the laws, administrative regulations, and provisions of the CSRC; the information disclosed by the purchaser is true, accurate, and complete and there is no false record, misleading statement, or major omission.
(4) It has submitted the professional opinions it issued thereby for the takeover in question to the internal examination organ for examination, and passed the examination.
(5) It has taken rigid confidentiality measures and rigidly implemented an internal firewall system while acting as a financial consultant.

(6) It has concluded an agreement on continuous supervision and guidance with the purchaser.[120]

10.104 It should be noted that the role of the financial consultant does not end when the takeover transaction is completed. Rather, there is a so-called 'period of continuous supervision and guidance', which usually lasts 12 months after the conclusion of the takeover transaction.

10.105 Hence, from the day on which the purchaser reports the takeover of the listed company to 12 months after conclusion of the takeover, the financial consultant shall, by way of daily routine communications and regular visits, etc, pay attention to the business situation of the listed company, and perform the duty of continuous supervision and guidance to the purchaser and the target company by considering the matters disclosed in the regular reports and interim reports of the acquired company, carrying out the following tasks:

(1) Supervising the purchaser in going through the formalities for equity transfer in a timely fashion and performing the obligations of reporting and announcement.
(2) Supervising and checking the normalized operation of the purchaser and the acquired company.
(3) Supervising and checking the situation with regard to the purchaser's performing public commitments.
(4) Checking, by considering regular reports from the acquired company, the situation with regard to implementing the follow-up plans by the purchaser, whether anticipated targets have been reached, whether there is a major difference between the implementation results and the contents previously disclosed, and whether the relevant profit-making expectation or the targets anticipated by the management staff have been achieved.
(5) Checking whether the situation with regard to implementation of relevant repayment plans as disclosed in the regular reports of the acquired company is consistent with the facts where the management buyout is involved.
(6) Supervising and checking the performance of other duties as stipulated in the takeover agreement.[121]

10.106 During the period of continuous supervision and guidance, the financial consultant shall, in combination with the quarterly reports, semi-annual reports, and annul reports disclosed by the listed company, issue opinions about continuous supervision and guidance and report them to the representative office within 15 days after the aforesaid regular reports are disclosed.

---

[120] 2006 Takeover Measures, Art 68.
[121] 2006 Takeover Measures, Art 71.

During the aforesaid period, if the financial consultant finds that the information **10.107**
disclosed by the purchaser in the report on the takeover of the listed company is
inconsistent with the facts, it shall urge the purchaser to faithfully disclose the relevant information, and report it to the CSRC, the representative office, and the
stock exchange in a timely fashion. Where the financial consultant rescinds the
authorization contract, it shall report it to the CSRC, the representative office, and
the stock exchange in written form in a timely fashion, explain the reasons for its
inability to continue to perform the duties of continuous supervision and guidance,
and make an announcement of such.[122]

Apart from information disclosure issues, the financial consultant is also under a **10.108**
duty to monitor whether there is any circumstance in which the interests of the listed
company may be injured. This may include the question of whether the target company has provided guarantee for, or loans to, the purchaser or the affiliated party
thereof. If the financial consultant finds any illegal or improper act, it shall report it
to the CSRC, the representative office, and the stock exchange in a timely fashion.[123]

As with the sponsor in the listing process, the financial consultant is essentially **10.109**
a gatekeeper in the Chinese takeover market. In order to enhance the utility of
this system, the CSRC has recently established a system of *Fendao Zhi* ('different
route') under which takeover applications sponsored by different financial consultants will be treated differently.[124] This system is expected to incentivize the
financial consultant to work well because financial consultants will receive differentiated treatment from the CSRC depending on their capacity and record of
compliance with the law and honesty.

10.11. Continuous Supervision

In practice, some problems with takeovers may occur or come to light after the **10.110**
transaction. To address this situation, the CSRC has put in place a system of continuous supervision on takeovers, including supervision by the financial consultant, supervision by branches of the CSRC, and restrictions on the transfer of shares
by the purchaser.

First, within 12 months after the takeover of a listed company, the financial consultant hired by the purchaser shall, within three days before each quarter, report **10.111**
to the representative office any investment, purchase, or selling of assets; affiliated
transactions and adjustment of main businesses; change of directors, supervisors,

---

[122] 2006 Takeover Measures, Art 71.
[123] 2006 Takeover Measures, Art 69.
[124] Binggou Chongzu Shenhe Fendao Zhi Shishi FangAn [Implementation Plan for the System
of Different Routes for the Approval of Mergers and Acquisitions] (issued by the CSRC on 13
September 2013).

or senior managers; relocation of employees; or fulfilment of commitments by the purchaser for the last quarter that may produce great effects on the listed.[125]

10.112 Second, the branches of the CSRC, according to the principle of prudent supervision, supervise and check the purchaser and the listed company after the conclusion of the takeover, by way of talking to the accounting firm that is retained to provide auditing services for the listed company, examining the fulfilment of continuous supervision and guidance duties by the financial consultant, and conducting regular and irregular on-site inspections, etc. If the CSRC finds that there is any significant difference between the actual situation and the contents disclosed by the purchaser, it shall pay key attention to the purchaser and the listed company and can order the purchaser to extend the period of continuous supervision and guidance of the financial consultant, and shall investigate and handle it according to law.[126]

10.113 Finally, in order to prevent the purchaser from opportunistic 'cut and run' behaviour, the shares of the target company as held by the purchaser are subject to a lock-up period: that is, they cannot be transferred within 12 months of the conclusion of the takeover. This rule does not apply however where the shares in the target company whose entitlements are held by the purchaser are transferred between different subjects under the same actual controller.[127]

10.12. Comments

10.12.1. Strengths

10.12.1.1. Encouraging takeovers by tender offer

10.114 Consistent with the principle of contestability of takeovers, China's takeover legal regime, as embodied in the 2006 Takeover Measures, is intended to encourage wealth-creating takeover activities to help restructure the national economy and optimize the allocation of resources. One of the government's overarching policy goals in the post-WTO era is the so-called *Guotui Minjin* (state capital retreating to let private capital in). Its purpose is to shunt state-owned enterprises (SOEs) into the private sector, retaining only a tiny core that the state deems crucial for national defence, energy security, and so on.[128] Therefore, in some sectors, the government is encouraging the consolidation of SOEs into large integrated conglomerates that

---

[125] 2006 Takeover Measures, Art 72.
[126] 2006 Takeover Measures, Art 73.
[127] 2006 Takeover Measures, Art 74.
[128] Guowuyuan Guanyu Guli Zhichi he Yindao Getisiyindeng Feiguoyouzhi Jingji Fazhan de Ruogan Yijian [Opinions of the State Council on Encouraging and Supporting the Development of Non-Public Ownership Economy] (promulgated by the State Council on 25 February 2007).

are intended to be global leaders in their field; in others, the state is reducing the level of its equity ownership, making a large number of SOEs available for private capital, including foreign capital. As a result, an estimated 4,000–5,000 SOEs are privatized each year, out of total remaining stock of roughly 135,000. The government has viewed takeover activity as a key driver of this restructuring and privatization process.[129]

10.115 The goal of encouraging takeovers by tender offer has been well illustrated in those significant changes, such as the permission of partial bids, the more flexible methods of payment allowed, and the more efficient systems for governmental approval and information disclosure. In accordance with the shareholding structure reform, the 2006 Takeover Measures set up a takeover regime with a clear emphasis on takeovers by tender offer. Previously, in order to gain corporate control, it was often necessary or highly desirable to purchase those shares by private agreement, for several reasons.

10.116 First, as noted earlier, before the 2005 shareholding structure reform, non-tradable shares represented about two thirds of the shares in most listed companies. It was virtually impossible to take over a company without acquiring part of those non-tradable shares. Second, due to the segregated equity structure, the price of non-tradable shares was systematically much lower than that of tradable shares in the same company.[130] In addition, it would be preferable to purchase a control block of non-tradable shares for reasons of speed and certainty, even though the purchase of non-tradable shares requires governmental approval.[131]

10.117 The third important reason lies in the ability to exempt the mandatory bid obligation. As noted earlier, like any other means of acquiring shares, takeover by private agreement would trigger the mandatory bid rule if the transfer of non-tradable shares caused the transferee to cross the 30 per cent threshold. To avoid the high cost of making a mandatory bid, acquirers would apply to the CSRC for an exemption. In the past, the CSRC frequently gave exemptions to allow takeovers to go ahead without making a bid to all target shareholders. By the end of 2000, all 121 takeovers by private agreement had successfully obtained exemption from the CSRC.[132]

---

[129] See Hui Huang, 'The New Takeover Regulation in China: Evolution and Enhancement' (2008) 42(1) *The International Lawyer* 153, 154.

[130] Because the non-tradable shares are not listed on the stock exchanges, they are priced at the net asset value per share. In practice, the price of the non-tradable shares has been significantly lower than the market price of the tradable shares. For example, in the 1994 Hengtong Investment case, the first instance of takeover by private agreement, the non-tradable shares were priced at CNY 4.3 per share while the market price of the tradable shares was around CNY 13. Guanghua Yu, 'Using Western Law to Improve China's State-Owned Enterprises of Takeovers and Securities Fraud' (2004) 39 *Val U L Rev* 339, 350.

[131] Securities Law, Art 101 (providing that the acquisition of state shares is subject to the approval of the relevant administrative departments).

[132] Bingan Li, 'A Discussion of the Exemption from the Mandatory Bid Rule' (2003) 18(6) *Falu Luntan [Legal Forum]* 50.

Table 2 CSRC exemptions from MBR from 2004 and 2012

Year	Total number of takeovers triggering the mandatory bid obligation	Total number of exemptions	Number of bids made according to decision of the CSRC
2004 (from 21 July)	42	38	4
2005	78	73	5
2006	164	157	7
2007	139	134	5
2008	58	57	1
2009	129	125	4
2010	123	122	1
2011	99	98	1
2012 (as of 16 December)	42	39	3
Total	874	843 (96.45%)	31 (3.55%)

The reason behind the CSRC's readiness to grant exemptions was largely the need for an active takeover market to facilitate the transfer of state shares as part of the grand economic reform plan. If an exemption could not be obtained, the mandatory bid rule would apply, and the resulting high cost would create strong disincentives to the acquisition of non-tradable shares.

10.118 Takeover by private agreement had therefore long been a preferred method of gaining corporate control in China, but this situation has begun to change under the 2006 Takeover Measures. Indeed, once all non-tradable shares are turned into tradable shares as a result of the reform, the problems of segregated equity structure and different prices for different shares will disappear. The previously loose exemption system, which has made takeover by private agreement a very cheap way to gain corporate control, is likely to be tightened. As discussed earlier, the 2006 Takeover Measures are much more restrictive than their 2002 predecessors with respect to the grounds upon which the CSRC could grant an exemption. Although the CSRC will continue to grant exemptions on a case-by-case basis, it has made it clear that the such exemption is now going to be much more difficult to obtain, and the mandatory bid rule will have real teeth.[133] Takeover by tender offer, therefore, is expected to become the main way to acquire shares with a view to gaining corporate control.

10.119 However, empirical evidence suggests that after 2006, the CSRC has not really tightened the granting of exemptions, as expected. Table 2 illustrates the readiness of the CSRC to grant exemptions from 2004 and 2012.[134]

---

[133] 'The CSRC's Answers to the Relevant Questions Asked by the Reporter from the Chinese Government Website Office About the New Takeover Measures' ('CSRC Answers'), available at http://www.gov.cn/zwhd/2006-09/17/content_389685.htm.
[134] Wei Cai, 'An Efficiency Approach to the Mandatory Bid Rule' (2013) 4 *Peking University Law Journal* 847, 854.

Finally, it should be noted that because the present shareholding structure reform **10.120**
is a gradual process, takeover by private agreement will remain a common method
of gaining corporate control for a certain period of time. A key feature of the 2005
reform is that it is a staged process, with non-tradable shares becoming tradable
incrementally, so as to spread the impact of the reform over several years. First,
the reform imposes a minimum 12-month lock-up on non-tradable shares following their conversion into tradable shares.[135] After this lock-up period, holders
of formerly non-tradable shares that hold more than 5 per cent of the company's
shares may only sell a limited number of shares: no more than 5 per cent of the
total shares within any rolling 12-month period, and no more than 10 per cent in
any rolling 24-month period. Besides, it is worth noting that, in order to further
alleviate concern regarding dilution effects on public investors from the conversion
of the non-tradable shares into tradable shares, the holders of non-tradable shares
in many companies have agreed to voluntary lock-up periods longer than the statutory requirements. The reform process is thus going to take time, given the large
number of non-tradable shares in the market.

10.12.1.2. Enhancing investor protection

The 2006 Takeover Measures strengthen the regulations that prevent opportunistic takeovers while at the same time encouraging bona fide takeovers. First, they **10.121**
set out a number of substantive requirements with respect to an investor's eligibility to make takeovers. Under Article 6, an investor is barred from taking over
any listed companies if it has certain problems; for example, investors that owe
a large amount of debt that has become due and payable, or investors that have
ever committed a major illegal act or have ever been suspected of being involved
in any major illegal act within the recent three years, may be barred from taking
over listed companies.[136] Second, when making a takeover bid to be paid in cash,
the bidder must deposit no less than 20 per cent of the total amount of the offered
price in the bank designated by the securities depository and clearing institution as
the performance guarantee.[137] This is to prevent a form of 'bluffing' in announcement of takeovers. Third, the shares acquired cannot be sold within 12 months of
the conclusion of the takeover, but this lock-up rule does not apply if the acquired
shares are to be transferred to the acquirer's associates.[138]

In order to ensure takeovers are done in a fair and market-oriented way, a new **10.122**
scheme concerning private financial consultants has been introduced to complement the CSRC's governmental enforcement of takeover law. In a takeover bid,
both the acquirer and the target need to engage qualified financial consultants,

---

[135] See Shangshi Gongsi Guquan Fenzhi Gaige Guanli Banfa [Measures on the Shareholding Structure Reform of Listed Companies] (promulgated by the CSRC on 4 September 2005), Art 27.
[136] 2006 Takeover Measures, Art 6.
[137] 2006 Takeover Measures, Art 36.
[138] 2006 Takeover Measures, Art 74.

such as investment bankers. The financial consultant performs a number of important functions, including the provision of professional services for their client, as well as the fulfilment of some duties of regulatory character. For example, the financial consultant for the acquirer should conduct a due diligence investigation into the acquirer's financial condition, provide professional services to help the acquirer plan and carry out the takeover, ensure the quality of the information disclosed by the acquirer, and supervise the behaviour of the acquirer within the 12-month period after the takeover is finished.[139] Thus, the financial consultant has a dual role to play: the first is as a commercial entity advancing the interests of its clients; the second is as a market participant with some important regulatory responsibilities. It is believed that this regulatory structure makes use of market disciplines and will improve the overall efficacy of the regulatory regime regarding takeovers.[140]

10.12.2. Weaknesses

10.123 Although China's takeover law, as amended in 2006, has improved significantly with respect to the making of takeover offers, there are a number of weaknesses in this area. Indeed, the 2006 reform has made some important innovations, but the workability of those innovations is undermined due to the lack of detailed and functional provisions, as well as some loopholes. An example is that while the law permits variation of offer terms subject to the approval of the CSRC, it raises more questions than it answers. For instance, what are the criteria applied by the CSRC in granting approval? If the bidder varies the offer by improving the consideration or offering an alternative form of consideration, would this entitle a person who has already accepted an offer under the bid to the improved consideration or to make a choice as to the form of consideration to be taken? In what circumstances can a bidder extend the offer period? And when is it permissible for a person who has accepted an offer to withdraw their acceptance?

10.124 There are even more serious problems with the rules in relation to the application of conditions and partial bids, which will now be discussed in detail.

10.12.2.1. Conditions in takeover bids

10.125 The 2006 Takeover Measures make a breakthrough by stipulating that tender offers may be subject to conditions.[141] But they do not provide useful guidance as to what conditions are permissible and how the conditions operate. This is problematic because the bidder may potentially use conditions to shift some of the bid's risk onto offerees in a way that has a coercive effect or lacks transparency. In order to prevent abuse, China may wish to look to the Australian experience, where the

---

[139] 2006 Takeover Measures, Art 65.
[140] CSRC Answers.
[141] 2006 Takeover Measures, Art 29(7).

conditions permitted to be included in takeover bids are carefully regulated. For instance, Australia prohibits maximum acceptance conditions;[142] conditions that allow the bidder to acquire securities from some but not all of the persons who accept offers;[143] conditions requiring approval to payment to officers or employees of the target company as compensation for loss of office or employment;[144] and conditions that turn upon the opinion of the bidder or its associates or the happening of an event that is within their sole control.[145]

10.126 Further, there are detailed rules on the use of so-called 'defeating conditions'— that is, conditions that entitle the bidder to rescind the takeover contract or which prevent it arising upon acceptance of offers. For instance, defeating conditions are permitted only if the offers specify a date (within 7–14 days before the end of the offer period) for giving notice of the status of the condition.[146] By such notice, offerees may be aware before the end of the offer period of the risk that the bidder may be entitled to walk away from the bid because of failure of the condition. This allows investors to hold off acceptance until this period. Moreover, the bidder may free the offers from the condition only by giving the target company notice in accordance with the law. Therefore, these rules help protect the interests of investors and ensure that the takeover market runs in a transparent and efficient manner.

10.12.2.2. Problems with the partial bid rule

10.127 As noted before, in an effort to encourage takeovers, the 2006 Takeover Measures permit partial takeovers in order to allow a bidder to take over a company with a considerably lower outlay than would be the case with a full takeover. There is however a serious defect in relation to the partial takeover rule from the perspective of the equality principle underpinning the Chinese takeover law.

10.128 Under Article 43, if the bidder in a partial bid receives acceptance for a greater number of shares than specified in the offer, each acceptance shall be pro-rated to the same proportion and the excess returned to target shareholders.[147] This form of partial bid appears to be a so-called pro-rata bid, which may exert coercive pressure on shareholders and cause uncertainty as to the number of shares ultimately sold. Indeed, by their nature, partial bids may prevent target company shareholders from having the opportunity to participate equally in the bid without coercion. In a successful partial bid, the control premium will have been paid only to those accepting shareholders. This may place coercive pressure on shareholders to accept the partial bid because if they do not, they may miss out on participation in the premium for control.

---

[142] Corporations Act, s 626.
[143] Corporations Act, s 627.
[144] Corporations Act, s 628.
[145] Corporations Act, s 629.
[146] Corporations Act, s 630(1).
[147] 2006 Takeover Measures, Art 43.

10.129 This is particularly so in the case of pro-rata bids where the accepting shareholders could in fact tender a higher proportion of their shares in the likely event of non-acceptance by some shareholders. For example, if a 29 per cent shareholder makes a pro-rata bid to acquire in total a little over 50 per cent and receives acceptance for 20 per cent of the shares from only some large shareholders, these accepting shareholders can actually sell their shares in full. This will have a strong coercive effect on target shareholders because unless they accept the offer, they will not participate in the control premium and would be left in the rump of minority shareholders. For this reason, pro-rata bids have been prohibited in Australia since 1986.[148]

10.130 Instead, Australia permits another form of partial bid, known as proportional bids, under which an offer is made for the same proportion of each shareholder's holding in the target company.[149] For example, if the 29 per cent shareholder makes a proportional bid for 50 per cent of every other shareholding and the holders of all outstanding shares accept the offer, the bidder would end up holding 64.5 per cent of the total shares. Proportional bids do not exert the same degree of coercive pressure as is the case with pro-rata bids. A failure to accept a proportional bid does not result in an increased proportion of the control premium going to accepting shareholders; therefore, there is no incentive in such a bid to rush to accept for fear of missing out.

10.131 It should be noted, however, that although proportional bids can ensure achievement of equality of opportunity among target shareholders, they shift to bidders the uncertainty as to the number of shares ultimately sold. In practice, it would be unusual for all target shareholders to accept a proportional bid. Therefore, a bidder must pitch a proportional bid at such a level as it estimates will take into account non-acceptances in order to attain the shareholding it wants to acquire. If there are more acceptances than expected, the bidder may have to acquire more shares and spend more than is necessary to gain corporate control. Thus, a trade-off must be set between considerations of equity between target shareholders and potential cost savings for bidders. It is submitted that the Australian experience merits serious consideration in the Chinese condition, as both countries aim to promote shareholder protection in accordance with the equality-of-opportunity principle.

10.12.3. Summary

10.132 China's takeover law has evolved in a gradualist way, with significant changes and developments in recent years. Along with other laws and regulations, the 2006 Takeover Measures have greatly enhanced China's takeover legal regime both in terms of form and substance. This comes at a time when the Chinese economy is undergoing strategic restructuring and China's capital markets are poised on the

---

[148] HAJ Ford et al, *Ford's Principles of Corporations Law* 1131 (12th edn: LexisNexis, 2005).
[149] Corporations Act, § 618.

brink of a new era thanks to the ongoing shareholding structure reform. The 2006 reform brings China's takeover law more closely into line with its counterparts in more developed economies, forming a sound basis for takeover activities in China.

The Chinese takeover law, however, is not immune to criticism, even though the law has generally been seen as a laudable achievement. In principle, China's takeover law should be carefully designed to achieve two goals: contestability of takeovers and investor protection. A comparative approach is taken to analysis of the principal elements of the Chinese takeover law. It is suggested that those rules regarding information disclosure and mandatory bid obligations are suitable for China, and there is no compelling reason to vary them. There are, however, some problems with certain aspects of the takeover law, in particular the application of conditions and the partial bid rule. The efficacy of the legal regime would be enhanced if those problems were addressed along the lines suggested in this chapter. **10.133**

11

TAKEOVERS OF LISTED COMPANIES (2)

11.1. Introduction	11.01	11.3.2. *Ex post* defences	11.32
11.2. Takeover Defences Under Chinese Law	11.04	11.4. Analysis and Implications	11.43
11.2.1. 2005 Securities Law and 2006 Takeover Measures	11.06	11.4.1. Widespread adoption of takeover defences	11.43
11.2.2. 2005 Company Law	11.12	11.4.2. Suggestions for improvement	11.52
11.2.3. 2006 Guidelines for Articles of Association	11.16	11.5. A New Regime for Takeover Defences	11.56
11.3. Takeover Defences in Practice	11.19	11.5.1. United States (Delaware law)	11.57
11.3.1. *Ex ante* defences	11.21	11.5.2. United Kingdom	11.61
		11.5.3. The way forward	11.64

11.1. Introduction

11.01 The issue of takeover defences has long been a subject of heated debate, largely because takeover defences are essentially a double-edged sword: on the one hand, they can be used as a means to protect target shareholders from undesirable takeovers or, if the transfer of corporate control becomes inevitable, create an active auction to maximize the sale price for target shareholders; on the other, there is a real risk that the target's management may abuse defensive tactics to thwart a hostile takeover for the purpose of entrenchment, regardless of whether the takeover would be beneficial for shareholders.

11.02 Internationally, different jurisdictions have adopted different laws on the issue of takeover defences. Naturally, each regulatory model has its advantages and disadvantages, and the efficacy of any law depends very much on the particular context in which it operates. Drawing upon international experiences, China formally established its legal regime for takeover defences in 2002. How has China transplanted foreign laws in relation to takeover defences? Are they properly adapted to the Chinese local conditions? Have they been effectively enforced in practice? How can the Chinese law be improved?

11.03 This paper seeks to shed light on these questions, examining both the law in the books and the law in action for takeover defences in China. It will first discuss the relevant rules governing takeover defences under Chinese law. This is followed by an in-depth empirical enquiry into the use of takeover defences, including *ex ante* defences and *ex post* defences. The empirical findings will then be used to inform and anchor theoretical analysis of the problems and prospects related to takeover defences in China.

11.2. Takeover Defences Under Chinese Law

The China Securities Regulatory Commission (CSRC) is the national securities regulator, with centralized power to oversee China's securities market, including the takeover of listed companies. In 2006, the CSRC set up a specialised committee known as the M&A and Restructuring Examination Committee (*Binggou Chongzu Shenhe Weiyuanhui*) to handle issues related to a wide range of takeover-related matters. This committee is composed of professionals and relevant experts in the takeover area whose function is to provide opinions about takeover regulation at the request of a functional department of the CSRC.   **11.04**

Due to the broad nature and wide variety of takeover defences, the legal provisions for takeover defences can be found in several laws as well as administrative rules promulgated by the securities market regulator, namely the CSRC. These include the 2005 *Securities Law of the People's Republic of China* (hereinafter 2005 Securities Law),[1] the 2006 *Measures for Regulating Takeovers of Listed Companies* (hereinafter 2006 Takeover Measures),[2] the 2005 *Company Law of the People's Republic of China* (hereinafter 2005 Company Law),[3] and the 2006 *Guidelines for Articles of Association of Listed Companies* (hereinafter 2006 Guidelines for Articles of Association).[4] They will be discussed in turn.   **11.05**

11.2.1. 2005 Securities Law and 2006 Takeover Measures

The 2005 Securities Law devotes a whole chapter to the issue of takeovers. This chapter has a total of 17 provisions, but no provision specifically addresses whether, and if so to what extent, takeover defences can be used. Article 101(2) authorizes the CSRC to promulgate detailed rules on takeovers. With this authorization, the CSRC has   **11.06**

---

[1] Zhonghua Renming Gongheguo Zhenquan Fa [Securities Law of the People's Republic of China] (promulgated by the Standing Commission of the National People's Congress, 29 December 1998, effective 1 July 1999, amended 28 August 2004, 27 October 2005, and 29 June 2013).
[2] Shangshi Gongsi Shougou Guanli Banfa [Measures for Regulating Takeovers of Listed Companies (2006 Takeover Measures)] (promulgated by CSRC on 31 July 2006 and effective from 1 September 2006, amended in 2008 and 2012).
[3] Zhonghua Renming Gongheguo Gongsi Fa [Company Law of the People's Republic of China (Company Law)] (promulgated by the Standing Commission of the National People's Congress, 20 December 1993, effective 1 July 1994, amended 25 December 1999, 28 August 2004, 27 October 2005, and 28 December 2013).
[4] Shangshi Gongsi Zhangcheng Zhiyin (2006) [Guidelines for the Articles of Association of Listed Companies] (promulgated by CSRC on 16 March 2006, amended 9 October 2008).

promulgated the 2006 Takeover Measures, which supersede the twin takeover regulations the CSRC issued in 2002.[5]

11.07 The 2006 Takeover Measures are currently the centrepiece of China's takeover legal framework, containing two key provisions in relation to the issue of takeover defences.

11.08 First, Article 8 is a general rule governing the use of takeover defences by reference to the directors' duties, stating that

> The directors, supervisors and senior managers of a target company shall assume the obligation of fidelity and diligence, and shall equally treat all the purchasers that intend to take over the said company.
>
> The decisions made and the measures taken by the board of directors of a target company for the takeover shall be good for maintaining the rights of the company and its shareholders, and shall not erect any improper obstacle to the takeover by misusing its authorities, nor may it provide any means of financial aid to the purchaser by making use of the sources of the target company or damage the lawful rights and interests of the target company or its shareholders.

11.09 This provision essentially uses the concept of directors' duties to regulate the employment of takeover defences, but China's legal regime for directors' duties is generally underdeveloped. Indeed, the legal texts on directors' duties in China are couched in simple and general terms, and the courts have not provided much further guidance on the meaning of directors' duties.[6] How then has Article 8 been enforced? And has it helped the development of the law of directors' duties in the context of takeovers?

11.10 Second, Article 33 specifically prohibits the use of certain takeover defences without the approval of the shareholder meeting, providing that

> During the period after the announcement of a takeover bid and before the completion of the takeover bid, except for conducting ordinary business operations and implementing resolutions made by the general meeting of shareholders, target company management should not cause major impacts on the assets, liabilities, entitlements or business performances of the target company by disposing of assets, engaging in external investments, adjusting the main businesses, providing guarantees or loans and others.

11.11 The basic tenet of this provision is that takeover defences must not be undertaken unless they are approved by shareholders at the general meeting. There are however some constraints on its application. Looking into the words of this provision, it seems that its application is subject to two conditions: (1) takeover defences

---

[5] For more discussion of the 2002 twin takeover regulations, see Hui Huang, 'China's Takeover Law: A Comparative Analysis and Proposals for Reform' (2005) 30(1) *Delaware Journal of Corporate Law* 145.

[6] Guangdong Xu, Tianshu Zhou, Bin Zeng, and Jin Shi, 'Directors' Duties in China' (2013) 14 *European Business Organization Law Review* 57.

must have major impacts on the assets, liabilities, entitlements, or business performances of the target company; (2) takeover defences must be undertaken after the announcement of takeover bids.[7] There is a further exemption when the takeover defence is carried out in the ordinary business of the company. As a consequence, under Article 33, a takeover defence may be lawfully adopted even without approval from shareholders, as long as it does not have a significant impact on company assets and liabilities, or it is taken before the announcement of a takeover bid, or it constitutes an ordinary business operation.

11.2.2. 2005 Company Law

11.12 Change of control is by its nature a major event for the company concerned, and thus it is of relevance to look at which corporate organ—the shareholder meeting or the board of directors—has power to make decisions on corporate control transactions, including the use of defensive tactics, under the company law of any given jurisdiction.

11.13 In China, the corporate governance system is basically shareholder-centred in that the shareholder meeting is the final decision-maker in relation to major issues of the company, including, but not limited to, electing and changing the directors and supervisors; making resolutions on increase or decrease in the company's registered capital; making resolutions on the merger, division, change of company form, disbanding, or liquidation of the company; and revising the articles of association of the company.[8] In contrast, the board of directors is generally accountable to the shareholder meeting, with powers to work out major business plans and submit them to the shareholder meeting for approval.[9]

11.14 Apart from the general division of power between the shareholder meeting and the board of directors, there are specific company law provisions which may affect the use of certain defensive tactics. For instance, the practice of poison pill, a widely used takeover defence in the US, runs afoul of Article 127 of the 2005 Company Law, which states:

> The issuance of shares shall comply with the principles of fairness and impartiality. The shares of the same class shall have the same rights and benefits. The same kind of shares issued at the same time shall be equal in price and shall be subject to the same conditions. The price of each share of the same kind purchased by any organization or individual shall be the same.[10]

11.15 Further, the practice of share purchase can hardly be used as a takeover defence, for it is tightly regulated under Article 143 of the 2005 Company Law. A company is prohibited from purchasing its own shares save in very special circumstances,

---

[7] Tang Xin and Xu Zhizhan, 'Fan Shougou Cuoshi de Hefaxing Jianyan' [An Examination on the Legitimacy of Anti-takeover Measures] (2008) 2 *Qinghua Faxue [Tsinghua Law Review]* 95.
[8] 2005 Company Law, Arts 38, 100.
[9] 2005 Company Law, Arts 47, 109.
[10] 2005 Company Law, Art 127.

including: (1) it reduces its registered capital; (2) it merges with another company that holds its shares; (3) it rewards the staff and workers of the company with its shares; or (4) a shareholder requests the company to purchase his shares because he holds objections to the resolution on the merger or division of the company adopted by the shareholder general meeting.[11]

11.2.3. 2006 Guidelines for Articles of Association

11.16 In China, the CSRC, as the regulator of the securities market, has issued various rules regarding the corporate governance of listed companies. Of particular relevance to takeover defences is the 2006 Guidelines for Articles of Association, which essentially provide a template for Chinese listed companies to make their articles of association. In this way, the CSRC aims to ensure that the articles of association of listed companies are standard and formal, thereby enhancing the level of law compliance and the quality of information disclosure.

11.17 It is made clear, however, that some variations to the template are allowed. Items in the 2006 Guidelines for Articles of Associations are meant to be the basic elements of the articles of association of listed companies. Without violating the relevant laws and regulations, the listed company can, depending on its particular circumstances, add items that are not contained in the 2006 Guideline for Articles of Association, or adjust the wording or sequencing of the items stipulated in the 2006 Guideline for Articles of Association. In the case that the listed company adds to or adjusts the compulsory elements of the 2006 Guidelines for Articles of Association to meet its practical needs, these variations should be highlighted when the board of directors makes public announcements to revise the articles of association.

11.18 Hence, it is possible for listed companies to introduce takeover defences by way of constitutional provisions, if two conditions are met. The first condition is a substantive rule under which the constitutional provision does not violate the relevant laws and regulations; the second is a procedural rule requiring the proper disclosure of the constitutional provision concerned.

11.3. Takeover Defences in Practice

11.19 The above laws and regulations make up the legal framework for takeovers of Chinese listed companies. This is a significant achievement, considering the short history of the Chinese securities market. It is not clear however whether the law has been enforced effectively to regulate the use of takeover defences. This section will thus empirically examine takeover defences in practice.

---

[11] 2005 Company Law, Art 143.

Depending on the time at which takeover defences are used, they can be broadly **11.20**
divided into two categories, namely *ex ante* defences and *ex post* defences. *Ex ante*
defences are introduced before the emergence of an imminent takeover offer, and
usually take the form of provisions in the articles of association of listed companies.[12] By contrast, *ex post* defences are initiated after a specific takeover threat
arises and, in addition to constitutional provisions, there are a variety of defensive
tactics. In general, *ex ante* defences are proactive, prophylactic and long-standing,
while *ex post* defences are reactive, targeted and one-time.

11.3.1. *Ex ante* defences

11.3.1.1. Methodology

As *ex ante* defences often take the form of constitutional provisions, it is necessary **11.21**
to examine the constitutions of listed companies in China. In a well-cited 2009
study, the researcher randomly selected 100 Chinese listed companies and then
used 40 of them as the sample for empirical analysis (without clearly explaining the criteria against which the 40 companies were selected).[13] Inspired by this
study, but seeking to reduce the problem of selection bias, this section examines
the constitutions of the 300 component companies in the Shanghai-Shenzhen
300 Index as of the end of 2013. This index was selected because it is designed to
reflect the overall situation of the Chinese securities market, including representative listed companies from both the Shanghai Stock Exchange and the Shenzhen
Stock Exchange.[14]

11.3.1.2. Research findings

The first important finding is that anti-takeover constitutional provisions are quite **11.22**
common among Chinese listed companies, particularly those with a dispersed
shareholding structure. Out of the 300 companies under study, more than half are
found to have adopted certain defensive measures in their constitutions. Further,
although the rest of the companies in the dataset do not have anti-takeover constitutional provisions, most of them have a controlling shareholder with a shareholding

---

[12] In a broad sense, *ex ante* defences may take other forms, such as the increase of shareholdings by way of direct acquisition of shares or cross-shareholding arrangements. These types of *ex ante* defences are essentially adopted by existing shareholders, and not the incumbent management of the target company. They are not the focus of the discussion here, as the legal concern over takeover defences primarily arises from the possibility of the target management abusing them for the purpose of entrenchment. In theory, constitutional provisions need to be approved by shareholders, but in practice, due to the agency costs inherent in the shareholder-management relationship, the management can exert significant influence on constitutional provisions to pursue their own interests.
[13] Zhang Fang, 'Shangshi Gongsi Zhangcheng Zhong Dongsi Xuanren Tiaokuan de Youxiaoxing Fenxi' [Legitimacy of Antitakeover Provisions on Election of Directors in the Constitutions of Listed Companies] (2009) 1 *Faxue [Legal Science]* 122.
[14] For more information on this index, see the website of China Securities Index Co Ltd, which issues the index: http://www.csindex.com.cn/sseportal/csiportal/zs/jbxx/report.do?code=000300&subdir=1.

Table 1 Types of anti-takeover constitutional provisions

	Constitutional Provisions
	Obstacles to the acquirer purchasing shares
1	Share acquisitions above certain thresholds need to be approved
	Obstacles to the acquirer electing new board members
1	Board may refuse to put forward proposals to the general meeting, including the proposal to nominate new board members
2	Raising the eligibility of shareholders to nominate board members
3	Prohibition against dismissal of management without causes
4	Staggered board
5	Qualifications of the chairperson and other board members
6	Golden/silver parachutes
	Others
1	Empowering a board of directors to take defensive measures without getting approvals from shareholders
2	Super-majority voting requirement to amend anti-takeover constitutional provisions

of 30 per cent or higher. Clearly, such a concentrated shareholding structure is by itself powerful in fending off hostile takeover threats. In other words, there is little need for those companies to adopt anti-takeover constitutional provisions.

11.23 Logically, in order to thwart a hostile takeover, the first line of defence is to prevent the acquirer from purchasing enough shares; if this fails, the next defensive tactic is to make it difficult for the acquirer to select new board members. In theory, therefore, anti-takeover constitutional provisions can be broadly grouped into three categories: (1) obstacles to the acquirer purchasing shares; (2) obstacles to the acquirer electing new board members; (3) others. The empirical study reveals that all three categories of provision have been adopted by Chinese listed companies. Table 1 presents the empirical findings.

11.24 In the first category, the anti-takeover constitutional provision usually requires that if a shareholder comes to hold more than 5 or 10 per cent of shares, it should notify the company and obtain approval from the board as well as the general meeting before it can acquire more shares. One particular company makes it clear that without notifying the board and obtaining its approval, the shares acquired by the shareholder do not carry rights to nominate board members.[15]

11.25 The second category contains most of the anti-takeover constitutional provisions used by Chinese listed companies, and can be further divided into several types. First, the incumbent board is empowered to review the nomination of new board members by shareholders. This implies that the incumbent board may, after

---

[15] See Article 38 of the constitution of the Shanghai-listed company of Meihua Jituan (trading code 600873) (revised 2013), which is available at http://www.sse.com.cn/assortment/stock/list/name.

reviewing the nomination motion, refuse to submit it to the general meeting for approval. In short, the right of nomination is ultimately vested in the hands of the board.

11.26 Second, some companies adopt provisions to heighten the substantive criteria for shareholders to nominate board members. The nominating shareholder is usually required to have a shareholding of 5 per cent or higher, and/or to have held shares for a minimum period of time (for example, 180 days). One company even required the election of directors to be supported by three quarters of all the shareholders that attended the shareholder meeting.

11.27 The third type of provision in this category is to impose restrictions on the dismissal of directors. Clearly, if the existing directors cannot be dismissed, the acquirer will not be able to appoint new directors. Many companies provide in their constitutions that directors should not be dismissed within their term of office without cause. The widespread use of such provision can be explained by reference to the historical development of Chinese company law. The Company Law 1993 explicitly prohibited the dismissal of management without cause,[16] but this provision was deleted in the 2005 Company Law revision. This means that the company can now dismiss its directors without cause. In practice, however, most companies have chosen to retain the requirement by way of constitutional provisions.[17]

11.28 Fourth, there is a so-called 'staggered board' provision, under which the term of office for the director is often set at three years, and only a certain proportion of the incumbent directors—usually one third—can be replaced at a general meeting of shareholders. The staggered board mechanism can cause delays and uncertainties in the acquirer's effort to obtain control in the boardroom. Suppose a company constitution divides the board of directors into three classes, and requires only one class of directors to be replaced in each general meeting. The acquirer will then have to wait for at least two general meetings to be held in order to obtain majority seats in the boardroom.

11.29 The fifth type of provision imposes demanding (sometimes unreasonable) qualification requirements for the chairperson and other board members. For instance, one such requirement is that for one to be elected as chairperson of the board of directors, he must have worked within the company for a specified period of time. Clearly, this makes it difficult for the acquirer to elect its own people—who will likely be outsiders to the company—to the board of the target company.

11.30 The sixth type is the so-called 'golden/silver parachute' provision, under which the incumbent management, including directors and senior managers, can receive compensation if they are dismissed before the expiry of their term of office in the

---

[16] Company Law 1993, Art 47.
[17] The CSRC seems to support this, as the above constitutional provision is still included under Article 79 of the 2006 Guidelines for Articles of Association which it issued for listed companies.

event of a takeover. The compensation may take different forms, such as cash and shares, and the value is usually substantial.

11.31 The above two categories contain most of the anti-takeover constitutional provisions adopted by Chinese listed companies, but there are also some other types of provision. For instance, under one company's constitution, if it is subject to a hostile takeover, except for the acquirer, any shareholder who individually or collectively holds 20 per cent or more of the total shares has the right to require, in writing, the board to take defensive measures which are not prohibited by the relevant laws and regulations. The board should immediately employ defences after receipt of such written document or resolution, and make announcement to the shareholders.[18] This means that the board can use defences simply at the request of large shareholders. Further, the constitutions of some companies provide that in order to amend anti-takeover provisions, the approval of shareholders representing three quarters or more of the voting rights of the shareholders who attend the general meeting is required. Hence, it would be very difficult to eliminate anti-takeover constitutional provisions once they have been put in place.

11.3.2. *Ex post* defences

11.3.2.1. Methodology

11.32 This section empirically examines the use of *ex post* defences by Chinese listed companies. In practice, for various reasons, disputes arising from the use of *ex post* defences have seldom been brought to the court or the CSRC; rather, the disputants often reach compromises and resolve the issue in private. This means that if one were to examine only cases handled by the court or the CSRC, the data would be grossly inadequate. Hence, this section tries to gather information about the use of *ex post* defences from several different sources, including two widely used Chinese law databases (*Beida Fabao* and *Beida Fayi*), the website of the CSRC, media reports, and existing literature.[19]

11.3.2.2. Research findings

11.33 The research reveals that various types of takeover defences have been used in the Chinese securities market.

11.34 The first is the so-called 'white knight', a practice of inviting a friendly acquirer to make a competing bid. A good example is the takeover battle between Guangfa Zhengquan (the target company) and Zhongxin Zhengquan (the acquirer), which

---

[18] See Article 43 of the constitution of the Shenzhen-listed company of Tiankang Shengwu (trading code 002100) (revised May 2013), available at http://disclosure.szse.cn/m/drgg002100.htm.

[19] This part also draws upon some research findings of a doctoral project Dr Juan Chen undertook under my supervision in relation to the takeover law in China. Juan Chen, *Examining the Transplantation of Takeover Law into China: Balancing Shareholder Protection with Efficiency* (PhD thesis, University of New South Wales, Sydney, Australia, 2013).

illustrates well how friendly acquirers can act together to defeat a takeover threat.[20] In September 2004 the hostile acquirer, Zhongxin Zhengquan, announced a takeover bid, offering to buy the remaining shares of the target company Guangfa Zhengquan at 1.25 Yuan per share. The target company responded to the hostile bid by setting up a company called Shenzhen Jifu, the shares of which were subscribed by the management and employees of Guangfa Zhengquan. Shenzhen Jifu obtained around 12.23 per cent of the target company shares from existing block holders. Shenzhen Jifu was however constrained by its financial capacity from making further share acquisitions.

11.35 Two other acquirers associated with the target company emerged at this point. The target company had cross-shareholding arrangements with two of its largest shareholders, Liaoning Chengda and Jilin Aodong, which held 24 per cent and 13.75 per cent of shares in the target company respectively. The target company was the second largest shareholder in Liaoning Chengda and the fifth largest shareholder in Jilin Aodong. The cross-shareholding tied the target company and its two largest shareholders together through their common economic interests. To preserve such common economic interests, the two largest shareholders conducted a number of negotiated share acquisitions from other holders of share blocks, which were aided by the incumbent management. After the negotiated share acquisitions, the three friendly acquirers—Shenzhen Jifu, Liaoning Chengda, and Jilin Aodong—jointly held 66.67 per cent of the target company's shares. The hostile bidder withdrew its offer as it was impossible for it to obtain majority shares even if all the remaining shareholders tendered their shares.

11.36 The second defence is to win support from minority shareholders and stakeholders for the purpose of fending off a hostile takeover threat. The failed hostile takeover attempt of ST Meiya is a typical case in point.[21] There, the target company was in severe financial distress for more than two years. The controlling shareholder of the company, which was the local state asset regulator, intended to transfer the 29 per cent of shares it held to the hostile acquirer, Wanhe Jituan. In September 2003, without consulting with and obtaining consent from the incumbent management, the controlling shareholder of ST Meiya entered into a share transfer agreement with the acquirer.

11.37 The disclosed contract met with strong opposition from the management of the target company. The incumbent management claimed, both in the media and in corporate meetings, that the intended transfer of shares would be detrimental to long-term corporate interests, because the acquirer mainly operated in a different

---

[20] Hanyao Shen and Hui Wang, 'Fanbinggou: Lilun Celue Shishi Anli' [Takeover Defences: Theories, Strategies, Implementation and Cases] (2007) 9 *Dongshihui [Directors and Boards]* 16.
[21] Aibing Lv, 'ST Meiya Shougou yu Fanshougou Dazhan' [Hostile Takeover and Takeover Defences surrounding ST Meiya]' (2004) 2 *Zhongguo Touzi [China Investment]* 12.

industry from that of the target company and thus would not be competent to run the target company. In order to win support from employees, the board of directors resolved to make a payment to their superannuation, which had been put off for a long time. Soon after the target management initiated these defensive measures, the existing controlling shareholder terminated the share transfer agreement with the hostile acquirer and entered into a new agreement with a friendly acquirer recommended by management.

11.38 Generally speaking, winning support from minority shareholders can defeat a hostile takeover attempt by leaving insufficient shareholding for hostile acquirers to obtain control. Additionally, as seen in this case, the support of relevant stakeholders such as employees may be an important consideration in SOE-related transactions. Strong opposition from minority shareholders and stakeholders may dissuade the state asset regulator from selling shares to a hostile acquirer, as it may give rise to concerns over social stability, currently a political priority of the Chinese government.

11.39 The third defence is to file complaints with the CSRC or the court. As the Chinese securities regulator, the CSRC is charged with reviewing takeover transactions, intervening in the transaction process, and mandating the relevant participants to take certain actions. If the complaints filed by certain parties lead to certain actions taken by the CSRC, they may defeat a hostile takeover attempt.

11.40 In China's first ever hostile takeover case, which happened in 1993, the takeover of Yanzhong Shiye (the target company) by Shenzhen Baoan (the acquirer), the target company's management filed a complaint with the CSRC accusing the acquirer of breaching relevant disclosure rules in relation to takeovers. The complainant also claimed that the bid was funded by bank loans, which was prohibited under Chinese law at that time. The CSRC intervened by mediating the dispute between the two parties. The validity of the share acquisition was upheld, but the acquirer undertook to retain management employment after obtaining control.[22]

11.41 Alternatively, a complaint may be made to the court. The civil litigation filed by Sanlian Shangshe against Guomei Dianqi provides a recent example of this defence.[23] In February 2008, by way of a judicial auction, Longji Dao obtained 10.9 per cent of shares of the target company, Sanlian Shangshe, but it was later revealed that Longji Dao was only a 'shadow' acquirer used by the real acquirer, Guomei Dianqi. Soon after the purchase of shares by Longji Dao, Guomei Dianqi announced a takeover of Longji Dao and indirectly obtained control of the target company. In December 2008, the target company filed a lawsuit at the High

---

[22] Junfeng Huang, '"Baoyan Fengbo" Ziben Shichang Binggou Diyi An' [Baoyan Takeover: the First Takeover in the Capital Market], *Zhongguo Zhengquan Bao [China Securities Daily]* 1 September 2008.
[23] Caizhou Yue, 'Sanlian Shangshe de Ziben Mozhou' [Capital Curse on Sanlian Shangshe] (2011) 8 *Zhongguo Lianshuo [China Chain Store]* 21.

Court of Shandong Province. The plaintiff claimed the indirect takeover made by Guomei Dianqi was initiated for malicious purposes and breached relevant disclosure rules regarding the takeover of a listed company. In March 2009 the case was thrown out by the court on the basis that the case was filed through an incorrect procedure and thus did not meet the criteria for case acceptance.[24]

Finally, listed companies may try to revise company constitutions for the purpose of thwarting hostile takeover offers. In the hostile takeover of Aishi Gufen by Dagang Youtian, for instance, after perceiving the takeover threat, the target company management initiated two amendments to its constitution in May 1999.[25] The first amendment added a requirement of approval from the incumbent board for nominating new board members. Under the second amendment, the eligibility requirement was made more stringent than the statutory standard for shareholders to nominate board members: only shareholders who separately or jointly held more than 10 per cent of shares in the target company consecutively for more than 180 days could nominate new members to the board. The hostile acquirer filed a complaint to the CSRC against the two amendments, and the CSRC ordered that the amendments be removed. **11.42**

11.4. Analysis and Implications

11.4.1. Widespread adoption of takeover defences

The empirical data in the previous section show that adoption of takeover defences is widespread in the Chinese securities market. The defences can be divided into two categories, namely *ex ante* and *ex post* defences: the former mainly take the form of anti-takeover constitutional provisions while the latter are effected in a multiplicity of ways. Also, many companies have adopted more than one type of anti-takeover constitutional provision. This widespread adoption of takeover defences may be attributable to a number of factors, which will now be discussed. **11.43**

11.4.1.1. Unclear law

As discussed earlier, the legal framework for takeover defences is quite vague, leaving a large grey area for many takeover defences. **11.44**

For instance, with regard to the restrictions on shareholders to bring forward proposals to the general meeting, particularly the proposal to nominate new board members, the current law is unclear on its legitimacy. Under Article 103 of the **11.45**

---

[24] High Court of Shandong Province, Minshi Caiding Shu [Civil Order] (2009) Lu Shang Chu Zi Di 2-1 Hao [Commercial case report, First instance, No 2-1].
[25] Hongtao Xu, 'Gongsi Fanshougou Falv Zhidu Yanjiu' [Research Report: The Regulation of Takeover Defences]' (Shenzhen Stock Exchange Research Center, 2006), http://www.szse.cn/UpFiles/Attach/1088/2006/04/19/1624072376.pdf, 39–40.

2005 Company Law, a shareholder who separately or jointly holds 3 per cent or more of the shares can put forward proposals to the general meeting.[26] This right should cover the proposal to nominate new board members. There has been an ongoing debate on whether the company can raise the shareholding requirement above the statutory rule.[27]

11.46 Further, the existing law is silent on the legitimacy of other types of anti-takeover constitutional provisions, including the staggered board provision and the provision imposing qualifications for new board members.

11.4.1.2. Legal loopholes

11.47 As discussed earlier, Article 33 of the 2006 Takeover Measures is not applicable if the following two conditions are not satisfied: (1) takeover defences must significantly change company assets and liabilities; (2) takeover defences must be taken after the announcement of takeover bids. This opens the floodgates for the use of many takeover defences.

11.48 This is illustrated in the use of *ex post* defences. For instance, in the case of Guangfa Zhengquan discussed earlier, the 'white knight' defensive tactic was used without the approval of the shareholders because, arguably the first condition was not satisfied—that is, the defence did not significantly change the assets, liabilities, entitlements, and business performance of the target company. Similarly, in the case of ST Meiya discussed earlier, the target management did not obtain the shareholders' approval to use the defence of winning support from relevant stakeholders, due to the absence of the second condition: technically, the defence was adopted before the announcement of a takeover bid.

11.4.1.3. Lax enforcement by the CSRC

11.49 In some cases, it is reasonably clear that the adoption of takeover defences is in violation of the law, but the CSRC has not taken appropriate action to regulate it.

11.50 For instance, the constitutional provision empowering the board of directors to take defensive measures without getting approval from shareholders runs afoul of the law for takeover defences. As discussed earlier, under the Chinese company law, the general meeting, rather than the board of directors, has the power to decide on major issues including takeovers. More specifically, Article 33 of the

---

[26] Company Law 2005, Art 103.
[27] Tang and Zhizhan, 'Fan Shougou Cuoshi de Hefaxing Jianyan' 95, 97 (arguing that Article 103 of the 2005 Company Law is a mandatory rule and thus the company cannot deviate from it); cf Zhang Siwei, 'Zhongguo Shangshi Gongsi Fanshougou Cuoshi de Falv Fenxi yu Sheji: Yi Xifang Changjian Fanshougou Cuuoshi Wei Zhongxin' [A Legal Analysis of Anti-takeover Measures in China's Listed Companies: Focused on the Common Anti-takeover Measures in the Western Countries] (2007) 1 *Gongsifa Pinglun [Comments on Company Law]* 127 (contending that it is lawful and desirable for the company to raise the nomination criteria).

2006 Takeover Measures requires approval from shareholders for certain types of takeover defences.

Further, serious doubt can be cast on the legitimacy of the constitutional provision **11.51** requiring approval from the board of directors for share acquisitions above certain thresholds. This is because it is a fundamental right for shareholders of listed companies to freely transfer their shares, subject to relevant disclosure requirements.

11.4.2. Suggestions for improvement

Since 2005, the CSRC has been implementing shareholding structure reform with **11.52** a view to reducing the level of concentration of ownership in Chinese listed companies. Many commentators expected the reform to usher in a new era of hostile takeovers in China, but to date the reality is that hostile takeovers remain rare in China. One contributing factor is the pervasive use of takeover defences. As discussed, this is due to problems with both the law and its enforcement. Hence, some suggestions for improvement will be made.

The empirical study shows that in practice, takeover disputes are dealt with mainly **11.53** by the CSRC, rather than the court. This is not surprising, given that the CSRC is a specialist regulatory body and thus is better equipped to deal with complicated cases such as takeover disputes. It is also good practice, as litigation is usually time-consuming and may itself be abused as a form of takeover defence. However, the CSRC enforcement has left a lot to be desired. First, the CSRC has not provided much guidance on the concept of directors' duties in the specific context of takeover cases; second, it has failed to take action against the adoption of certain takeover defences which blatantly contravene relevant laws.

On the other hand, the law on takeover defences is in need of improvement. First, **11.54** the law needs to clarify the legitimacy of those controversial anti-takeover constitutional provisions. Some commentators have argued that to facilitate takeovers in China, all *ex ante* takeover defensive provisions should be prohibited.[28] This suggestion needs to be reconsidered, as it is overly rigid to impose such a blanket ban. In some circumstances, the use of anti-takeover defences may be justified. For instance, the staggered board provision is widely adopted in the US. To be sure, there is a heated debate on such provision, but the debate has not been conclusive. One side of the debate argues that such provision may serve some useful purposes, such as maintaining the continuity of business policies and helping the target management to secure a better bid.[29] It is not prudent for China to jump to any final conclusion before the debate is finished.

---

[28] See eg Wei Cai, 'Hostile Takeovers and Takeover Defences in China' (2012) 42(3) *Hong Kong Law Journal* 1, 34.
[29] Richard H Koppes, Lyle G Ganske, and Charles T Haag, 'Corporate Governance Out of Focus: The Debate Over Classified Boards' (1999) 54 *Business Lawyer* 1023. But see Lucian

11.55 Second, it is necessary to reform the scope of application of Article 33 of the 2006 Takeover Measures. As discussed earlier, Article 33 applies only if a takeover defence is adopted after the announcement of a takeover bid. This is a loophole, as the target management may adopt a takeover defence before the actual announcement of a bid if they reasonably believe a bid might be imminent. Also, it would help if the CSRC could provide guidance on what constitutes 'major impacts on the assets, liabilities, entitlements or business performances of the target company'.

11.5. A New Regime for Takeover Defences

11.56 From a comparative perspective, China's legal framework for takeover defences, with the 2006 Takeover Measures as its core, is an instance of legal transplant from overseas jurisdictions. As will be discussed, Article 8 of the 2006 Takeover Measures generally draws upon the US experience, while Article 33 clearly borrows from the UK experience in relation to the application of some selected defensive measures. The following part will thus look at foreign experiences at length and, based on such examination, propose a new regime for takeover defences in China.

11.5.1. United States (Delaware law)

11.57 In the US takeover defence regime, as represented by Delaware law, the directors of target corporations are empowered to institute a wide variety of defensive measures in response to hostile takeovers.[30] Obviously, target management enjoy substantial discretionary power. In order to prevent target management from abusing their power to take defensive measures (for the sole purpose of entrenchment), US takeover law imposes levels of judicial review depending on the perceived possibility of management opportunism.[31] When target management adopts a defensive measure against a hostile bid, Delaware law applies the 'modified business judgment rule', under which the directors are required to show that after a "good faith and reasonable investigation", they saw a danger to corporate policy and effectiveness'.[32]

11.58 In 1985, the Delaware Supreme Court decided a leading case regarding takeover defences: *Unocal Corp v Mesa Petroleum Co.*[33] In this case, the court made several

---

Bebchuk, John C Coates, and Guhan Subramanian, 'The Powerful Antitakeover Force of Stagged Boards: Theory, Evidence, and Policy' (2002) 54 *Stanford Law Review* 887.

[30] See Robert C Clark, *Corporate Law* (A A Balkema,1986) 581–2 (offering an explanation of various defensive measures).

[31] Richard Painter and Christian Kirchner, 'Takeover Defenses under Delaware Law, the Proposed Thirteenth EU Directive and the New German Takeover Law: Comparison and Recommendations for Reform' (2002) 50 *American Journal of Comparative Law* 452.

[32] Painter and Kirchner, 'Takeover Defenses' (quoting Cheff v Mathes, 199 A.2d 548, 555 (Del. 1964)).

[33] 493 A.2d 946 (Del. 1985).

important developments concerning the judicial review of target management's use of anti-takeover defences. The court held that the board of the target corporation 'has an obligation to determine whether the offer is in the best interests of the corporation and its shareholders'.[34] Having established this general principle, the court then proceeded to articulate the directors' duties in the context of takeovers. According to this case, the defendants, namely the target company directors, are now required to show (1) 'that they had reasonable grounds for believing that a danger to corporate policy and effectiveness existed because of another person's stock ownership', and (2) that 'it [the defensive measure] must be reasonable in relation to threat posed'.[35] The court went on further to discuss the relational requirement, stating:

> This entails an analysis by the directors of the nature of the takeover bid and its effect on the corporate enterprise. Examples of such concerns may include: inadequacy of the price offered, nature and timing of the offer, questions of illegality, the impact on 'constituencies' other than shareholders (i.e., creditors, customers, employees, and perhaps even the community generally), the risk of nonconsummation, and the quality of the securities being offered in the exchange.... While not a controlling factor, it also seems to us that a board may reasonably consider the basic stockholder interests at stake, including those of short term speculators, whose actions may have fueled the coercive aspect of the offer at the expense of the long term investor.[36]

It is worth noting here that the defendant, not the plaintiff, bears the burden of proof.[37] In this way judicial review acts as a deterrent to abusive use of takeover defences.[38]

Revlon Inc v MacAndrews & Forbes Holdings, Inc further developed judicial review concerning the duties of target management when using defensive measures.[39] Under *Revlon*, directors' duties will change once the board reasonably believes that the sale of the company is inevitable or the board takes steps to put the company

11.59

---

[34] 493 A.2d 946 (Del. 1985) at 954.
[35] 493 A.2d 946 (Del. 1985) at 955 (citations omitted).
[36] 493 A.2d 946 (Del. 1985) at 955–6 (footnotes omitted).
[37] See John H Farrer, 'Business Judgment and Defensive Tactics in Hostile Takeover Bids' (1989) 15 *Canadian Business Law Journal* 15, 22 (describing *Unocal*).
[38] Under the traditional business judgment rule, the burden of proof lies on the plaintiff unless there is a conflict of interest in the case. See Robert B Thompson and D Gordon Smith, 'Toward a New Theory of the Shareholder Role: "Sacred Space" in Corporate Takeovers' (2001) 80 *Texas Law Review* 261, 277–8. Before 1985, however, director-instituted defensive measures did not constitute express conflicts of interest and thus the courts required the plaintiff to present evidence of lack of sufficient investigation, lack of good faith, and so on. This is called the 'deferential review of the traditional business judgment rule': See Parter v Marshall Field & Co., 646 F.2d 271 (7th Cir 1981); Johnson v Trueblood, 629 F.2d 287 (3d Cir 1980). Accord Stotland v GAF Corp, No 6876, 1983 Del Ch LEXIS 477 (Del Ch Sept 1, 1983). In *Unocal*, the court stated that there exists an 'omnipresent spectre' of conflict of interest in the use of takeover defences, even though this conflict falls short of the express conflict in the traditional cases, such as a self-dealing transaction; based on this conflict, the court switched the burden of proof to the defendants. *Unocal*, 493 A.2d at 954–5.
[39] 506 A.2d 173 (Del 1985).

up for sale.⁴⁰ Upon this triggering situation, the directors must discharge their duties by obtaining the highest price for shareholders, rather than maintaining the corporate enterprise, and cannot adopt a defence for the purpose of giving absolute priority to a non-shareholder constituency.⁴¹

11.60 Thus, the defences permitted by *Unocal* could be a breach of the directors' fiduciary duty if the company is in the same situation as *Revlon*. Two subsequent cases, *Paramount Communications, Inc v Time, Inc*⁴² and *Paramount Communications, Inc v QVC Network Inc*,⁴³ offered some guidance to distinguish defensive transactions that put a company into a *Revlon* situation from transactions that do not. If a transaction contemplates a change in control of the target company, for example, by selling a control block of the target's stock to a single person or corporation, then the *Revlon* duty would be imposed on the target's management; otherwise, only the *Unocal* duty would apply.⁴⁴ In short, under Delaware law, the use of defensive measures is a matter that falls within the business discretion of the target's directors and officers.

11.5.2. United Kingdom

11.61 In the UK, the conduct of target management in the context of takeovers is regulated by both the common law and a voluntary code of conduct known as the City Code on Takeovers and Mergers (City Code).⁴⁵ Under the common law in the UK, the directors of the target company are subject to equitable principles of fiduciary law and are required to act bona fide in the interests of the company when using defensive tactics.⁴⁶ This fiduciary duty-based system is very similar to that of the US, even though there may be some differences in the contents or judicial interpretations of the amorphous notion of fiduciary duty.⁴⁷ Of more interest, however, is the new method through which the City Code puts in place a system of checks and balances on the use of defences by the target's management.

11.62 The framework regulating the use of defences by the target directors in the City Code exhibits a sharp contrast with that of US law. The City Code is a voluntary agreement issued and administered by the Panel on Takeovers and Mergers in the

---

⁴⁰ 506 A.2d 173 (Del 1985) at 182.
⁴¹ 506 A.2d 173 (Del 1985). Other states, however, allow the target directors to consider the interests of non-shareholder constituencies in the context of takeovers. Furthermore, 'Connecticut. . . requires directors to consider non-shareholder constituencies in change of control transactions'. See Painter and Kirchner, 'Takeover Defenses' 453.
⁴² 571 A.2d 1140 (Del 1989).
⁴³ 637 A.2d 34 (Del 1994).
⁴⁴ Painter and Kirchner, 'Takeover Defenses' 453.
⁴⁵ The Panel on Takeovers and Mergers, *The Takeover Code* (2006).
⁴⁶ Farrer, 'Business Judgment'.
⁴⁷ For a relatively detailed comparison of the directors' duties in the context of takeovers in several commonwealth countries, see eg Farrer, 'Business Judgment'; James Mayanja, 'Reforming Australia's Takeover Defence Laws: What Role for Target Directors? A Reply and Extension' (1999) 10 *Australian Journal of Corporate Law* 162, 164.

City of London since 1968. The Panel is a self-regulatory organization in charge of takeover and merger transactions.[48] Although the City Code does not have the force of law, it has gained tremendous influence, because it 'represents the collective opinion of those professionally involved in the field of takeovers as to good business standards and as to how fairness to shareholders can be achieved'.[49] Furthermore, the City Code's influence is based on the fact that it has been well enforced by a powerful self-regulating organization, the Panel.[50]

Under the strict 'neutrality rule' in Principle 7 of the City Code, it is forbidden for the target's management to adopt 'any action... which could effectively result in any bona fide offer being frustrated or in the shareholders of the offeree company being denied the opportunity to decide on its merits'.[51] Further, the City Code makes it clear that once an offer has been made or appears to be imminent, all defensive transactions which could frustrate the bid must be approved by shareholders at the general meeting.[52] Thus, in the City Code, the shareholders, rather than the directors, have the final say with respect to the employment of defensive measures. **11.63**

11.5.3. The way forward

The Chinese legislative attitude toward defensive tactics, as shown in the relevant provisions of the 2006 Takeover Measures, seems to discourage the use of defences to avoid opportunism. This orientation is desirable because at the present stage of economic development in China, the benefits of takeover activities are urgently needed; thus, the law should ensure the contestability of takeovers. Target directors might misuse the defences, as conflicts of interest are inherent in them. Moreover, such abuses would inhibit takeovers, thus depriving people of various benefits such as efficient allocation of scarce resources, mechanisms of monitoring corporate management, etc. This does not suggest, however, that China needs to wholly abandon the use of such defences. **11.64**

Rather, the goal is to design an effective mechanism to eliminate the abuse of defences but at the same time preserve the use of defences for proper purposes. There are two main reasons for this. First, the debate about the value of takeovers is unsettled. Even though it is submitted that China should encourage takeover **11.65**

---

[48] See Tunde I Ogowewo, 'Is Contract the Juridical Basis of the Takeover Panel?' (1997) 12 *Journal of International Banking Law* 15 (concluding that the Takeovers Panel relies on a self-regulatory system, and has neither legislative backing nor a contractual basis).

[49] City Code, Introduction, § 1, para (a).

[50] If a person or business who is authorized to conduct investment activity within the UK fails to comply with the City Code, the Panel may sanction that person or business by withdrawing its authorization. See City Code, para 1(c). The deliberations of the panel, however, may be subject to judicial review by the court. See *R v Takeover Panel, ex p Datafin plc* [1987] 1 All ER 564.

[51] City Code, Principle 7.

[52] City Code, Rule 21.1.

activities, China cannot push this inclination to an unlimited extreme without consideration of the potential harms associated with takeovers. Second, and more visibly, the defences could be properly used by target management for the benefits of the shareholders. It is important to note that the shareholder protection principle has two aspects: (1) protection of shareholders from management' opportunism, and (2) protection of shareholders from corporate raiders. Target management could protect shareholders by using anti-takeover defences to thwart genuinely undesirable takeovers.

11.66 Further, in a contested takeover some defences could be employed to instigate an auction, which would get the shareholders the highest possible price for their assets.[53] Even assuming that the target's management will act in a self-interested way, some commentators have argued that some, but not all, target stock buybacks may increase shareholder wealth as a result of the instigated auction.[54] Statistical data have shown that the takeover premiums paid for US companies are higher than those paid for European companies, which suggests that the defences used widely in the US could raise the premiums for shareholders.[55] Still, there is leeway for the use of defensive tactics to benefit shareholders, leaving the indiscriminate prohibition of defensive measures as too simplistic a remedy.

11.67 Thus, the issue of how to regulate takeover defences needs to be handled delicately to fulfil the dual goals of contestability of takeovers and shareholder protection. As discussed earlier, China's regulatory regime for takeover defences is riddled with problems, and has not been effectively implemented in practice. An in-depth analysis is now undertaken to examine whether, and if so how, foreign experiences can be utilized to inform the improvement of China's takeover law and how they can adapt themselves to the Chinese local situation.

11.5.3.1. The US model cannot take root in China

11.68 The characteristic feature of the US model is that management is granted wide discretion to implement defensive measures, subject to intense judicial supervision

---

[53] See eg Lucian A Bebchuk, *The Case for Facilitating Competing Tender Offers* (1982) 95 *Harvard Law Review* 1028, 1034–8; Ronald J Gilson, 'A Structural Approach to Corporations: The Case Against Defensive Tactics in Tender Offers' (1981) 33 *Harvard Law Review* 819, 868–75; Ronald J Gilson, 'Seeking Competitive Bids Versus Pure Passivity in Tender Offer Defenses' (1982) 35 *Harvard Law Review* 51.

[54] Michael Bradley and Michael Rosenzweig, 'Defensive Stock Repurchases' (1986) 99 *Harvard Law Review* 1377; Jonathan R Macey and Fred S McChesney (1985) 'A Theoretical Analysis of Corporate Greenmail' 95 *Yale Law Journal* 13. But see Jeffrey N Gordon and Lewis A Kornhauser, 'Takeover Defense Tactics: A Comment on Two Models' (1986) 96 *Yale Law Journal* 295 (arguing that the target stock buybacks are unlikely to increase shareholder wealth as a general matter).

[55] Christian Kirchner and Richard W Painter, 'European Takeover Law—Toward a European Modified Business Judgment Rule for Takeover Law' (2000) 2 *Eur Bus Org L Rev* 353, 379–81. But see Frank H Easterbrook and Daniel R Fischel, 'Auctions and Sunk Costs in Tender Offers' (1982) 35 *Harvard Law Review* 1, 8 (arguing that diversified shareholders who own both bidder and target company stock should be indifferent to bid price maximization).

protecting the shareholder from abuse of the defences. The courts, rather than the directors, are the arbiters of the proper use of specific defences in particular situations and thus play a central role in the US model. The work is difficult and requires judges who are experienced enough to fulfil this mission. In Delaware, where the majority of America's largest corporations are incorporated, corporate matters account for the bulk of the workload of Delaware's judges on the court of chancery.[56] In order to handle disputes quickly and effectively, those judges have necessarily developed extensive and notable experience in corporate law issues. All corporate matters are originally heard by the Delaware Court of Chancery and any appeals are taken to the Delaware Supreme Court.[57] The judges who sit on both courts are highly valued in Delaware and building a team of such highly qualified judges is extremely difficult.[58]

11.69 Obviously, there is a long way for China to go to set up a comparable team of judges who are able to effectively resolve complex takeover disputes. A lack of qualified judges is a key factor in rejecting the idea of importing the US model into China. The empirical study discussed earlier reveals that the Chinese courts have not played any meaningful role in the development of the concept of directors' duties in the specific context of takeover defences.

11.70 Additionally, China's commercial environment is significantly different from that of the US, which provides strong disincentives to the misuse of defences. There are, among other things, at least four important factors worth noting. First, in the US, management has long accepted the notion of shareholder primacy as a product of law and acculturation. As a socialist state, however, China has to give more consideration to the benefits of the employees of companies being taken over and the maintenance of social stability. This attenuates the board's sense of accountability to shareholders in China. The anti-takeover defences could be justified for employee considerations, even if they are not in the best interests of shareholders. Worst of all, concern with employee benefits could be manipulated as a pretext for misusing defences.

11.71 Second, the heavy institutional investor ownership in large public firms in the US makes management highly sensitive to public shareholder interests in considering a takeover bid, based on the fact that board members are elected by shareholders on a yearly basis. In contrast, the role played by institutional investors in corporate governance in China is rather weak, and the term of directorship can be as long as

---

[56] Robert B Thompson, 'Takeover Regulation after the 'Convergence' of Corporate Law' (2002) 24 *Sydney Law Review* 323, 334.
[57] Thompson, 'Takeover Regulation'.
[58] Delaware has a number of assets that are specific to its status as the foremost purveyor of state-of-the-art corporate law. As Professor Romano has noted, these assets include the state's 'comprehensive body of case law, judicial expertise in corporation law, and administrative expertise in the rapid processing of corporate fillings.' Roberta Romano, *The Genius of American Corporate Law* (Aei Press, 1993) 39.

three years in China. Third, independent directors in the US place important checks and balances on the use of defences.[59] This internal control within the board over the decision-making process is lacking in China. Finally, executive compensation in the US discourages management from using defences for entrenchment purposes. Stock options account for a large percentage of compensation provided to US managers.[60] Because a takeover always accelerates the vesting of options, managers are reasonably inclined to accept premium bids and could possibly make a large fortune overnight. Stock options, however, are not yet widely used in China as a form of compensation and, thus, cannot provide incentives for managers to accept a takeover bid that would increase the shareholders' value.

11.72 In fact, the US model has itself received increasing criticism recently for weak shareholder protection and the unclear application of fiduciary duty precedent in the context of takeovers.[61] As discussed earlier, the courts now apply a 'modified business judgment rule' established in *Unocal* to limit managerial discretion and protect shareholders who complain that defences are abused. This rule, however, seems impotent. In 2001, Robert B Thompson and Gordon Smith published the results of a survey showing that of all Delaware cases applying the *Unocal* framework, few involved the invalidation of takeover defences by the courts.[62] They also found that the number of *Unocal* claims decided by the Delaware courts had dramatically declined.[63] Thus, they concluded that '*Unocal*, as currently structured[,] does not provoke judicial scrutiny of director defensive tactics that is at all "enhanced," as compared to the review provided under the traditional business judgment standard'.[64] Because the courts often defer to the judgement of management when defences are used, most case law under *Unocal* permits defensive measures to remain in place.[65]

11.73 The reasons for the deficiency in the checks put on the target management's ability to use defences under *Unocal* largely lies in the 'modified business judgement

---

[59] See Stephen M Bainbridge, 'Director Primacy in Corporate Takeovers: Preliminary Reflections' (2002) 55 *Harvard Law Review* 791, 809; Mark Gordon, 'Takeover Defenses Work. Is That Such a Bad Thing?' (2002) 55 *Harvard Law Review* 819, 831; but see John C Coates et al, 'The Powerful Antitakeover Force of Staggered Boards: Further Findings and a Reply to Symposium Participants' (2002) 55 *Harvard Law Review* 885, 898 (arguing that having a majority of independent directors does not address the concern that defensive tactics might be abused).

[60] David Yermack, 'Do Corporations Award CEO Stock Options Effectively?' (1995) 39 *Journal of Financial Economics* 237, 238.

[61] See eg Robert B Thompson, 'Takeover Regulation' (arguing that the anti-takeover regimes of 'Australia, the United Kingdom, and other common law countries with developed securities markets do a better job of protecting shareholder space to make corporate decision in a takeovers context when the interests of directors may diverge from those of shareholders').

[62] Thompson and Smith, 'Toward a New Theory of the Shareholder Role'.

[63] Thompson and Smith, 'Toward a New Theory of the Shareholder Role', 283.

[64] Thompson and Smith, 'Toward a New Theory of the Shareholder Role', 284–6.

[65] In *Moran v Household Int'l, Inc*, 500 A.2d 1346, 1357 (Del 1985), the Delaware Supreme Court upheld a 'flip over' poison pill, which would allow remaining target shareholders to buy the acquirer's stock at half price if the acquirer merged the target corporation with the acquirer corporation after a hostile tender offer. The court pointed out that the pill was designed to protect the

rule' itself. As discussed earlier, this rule has introduced three significant components. To begin with, a procedural change shifts the burden of proof onto the defendant. This would be expected to have had a positive impact, but in fact has failed to have made any perceptible difference. Second, defendants are required to prove that 'they had reasonable grounds for believing that a danger to corporate policy and effectiveness existed', and this evidentiary obligation could be discharged by 'a showing of good faith and reasonable investigation'.[66] This has turned out to be too easy a task, because 'anything seems to satisfy the showing of a threat, including an assertion that shareholders misperceive the value of the company'.[67] Finally, the proportionality test seems to have suffered more serious problems. In 1995, when *Unitrin, Inc v American General Corp.* was decided,[68] this test was interpreted to be dependent on whether the defensive tactics were 'coercive' or 'preclusive'.[69] The terms 'coercive' and 'preclusive' are so restrictively defined as to only include the most dramatic situations where the shareholders have no opportunity to exit. If the directors could be removed by a proxy vote over a two-year period, for example, the court would consider the test met, even though the defences would have excluded shareholders from making a takeover decision.

11.74 Thus, Delaware law appears to be far from ideal from the perspective of shareholder protection. Recent statistical evidence has shown a low probability of success for hostile takeovers in the US.[70] Obviously, this is not the outcome China would presently like to encourage. It is almost certain that the situation would be much worse if China were to import the US system unchanged, because Chinese judges are far less experienced than their American counterparts and would be far more hesitant to intervene in corporate matters, leaving management with greater discretion on the use of defences.

11.5.3.2. The City Code, while illuminating, is unsuitable for China

11.75 As shown before, the main feature of the City Code is that it makes shareholders the final arbiters on the acceptability of takeover defences. Directors in this system play a largely passive role: the defence may be used only if the shareholders approve it in advance. Under this system, the target's shareholders will have an opportunity during the takeover bid to consider a tender offer on its merits and refuse approval

---

corporation's shareholders against a two-tier coercive offer by assuring that shareholders on the back end of a tender offer were adequately compensated. The Delaware Supreme Court rejected the claims that such a pill was not authorized by statute and that the pill violated the director's fiduciary duties.

[66] *Unocal*, 493 A.2d at 955.
[67] Thompson, 'Takeover Regulation'.
[68] 651 A.2d 1361 (Del 1995).
[69] 651 A.2d 1361 (Del 1995) at 1367 (citing *Paramount Communications, Inc v QVC Network Inc*, 637 A.2d 34, 45–46 (Del. 1994)). The court held that 'if the board of directors' defensive response is not draconian (preclusive or coercive) and is within a "range of reasonableness," a court must not substitute its judgment for the board's': at 1388.
[70] Kirchner and Painter, 'European Takeover Law'.

of defensive tactics which would thwart an offer that might otherwise be beneficial to shareholders. Therefore, in theory, the City Code could yield the best protection for shareholders against management opportunism.

11.76 Another benefit of this system is that the complex and bewildering issues of directors' duties are not as pivotal as in the US model because shareholders themselves determine the use of defences and, in fact, the ultimate destiny of the company. This is a very important consideration for China—as found in the empirical study earlier, the concept of directors' duties, particularly in the context of takeover defences, is quite underdeveloped in China.

11.77 This, by its nature, reflects the different attitudes toward the allocation of power between directors and shareholders. Clearly, takeovers result in a change of control and thus have material effects on a company. In the face of such a critical event, it appears that a system such as the City Code is preferable to the US system because under the City Code, shareholders, as the ultimate owners of the company, have an opportunity to express their opinion in respect of their property rights, instead of managers making the decisions on their own in their capacity as agents.[71] Again, this fits well with the Chinese company law, which treats the shareholder meeting as the highest organ of corporate power and requires its approval for major corporate matters, including takeovers.

11.78 The City Code is viewed positively by both academics and legislators. Many commentators have advocated the City Code model and urged their own countries to move in that direction.[72] In Australia, it has been argued that directors should desist from taking any action that may have the foreseeable effect of blocking a takeover without the prior consent of the shareholders.[73] American scholars also expressed their preference for the City Code, arguing that it 'both addresses possible defects in the takeover process and ensures that shareholders, not management, have the ultimate say on whether a takeover proceeds'.[74] Many countries, including Commonwealth countries such as New Zealand and European Union

---

[71] A counterargument is made that in a relatively efficient financial market, the shareholder choice standard like the City Code would encourage the 'managers to adopt strategies that make hostile bids less likely to occur, even if those strategies reduce the ultimate value of the corporation to the shareholders.' See Michael L Wachter, 'Takeover Defense when Financial Markets Are (Only) Relatively Efficient' (2003) 151 *University of Pennsylvania Law Review* 787, 794.

[72] See eg Farrer, 'Business Judgment'; Michael C Jensen, 'Takeovers: Their Causes and Consequences' (1988) 2 *Journal of Economic Perspectives* 21, 44.

[73] James Mayanja, 'Reforming Australia's Takeover Defence Laws' (arguing that '[t]o achieve effective shareholder protection in transactions involving the transfer of corporate control,... This, in turn, can be achieved by requiring prior shareholder approval of any action proposed to be taken by directors which may have the foreseeable effect of blocking an offer').

[74] See eg Lucian Arye Bebchuk and Allen Ferrel, 'Federalism and Corporate Law: The Race to Protect Managers from Takeovers' (1999) 99 *Columbia Law Review* 1193.

member states such as Ireland, as well as many others,[75] have adopted a similar model to the City Code.

The City Code, however, is also beset by a number of serious problems in practice. Notably, the so-called collective action problems, including widespread rational apathy among shareholders and free-riding, have discounted the function of the shareholders' meeting as an effective mechanism.[76] It has been argued that the approval process of the City Code is 'in most cases impossible to use because the notice and preparation period for a general shareholders' meeting is too long'.[77] Especially in the context of takeovers, which are by nature time-sensitive commercial arrangements, the time the shareholders have before reaching a decision is critical and always very limited. The shareholders' meeting would take considerable time even if the shareholders are willing to take part in the meeting, and the delay would prevent the directors from making proper use of defences to ward off bids offering an inadequate price or posing threats to the company. **11.79**

This problem is particularly severe and disconcerting in China, where shareholders consist mostly of retail investors who are more inclined to exhibit rational apathy and free-riding. Further, due to monetary constraints and the problems imposed by communication and transportation systems in need of modernization, it is not surprising that the time taken to hold a shareholders' meeting in China would be much longer than that taken in countries that adhere to the City Code model. Furthermore, the frequent shareholders' meetings would result in considerable costs to corporations. Thus, the City Code model cannot be imported wholesale into China. The City Code, however, illuminates a step in the right direction, in that it provides shareholders with an opportunity to decide the use of defences. **11.80**

11.5.3.3. Reform proposal: shareholders ex post veto the use of defences

A system in which shareholders could, *ex post*, veto the use of defences by management could overcome the problems of time and costs associated with *ex ante* shareholder approval.[78] This approach enjoys two significant advantages. On the one hand, it shares a key feature of the City Code, because shareholders are granted an opportunity to approve or disapprove of defensive measures from their own perspective and thus could be best protected in the takeover context. On the **11.81**

---

[75] See eg Guido A Ferrarini, 'Share Ownership, Takeover Law and the Contestability of Corporate Control', at 15–16, nn 64–76, available at http://papers.ssrn.com/sol3/papers.cfm?abstract_id=265429 (providing a detailed list of twenty other countries following the model of the City Code).

[76] See Frank H Easterbrook and Daniel R Fischel, *The Economic Structure of Corporate Law* (Harvard University Press, 1991) 82–9 (discussing this problem in detail). See also Paul Redmond, 'The Reform of Directors' Duties' (1992) 15 *University of New South Wales Law Journal* 86, 92 (discussing the same issue in depth).

[77] Christian Kirchner and Richard Painter, 'Takeover Defenses under Delaware Law, the Proposed Thirteenth EU Directive and the New German Takeover Law: Comparison and Recommendations for Reform' (2002) 50 *American Journal of Comparative Law* 451, 457.

[78] Hui Huang, 'China's Takeover Law' 193–6.

other, management could respond quickly to takeovers and avoid any disastrous delay. This flexibility is necessary in a rapidly changing and complex commercial environment. Some commentators believe that a target's board is in a better position to make the initial decision on the use of takeover defences because 'a firm's true economic value is visible to well-informed corporate directors but not to [the] company's shareholders or to potential acquirers'.[79] Further, compared to the City Code, where every defence needs to be approved by the shareholder meeting, this system would result in a reduction of shareholder meetings because shareholders would not meet to veto a defence that they think is in their best interests. Thus, the costs incurred by the company would be diminished.

11.82 At the heart of this system, shareholders would have the opportunity to veto defensive measures immediately after they are implemented. The willingness of shareholders to exercise their veto power, especially institutional investors, is reinforced by the fact that in the context of takeovers, the possibility of gain or loss due to a notable change in the share price is large. This creates an opportunity to reap handsome short-term profits based on the premium offered by the bids. So, even assuming a sceptical attitude toward institutional shareholders' activism,[80] it is reasonable to make an exception and argue that they will take an active role in response to takeovers, in light of the short-term profits that such conduct might generate. The shareholders would only veto undesirable defences (ie those that materially harm them), and as such shareholder meetings would not be held with excessive frequency, leaving shareholders to concentrate their limited time, money, energy, and interests in attending truly important meetings. With the help of modern technology such as the Internet, the veto system could be more feasible and function more efficiently.

11.83 It is important, however, to note that the collective action problem connected with the shareholders' meeting would still exist in this system. To alleviate the concern that the directors would enjoy virtually full discretion if shareholders seldom hold meetings, the shareholders could *ex ante* set out the types of defensive measures available to the directors in the annual meeting. Since the defences would materially impact the company, they must be approved by a special majority according to the Company Law.[81] The directors could only use those approved defences in appropriate circumstances—for example, to repel a bid at an insufficient price. This approval would have to be renewed over a specified period of time, such as one year, as decided by shareholders in the annual meeting. If it is found that the directors have misused certain defences, the shareholders would be able to remove

---

[79] Bernard Black and Reinier Kraakman, *Delaware's Takeover Law: The Uncertain Search for Hidden Value* (2002) 96 *Northwestern University Law Review* 521, 521–2.
[80] Frank H Easterbrook and Daniel R Fischel, *The Economic Structure of Corporate Law* 80 (1991).
[81] Company Law, Arts 44, 104 (stipulating that resolutions on the merger, division, or dissolution of the company adopted by the shareholders' general meeting require more than two-thirds of the voting rights held by the shareholders present at the meeting).

those defences from the approval list at the next annual meeting. Alternatively, shareholders would be able to retain those removed defences if they are deemed necessary thereafter. In other words, the list is decided by shareholders, not directors or, specifically, legislators, as seen in China's pre-2006 legislator-based model. This model would provide the shareholders with enough flexibility to adjust the list according to changing situations and create a further check on the discretionary power of the directors. This added measure would impose fewer costs on the company and the shareholders, because annual meetings would continue to be held.

11.84 The appropriateness of this new anti-takeover scheme in China is further bolstered by the fact that the Company Law has already put many limits on the use of defences. As discussed earlier, some widely used defensive measures in the US, such as poison pills and share buyback, cannot be used in China. Further, under Chinese company law, all major measures, including issuing new shares, amending the articles of association, and increasing or reducing the company's capital, need shareholders' approval. In short, China's general company law framework has, in fact, ruled out many US defences and, therefore, decreased the possibility of the misuse of defences by directors.

11.85 Finally, the reform proposal is fundamentally consistent with the suggestion of Professors Bernard Black and Reinier Kraakman that emerging economies should adopt a self-enforcing model due to the prevalence of insider-controlled companies and the weakness of other institutional, market, cultural, and legal constraints.[82] In this self-enforcing model, shareholders could better protect themselves from management opportunism through shareholder meetings, with minimal resort to legal authority, including courts and regulators. This would offer a solution to the problem, identified in the empirical study earlier, that the court and the CSRC has not effectively enforced the law to regulate the use of takeover defences. In conclusion, as an emerging economy, China should model its takeover law on this self-enforcing model for the purpose of shareholder protection while simultaneously preserving managerial discretion.

---

[82] Bernard Black and Reinier Kraakman, 'A Self-Enforcing Model of Corporate Law' (1996) *109 Harvard Law Review* 1911, 1932; Robert B Thompson, 'Takeover Regulation' (stating that '[m]y preference is for a greater reliance on shareholder self-help in resolving disputes about the extent of takeover regulation').

12

THE REGULATION OF FOREIGN M&A

12.1. Introduction	12.01	12.4.1. Equity M&A vs asset M&A	12.26
12.2. Legal Framework for Foreign M&A in China	12.07	12.4.2. Restrictions on round-tripping investments	12.30
12.2.1. Overview	12.07	12.4.3. Approval and registration	12.35
12.2.2. Foreign M&A of Chinese listed companies	12.09	12.4.4. Pricing and payment	12.45
12.3. The 2006 Foreign M&A Regulation: Overview	12.14	12.5. Regulation of Special Purpose Vehicles	12.61
12.3.1. Scope of coverage	12.14	12.5.1. Overview	12.61
12.3.2. The approval authority	12.19	12.5.2. VIE structure	12.65
12.3.3. Interaction with other laws and regulations	12.22	12.6. National Security Review	12.70
		12.6.1. Overview	12.70
12.4. The 2006 Foreign M&A Regulation: Basic Rules	12.26	12.6.2. Central features	12.74
		12.6.3. Comments	12.93
		12.7. Summary	12.100

12.1. Introduction

12.01 With China's entry into the World Trade Organization (WTO), the gradual opening of previously closed industry sectors to foreign investment and the continued strong growth of the Chinese economy, M&A activity has become an increasingly attractive alternative to greenfield investment for foreign investors. In the 1980s, the first wave of foreign direct investment (FDI) in China mostly took the form of joint ventures, including equity joint venture enterprises (EJV) and contractual joint venture enterprises (CJV). A second wave followed in the 1990s in the form of wholly foreign-owned enterprises (WFOE). The EJV, CJV, and WFOE have traditionally been the three main forms of foreign-invested enterprises (FIE) in China.[1]

12.02 Now a third wave—foreign M&A (M&A by foreigners, or inbound cross-border M&A)—is gaining strength in China. Until China's accession to the WTO in 2001,

---

[1] For more detailed discussion of FIEs, see Hui Huang, 'The Regulation of Foreign Investment in Post-WTO China: A Political Economy Analysis' (2009) 23(1) *Columbia Journal of Asia Law* 185.

China appeared to often encourage foreigners to form joint ventures or set up WFOEs, while explicitly discouraging M&A. But it has since gradually loosened the regulations that govern foreign M&A of Chinese assets, including state-owned assets, and has made explicit moves to facilitate foreign M&A. As a result, during the past decade, foreign M&A transactions have experienced significant growth in China.

The rapid increase in foreign M&A activity in China can be explained on a number of grounds. On the one hand, it is not surprising, given the benefits it can provide to foreign investors. Foreign investors are becoming more inclined to invest in China by merging or acquiring existing Chinese companies, particularly the leading players in the fields, because M&A transactions offer foreign investors immediate market access with minimal business risk, and the acquired business can be converted to FIEs to receive favourable treatment. **12.03**

On the other hand, the Chinese government generally welcomes foreign M&A. First, foreign investors are important as they bring in the capital, advanced technologies, and management skills that China needs. Second, it is hoped that foreign M&A activity can play a useful role in carrying out the grand plan of strategically restructuring China's national economy. At present, one of the key challenges for the Chinese government is the on-going process of state-owned enterprises (SOE). The policy goal is to shunt the vast majority of SOEs into the private sector, retaining only a tiny core that the state deems crucial for national defence, energy security, and so on. Therefore in most sectors, a large number of SOEs are now being made available for private capital, including foreign capital. This bodes well for the development of foreign M&A in China. **12.04**

At the same time, the Chinese government is concerned that foreigners may swoop in and buy their way to dominance in key sectors of the economy, and has responded by introducing more control on foreign M&A. A report conducted by the Development Research Centre under the State Council in 2006 showed that foreign investors controlled the top five businesses in all the industrial sectors that were open to foreign investments, and also controlled most of the assets in 21 out of the 28 leading industrial sectors in China.[2] This is certainly an alarming situation and as such, drawing upon the international practice, China has now established a more stringent screening process for foreign investment through M&A. This is evidenced by the introduction of, among other things, the 'national economic security' review and the antitrust review with respect to foreign M&A in 2006. **12.05**

China's current policy towards foreign M&A was explained in the 11th Five-year Plan for Utilizing Foreign Investment, published by the National Development and Reform Commission (NDRC) in November 2006. It states that priority will be given to quality rather than quantity of foreign investment, and sets forth a clear industrial policy that prioritizes geographical areas, industrial sectors, levels of technology, **12.06**

---

[2] Qi Wu, *China Regulates Foreign Mergers for More Investment* (2006), Embassy of the PRC (USA), http://www.china-embassy.org/eng/gyzg/t271391.htm.

environmental protection, and efficient use of natural resources. In response to perceived rising concern over foreign acquisitions of leading Chinese firms in critical sectors, the Plan provides for increased supervision of sensitive acquisitions to ensure that what are termed 'critical industries and enterprises' remain under Chinese control.

12.2. Legal Framework for Foreign M&A in China

12.2.1. Overview

12.07 Foreign M&A laws operate as a supplement to domestic M&A laws in that they set out additional government approval requirements. Consistent with the gradualist nature of the 'Open Door Policy', China's law governing foreign M&A has evolved in an accretive way in response to problems. This has resulted in a large and bewildering body of rules applicable to foreign M&A in China.

12.08 In response to this problem, great efforts have been made to tidy up relevant regulations in this area. China first issued the Tentative Provisions on the M&A of Domestic Enterprises by Foreign Investors in 2003, which were superseded by the Provisions on the M&A of Domestic Enterprises by Foreign Investors in 2006 (2006 Foreign M&A Regulation).[3] The 2006 document represented a substantial amendment and expansion of its 2003 predecessor, setting up a comprehensive and systematic legal framework for foreign M&A in China.[4] In 2009, the 2006 Foreign M&A Regulation was revised by the Ministry of Commerce's Provisions on M&A of Domestic Enterprises by Foreign Investors mainly to delete its antitrust provisions in favour of the Anti-monopoly Law, which came into effect in 2008.[5] Please note that as a result of the 2009 revision, the numbering of the provisions in the 2006 Foreign M&A Regulation has changed. Reference is thus made in this chapter to the 2006 Foreign M&A Regulation as revised in 2009.

12.2.2. Foreign M&A of Chinese listed companies

12.09 The preceding chapters have discussed the law governing takeovers of listed companies in China. The law is applicable to both domestic acquirers and foreign

---

[3] Guanyu Waiguo Touzizhe Binggou Jingnei Qiye de Guiding [Provisions on the M&A of Domestic Enterprises by Foreign Investors] (promulgated in August 2006 by Minister of Commerce, State-owned Assets Supervision and Administration Commission, State Administration of Taxation, State Administration for Industry and Commerce, China Securities Regulatory Commission, State Administration of Foreign Exchange).

[4] Hui Huang, 'China's New Regulation on Foreign M&A: Green Light or Red Flag?' (2007) 30(3) *The University of New South Wales Law Journal* 804.

[5] Shangwubu Guangyu Waiguo Touzizhe Binggou Jingnei Qiye de Guiding [Ministry of Commerce's Provisions on M&A of Domestic Enterprises by Foreign Investors] (issued by the Ministry of Commerce on 22 June 2009).

acquirers. But as to takeovers of listed companies by foreigners, there is a separate group of regulations in addition to those for domestic acquirers.

12.2.2.1. Acquisition of non-A-shares

As discussed in the preceding chapters, there are several different types of shares in Chinese listed companies, including A-shares, B-shares, and foreign stock exchange-listed shares such as H-shares and N-shares. Non-A-shares such as B-shares and H-shares are specifically designed for foreign investors to invest in Chinese listed companies. As all types of shares hold the same voting rights, it is theoretically possible to acquire shares other than A-shares to gain control of Chinese listed companies. Hence, there are basically three ways to take over Chinese listed companies. First, takeovers can be carried out by acquiring B-shares. For example, in 1995, the US auto giant Ford acquired a sufficient number of B-shares in Jianglin Auto, becoming the second largest shareholder in the latter. The second way is to acquire foreign stock exchange-listed shares such as H-shares or N-shares. A good example can be found in the US beverage company Anheuser-Busch becoming the second largest shareholder of Tsingtao Beer in 2002 through the acquisition of H-shares in Tsingtao Beer on the Hong Kong Stock Exchange. Finally, foreigners can take over Chinese listed companies by acquiring A-shares. **12.10**

As less restriction is imposed on transactions involving non-A-shares by foreigners, takeovers through acquisition of B-shares or H-shares are simpler compared to those though A-share purchases. But the problem is that, as noted previously, non-A-shares generally account for a small proportion of shares in Chinese listed companies. This makes it impossible to effect corporate control transactions by acquiring non-A-shares in most cases. Therefore, in practice, acquiring A-shares has been the main way for foreigners to take over Chinese listed companies. **12.11**

12.2.2.2. Acquisition of A-shares

The policy on acquisition of A-shares by foreigners has evolved over time from a strict prohibition to a conditional facility. In 1995, two Japanese companies (Isuzu Motors and Itochu Trading) gained control of a Chinese listed company named Beijing Light Bus after acquiring non-tradable A-shares of the target by private agreement. This has been recorded as the first instance of a foreign takeover of a Chinese listed company. The Chinese government responded quickly to this case by promulgating a rule to put a temporary ban on foreigners acquiring non-tradable A-shares of Chinese listed companies.[6] **12.12**

As China's economic reform continued to progress, the government came to realize the useful role foreigners could play in its SOE reform. The government started **12.13**

---

[6] Zanting jiang Shangshi Gongsi Guojiagu he Farengu Zhuanrang Geiyu Waishang de Tongzhi [Notice on the Suspension of Transfer of State Shares and Legal Person Shares of Listed Companies to Foreign Investors] (promulgated by the State Council in September 1995).

trying to restructure SOEs by utilizing foreign investment after 1998. Hence, the blanket ban on foreign M&A of Chinese listed companies has been gradually relaxed through a string of rules, some of which include:[7]

- In August 1999, the State Economic and Trade Commission promulgated a rule to permit foreigners to acquire SOEs, including listed companies.[8] However, this rule lacks specific and functional provisions so as to undermine its workability.
- In November 2001, several government agencies issued a rule to allow foreigners to acquire non-tradable shares *indirectly* through FIEs such as WFOE.[9]
- In November 2002, a rule was published by the government to facilitate foreigners acquiring non-tradable shares.[10] This rule establishes a clear legal framework for foreign acquisition of non-tradable A-shares, but the procedure required for transactions is criticized to be too burdensome. Hence, this rule has been modestly used in practice.
- In January 2003, several government agencies issued a rule to guide the utilization of foreign investment to restructure SOEs.[11] It should be noted that this rule excludes listed companies and financial enterprises from its coverage.
- In March 2003, a general rule was issued to govern the foreign acquisition of domestic enterprises, including listed companies. As noted earlier, it was significantly revised in 2006 and 2009.[12]
- In December 2005, several government agencies published a rule to encourage strategic investment in listed companies by foreign investors against the background of the shareholding structure reform.[13] The acquisition of A-shares here must be as a strategic long-term investment. This rule makes a breakthrough in the policy on foreign M&A of Chinese listed companies, in that it extends far beyond merely allowing foreigners to acquire minority shareholdings in

---

[7] For a more detailed discussion of the historical development of China's law governing foreign M&A involoving listed companies, see Lusong Zhang, *Regulation of Foreign Mergers and Acquisitions involving Companies Listed in China* (London: Kluwer Law International, 2007) 29–35.

[8] Waishang Shougou Guoyou Qiye de Zanxing Guiding [Tentative Rules on Foreign Acquisitions of State-owned Enterprises] (promulgated by the State Economic and Trade Commission in August 1999).

[9] Guanyu Shangshi Gongsi Sheji Waishang Touzi Youguan Wenti de Ruogan Yijian [Several Opinions on the Issues regarding Foreign Investment in Listed Companies] (promulgated by the MOFTEC and CSRC in November 2001).

[10] Guanyu xiang Waishang Zhuanrang Shangshi Gongsi Guoyougu he Farengu Youguan Wenti de Tongzhi [Notice on Relevant Issues Regarding the Transfer to Foreign Investors of State Shares and Legal Person Shares of Listed Companies] (promulgated by the Ministry of Finance, the CSRC, the State Economic and Trade Commission in November 2002).

[11] Liyong Waizi Gaizu Guoyou Qiye Zanxing Guiding [Interim Provisions on the Utilization of Foreign Investment to Restructure State-owned Enterprises] (promulgated in January 2003).

[12] Guanyu Waiguo Touzizhe Binggou Jingnei Qiye de Guiding [Provisions on the M&A of Domestic Enterprises by Foreign Investors] (promulgated in 2006, amended in 2009).

[13] Waiguo Touzizhe dui Shangshi Gongsi Zhanlue Touzi Guanli Banfa [Administrative Measures for the Strategic Investment in Listed Companies by Foreign Investors] (promulgated in December 2005).

Chinese listed companies. Under this rule, foreign investors can acquire a large holding (at least 10 per cent) in Chinese listed companies and are thus able to acquire control.

12.3. The 2006 Foreign M&A Regulation: Overview

12.3.1. Scope of coverage

Under the 2006 Foreign M&A Regulation, there are two types of M&A that foreigners can undertake in China, namely 'Equity M&A' and 'Asset M&A'.[14] 'Equity M&A' occurs where a foreign purchaser acquires existing shares, or subscribes to a capital increase in a non-FIE domestic enterprise, and then converts the acquired enterprise into an FIE. It should be noted that the 2006 Foreign M&A Regulation defines a non-FIE domestic enterprise as a 'domestic company', because the Equity M&A of FIE by foreigners is basically governed by specific FIE regulations. **12.14**

On the other hand, the term 'Asset M&A' refers to transactions involving both the establishment by a foreign investor of an FIE and then its acquisition of a domestic enterprise by purchasing its assets through the FIE; or a foreign investor purchasing the assets of a domestic enterprise and then using those assets to establish a new FIE to operate those assets. Importantly, Asset M&A targets include all types of domestic enterprises, including FIEs. In other words, unlike Equity M&A, the Asset M&A of FIEs by foreigners also falls within the ambit of the 2006 Foreign M&A Regulation. **12.15**

Hence, the 2006 Foreign M&A Regulation is generally applicable to foreign M&A of all types of domestic enterprises, with the exception of equity acquisition of FIEs, which is governed by specific FIE regulations. **12.16**

It should be noted that, even for equity acquisition of FIEs, the 2006 Foreign M&A Regulation is of high relevance.[15] First, for the so-called 'investment company' (*touzixing gongsi*) which is established by a foreign investor inside the territory of China in accordance with the law, its M&A of domestic enterprises shall be governed by the 2006 Foreign M&A Regulation. The investment company is a special type of FIE, in that it is established for the purpose of making investments and thus is different from productive FIEs. In practice, the investment company is normally used by foreigners as a holding company to manage multiple productive FIEs in China. **12.17**

Second, where the specific FIE regulations are silent on certain issues of M&A transactions involving FIEs, those issues will be determined under the 2006 Foreign **12.18**

---

[14] 2006 Foreign M&A Regulation, Art 2.
[15] 2006 Foreign M&A Regulation, Art 52.

M&A Regulation. This may occur in the following three circumstances: (1) where a foreign investor purchases the equity of a FIE or subscribes to increased capital of a FIE, it shall be subject to the specific FIE regulations on alteration in investors' share right of foreign investment enterprises. If there is no such applicable provision, it shall be handled by reference to the 2006 Foreign M&A Regulation; (2) where a foreign investor merges or acquire a domestic enterprise through its FIE established in China, it shall be subject to the relevant provisions on merger and division of FIEs, and the relevant provisions on domestic investment by FIEs. If there is no such applicable provision, it shall be handled by reference to the 2006 Foreign M&A Regulation; (3) where a foreign investor merges a domestic limited liability company and reauthorizes it into a joint-stock company, or the domestic company is a joint-stock company, it shall be subject to the relevant provisions on establishment of foreign investment joint-stock companies. If there is no such applicable provision, it shall be handled by reference to the 2006 Foreign M&A Regulation.

12.3.2. The approval authority

12.19 China has a complicated approval regime in relation to foreign M&A. A single M&A transaction may need approvals from multiple government agencies, depending on a number of factors such as the structure of the deal, the nature of the target, and the outcome of the transaction.

12.20 The difficulty with the approval regime is compounded by the frequent government organizational reform in which a number of government agencies are reshuffled. For example, after the 2003 reform, the Ministry of Foreign Trade and Economic Cooperation (MOFTEC) was replaced by Ministry of Commerce (MOFCOM) and the State Economic and Trade Commission displaced in favour of the National Development and Reform Commission (NDRC).

12.21 Under the 2006 Foreign M&A Regulation, the MOFCOM is positioned as the final approval authority for foreign M&A transactions.[16] To make the approval process more efficient, approval power will be exercised by the MOFCOM itself or its provincial branches ('provincial approval authority'), depending on factors such as the value of the transaction. However, if the FIE established after the M&A falls into the special category of FIEs whose establishment needs to be approved by the MOFCOM in accordance with the laws, administrative regulations or departmental rules, the provincial approval authority shall transfer the application documents to the MOFCOM for the final approval.

12.3.3. Interaction with other laws and regulations

12.22 The 2006 Foreign M&A Regulation sets up a comprehensive framework for foreign M&A, containing rules which are generally applicable to foreign M&A

---

[16] 2006 Foreign M&A Regulation, Art 10.

transactions. Due to the complexity of such transactions, however, some foreign M&A transactions may give rise to special legal issues which are governed by other laws and regulations. The 2006 Foreign M&A Regulation provides a signpost to those laws and regulations, rendering itself the centrepiece of China's foreign M&A law.

Under Article 3 of the 2006 Foreign M&A Regulation, in mergers and acquisitions of domestic enterprises, foreign investors shall comply with the laws, administrative regulations, and departmental rules and adhere to the principles of fairness, reasonableness, compensation for equal value, and honesty and good faith, and shall not create excessive concentration, eliminate or hinder competition, disturb the social economic order, harm societal public interests, or lead to the loss of state-owned assets.[17] **12.23**

More specifically, the 2006 Foreign M&A Regulation makes reference to the following legal issues: **12.24**

(1) As noted above, foreign M&A transactions shall not create excessive concentration, or eliminate or hinder competition.[18] This means that foreign M&A transactions need to comply with China's antitrust law.
(2) In mergers and acquisitions of domestic enterprises, foreign investors shall comply with the requirements regarding the investors' qualifications, as well as relevant industrial, land, and environmental protection policies.[19]
(3) If a foreign M&A transaction involves transfer of state-owned assets or management of state-owned equity in public listed companies, it shall comply with the relevant laws and regulations on the administration of state-owned assets.[20] Approval may need to be obtained from relevant government agencies such as the Ministry of Finance, the National Development and Reform Commission (NDRC), and the State Owned Asset Supervision and Administration Commission (SASAC).
4) If a new FIE is to be set up after foreign M&A, it needs to comply with the rules governing the establishment of FIEs, and register with the relevant regulatory agency, namely the State Administration for Industry and Commerce (SAIC) or its authorized local branch. Further, if the target of foreign acquisition is a listed company, the foreign investor shall also apply to the CSRC in accordance with the Administration Rules on Foreign Investors' Strategic Investment in Listed Companies.[21]

---

[17] 2006 Foreign M&A Regulation, Art 3.
[18] 2006 Foreign M&A Regulation, Art 3.
[19] 2006 Foreign M&A Regulation, Art 4. A very important instrument setting out China's industry policy is the Waishang Touzi Chanye Zhidao Mulu [Catalogue for the Guidance of Foreign Investment Industries]. It has been revised several times to keep up with the rapidly changing society in China. Under this document, industries are grouped into three categories: 'encouraged', 'restricted', and 'prohibited'.
[20] 2006 Foreign M&A Regulation, Art 5.
[21] 2006 Foreign M&A Regulation, Art 6.

5) All parties involved in the foreign M&A transactions shall pay the taxes and accept the supervision of taxation authorities in accordance with China's relevant laws and regulations on taxation.[22]

6) All parties involved in the foreign M&A transactions shall comply with China's relevant laws and regulations on foreign exchange control, and shall promptly go through all procedures on approval, registration, putting on records, and alteration regarding foreign exchange with the competent foreign exchange administrative authorities, namely the State Administration of Foreign Exchange of the People's Republic of China (SAFE) or its branches.[23]

12.25 In short, the MOFCOM acts as the umbrella approval authority, co-ordinating the complex approval process. In the end, all application materials, including approvals from other relevant government bodies, are to be put together and sent to the MOFCOM for the final stamp.

12.4. The 2006 Foreign M&A Regulation: Basic Rules

12.4.1. Equity M&A vs asset M&A

12.26 As noted earlier, the 2006 Foreign M&A Regulation provides for two main ways to buy Chinese businesses, namely equity M&A and asset M&A. This brings the options for doing M&A in China in line with those of major overseas jurisdictions. Foreign investors may purchase shares in the target, either by acquiring existing shares from a seller or by acquiring newly issued shares from the target, or purchase the assets.

12.27 The pros and cons of equity M&A vis-à-vis asset M&A in China are similar to those in other jurisdictions. Under Article 13, in equity acquisition, the foreign acquirer shall succeed to the credits and debts of the target, while this is not the case for asset acquisition. The foreign investor, the merged domestic enterprise, the creditors, and other parties can opt out of the above rule by reaching an agreement on the disposition of the claims and debts of the merged domestic enterprise, provided that the agreement shall not damage a third person's interests or public interests. The agreement on disposition of the claims and debts shall be submitted to the approval authority.[24]

12.28 Insulation from succession liabilities represents a major advantage of asset M&A, particularly in China, where many companies have complicated and sometimes hidden liabilities. However, asset M&As are usually more complicated to complete. At least 15 days prior to the submission of application documents to the

---

[22] 2006 Foreign M&A Regulation, Art 7.
[23] 2006 Foreign M&A Regulation, Art 8.
[24] 2006 Foreign M&A Regulation, Art 13.

relevant approval body by the foreign investors, the domestic enterprise that sells assets shall notify all creditors, and shall make a public announcement on the newspaper of provincial level or above published nationwide.[25] The notified creditors can require security for their debts or ask for discharge of their debts before the foreign M&A transaction is completed.

In practice, to protect the interests of the target employees, an 'employee settlement plan' must usually be included in the deal and be subject to government approval. This applies to both equity and asset transactions.   **12.29**

12.4.2. Restrictions on round-tripping investments

After the foreign M&A transaction, the foreign party must have at least 25 per cent shareholding in the resultant entity in order to enjoy favourable treatment for FIEs. If the contribution made by a foreign investor to the registered capital of the FIE established after the merger or acquisition is less than 25 per cent, the enterprise shall not enjoy favourable treatments for FIEs, and it shall be subject to relevant provisions on contracting a foreign loan applicable to a non-FIE when the enterprise intends to contract a foreign loan, unless otherwise provided in relevant laws and regulations. The approval authority shall, when issuing the FIE approval certificate (Approval Certificate), indicate on the certificate the following words: 'foreign investment contribution is less than 25%.' The registration administrative authority and the foreign exchange administrative authority shall also, when issuing the business licence of FIE and the foreign exchange registration certificate, indicate on them the words: 'The foreign investment contribution is less than 25%.'[26]   **12.30**

In order to prevent so-called round-tripping investments, where Chinese entities go overseas to set up an off-shore company and then use it to invest back in China for the purpose of obtaining favourable FIE treatment, relevant measures are put in place regarding how to determine foreign investment and the satisfaction of the 25 per cent requirement.   **12.31**

Basically, if any domestic company, enterprise, or natural person merges its affiliated domestic company by way of a company legally established or controlled by the aforesaid domestic company, enterprise, or natural person in a foreign country or region, the foreign investment enterprise established after the merger shall not be treated as a foreign investment enterprise.[27] The logic is that the acquisition is ultimately made by a Chinese domestic company and not really by foreign investors.   **12.32**

Two important points need to be noted about the above rule. First, if the overseas company purchases any increased capital of the domestic company, or the   **12.33**

---

[25] 2006 Foreign M&A Regulation, Art 13.
[26] 2006 Foreign M&A Regulation, Art 9.
[27] 2006 Foreign M&A Regulation, Art 9.

enterprise established after the merger by the overseas company increases capital to a proportion of 25 per cent of its registered capital, then the acquisition will qualify for FIE incentives. Second, if the contribution made by a real foreign investor other than the actual controller is more than 25 per cent of the registered capital of the enterprise established according to this paragraph, the enterprise may be treated as a foreign investment enterprise.

12.34 Finally, Article 55 stipulates that any subsequent change in the nationality of the individual shareholders of a domestic company will not affect the FIE status of the company.

12.4.3. Approval and registration

12.35 Both equity and asset M&A need to comply with relevant approval and registration requirements as provided for under Chapter 3 of the 2006 Foreign M&A Regulation.

12.36 In the case of equity M&A, the foreign investor shall, pursuant to the total investment amount of the foreign investment enterprise under planned establishment, the type of the enterprise, and the industry it engages in, submit the following documents to the approval authority with the corresponding approval power in accordance with the laws, administrative regulations, and departmental rules on establishment of foreign investment enterprises:

(1) The resolution of the shareholders of the merged domestic limited liability company on unanimous consent of the foreign investor's equity merger, or resolution of the shareholders' meeting of the merged domestic stock limited company on consent of the foreign investor's equity merger.
(2) The application for the merged domestic company to be modified in accordance with the law into and be established as a foreign investment enterprise.
(3) The contract and articles of association of the foreign investment enterprise established after the merger.
(4) The agreement on the foreign investor's purchase of the shareholders' equity of the domestic company or on the subscription of the domestic company to increase capital.
(5) The financial auditing report of the merged domestic company in the previous accounting year.
(6) The identification certificate or incorporation certificate and the credit certificate of the investor notarized and attested according to law.
(7) The statement on the enterprises invested in by the merged domestic company.
(8) The business licences (duplicates) of the merged domestic company and of the enterprises in which it invests.
(9) The plan for re-settlement of the merged domestic company's employees.
(10) The documents required in articles 13, 14, and 15 hereof.

Where the business scope, scale, and obtainment of land use rights of the foreign investment enterprise established after the merger involves permits from other relevant governmental departments, the relevant permit documents shall be submitted along with those provided for in the preceding paragraph.[28]

12.37

Under Article 22, the equity purchase agreement and capital increase agreement for the domestic company shall be governed by Chinese laws, and shall include the following contents:

12.38

(1) Information regarding each party to the agreements, including its name, its domicile, and the name, position, and nationality, etc. of its legal representative.
(2) The proportions and price of the purchased equity or the capital increased from subscription.
(3) The term and method for performance of the agreements.
(4) The rights and obligations of each party to the agreements.
(5) The liabilities for breach of the agreement and settlement of disputes.
(6) The date and place for conclusion of the agreements.

In the case of asset M&A, the foreign investor shall, pursuant to the total investment amount of the foreign investment enterprise under planned establishment, the type of the enterprise, and the industry in which it is engaged, submit the following documents to the approval authority with the corresponding approval power in accordance with the laws, administrative regulations, and departmental rules on establishment of foreign investment enterprises:

12.39

(1) The resolution of the property holders or authority of the domestic enterprise on agreeing to sell the assets.
(2) The application for the establishment of the foreign investment enterprise.
(3) The contract and articles of association of the foreign investment enterprise to be established.
(4) The agreement concluded between the foreign investment enterprise to be established and the domestic enterprise on purchase of assets, or the agreement concluded between the foreign investor and the domestic enterprise on assets purchase.
(5) The articles of association and business licence (duplicates) of the domestic enterprise subject to the merger or acquisition.
(6) The evidence of notice and public announcement to creditors by the domestic enterprise subject to the merger or acquisition, and a statement on whether or not any objection has been made by creditors.
(7) The identification certificate or incorporation certificate and the credit certificate of the investor notarized and attested according to law.

---

[28] 2006 Foreign M&A Regulation, Art 21.

(8) The plan for employee re-settlement of the domestic enterprise subject to the merger or acquisition.
(9) the documents whose submission is required in Articles 13, 14, and 15 hereof.

12.40 Where the assets of the domestic enterprise purchased and operated in accordance with the preceding paragraph involve permits from other relevant governmental departments, the relevant permit documents shall be submitted along with those provided for in the preceding paragraph.

12.41 Where a foreign investor purchases the assets of a domestic enterprise by agreement and invests such assets in establishing a foreign investment enterprise, it shall not, prior to the establishment of the foreign investment enterprise, operate any business with such assets.

12.42 Under Article 24, the asset purchasing agreement shall be governed by the laws of China, and shall include the following contents:

(1) Information of each party to the agreements, including its name and domicile, and the name, position, and nationality, etc, of its legal representative.
(2) The list and price of the assets under planned purchase.
(3) The term and method for performance of the agreements.
(4) The rights and obligations of each party to the agreements.
(5) The liabilities for breach of the agreement and settlement of disputes.
(6) The date and place for conclusion of the agreements.

12.43 The approval authority shall, unless otherwise provided for, decide, in accordance with the law, whether or not to grant the approval within 30 days as of the receipt of all the documents submitted. If the approval authority decides to grant the approval, it shall issue a certificate of approval.[29]

12.44 Article 26 sets out registration requirements. In the case of asset M&A, the foreign investor shall, within 30 days as of the receipt of the approval certificate, apply to the administrative authority of registration for making registration of establishment and obtaining the FIE business licence. In the case of equity M&A, the merged domestic company shall, in accordance with the 2006 Foreign M&A Regulation, apply to the original registration administrative authority for registration of modification and obtaining the foreign investment enterprise's business licence. If the original registration administrative authority has no jurisdiction of registration, it shall, within ten days as of the receipt of the application documents, transfer them to an administrative authority of registration with the jurisdiction for handling the registration, and meanwhile attach the domestic company's registration files.

---

[29] 2006 Foreign M&A Regulation, Art 25.

12.4.4. Pricing and payment

12.4.4.1. Overview

12.45 Under Article 14, the transaction price should be based on the valuation conducted by an asset valuation institution in relation to the equity interest to be transferred or of the assets to be sold. Several points are to be noted here.

12.46 First, the parties to a foreign M&A transaction may agree on an asset valuation institution which is established within the territory of China in accordance with the law. Second, the valuation shall be conducted by adopting internationally recognized valuation methods. Third, it is prohibited to transfer equity interest or sell assets at a price significantly lower than the valuation result for the purpose of transferring capital out of China in a disguised way. Finally, when a foreign investor merges a domestic enterprise, resulting in the change of ownership of state equity rights or transfer of state-owned assets, the valuation shall be made in accordance with the relevant provisions on the administration of state-owned assets.

12.47 Under Article 17, the methods of payment used in foreign M&A transactions can be flexible, as long as they conform to China's relevant laws and administrative regulations. The methods include, but are not limited to, cash and equity rights. Where a foreign investor uses the currency of RMB it lawfully owns as the means of payment, it shall be subject to the approval of the foreign exchange administrative authority. Where a foreign investor uses the equity rights it is entitled to dispose of as the means of payment, it shall be subject to a set of rules contained in Chapter 4 of the 2006 Foreign M&A Regulation, which will now be discussed.

12.4.4.2. Conditions for payment in equity rights

12.48 Under Article 27, the term 'M&A of a domestic company by a foreign investor using equity rights to pay' is used to refer to a situation in which the shareholder of an overseas company using its equity in the overseas company as the payment, or an overseas company using the shares it additionally issues as the payment, purchases existing equity rights or newly issued shares in a domestic company. Essentially, this represents the so-called share–swap transaction: shares in an overseas company are used by foreigners as payment to acquire shares in a Chinese domestic company.

12.49 There are strict requirements on qualification of the overseas company whose shares can be used as payment in foreign M&A transactions. First, it shall be legally established and its registration place shall have a sound company law system. Second, the company and its management shall have not been punished by relevant regulatory authorities in the recent three years. Finally, except in the case of the special purpose companies that we will go on to discuss, the overseas company shall be a listed company, and the listing place shall have a sound legal system for securities transactions.[30]

---

[30] 2006 Foreign M&A Regulation, Art 28.

12.50 Apart from the qualification requirements on the overseas company, further conditions are set out on the equity in the company, including: (1) the equity is lawfully held by the foreigner and can be transferrable according to law; (2) the equity is free from any dispute over ownership, any pledge or any other property encumbrance; (3) the equity shall be listed on an overseas open and lawful securities exchange market (excluding over-the-counter markets); (4) the trading price of the equity has been stable in the latest year.[31]

12.51 Finally, under Article 30, the domestic company or its shareholders in a foreign M&A transaction shall employ a market intermediary institution established and registered in China to act as its consultant ('M&A Consultant'). The M&A Consultant shall satisfy the following qualification requirements: (1) to be with good credit standing and experience in relevant industries; (2) to be without record of serious violation of law or regulation; (3) to be with the ability to investigate and analyse the legal system in the registration and listing place of the overseas company as well as the financial status of the overseas company.[32]

12.52 The M&A Consultant shall conduct a due diligence investigation on the following issues: (1) the authenticity of application documents regarding the foreign M&A transaction; (2) the financial status of the overseas company; and (3) whether the transaction is in compliance with the relevant provisions of the 2006 Foreign M&A Regulation. After the investigation, the M&A Consultant shall issue a report to give clear and professional advice on the aforementioned issues.

12.4.4.3. Approvals for payment in equity rights

12.53 The scrip-based foreign M&A transaction is subject to a heightened level of examination and approval from the MOFCOM.

12.54 Under Article 32, in the case of M&A of a domestic company by a foreign investor using equity rights to pay, the foreign investor shall submit an application to the MOFCOM, and the domestic company shall also submit the following documents in addition to the documents which are required under Chapter 3 of the 2006 Foreign M&A Regulation as discussed earlier: (1) a statement on alteration in equity and material assets of the domestic company in the latest year; (2) the M&A Consultant's report; (3) the certificate of incorporation or the identity certificate of the domestic company, the overseas company involved in the M&A transaction, and the shareholders of these companies; (4) a statement on shareholding status of the shareholders of the overseas company and the name list of shareholders who hold more than 5 per cent of the equity of the overseas company; (5) the articles of association of the overseas company and statement on external guarantee provided

---

[31] 2006 Foreign M&A Regulation, Art 29. The third and fourth conditions as listed above are not applicable to the special purpose companies.
[32] 2006 Foreign M&A Regulation, Art 31.

by the overseas company; (6) the audited financial statements of the overseas company in recent years and a statement on stock transactions in the latest six months.

12.55 The MOFCOM shall make an examination of the application within 30 days as of the receipt of all application documents as required, and if the application can satisfy the conditions, it shall issue a certificate of approval and indicate the following words on the certificate: 'a foreign investor merges a domestic company by equity merger, which is valid within six months as of the issuance of a business license.'[33]

12.56 Within 30 days as of receipt of the certificate discussed above, the domestic company shall go through the procedure on registration of alteration with the competent administrative authority of registration and the foreign exchange administrative authority, and the administrative authority of registration and the foreign exchange administrative authority shall respectively issue the business licence for a foreign investment enterprise and the foreign exchange registration certificate to the domestic company, on which it shall indicate the words 'valid within eight (8) months as of its issuance'. When the domestic company goes through the procedure on registration of alteration with the administrative authority of registration, it shall in advance submit the application for equity alteration, an amendment to the articles of association, and the agreement on equity transfer signed by the legal representative of the domestic company for the purpose of restoration of equity structure.[34]

12.57 Under Article 35, within six months as of the issuance of the business licence, the domestic company or its shareholders shall apply to the MOFCOM and the foreign exchange administrative authority for approval and registration of establishment of foreign investment enterprise with respect to the equity of the overseas company held by the domestic company.

12.58 In addition to the documents to be submitted to the MOFCOM as required in the Provisions on Approval of Investment in and Establishment of Overseas Enterprises, the parties to a foreign M&A transaction shall also submit the approval certificate and the business licence of the foreign investment enterprise with the indication as previously mentioned. After the MOFCOM approves the domestic company or its shareholders to hold the equity in the overseas company, it shall issue the Approval Certificate of Overseas Investment by Chinese Enterprises to the domestic company, and shall also reissue an approval certificate for the foreign investment enterprise without the indication previously described.

12.59 Within 30 days as of receipt of an approval certificate for the foreign investment enterprise where the MOFCOM does not indicate any conditions, the domestic company shall apply to the administrative authority of registration and the

---

[33] 2006 Foreign M&A Regulation, Art 33.
[34] 2006 Foreign M&A Regulation, Art 34.

foreign exchange administrative authority for re-issuance of the business licence for a foreign investment enterprise and the foreign exchange registration certificate without indication.

12.60 Finally, the domestic company and its shareholders should go through the procedure on registration of taxation alteration with the competent taxation authority, with the approval certificate and the business license without indication as issued by the MOFCOM and the registration administrative authority.[35]

12.5. Regulation of Special Purpose Vehicles

12.5.1. Overview

12.61 A Special Purpose Vehicle (SPV) is defined as an overseas entity, directly or indirectly controlled by a domestic Chinese company or a natural person (PRC Founder), and specifically established for the purpose of an overseas listing of the PRC Founder's interests in the domestic enterprise. The PRC Founder can establish an SPV and then use the SPV as an acquiring vehicle to get the domestic Chinese enterprise listed overseas by swapping its shares in the domestic enterprise for shares in the SPV. This process is essentially a reverse takeover, as discussed in Chapter 10.

12.62 Apart from the general requirements for payment in equity rights as discussed earlier, the 2006 Foreign M&A Regulation devotes a whole section to setting out special rules for the SPV.[36] These rules require the establishment of SPVs to follow several complicated approval requirements.

12.63 Basically, the PRC Founder intending to incorporate an SPV must apply to MOFCOM for approval and, after obtaining this approval, must complete registration with the local SAFE authorities for permission to conduct an overseas investment. When an SPV is used as an acquiring vehicle to get a Chinese domestic enterprise listed abroad, the total value of the shares of an SPV listed abroad cannot be lower than the value of the equities of the domestic enterprise concerned as appraised by a Chinese asset appraisal institution. This share–swap arrangement requires approval from MOFCOM and the overseas listing of the SPV is subject to the approval of CSRC.

12.64 Within 30 working days of the SPV listing on an overseas exchange, the Chinese domestic company must report to MOFCOM on the status of the overseas listing (inclusive of a repatriation plan of raised funds) and apply for an FIE approval certificate. After obtaining the approval certificate and completing the repatriation

---

[35] 2006 Foreign M&A Regulation, Art 38.
[36] 2006 Foreign M&A Regulation, Part 3 of Chapter 4.

of all profits and dividends derived from the SPV to China, the domestic company shall apply to SAIC and SAFE for a FIE business licence and a foreign exchange registration certificate. After the SPV is listed overseas and the equity transaction is consummated, its shares can be used as the payment method to acquire further domestic companies.

12.5.2. VIE structure

To date, very few Chinese companies, if any at all, have gone through the above complex approval process to establish SPVs for the purposes of getting listed overseas. As an alternative, the Variable Interest Entity (VIE) structure has been used. **12.65**

The VIE structure was used before 2006 when the MOFCOM imposed stringent approval requirements on the SPV for the first time. Indeed, the VIE structure was originally designed to circumvent the restrictions the Chinese government put on foreign direct investment in specific economic sectors like education, finance, media, and telecommunications. Under the VIE structure, foreign investors typically form a WFOE in China, which in turn enters into a series of contracts with a domestic company having the required licences to operate in the restricted/prohibited economic sectors. There are various contractual instruments, including call options, equity pledges, and service or consulting agreements. The common effect of those different forms of contractual instruments is that the VIE is obliged to submit to the control of the WFOE and to transfer all profits to the WFOE. In short, VIE allows foreign forms to contractually control—albeit not legally own Chinese companies in restricted sectors. **12.66**

If the foreign firm is actually established by the Chinese controller of the domestic company, then the VIE structure essentially becomes a vehicle to achieve the purpose of getting the domestic company listed overseas. The famous Chinese internet portal, Sina, first employed this VIE structure to get listed in the US, and thus this listing model is also called the 'Sina Model'. This model has been followed by other Chinese companies operating in restricted sectors, such as Alibaba, Baidu, and New Oriental Education. **12.67**

After 2006, the SPV route was effectively blocked due to the close-to-zero rate of success in gaining approval from the MOFCOM. The VIE structure has since been resorted to by Chinese businesses that operate in non-restricted sectors. As the VIE structure uses contractual instruments, rather than legal ownership, to effect the transfer of economic interests from Chinese domestic businesses to overseas firms, the relevant approval requirement does not apply. This has attracted more attention to the legal status and risk of the VIE structure. **12.68**

The VIE structure is essentially an effort to avoid the relevant law in China, and its legitimacy has never been clear. Thus far the Chinese government has maintained what I would call 'strategic ambiguity' on this issue to allow flexibility in striking a **12.69** balance between competing needs: on the one hand, it needs to keep a tight grip on foreign investment and thus cannot expressly legitimize the VIE structure; on the other, if the VIE structure were to be expressly clamped down on, it would not be able to meet Chinese businesses' need to get listed overseas. Taking into account the above factors, it is unlikely that the situation will change drastically in the near future.

12.6. National Security Review

12.6.1. Overview

12.70 The national security review has been in force since 2006, for at least two main reasons. First, there is mounting concern that foreign interests are accumulating capacity and market share in China, without commensurate oversight by the Chinese government. Second, this problem was further realized when Chinese companies went overseas to conduct takeovers and found that many countries, including the US, had actually put in place relevant measures to resist foreign M&A in the name of economic patriotism and security. It has been suspected that the adoption of national economic security was prompted by the failure of Chinese oil giant China National Offshore Oil Corporation (CNOOC) to bid for the California-based company Unocal in 2005.[37] In other words, China might have learnt to tighten its grip on foreign M&A simply by following internationally accepted practice.

12.71 According to Article 12 of the 2006 Foreign M&A Regulation, the parties to an M&A transaction must report to and seek approval from MOFCOM if the foreign investor intends to gain control of a domestic company in a 'key industry', or the transaction involves transfer of a domestic enterprise's actual control over a 'famous trade mark', or 'time-honoured brand', or factors that may have a potential or actual impact on China's national economic security. If the parties fail to do so, MOFCOM and other relevant government agencies may demand that the parties terminate the transaction or implement measures to eliminate the adverse impact on national economic security caused by the takeover.[38] This provision seems to authorize a security review of economic or cultural issues, and therefore has been categorized as either 'economic security' or 'cultural security'.[39]

12.72 The above provision is more like a policy statement than a legal requirement, as it is framed in very general terms and lacks workability. Subsequent regulations issued by the Chinese government give further substance to the review regime.

---

[37] The CNOOC actually withdrew after the US Congress passed a joint resolution demanding that the US President block the deal. The US national security review regime will be discussed later in the chapter.

[38] 2006 Foreign M&A Regulation, Art 12.

[39] Hui Huang, 'The Regulation of Foreign Investment in Post-WTO China: A Political Economy Analysis' (2009) 23(1) *Columbia Journal of Asia Law* 185.

In 2010, the State Council made clear its intention to establish a workable national security review regime;[40] subsequently, in February 2011, it issued the Notice of the General Office of the State Council on the Establishment of the Security Review System for Mergers and Acquisitions of Domestic Enterprises by Foreign Investors (State Council Notice on Security Review of Foreign M&A).[41] The State Council Notice was further implemented by the MOFCOM's interim provisions in March 2011, and finalized in August of the same year (MOFCOM Implementing Provisions on Security Review of Foreign M&A).[42] These two documents significantly improve the workability of China's legal regime for the national security review. Below is a discussion of the central features of this regime.

12.73

12.6.2. Central features

12.6.2.1. Scope of the security review

Under Article 1(1) of the State Council Notice on Security Review of Foreign M&A, the security review of foreign M&A covers two main areas: (1) foreign investors' M&As of domestic military industrial enterprises and supportive military industrial enterprises, enterprises surrounding major and sensitive military facilities, and other entities relating to national defence security; (2) foreign investors' M&As of domestic enterprises relating to important agricultural products, important energies and resources, important infrastructural facilities, important transportation services, key technologies, manufacturing of major equipment, etc., which relate to national security, and whose actual controlling power may be obtained by foreign investors.

12.74

Further guidance is provided on two important terms used in the above provision. The first term is 'merger or acquisition of a domestic enterprise by a foreign investor', which is defined as referring to any of the following circumstances: (1) a foreign investor purchases the equity shares of a domestic non-foreign-funded enterprise or subscribes to the increased capital of a domestic non-foreign-funded enterprise, and thus changes such domestic enterprise into a foreign-funded enterprise; (2) a foreign investor purchases the equity shares from the Chinese shareholders of a domestic foreign-funded enterprise or subscribes to the increased capital of a domestic foreign-funded enterprise; (3) a foreign investor establishes

12.75

---

[40] Guowuyuan guanyu Guli he Yindao Minjian Touzi Jiankang Fazhan de Ruogan Yijian [Several Opinions of the State Council on Encouraging and Guiding the Healthy Development of Private Investment] (issued by the State Council, 12 May 2010).

[41] Guowuyuan Bangongting guanyu Jianli Waiguo Touzizhe Bingou Jingnei Qiye Anquan Shencha Zhidu de Tongzhi [Notice of the General Office of the State Council on the Establishment of the Security Review System for Mergers and Acquisitions of Domestic Enterprises by Foreign Investors] (issued by the State Council on 3 February 2011, effective 3 March 2011).

[42] Shangwubu Shishi Waiguo Touzizhe Binggou Jingnei Qiye Anquan Shencha Zhidu de Guiding [Provisions of the Ministry of Commerce on the Implementation of the Security Review System for Mergers and Acquisitions of Domestic Enterprises by Foreign Investors] (issued by the Ministry of Commerce on 25 August 2011, effective 1 September 2011).

a foreign-funded enterprise through which it purchases by agreement the assets of a domestic enterprise and operates such assets, or through which it purchases the equity shares of a domestic enterprise; or (4) a foreign investor directly purchases the assets of a domestic enterprise, and then invests such assets to establish a foreign-funded enterprise to operate such assets.[43]

12.76 The second important term is 'obtainment of actual controlling power by a foreign investor', which is defined as meaning that a foreign investor becomes the controlling shareholder or actual controller of a domestic enterprise through merger or acquisition under any of the following circumstances: (1) the total shares held by a foreign investor and its parent holding company and controlled subsidiary companies after merger or acquisition account for not less than 50 per cent; (2) the total shares held by multiple foreign investors after merger or acquisition account for not less than 50 per cent in total; (3) The total shares held by a foreign investor after merger or acquisition account for less than 50 per cent, but the voting power it holds according to the stocks it holds is enough to have a material impact on the resolution of the shareholders' meeting, the general assembly of shareholders, or the board of directors; or (4) any other circumstance which leads to the transfer of the actual controlling power of a domestic enterprise on business decisions, financial affairs, personnel, technologies, etc. to a foreign investor.[44]

12.77 Further, the MOFCOM stipulates that whether a merger or acquisition of a domestic enterprise by a foreign investor falls within the scope of M&A security review shall be determined from the substance and actual impact of the transaction. No foreign investor shall substantially evade the M&A security review in any form, including but not limited to holding shares on behalf of others, trust, multilevel reinvestment, leasing, loans, agreement-based control, and overseas transactions.[45]

12.78 Hence, the scope of security review is broad and can be divided into two categories, namely defence-related industries and other important industries such as agricultural products, natural resources, energy, and critical infrastructure. The threshold for security review varies with categories. For the second category, review is required only when the foreign investor acquires actual control of the Chinese enterprise; this 'actual control' requirement does not, however, apply to transactions falling into the first category—that is, transactions affecting the defence sector will be reviewed regardless of whether the foreign investor acquires actual control.

12.6.2.2. Content of the Security Review

12.79 Article 2 of the State Council Notice on Security Review of Foreign M&A sets out some details on the content of the review:

---

[43] State Council Notice on Security Review of Foreign M&A, Art 1(2).
[44] State Council Notice on Security Review of Foreign M&A, Art 1(3).
[45] MOFCOM Implementing Provisions on Security Review of Foreign M&A, Art 9.

(1) The influence of M&A transactions on national defence security, including the ability to produce domestic products and provide domestic services required for national defence and the relevant equipment and facilities.
(2) The influence of M&A transactions on the stable operation of the national economy.
(3) The influence of M&A transactions on the order of basic social life.
(4) The influence of M&A transactions on the capacity of research and development of key technologies involving national security.

This provision, coupled with the provisions on the scope of review as previously discussed, suggests that the security review is given a broad mandate. Under the State Council Notice on Security Review of Foreign M&A, the review regime is simply referred to as 'security review' (*Anquan Shencha*), leaving some ambiguity with regard to the nature of this review: what is meant by 'security'? is it just national security? Indeed, when issuing the State Council Notice on Security Review of Foreign M&A, the State Council stated that the review regime was set up 'to guide the orderly development of mergers and acquisitions of domestic enterprises by foreign investors and safeguard *national security*'.[46] Within the common western definition, the term 'national security' is usually limited to national defence issues. Clearly, the concept of 'national security' in China has a much broader meaning, which may have different aspects, such as 'national defence security', 'national economic security', and even 'national cultural security'. **12.80**

12.6.2.3. Work mechanism of the security review

Under Article 3 of the State Council Notice on Security Review of Foreign M&A, a system of joint ministerial meeting for the security review of M&A of domestic enterprises by foreign investors (hereinafter referred to as 'joint meeting') shall be established to assume the specific work of security review of mergers and acquisitions. Members of the joint meeting shall, as led by the State Council and organized by the National Development and Reform Commission and the Ministry of Commerce, and jointly with other relevant departments, carry out the security review of M&A in the industries and fields involved in M&A by foreign investors. **12.81**

The primary responsibilities of the members of the joint meeting include: analysing the influence of mergers and acquisitions of domestic enterprises by foreign investors on national security; studying and co-ordinating the major issues on the security review of mergers and acquisitions of domestic enterprises by foreign investors; and if security review is necessary, conducting a security review of the transactions for the mergers and acquisitions of domestic enterprises by foreign investors and making decisions. **12.82**

---

[46] State Council Notice on Security Review of Foreign M&A, notice (emphasis added).

12.6.2.4. Procedure of the security review

(1) Initiation of the review

12.83 The security review can be instituted in three ways. First, the foreign investor involved in a foreign M&A transaction shall file an application with the Ministry of Commerce according to the State Council Notice on Security Review of Foreign M&A. If the transaction falls within the scope of the security review, the Ministry of Commerce shall request members of the joint meeting to review such transaction within five workdays.[47] Where a merger or acquisition involves two or more joint foreign investors, they may jointly apply or designate one foreign investor to apply for merger and acquisition security review to the Ministry of Commerce.[48]

12.84 Second, where the relevant department of the State Council, a national industrial association, an enterprise of the same profession, or an upstream or downstream enterprise deems it necessary to conduct a security review of the merger or acquisition of a domestic enterprise by a foreign investor, it may put forward suggestions on the security review of the merger or acquisition via the Ministry of Commerce. Third, members of the joint meeting may take the initiative to decide to conduct a security review if they do deem it necessary.

12.85 An applicant shall, when filing a formal application for merger and acquisition security review with the Ministry of Commerce, submit the following documents:

(1) A written application for merger and acquisition security review and a description of the transaction signed by the legal representative or the authorized representative of the applicant.
(2) A foreign investor's identity certificate or certificate of registration and credit certification documents, which are notarized or authenticated in accordance with law; the legal representative's identity certificate or the power of attorney issued by the foreign investor to the authorized representative and the authorized representative's identity certificate.
(3) A description of a foreign investor and its affiliated enterprises (including its actual controller and persons acting in concert), and its relationship with the government of the relevant country.
(4) A description of the domestic enterprise to be merged or acquired, the bylaws, business licence (photocopy), and audited financial statements of its previous fiscal year, the organizational charts before and after its merger or acquisition, and a description and the business licences (photocopy) of the enterprises in which it has invested.
(5) The contract on and bylaws of or partnership agreement on the foreign-funded enterprise to be established after merger or acquisition and a list of the

---

[47] State Council Notice on Security Review of Foreign M&A, Art 4(1).
[48] MOFCOM Implementing Provisions on Security Review of Foreign M&A, Art 1.

members of the board of directors to be appointed by the shareholders and the general manager to be employed or partners and other senior managerial personnel.

(6) In the case of any equity-based merger or acquisition transaction, the equity transfer agreement or the agreement on the foreign investor's subscription to additional capital of the domestic enterprise, the shareholders' resolutions of the merged or acquired domestic enterprise, resolutions of the shareholders' meeting, and relevant asset evaluation reports.

(7) In the case of any asset-based merger or acquisition transaction, a resolution on the consent of the domestic enterprise's governing authority or holder of title to assets to the sale of the assets, an asset sales agreement (including a list of the assets to be purchased and their condition), information on all parties to the agreement, and relevant asset evaluation reports.

(8) An explanation of the impact of the voting rights to be enjoyed by a foreign investor after merger or acquisition on the execution of the resolutions of shareholders' meeting or shareholders' assembly or board of directors and the partnership affairs, an explanation of other circumstances resulting in the transfer of the actual controlling powers in such aspects of the domestic enterprise as operational decision-making, finance, personnel, and technology to the foreign investor or its domestic or overseas affiliated enterprise, and agreements or documents related to the aforesaid circumstances.

(9) Other documents required by the Ministry of Commerce.[49]

12.86 Where the application documents for M&A security review submitted by an applicant are complete and comply with statutory requirements, the Ministry of Commerce shall notify the applicant in writing of its acceptance of the application. Where the transaction falls within the scope of M&A security review, the Ministry of Commerce shall notify the applicant in writing within 15 working days, and within five working days thereafter shall submit it to the joint ministerial meeting for review. The applicant shall not execute the merger or acquisition transaction within 15 working days from the date of written notification of acceptance of application, and the local department of commerce shall not examine and approve the merger or acquisition transaction. If the Ministry of Commerce does not notify the applicant in writing within 15 working days, the applicant may proceed to handle the relevant formalities in accordance with relevant state laws and regulations.[50]

12.87 It should be noted that to improve the efficacy of the review regime, the MOFCOM encourages parties to engage in pre-application consultation with it. Specifically, an applicant may, before filing a formal application for M&A security review with

---

[49] MOFCOM Implementing Provisions on Security Review of Foreign M&A, Art 5.
[50] MOFCOM Implementing Provisions on Security Review of Foreign M&A, Art 6.

the Ministry of Commerce, submit a consultation application to the Ministry of Commerce regarding the procedural issues related to its merger or acquisition of a domestic enterprise to discuss the relevant situations in advance. Such advance consultation is not a necessary procedure for filing a formal application, and the consultation results do not have any binding force or legal effect and do not serve as a basis for filing a formal application.[51]

(2) **Conduct of the review**

12.88 The review is a two-stage process, including a general review and a special review. The joint meeting shall first conduct a general security review of the merger or acquisition transaction, and then conduct a special review if the transaction fails to pass the general review. The parties to the merger or acquisition transaction shall co-operate in the security review work of the joint meeting, provide materials and information required for the security review, and accept the relevant inquiries.[52]

12.89 The general review shall be conducted in the form of soliciting opinions in writing. Members of the joint meeting shall, after receiving the application of the Ministry of Commerce for the security review of a merger or acquisition, solicit in writing the opinions of the relevant departments within five working days. The relevant departments shall put forward written opinions within 20 working days after receiving the letter soliciting their opinions. If the relevant departments concurrently hold that the merger or acquisition transaction will not affect the national security, a special review is not required, and members of the joint meeting shall put forward review opinions within five working days after receiving all written opinions, and notify the Ministry of Commerce in writing of their own opinions.

12.90 If any department holds that the merger or acquisition transaction may affect national security, members of the joint meeting shall start the special review procedure within five working days after receiving such opinions. Members of the joint meeting shall, after starting the special review procedure, organize a security appraisal of the merger or acquisition, review it by taking into consideration the appraisal opinions, and put forward comments if a consensus has been basically reached; or request the State Council to make a decision if there is any major dissent. Members of the joint meeting shall complete the special review within 60 working days from the date of starting the special review procedure, or request the State Council to make a decision. Members of the joint meeting shall notify the Ministry of Commerce in writing of their own review opinions.

(3) **Outcome of the review**

12.91 The Ministry of Commerce shall notify the applicant in writing of the opinions on the security review of merger or acquisition. The applicant may, during the security

---

[51] MOFCOM Implementing Provisions on Security Review of Foreign M&A, Art 4.
[52] State Council Notice on Security Review of Foreign M&A, Art 4(3).

review of merger or acquisition, apply to the Ministry of Commerce to amend the transaction plan or cancel the merger or acquisition.

Where the merger or acquisition of a domestic enterprise by a foreign investor has produced or may produce a material impact on national security, members of the joint meeting shall require the Ministry of Commerce to terminate the transaction between the parties concerned jointly with the relevant departments, or transfer the relevant equities or assets, or take other effective measures to eliminate the effect of such merger or acquisition on national security. **12.92**

12.6.3. Comments

With the promulgation of the State Council Notice on Security Review of Foreign M&A and the MOFCOM Implementing Provisions on Security Review of Foreign M&A, China has now established a relatively complete regime for conducting security review in relation to foreign M&A transactions, setting out rules on important issues such as the review scope, the review content, the work mechanism and the procedure. It should be noted that the security review of M&A of domestic financial institutions by foreign investors is not governed by the regime above, and is subject to provisions which are made separately.[53] Another point to note is that the regime applies to M&A by investors from Hong Kong Special Administrative Region, Macao Special Administrative Region and Taiwan region.[54] **12.93**

Despite the improvement, the regime is still vague in many respects. Terms such as 'key industries', 'well-known brand', and 'national economic security' are not defined. Also, under Article 2 of the State Council Notice on Security Review of Foreign M&A, it is unclear what is meant by terms such as 'stable operation of the national economy', 'order of basic social life', and 'key technologies involving national security'. **12.94**

In practice, China's security review of foreign M&A transactions has not yet been exercised to date. This is mainly because the review can easily become politicized and thus may harm diplomatic relations between trading nations. Despite the lack of enforcement, the mere existence of the review regime is of significance, in that it may deter egregious cases in the first instance, and can allow the Chinese government to act in cases of real necessity. At the same time, China needs to continue to improve its security review regime, so as to reassure foreign investors that China is not shutting the door to foreign M&A transactions but is simply ensuring that they are conducted in a mutually beneficial way. **12.95**

In fact, the security review for foreign M&A transactions is not unique to China, but is actually an international practice. As noted earlier, China's national security review regime is actually a legal transplant of overseas experiences, notably the US. **12.96**

---

[53] State Council Notice on Security Review of Foreign M&A, Art 5(4).
[54] State Council Notice on Security Review of Foreign M&A, Art 5(5).

12.97 In the US, the national security review of foreign investment is conducted by the Committee on Foreign Investment in the United States (CFIUS). The Exon-Florio amendment of 1988 to the Defense Production Act of 1950 authorizes the US President to block 'mergers, acquisitions, or takeovers' involving foreign entities if they are deemed to threaten national security.[55] The CFIUS provides advice to the President on the national security review of foreign investment. As an organization, the CFIUS is constructed as an interagency committee chaired by the Treasury Department and consisting of members drawn from relevant department and agencies such as the Departments of State, Defense, Justice, Energy, and Homeland Security, and the US Trade Representative. Traditionally, the US concept of 'national security' was focused on defence issues, but it was significantly expanded by the Foreign Investment and National Security Act of 2007 to cover non-defence-related areas such as critical infrastructure and energy concerns.[56] In sum, the US definition of 'national security' is also very broad now.

12.98 In Australia, foreign investment is regulated by the Foreign Acquisitions and Takeovers Act 1975 (FATA) and by the Australian government's Foreign Investment Policy (Policy). The FATA allows the Treasurer or his delegate to review investment proposals to decide if they are contrary to Australia's national interest. The Treasurer is assisted by the Foreign Investment Review Board (FIRB), a body composed of four part-time members (who are not public servants) and a full-time executive member. Hence, Australia's national security review is based on a 'national interest' test, and the Treasurer has flexibility in applying the test and ultimately deciding whether to prohibit or impose conditions on particular investments.

12.99 The Australian 'national interest' approach is similar to the Chinese definition of national security, in that they both extend the traditional idea of national security of defence to encompass national economic issues.[57] But the 'control' threshold of the Australian approach seems to be more stringent than that of China (more than 50 per cent of the equity, shares, or voting rights in an enterprise). The Australian 'national interest' review will be triggered if a foreign investor proposes to acquire 15 per cent or more in an Australian entity which is above a certain size and in sensitive or specially regulated sectors; if the proposed acquisition is by a foreign government or related entity, it should be subject to the review regardless of whether the acquisition is above 15 per cent or not. In 2010, the Australian government further expanded the concept of control to include circumstances in which a person

---

[55] 50 U.S.C. App §2170.
[56] Kevin B Goldstein, 'Reviewing Cross-Border Mergers and Acquisitions For Competition and National Security: A Comparative Look at How the United States, Europe and China Separate Security Concerns From Competition Concerns in Reviewing Acquisitions by Foreign Entities' (2010–2011) 3 *Tsinghua China Law Review* 215, 224–7.
[57] Vivienne Bath, 'Foreign Investment, the National Interest and National Security—Foreign Direct Investment in Australia and China' (2012) 34 *Sydney Law Review* 5, 23.

and its associates are able to determine the policy of the company in relation to any matter. This change is potentially broad enough to capture interests including structures using converting instruments, economic-only interests, and derivatives or swap positions in Australian entities or offshore entities with Australian assets.[58]

12.7. Summary

Drawing upon international experiences, China has established a relatively complete legal framework for foreign M&A transactions. At a policy level, it aims to facilitate foreign M&A transactions while protecting China's national economic security. On the one hand, it provides some much needed clarity on the rules to be followed in carrying out M&A transactions, which will reduce transaction costs in foreign M&A activity; on the other, it introduces more stringent approval requirements in response to the underlying concern that foreign interests are accumulating capacity and market share in China without commensurate oversight by the Chinese government. The law is certainly not intended to discourage foreign investments across the board, but rather to promote those that are conducive to the Chinese economic development. 12.100

Some uncertainties remain as to the implementation of relevant government approval requirements, particularly the national economic security review, even though the Chinese government has recently made great efforts to provide more guidance. This problem is not unique to China, however. The nature of the national economic security review dictates the consideration of legal and non-legal factors. How China implements the national economic security review will thus depend on the way in which similar review requirements are conducted overseas, particularly in relation to transactions implicating Chinese businesses. 12.101

---

[58] Greg Golding, 'Australian Regulation of Foreign Direct Investment by Sovereign Wealth Funds and State-owned Enterprises: Are Our Rules Right?' (2010) 38 *Australian Business Law Review* 215, 225.

INDEX

administrative liability *see under* liability
agency costs 10.54, 11.20
    takeovers, and 10.49
Agricultural Bank of China (ABC) 1.09, 1.17
    listed 1.18
Agricultural Development Bank of China 1.10, 1.19
Asset Management Association of China 9.117
attorneys' fees 6.70–6.75
    contingency fees/risk agency fees 6.72–6.74
        exclusions from 6.74–6.75
Australia
    Australian Prudential Regulatory Authority (APRA) 2.64
    Australian Securities and Investment Commission (ASIC) 2.23
        role 2.64
    disclosure
        continuous disclosure 5.16, 5.17
        disclosure-based regulation 3.11
    foreign investment, regulating 12.97–12.98
        control 12.99
        national interest 12.99
    insider trading
        front-running 8.41
    market manipulation 7.50
        intent 7.59, 7.63
    qualified investors for fund shares 9.89
    regulatory staffing level 2.51
    relevant interests in securities 10.92
    Reserve Bank of Australia 2.65
    takeovers
        associates 10.64, 10.65
        blocking takeovers 11.78
        compulsory buyouts 10.90
        conditions in takeover bids 10.125
        disclosure of substantial shareholdings 10.99
        mandatory bid rule 10.68, 10.71
        mandatory bid rule, exemptions from 10.76
        proportional/partial bids 10.130–10.131
        shareholder protection/Eggleston principle 10.57
    'twin peaks' model of regulation 2.64–2.65

backdoor listing *see under* takeovers of listed companies
Bank of China (BOC) 1.09, 1.17
    listed 1.18
banking 1.08–1.10, 1.16–1.24

bad loans 1.69, 2.58
banking/non-banking financial institutions 1.20
    central bank *see* Peoples' Bank of China (PBC)
    Chinese banks 1.16–1.22
    dominant position of banking system 1.46
    foreign banks 1.23–1.24
        national treatment 1.24
        relatively small size 1.48
        types of 1.23
    interest rates 2.10
    joint-stock commercial banks 1.20, 2.13
        relatively small size 1.48
    lending business 2.10
    modernization and innovation 2.56
    non-performing loans *see* non-performing loans
    private enterprises accessing banking loans, difficulty of 1.49
    regulation 2.12–2.18
        CBRC *see* China Banking Regulatory Commission (CBRC)
        lack of regulatory independence 2.41–2.43
        non-performing loans 2.15–2.18
    state-owned commercial banks 1.16–1.18
        mainstay of banking system, as 1.48
        presidents of state-owned banks, strong position of 2.42, 2.43
    state-owned financial institutions favouring SOEs 1.49
    state-owned policy banks 1.19, 2.13
bond markets *see under* stock exchanges

characteristics of China's financial markets 1.45–1.61
    gaming nature of the markets 1.58–1.61
    inefficiency in financial system 1.49
    policy market *see* policy market
    share ownership patterns in listed companies *see under* listed companies
    state ownership of financial institutions 1.48–1.49
    unbalanced market structure 1.45–1.47
China Banking Regulatory Commission (CBRC) 1.13, 2.12–2.14
    foreign banks 1.24
    housing market *see* housing market/mortgages
    lack of regulatory independence 2.41–2.43
    market conduct and prudential regulation 2.14
    non-performing loans *see* non-performing loans
    objectives as banking regulator 2.13

China Banking Regulatory Commission
    (CBRC) (*Cont.*)
  regulatory strategy 2.17
  role 2.03
  SIFs, regulating 9.06
    fund custodians 9.40
  supervisory powers/banking 'watchdog' 2.08,
    2.12
China Development Bank 1.10, 1.19
China Insurance Regulatory Commission
    (CIRC) 1.13
  lack of regulatory independence 2.41
  principal duties and responsibilities 2.19–2.21
  role 2.03, 2.19
  SIFs, regulating 9.06
China Securities Regulatory Commission
    (CSRC) 1.13, 2.22–2.28, 2.29
  administrative review, subject to 2.27–2.28
  approval regime 3.31–3.47, 4.04
    comments 3.46–3.47
    IEC *see* Issuance Examination Committee
    overview 3.31–3.33
  corporate governance for listed companies 11.16
  delisting 5.82
  encouraging growth of institutional
    investors 1.52
  inside information 8.21
    modified use test, adoption of 8.31–8.32
  insider trading 8.09, 8.13
    enforcement 8.49, 8.54, 8.66–8.67
    front-running 8.40–8.42
  IPOs, CSRC regulation of *see* initial public
    offerings, CSRC regulation of
  lack of regulatory independence 2.41
  markets operated by the stock exchanges 1.26
  powers 2.24–2.26
  principal function and regulatory duties 2.23
  resource constraints 2.48–2.52
    regulatory staffing level 2.51
  revolving door phenomenon/regulatory
    capture 2.52–2.54
  role and responsibilities 2.03, 2.22
  sanctions 2.26
  shareholding structure reform 1.33
  SIFs, regulating 9.06, 9.16
    fund custodians 9.40, 9.43, 9.46
    fund management companies 9.18–9.19, 9.22,
      9.23, 9.31
    fund services institutions 9.99, 9.105, 9.111
    investment rules 9.71–9.72
    non-publicly offered funds 9.88, 9.97
    public offering of funds 9.57–9.58, 9.60,
      9.62–9.64
    sanctions 9.34–9.35
    termination of manager role 9.37–9.38
  sponsorship supervisory measures *see under*
    sponsorship
  stock exchanges, supervising/monitoring 2.31

  substantial asset transactions,
    approving 5.52–5.55
  takeovers of listed companies 10.42, 11.04
    continuous supervision 10.104–10.113
    CSRC checks 10.112
    disclosure of substantial shareholdings 10.95
    disputes dealt with by CSRC 11.53
    financial consultants' role 10.103–10.111
    lax enforcement by CSRC 11.49–11.50, 11.53
    M&A and Restructuring Examination
      Committee 10.42, 11.04
    mandatory bid rule, exemption from
      10.73–10.76, 10.117–10.119
    rules on takeovers, making 11.06
    shares lock-up period 10.113
    variation of terms of offers 10.88, 10.123
civil liability *see under* liability
civil litigation
  attorney fees 6.70–6.75
  compensation *see* compensation/damages
  court fees 6.77
  forms of litigation 6.59–6.77
    Chinese law from a comparative perspective
      6.59–6, 6.63
    class actions 6.59–6.60, 6.63, 6.75
    criticisms and responses 6.64–6.79
    individual actions 6.59–6.60, 6.62
    joint actions 6.60–6.63
  inefficient use of limited judicial resources 6.65
  jurisdiction of the court 6.54–6.58
    courts unsympathetic to securities civil
      suits 6.57
    geographical jurisdiction 6.54–6.55
    hierarchical jurisdiction 6.54
    local protectionism 6.58
  limitation 6.50–6.53
    counting the limitation period 6.51–6.52
  procedural rules of 6.39–6.73
  prerequisite procedure 6.39–6.49
    benefits of 6.47–6.48
    criticisms of 6.46, 6.49
    prior criminal judgment or administrative
      sanction required 6.39
    procedural and evidential effects 6.40–6.41
  substantive rules for misrepresentation actions *see
    under* misrepresentation, liability for
  Supreme Peoples' Court circulars on hearing
    securities fraud civil cases 8.70–8.71
  test suits 6.66–6.67
civil servants
  private sector employment 2.54
companies
  joint-stock companies 4.06, 10.04
  limited liability companies 4.06
  listed companies *see* listed companies
compensation/damages 6.34–6.38
  actual loss 6.34
  benchmark day 6.35

Index

calculation of 6.34–6.38
expert witnesses, use of 6.38
insider trading 8.47
measure of damages 6.36–6.37
compulsory buyouts *see under* takeovers of listed companies
continuous disclosure *see under* disclosure
Construction Bank of China (CBOC) 1.09, 1.17
listed 1.18
corporate governance of listed companies 5.19–5.73
CSRC rules 11.16
delisting *see* delisting
independent directors *see under* directors of listed companies
institutional investors, weak role of 11.71
lack of management supervision 10.54
listing suspension *see* suspension of listing
overview 5.19–5.21
problem of corporate governance in China 10.54–10.55
related party transactions *see* related party transactions
shareholder meeting as final decision-maker on major issues 11.13
substantial asset transactions *see* substantial asset transactions
takeovers, and 10.49–10.52
court fees 6.77
courts, jurisdiction of 6.54–6.58
courts unsympathetic to securities civil suits 6.57
geographical jurisdiction 6.54–6.55
hierarchical jurisdiction 6.54
local protectionism 6.58
criminal liability *see under* liabilities
currency
exchange rate 2.09
foreign investors 10.34
incomplete convertibility 10.25
issuing and controlling 2.07
policy 1.67
restricted foreign currency policy 10.25
role of PBC
currency-issuing role 2.07
currency-stabilizing role 2.08

delisting 5.03
criteria 5.75
information disclosure 5.76
special treatment measures 5.77–5.79
under-enforcement of delisting regime 5.80–5.82
directors of listed companies
boards of directors 5.36
accountability to shareholders 11.13, 11.70
related party transactions, approving 5.69–5.70
substantial asset transactions, approving 5.47–5.51
conflicts of interest 5.69

directors' duties concept underdeveloped 11.76
independent directors 5.02, 5.22–5.37
comments 5.35–5.37
definition of 5.23
duties of good faith and diligence 5.24
general requirements 5.23–5.26
independence requirement 5.27–5.28
powers and responsibilities 5.32–5.34
qualifications 5.27–5.28
selection process 5.29–5.30
substantial asset transactions, approving 5.49
tenure 5.31
training 5.25
'related directors', definition of 5.69–5.70
shareholders electing and changing directors/supervisors 11.13
supervisory boards 5.36
takeovers 11.08–11.09
defences, and *see under* takeover defences
see also takeovers of listed companies
disclosure/disclosure of information
affirmative duties in information disclosure regime 7.03
continuous disclosure 5.14–5.18
meaning of 5.01
costs of 10.59
disclosure-based vs merits-review regulation 3.01–3.13
fabricating or disseminating false information 7.02–7.04
see also market misconduct
insider information *see under* insider trading
IPO information disclosure requirements *see under* initial public offerings (IPOs)
listed companies, information disclosure by *see under* listed companies
listing suspension and delisting, information disclosure requirements for 5.76
major events *see* major events
market efficiency, and 3.14–3.22
disclosure-based regulation 3.02, 3.11
ECMH *see* Efficient Capital Market Hypothesis
forms of disclosure 3.20–3.22
mandatory disclosure 3.17–3.19
misrepresentation *see* misrepresentation, liability for
periodic disclosure 5.01
related party transactions, information disclosure in 5.73
reports *see* reports
securities offerings requirements *see under* securities offerings by listed companies
SIFs
conflicts of interest in 9.27–9.29
information disclosure rules 9.76–9.78
substantial asset transactions, information management in 5.56–5.59

disclosure/disclosure of information (*Cont.*)
  takeovers
    disclosure of substantial
      shareholdings 10.95–10.100
    financial consultants 10.106–10.108
    tender offers, information disclosure 10.86

Efficient Capital Market Hypothesis 3.14–3.22
  forms of 3.15–3.16
exchange rate 2.09
Export-import Bank of China 1.11, 1.19

fees *see* attorneys' fees; court fees
financial consultants *see under* takeover of listed companies
financial crisis *see* global financial crisis
financial institutions, state ownership of 1.48–1.49
  favouring SOEs 1.49
financial markets 1.01–1.73
  characteristics of *see* characteristics of China's financial markets
  China and global financial markets *see* global financial markets, China and
  evolution 1.07–1.14
    before 1978: no financial regulation in true sense 1.07–1.08
    1978–1992: centralized and single regulator 1.09–1.12
    1992–present: multiple sector-based regulators 1.13–1.14, 2.03
  meaning of 1.01–1.02
  opening up 1.67
  overview 1.15–1.44
    banking *see* banking
    insurance market *see* insurance market
    securities market *see* securities market
  regulation *see* financial regulatory framework
  regulator *see* China Securities Regulatory Commission (CSRC)
  submarkets 1.03
  underdeveloped nature of 1.66–1.67
financial modernization and innovation 2.55–2.59
financial products 1.01
financial regulatory framework 2.01–2.86
  characteristics and problems 2.39–2.59
    challenges of financial modernization and innovation 2.55–2.59
    lack of regulatory independence 2.39–2.47
    resource constraints and regulatory capture 2.48–2.54
  current financial regulatory structure 2.03–2.38
    banking regulation 2.12–2.18
    central banking 2.06–2.11
    insurance regulation 2.19–2.21
    sector-based 1.13–1.14, 2.03–2.05, 2.55, 2.73, 7.10
    securities regulation 2.22–2.38

  future of 2.60–2.84
    major structural models *see* major structural models of financial regulation
    short and long term suggestions for China 2.72–2.84
  'one bank, three commissions' 1.14
  separate operation, separate regulation policy 1.14
foreign direct investment 12.01
foreign M&A, regulation of 12.01–12.101
  2006 foreign M&A regulation: basic rules 12.26–12.60
    approval and registration 12.35–12.44
    equity M&A vs asset M&A 12.26–12.29
    pricing and payment 12.45–12.60
    restrictions on round-tripping investments 12.30–12.34
  2006 foreign M&A regulation: overview 12.14–12.18
    approval authority 12.19–12.21
    interaction with other laws and regulations 12.22–12.25
    scope of the coverage 12.14–12.18
  asset M&A 12.14–12.15, 12.26–12.29
  equity M&A 12.14, 12.26–12.29
  growth of 12.02–12.04
  increased control on 12.05
  legal framework for foreign M&A in China 12.07–12.13
    acquisition of A-shares 12.12–12.13
    acquisition of non-A-shares 12.10–12.11
    foreign M&A of Chinese listed companies 12.09–12.13
    overview 12.07–12.08
  M&A Consultants 12.51–12.52, 12.54
  national security review *see* national security review
  policy on 12.06
  pricing and payment 12.45–12.60
    approvals for payment in equity rights 12.53–12.60
    conditions for payment in equity rights 12.48–12.52
    overview 12.45–12.47
  special purpose vehicles, regulation of 12.61–12.69
    definition of 'special purpose vehicle' 12.61
    overview 12.61–12.64
    Variable Interest Entity structure 12.65–12.69
fund associations *see under* securities investment funds (SIFs)
fund services institutions 9.98–9.114
  duties of 9.99
  overview 9.98–9.101
  registration/recordation formalities 9.99
  types of 9.102–9.114
    fund investment advisory institutions 9.109
    fund rating institutions 9.110–9.111
    fund sale institutions 9.103

Index

fund shares registration
    institutions 9.105–9.106
fund trading payment institutions 9.104
fund valuation institutions 9.107–9.108
law firms and accounting firms 9.112–9.113
other fund services institutions 9.114
see also securities investment funds
funds, investment *see* securities investment funds (SIFs)
futures exchanges
    commodity futures 1.36
    financial futures 1.36–1.37

Germany 2.63
    continuous disclosure 5.16
    SIFs, contractual/trust fund form of 9.09, 9.11
global financial crisis 1.49, 3.12
    effects on China 1.62–1.65, 1.67
    implications for China 1.62–1.69
global financial markets, China and 1.62–1.73
    global financial crisis *see* global financial crisis
    Shanghai as new global centre 1.70–1.73

Hong Kong 1.70, 9.14
    backdoor listing 10.17
    disclosure
        continuous disclosure 5.16
        disclosure-based regulation 3.11
    financial centres, as 1.70–1.73
    qualified investors for fund shares 9.89
    securities offerings 4.03
housing market/mortgages
    growth of 1.69, 2.18, 2.58
    high volume of mortgages as bank loan risk 2.18

individual investors 1.50
individual ownership 10.28
Industrial and Commercial Bank of China (ICBC) 1.09, 1.17
    listed 1.18
information *see* disclosure/disclosure of information
initial public offerings (IPOs) 4.05
    backdoor listing as alternative 10.17
    CSRC regulation of *see* initial public offerings, CSRC regulation of
    criteria for 4.10–4.75
        CSRC regulation *see* initial public offerings, CSRC regulation of
        IPO and listing on the main board market 4.16–4.47
        securities law 4.10–4.14
    information disclosure requirements 4.88–4.106
        IPO and listing on main board 4.88–4.95
        IPO and listing on second board 4.96–4.106
    pricing of shares *see* share prices/pricing
    procedure *see* initial public offerings, procedure for

stock exchange listing rules 4.69–4.75
    Shanghai Stock Exchange 4.70–4.71
    Shenzhen Stock Exchange 4.72–4.75
underwriting *see* underwriting
initial public offerings, CSRC regulation of 4.15–4.68
    IPO and listing on main board market 4.16–4.47
        finance and accounting 4.34–4.43
        independence 4.20–4.25
        procedure 4.80–4.82
        qualification for issuers 4.17–4.19
        standardized operation 4.26–4.33
        utilization of raised funds 4.44–4.47
    IPO and listing on second board market 4.48–4.68
        finance and accounting 4.54–4.57
        independence 4.58
        issuers, conditions for 4.49–4.50
        qualification for issuers 4.51–4.53
        standardized operation 4.59–4.66
        utilization of raised funds 4.67–4.68
initial public offerings, procedure for 4.76–4.87
    IPO and listing on main board 4.76–4.86
        CSRC approval 4.80–4.82
        issuance 4.83–4.84
        listing 4.85
        shareholder resolution 4.77–4.78
        sponsor and application 4.79
    IPO and listing on second board 4.87
innovation 2.55–2.59
insider trading 5.56, 8.01–8.78
    background 8.05–8.09
        extent of insider trading widespread 8.08–8.09
        regulatory framework 8.05–8.07
    beneficial effects of 8.02
    bull markets, insider trading more likely to occur in 8.53
    detrimental effects of 8.02
    enforcement of insider trading law 8.43–8.75
        analysis and policy implications 8.61–8.75
        criminal prosecutions 8.58–8.60
        CSRC enforcement 8.49, 8.54, 8.66–8.67
        empirical data: 1991–2011 cases 8.48–8.60
        empirical data, findings from 8.51–8.60
        empirical data, methodology 8.48–8.50
        increase in number of insider trading cases 8.61
        overview of enforcement mechanism 8.43–8.47
        private enforcement 8.68–8.75
        public enforcement 8.63–8.67
    equality-of-access theory 8.35, 8.36, 8.41–8.42
    front-running 8.38–8.42
    increasingly prohibited 8.03
    inside information 8.16–8.21
        definition of 'inside information' 8.16, 8.19–8.20
        major events, disclosure of 8.18
        'other information' 8.21

insider trading (*Cont.*)
   types of facts regarded as inside
      information 8.17
   insiders 8.10–8.15
      corporate insiders 8.11, 8.37
      persons obtaining illegally non-public
         information 8.15
      regulatory officials 8.12
      temporary or constructive insiders 8.12, 8.37
   M&A information, majority of cases based
      on 8.57
   meaning of 8.01
   most practised form of market abuse 8.01
   subjective elements 8.22–8.32
      criminal liability 8.22
      knowledge 8.25
      modified use test 8.31–8.32
      negligence 8.23–8.24
      'obviously abnormal' transactions 8.28–8.29
      presumption that inside information
         possessed 8.27
      rebutting presumption of inside information
         possession 8.30
      reversing burden of proof 8.26–8.27
      'use or possession' debate 8.30–8.32
   what constitutes insider trading in
      China 8.10–8.42
      subjective elements 8.22–8.32
      theoretical basis of China's insider trading
         law 8.33–8.42
      what is inside information 8.16–8.21
      who is an insider 8.10–8.15
institutional investors 1.52
   Qualified Domestic Institutional Investors 10.34
   Qualified Foreign Institutional Investors 10.34
   Renminbi Qualified Foreign Institutional
      Investors 10.34
   weak role in corporate governance 11.71
insurance market 1.08, 1.11
   growth in 1.43–1.44
   modernization and innovation 2.56
   oligopoly, as 1.44
   regulation 2.19–2.21
      CBRC *see* China Insurance Regulatory
         Commission (CIRC)
   state-owned insurance companies having largest
      market share 1.48
interest rates 2.10–2.11
   bank profits 2.10
   liberalization 2.11
interim reports *see under* reports
investment funds *see* securities investment funds
   (SIFs)
Issuance Examination Committee (IEC) 3.32–3.47
   comments 3.46–3.47
   composition 3.32
   constitution and term 3.35–3.37
   Main Board IEC 3.34, 3.35
   powers and duties 3.38–3.41
   Second Board IEC 3.34, 3.35
   work procedure 3.32, 3.42–3.45

Japan 2.63
   SIFs, contractual/trust fund form of 9.09–9.10

liability
   administrative liability 7.38–7.39, 8.43
   civil liability 7.44–7.47, 8.43
   criminal liability 7.40–7.43, 8.22, 8.43
      intent 8.22
   defences to 6.22–6.24
   joint and several liability 6.21
   market manipulation, for *see under* market
      manipulation
   misrepresentation *see* misrepresentation,
      liability for
   proportional liability 6.21
listed companies
   articles of association
      2006 Guidelines for Articles of
         Association 11.16–11.18
      variations to template 11.17
   bonus shares given instead of cash
      dividends 1.60
   corporate governance of *see* corporate governance
      of listed companies
   CSRC encouraging growth of institutional
      investors 1.52
   directors *see* directors of listed companies
   information disclosure 5.04–5.18
      comments 5.14–5.18
      reports *see* reports
   IPOs *see* initial public offerings (IPOs)
   listed status as scarce commodity 5.81
   listing *see* securities listing
   securities offerings *see* securities offerings by listed
      companies
   share ownership patterns in 1.50–1.53
      distribution of share ownership in 1.51–1.53
      high level of concentration in
         shareholding 10.14, 10.44
      individual participation in stock
         markets 1.50
      state ownership very high 1.51, 10.44, 10.54
   shareholding structure in listed
      companies 10.21–10.38
      A-shares 10.22–10.24
      B-shares 10.23–10.24
      different types of shares 10.21–10.24
      H-shares 10.22, 10.24
      N-shares 10.22
      reasons behind the structure 10.25–10.30
      recent developments 10.31–10.38
   special treatment measures 5.77–5.79
listing *see* securities listing
listing suspension *see* suspension of listing

Index

major events 5.08–5.10, 5.76
  change of control 11.12
  inside information, and 8.18
  SIFs, and 9.31
major structural models of financial
    regulation 2.61–2.65
  comparison of structural models 2.67–2.71, 2.81
  'integrated regulation' model 2.63, 2.69–2.71, 2.80–2.81
  'sectoral regulation' model 2.61–2.62, 2.67–2.68
  'twin peaks' model 2.64–2.65, 2.69, 2.71, 2.80–2.81, 2.83
management buyouts *see under* takeovers of listed companies
mandatory bid rule *see under* takeovers of listed companies
market misconduct 7.01–7.72
  comments 7.48–7.72
  definition of 'market manipulation' 7.13, 7.48
    artificiality-based definition 7.50–7.56
    critique of 7.48–7.49
    intent, role of 7.49, 7.50, 7.57–7.72
    international experience 7.66–7.71
  intent 7.49, 7.50, 7.57–7.72
    Australia 7.59, 7.63
    circumstantial evidence 7.64
    difficulty of proving intention 7.63–7.64
    indispensable in differentiating transactions 7.72
    inferring intent 7.64–7.65
    pivotal nature of intention 7.60
    role of 'intent' 7.57–7.65
    socially desirable transactions as manipulative 7.61–7.62
    United Kingdom 7.69–7.71
    United States 7.67–7.68
  legal liabilities for market manipulation 7.37–7.47
    administrative liability 7.38–7.39
    civil liability 7.44–7.47
    criminal liability 7.40–7.43
  market manipulation 7.13–7.47
  attempts to commit trade-based market manipulation 7.17
    history 7.14–7.16
    motivations for 7.18
    overview 7.13–7.18
  types of misconduct 7.02–7.12
    churning 7.06
    fabricating or disseminating false information 7.02–7.04
    fraud by a securities firm and its employees 7.05–7.06
    'matched orders' 7.20, 7.29, 7.31, 7.49, 7.61, 7.67
    misappropriating public funds 7.11
    misappropriating securities/funds 7.06
    prohibited trading acts 7.07–7.12
    unlawfully using another's account 7.08–7.09

    unqualified capital in stock market 7.10
    'wash sales' 7.20, 7.29–7.31, 7.49, 7.61, 7.67
  what constitutes market manipulation 7.19–7.36
    Article 77(1)(a) 7.22–7.28
    Article 77(1)(b) and (c) 7.29–7.31
    Article 77(1)(d) 7.32–7.36
    overview 7.19–7.21
mergers and acquisition (M&A)
  foreign M&A, regulation of *see* foreign M&A, regulation of
  takeovers, and 10.05–10.06
  see also takeovers of listed companies
merits-review regulation *see under* securities offerings
Ministry of Commerce (MOFCOM) 12.20–12.21, 12.25
  approvals for payment in equity rights 12.53–12.60
  economic security/cultural security 12.71
  national security review *see* national security review
  special purpose vehicles 12.63–12.64, 12.66, 12.68
Ministry of Finance 2.04
misconduct *see* insider trading; market misconduct
misrepresentation, liability for 6.01–6.81
  causation 6.25–6.33
    correction date 6.29
    exposure date 6.29–6.31
    misrepresentation date 6.29
    presumed reliance or causality 6.26
    rebutting presumption of reliance 6.27–6.28, 6.32–6.33
  comments 6.78–6.81
  compensation 6.34–6.38
    actual loss 6.34
    benchmark day 6.35
    expert witnesses, use of 6.38
    measure of damages 6.36–6.37
  development of securities civil liability 6.07–6.12
    legal basis for civil suits in statute 6.11
  excluded transactions 6.15
  false recording 6.17–6.18
  forms of litigation *see under* civil litigation
  forms of securities misrepresentation 6.17–6.19
  improper disclosure 6.17–6.18
  inducing investors to purchase or sell 6.19
  'investor', meaning of 6.14
  jurisdiction 6.54–6.58
    courts unsympathetic to securities civil suits 6.57
    geographical jurisdiction 6.54–6.55
    hierarchical jurisdiction 6.54
    local protectionism 6.58
  liability
    defences to 6.22–6.24
    joint and several liability 6.21
    proportional liability 6.21

misrepresentation, liability for (*Cont.*)
   limitation 6.50–6.53
      counting the limitation period 6.51–6.52
      material omissions 6.17–6.18
      misleading statements 6.17–6.18
      primary and secondary markets 6.16
      procedural rules of civil litigation 6.39–6.73
         jurisdiction of the court 6.54–6.58
         prerequisite procedure *see under* civil litigation
         statute of limitation 6.50–6.53
      'securities market', meaning of 6.14
      substantive rules of civil litigation 6.13–6.38
         calculation of compensation 6.34–6.38
         causation 6.25–6.33
         defences to liability 6.22–6.24
         'misrepresentation', definition of 6.17–6.19
         scope of application 6.13–6.16
         scope of defendants 6.20–6.21
      types of legal liabilities 6.01–6.06
         administrative liability 6.01
         civil liability 6.05
         criminal liability 6.02–6.04
         ordinary fault-based liability 6.23
         presumed fault-based liability 6.24
         strict liability 6.22, 6.23
money markets
   meaning of 1.03
   National Audit Office 2.04
mortgages *see* housing market/mortgages

National Development and Reform Commission 2.04, 3.31, 4.81
   foreign M&A 12.06, 12.20, 12.34, 12.81
national security review 12.70–12.99
   central features 12.74–12.92
      content of security review 12.79–12.80
      control 12.76
      national interest 12.71, 12.74, 12.78, 12.99
      procedure of security review 12.83–12.92
      scope of security review 12.74–12.78
      work mechanism of security review 12.81–12.82
   comments 12.93–12.99
      Australia 12.98–12.99
      lack of enforcement 12.95
      key terms not defined 12.94
      United States 12.97
   overview 12.70–12.73
      economic security/cultural security 12.71
      establishment of national security review regime 12.73
   procedure of security review 12.83–12.92
      conduct of review 12.88–12.90
      initiation of review 12.83–12.87
      outcome of review 12.91–12.92
non-performing loans 1.67, 2.15–2.18
   Central Huijin established 2.16

offerings *see* securities offerings; securities offerings by listed companies
off-exchange markets 1.38–1.42
   over-the counter market (OTC) 1.42
   Regional Equity Trading Markets (RETM) 1.41
   Third Markets Board (TMB) 1.40
   underdeveloped 5.81
over-the-counter market (OTC) 1.42

Peoples' Bank of China (PBC) 1.08, 1.09, 1.12–1.14
   central bank, role as 2.06–2.07
   currency
      currency-issuing role 2.07
      currency-stabilizing role 2.08
      interest rate, setting 2.10
   functions 2.07
   government bank, as 2.07
   governor 2.39
   lack of regulatory independence 2.39–2.40
   monetary policy and stability of financial system, responsibility for 2.03, 2.06
periodic reports *see under* reports
policy market 1.54–1.57
   controls through newspaper editorials 1.56
   stock market resulting of government policies 1.54
Postal Savings Bank of China 1.22
post-listing issues 5.01–5.82
   corporate governance of listed companies *see* corporate governance of listed companies
   information disclosure by listed companies *see under* listed companies
prerequisite procedure *see under* civil litigation
prices/pricing *see* share prices/pricing
private enterprises
   accessing banking loans, difficulty of 1.49
   growing China's economy 1.49

Regional Equity Trading Markets (RETM) 1.41
regulatory capture 2.52–2.54
regulatory framework *see* financial regulatory framework
related party transactions 5.60–5.73
   approval requirements 5.69–5.72
      board of directors' approval 5.69–5.70
      shareholder approval 5.69, 5.71–5.72
   definition of 5.62–5.69
      'connection relationship', definition of 5.62
      'transactions', definition of 5.68
   information disclosure 5.73
   'related directors', definition of 5.69–5.70
   'related shareholders', definition of 5.72
reports
   interim reports 5.08–5.13
      exemption from 5.13
      major events 5.08–5.10
      postponement of 5.12
      timing 5.11

Index

periodic reports 5.04–5.07
  annual reports 5.04
  half-yearly reports 5.05
  quarterly reports 5.07
  written examination opinions 5.06
revolving door phenomenon 2.52–2.54
risk agency fees *see under* attorney fees

Securities Association of China (SAC) 1.50, 4.145–4.146
securities investment funds (SIFs) 9.01–9.117
  closed-end funds 9.47, 9.48, 9.63, 9.80
  economic functions 9.03
  fund associations 9.115–9.117
    functions of 9.116
    national fund association 9.117
    nature of 9.115
  fund custodians 9.39–9.46
    conditions to serve as fund custodian 9.41
    functions of 9.42–9.44
    nature of 9.40
    termination of 9.45–9.46
  fund managers/management 9.06, 9.15–9.38
    central role of managers 9.06, 9.15
    companies or partnerships as managers 9.16
    formation of fund management companies 9.17–9.19
    qualification of employees of fund management companies 9.20–9.22
  fund management institutions for publicly offered funds
    conflicts of interest 9.27–9.29
    fiduciary duties 9.24–9.30
    functions/duties of fund management institution 9.23–9.31
    major events, reporting 9.31
    priority given to interests of fund shareholders 9.30
    sanctions and remedies 9.32–9.35
    termination of manager role 9.36–9.38
  fund services institutions *see* fund services institutions
  fund share trading, subscription and redemption 9.66–9.70
    conditions for listing and trading fund shares 9.67
    redemption 9.69–9.70
    subscription 9.69–9.70
    termination of listing and trading 9.68
  fund unit holders 9.47–9.54
    fund shareholders' meetings 9.51–9.52, 9.54
    fund shareholders' rights 9.49–9.50
    general offices 9.53, 9.54
    operating mode of a fund 9.47–9.48
  important features of 9.02
  investment of publicly offered funds and information disclosure 9.71–9.78
    information disclosure rules 9.76–9.78
    investment rules 9.71–9.75
  legislative framework 9.04–9.05
  meaning of 'securities investment funds' 9.01
  non-publicly offered funds 9.88–9.97
    definition of 'non-publicly offered fund' 9.88–9.90
    differences between publicly/non-publicly offered funds 9.90
    fund contracts 9.92–9.94
    investments, wide scope of 9.97
    limited partnerships, funds established using 9.94
    offering process 9.92–9.95
    qualified investors 9.88–9.89
    transfer of shares 9.96
  open-end funds 9.47, 9.48
  organizational structure 9.07–9.54
    contractual funds adopted by China 9.14
    contractual/trust fund form 9.09–9.12
    corporate form of SIFs 9.08
    fund custodians 9.39–9.46
    fund managers 9.15–9.38
    fund unit holders 9.47–9.54
    structural differences between corporate/contractual funds 9.13
  public offerings 9.55–965
    definition of 'public offering' 9.55
    offering process 9.61–9.65
    paying fund managers and custodians 9.59
    registration 9.57–9.58, 9.60
    requirements of contents of fund contracts 9.59
  publicly offered funds 9.55–9.87
    exercise of rights by fund shareholders 9.83–9.87
    fund share trading, subscription and redemption 9.66–9.70
    fund shareholders' meetings 9.83–9.87
    investment of publicly offered funds and information disclosure 9.71–9.78
    modification of fund contract/liquidating fund assets 9.79–9.80
    public offerings 9.55–9.65
    termination of fund contract/liquidating fund assets 9.81–9.82
  rat trading/front running 9.25–9.26
  regulators 9.06
securities listings 4.01–4.172
  benefits and costs of listing 4.06–4.09
    advantages of listing and quotation 4.08
    disadvantages of listing 4.09
  IPOs *see* initial public offerings (IPOs)
  listings vs offerings 4.01–4.05
  post-listing issues *see* post-listing issues
  pricing *see* share prices/pricing
  sponsorship *see* sponsorship
  underwriting *see* underwriting
securities market 1.25–1.42
  futures exchanges *see* futures exchanges

Index

securities market (Cont.)
  gaming nature of 1.58–1.61
  modernization and innovation 2.56
  nature of 1.03
  off-exchange markets *see* off-exchange markets
  primary market 1.05
  recent developments 10.31–10.38
    divide of A and B shares 10.34–10.36
    divide of tradable/non-tradable shares 10.37–10.38, 10.46
    market segregation, addressing problem of 10.31–10.33
    shareholding structure reform 10.37–10.38
  regulation 2.22–2.38
    CSRC *see* China Securities Regulatory Commission (CSRC)
  secondary market 1.05–1.06
  stock exchanges *see* stock exchanges
securities offerings 3.01–3.96
  CSRC approval regime *see under* China Securities Regulatory Commission (CSRC)
  disclosure and market efficiency *see* disclosure and market efficiency
  evolution of China's fundraising regulation 3.04–3.08
    1990–1999: Pei E Zhi (quota system) 3.04–3.05
    1999–present: He Zhun Zhi (approval/merit-review system) 3.06–3.08
    future development 3.09–3.13
  listed companies *see* securities offerings by listed companies
  regulatory model: disclosure-based vs merits-review 3.01–3.13
    disclosure-based regulation 3.02
    merits-review regulation 3.03
  regulatory structure: public offerings vs private placement 3.23–3.30
    comments 3.29–3.30
    private placement 3.27–3.28
    public offerings 3.25–3.26
securities offerings by listed companies 3.48–3.96
  disclosure requirements 3.85–3.96
    comments 3.94–3.96
    CSRC approval, disclosure relating to 3.90–3.91
    general requirements 3.85–3.87
    issuance, disclosure relating to 3.92–3.93
    shareholder resolutions, disclosure relating to 3.88–3.89
  private placement 3.70–3.73
    definition of 'private placement' 3.71
    merits review criteria 3.72–3.73
  procedure for offering securities 3.74–3.84
    CSRC approval 3.80–3.83
    issuance 3.84
    shareholders resolutions 3.75–3.79
  public offerings 3.50–3.69
    general merits review criteria 3.50–3.58
    special requirements for offerings of convertible corporate bonds 3.63–3.669
    special requirements for offerings of shares 3.59–3.62
securitization 1.66, 1.69, 2.58
self-regulatory organizations (SROs) 2.05
Shanghai as new global centre 1.70–1.73
share prices/pricing 4.143–4.160
  price artificiality 7.50–7.56
    forces of supply and demand behind the price 7.54–7.55
    historically unusual prices 7.52–7.53
  price enquiry participants 4.144–4.149
  procedure for price enquiry 4.150–4.160
  share-price related sensitive information
    disclosure/protection of 5.57–5.59
    insider trading, and 8.20
    sensitivity to government policies 1.55, 8.20
  strategic investors 4.159–4.160
shareholders
  apathy and free-riding 11.80
  compulsory buyouts 10.90
  controlling shareholders
    related party transactions 5.60
  corporate governance, and 11.13
  CSRC shareholding structure reform 1.33, 11.52
  decision-makers 11.13
  fund shareholders
    exercise of rights by 9.83–9.87
    meetings 9.83–9.87
    priority given to interests of 9.30
  fund unit holders 9.47–9.54
    fund shareholders' meetings 9.51–9.52, 9.54
    fund shareholders' rights 9.49–9.50
  IPOs shareholder resolution 4.77–4.78
  listed companies, shareholding structure in *see under* listed companies
  managers, monitoring 10.54
  related party transactions, approving 5.69, 5.71–5.72
  'related shareholders', definition of 5.72
  securities offerings by listed companies
    shareholders' resolutions 3.75–3.79
    shareholders' resolutions, disclosure relating to 3.88–3.89
  shareholder protection in takeovers 10.56–10.59
    conflicting with economic objectives 10.59
    enhancing investor protection 10.121–10.122
    mandatory bid rule 10.69, 10.70
  shareholders' meetings as highest organ of corporate power 11.77
shares *see* shares
substantial asset transactions, approving 5.47–5.51
takeover defences 11.10–11.11

Index

shares 1.27–1.35
  A-shares 1.28, 1.29, 1.31–1.32, 10.22–10.24, 10.25
    acquisition of 12.12–12.13
    market opened up to foreigners 10.34
    subsets 10.13, 10.43
  B-shares 1.28, 1.31–1.32, 10.23–10.24, 10.25, 12.10
    available to domestic purchasers to buy with foreign currency 10.35
  distinction between A-shares/B-shares blurring over time 10.34–10.36, 10.46
  foreign M&A
    acquisition of A-shares 12.12–12.13
    acquisition of non-A-shares 12.10–12.11
  H-shares 1.34, 10.22, 10.24, 12.10
  individual investors 1.50
  institutional investors *see* institutional investors
  joint stock companies only issuing 10.04
  listed companies *see under* listed companies
  market segmentation 1.27, 1.30
  N-shares 1.34, 10.22, 12.10
  share ownership patterns in listed companies 1.50–1.53
    distribution of share ownership in listed companies 1.51–1.53
    individual participation in stock markets 1.50
  share price *see* share price/pricing
  state ownership 1.51
  tradable/non-tradable shares 1.32–1.33, 10.31, 10.43, 10.116
    fundamental problem with Chinese stock market, as 10.31
    reform of shareholding structure 10.37–10.38, 10.46, 10.118, 10.120
'Socialist Transformation' Policy 1.07
special purpose vehicles *see under* foreign M&A, regulation of
sponsorship 4.107–4.141
  overview 4.107–4.111
    nature/role of sponsors 4.108
    sponsorship in securities listings 4.110
    sponsorship in securities offerings 4.109
  procedures for sponsorship business 4.128–4.133
  qualifications of sponsor representatives 4.113
  qualifications of sponsors 4.112
  responsibilities of sponsors 4.114–4.127
    assisting CSRC examination 4.121
    continuous supervision and guidance after issuance 4.122, 4.126
    due diligence 4.115
    guidance and training to issuers 4.116
    information, checking 4.118–4.119
    issuance sponsor letter/listing sponsor letter, submitting 4.120
    monitoring and reporting duties about other professionals 4.127
    sponsorship agreement, concluding 4.117
    supervision of issuer 4.114

supervisory measures of CSRC/ legal liabilities 4.134–4.141
  applications, CSRC approval and revocation of 4.135
  CSRC's sponsorship credit supervision system 4.134
  sanctions 4.136–4.141
state assets, protecting 10.26–10.27, 10.29
state-owned enterprises (SOEs) 1.08
  financial institutions, state ownership of 1.48–1.49
  favouring SOEs 1.49
  listed companies spun-off from 5.60, 5.81, 10.27, 10.93
  policy of moving SOEs into private sector 10.114
  preventing uncontrolled sale of 1.32
  raising funds for/rescuing 1.54, 3.04, 10.30
  restricting exposure of 7.12
  state ownership as highest form of ownership 10.27
stock exchanges 1.05, 1.08, 1.25–1.35, 2.29–2.38
  bond markets 1.35
    underdevelopment of 1.46
  council 2.45–2.46
  CSRC supervising/monitoring 2.31, 2.45–2.47
  foreign investors 1.67
  IPO listing rules 4.69–4.75
  judicial review 2.35–2.38
  listing rules 2.33
  membership-based mutual organizations 2.45
  officers 2.46
  regulatory role 2.29–2.34
    lack of regulatory independence 2.44–2.47
    rule-making 2.30, 2.32–2.33
    sanctions 2.34
  Shanghai Stock Exchange 1.11, 1.25–1.26, 1.38–1.39
    IPO listing rules 4.70–4.71
    main board market 1.26
  shares *see* shares
  Shenzhen Stock Exchange 1.11, 1.25–1.26, 1.38–1.39
    IPO listing rules 4.72, 4.75
    SME Board and GEM (Growth Enterprise Market) 1.26, 1.40, 3.34, 5.82
  size 1.25
  trading rules 2.32
substantial asset transactions 5.38–5.59
  CSRC approval 5.52–5.55
  directors and shareholders' approval 5.47–5.51
  information management 5.56–5.59
  nature of 5.38
  principles and standards 5.40–5.46
  regulatory regime 5.39
supervisors, boards of 5.36
suspension of listing
  criteria 5.74
  information disclosure 5.76
  special treatment measures 5.77–5.79
suspension of trading 5.03

Takeovers and Reorganizations
    Committee 5.39, 5.54
takeover defences 11.01–11.85
  abuse of defensive tactics 10.59, 11.01
  analysis and implications 11.43–11.55
    lax enforcement by CSRC 11.49–11.50, 11.53
    legal loopholes 11.47–11.48
    suggestions for improvement 11.52–11.55
    unclear law 11.44–11.45
    widespread adoption of takeover
      defences 11.43–11.51
  defences under Chinese Law 11.04–11.18
    2005 Company Law 11.12–11.15
    2005 Securities Law and 2006 Takeover
      Measures 11.06–11.11
    2006 Guidelines for Articles of
      Association 11.16–11.18
  employee considerations 11.70
  ex ante/anti-takeover constitutional
      provisions 11.17–11.18, 11.21–11.31, 11.54
    amending anti-takeover provisions 11.31
    defences at request of large shareholders, use
      of 11.31
    'golden/silver parachute' provisions 11.30
    obstacles to acquirer electing new board
      members 11.23, 11.25–1130
    obstacles to acquirer purchasing
      shares 11.23–11.24
    qualification requirements for board
      members 11.29
    restrictions on dismissal of directors 11.17
    staggered board provision 11.28, 11.54
  ex post defences 11.32–11.42
    filing complaints with court 11.41
    filing complaints with CSRC 11.39–11.40
    revision of company constitutions 11.42
    support from minority shareholders/
      stakeholders 11.36–11.38
    'white knights' 11.34–11.35
  legal provisions for takeover defences 11.05
  M&A and Restructuring Examination
      Committee 10.42, 11.04
  new regime for takeover defences 11.56–11.85
    United States (Delaware Law) 11.57–11.60
  poison pills 11.14
  share purchase 11.15
  takeover defences in practice 11.19–11.42,
      11.53–11.54
    ex ante defences: methodology 11.21
    ex ante defences: research findings 11.22–11.31
    ex post defences: methodology 11.32
    ex post defences: research findings 11.33–11.42
  way forward 11.64–11.85
    City Code unsuitable for China 11.75–11.80
    reform proposal: shareholders *ex post* veto use of
      defences 11.81–11.85
    US model cannot take root in
      China 11.68–11.74

takeovers of listed companies 10.01–10.33
  backdoor listing
    alternative to IPOs, as 10.17
    disadvantages 10.17
    regulating 10.18–10.20
  benefits of takeovers 10.49–10.50
  comments 10.114–10.133
    strengths: encouraging takeovers by tender
      offer 10.114–10.120
    strengths: enhancing investor
      protection 10.121–10.122
    summary 10.132–10.133
    weaknesses: conditions in takeover
      bids 10.125–10.126
    weaknesses: problems with partial bid
      rule 10.127–10.131
  compulsory buyouts 10.89–10.91
    equal treatment of target shareholders 10.89
  continuous supervision 10.110–10.113
    CSRC checks 10.112
    financial consultants' role 10.104–10.108,
      10.110–10.111
    shares lock-up period 10.113
  corporate governance, takeovers beneficial to 10.49
  defences *see* takeover defences
  disclosure of substantial
      shareholdings 10.95–10.100
    broad disclosure with respect to substantial
      shareholders 10.95
    purpose 10.95
    thresholds 10.96, 10.99–10.100
    'toeholds' 10.99
  economic value of takeovers, debate
      over 10.49–10.53
  equal opportunity principle 10.61, 10.86, 10.89,
      10.127, 10.131
  financial consultants 10.101–10.109
    commitments in financial consultancy
      reports 10.103
    continuous supervision and guidance period,
      role in 10.104–10.108, 10.110–10.111
    gatekeeper, as 10.109
    new scheme of differentiated treatment 10.109,
      10.122
    requirement of independence 10.101
    role in takeover process 10.102–10.104, 10.122
  guiding principles for takeover
      regulation 10.47–10.60
    contestability of takeovers 10.49–10.55
    shareholder protection 10.56–10.59
    Three Gong principles 10.47–10.48, 10.69
  hostile takeovers 1.32, 10.10–10.13, 10.49
    abuse of defensive tactics 10.59
    see also takeover defences
    business disruption/lost productivity,
      causing 10.51
    emphasis on short-term gains as response
      to 10.51

358

indirect takeovers 10.92
legal framework 10.39–10.41
M&A and Restructuring Examination Committee 10.42, 11.04
management buyouts 10.93–10.94
  political and ethical issues 10.93
  regulation of 10.94
mandatory bid rule 10.12, 10.61–10.76
  'associates', meaning of 10.63–10.64
  associates/parties acting in concert, votes of 10.63, 10.65
  calculating shareholding 10.63–10.67
  different means of acquisition triggering rule 10.62
  exemptions from 10.73–10.76, 10.117–10.119
  investor protection 10.69, 10.70
  mitigating harshness of the rule 10.70–10.76
partial bids
  full/partial bids in tender offers 10.77–10.78, 10.115
  mandatory bid rule 10.72
  problems with partial bid rule 10.127–10.131
  pro-rata bids 10.128–10.129
private agreement, takeover by 10.43–10.44, 10.62, 10.117–10.118, 10.120
regulator, CSRC as 10.42, 11.04
shareholding structure in listed companies see under listed companies
takeover activities 10.43–10.46
takeover law 10.60
  supplement to general law of contract, as 10.02
tender offers
  conditions in takeover bids 10.125–10.126
  conducting the takeover bid 10.86–10.88
  defeating conditions 10.126
  encouraging 10.114–10.120
  equal opportunity principle 10.86
  full/partial bids 10.77–10.78, 10.115
  information disclosure 10.86–10.87
  offer period/reasonable time to consider 10.87
  payment methods 10.79, 10.115
  pricing rules 10.80–10.85
  rules 10.77–10.88
  takeover by 10.43, 10.45–10.46, 10.62
  variation of terms of offers 10.88, 10.123
terminology 10.03–10.08
  corporate control transaction, meaning of 10.07
  'takeover', meaning of 10.04–10.06
transaction-specific disclosure 3.32
typology 10.09–10.20
  friendly takeovers 10.10
  horizontal, vertical and conglomerate takeovers 10.14–10.15
  hostile takeovers 1.32, 10.10–10.13
  normal/forward takeovers 10.16
  reverse takeovers/backdoor listing 10.16–10.20

Third Markets Board (TMB) 1.40
trading of securities, suspension of see suspension of trading

underwriting 4.161–4.172
  'best-effort' underwriting 4.164
  'classic' underwriting 4.162
  'firm-commitment' underwriting 4.163
  functions of underwriting 4.161
  overview 4.161–4.164
  specific rules 4.165–4.172
United Kingdom
  disclosure
    continuous disclosure 5.16
    disclosure-based regulation 3.11
  Financial Conduct Authority 2.84
  Financial Services Authority 2.63, 2.64
  insider trading 8.62
  institutional investors 1.52
  insurance 1.44
  'integrated regulation' model 2.63, 2.74, 2.84
  London Stock Exchange 4.107
  market manipulation 7.69–7.72
  Prudential Regulatory Authority 2.84
  qualified investors for fund shares 9.89
  regulatory staffing level 2.51
  takeovers
    City Code on Takeovers and Mergers 10.68, 11.61–11.63, 11.75–11.80
    City Code: positive views of 11.78
    City Code: problems in practice 11.79
    collective action problems 11.79
    fiduciary duties of target company directors 11.61
    mandatory bid rule 10.68
    'neutrality rule' 11.63
    Panel on Takeovers and Mergers 11.62
    shareholders as final arbiters on offers/defences 11.63, 11.75–11.77
  'twin peaks' model of regulation 2.84
  unit trusts 9.09, 9.12
United States 1.14
  backdoor listing 10.17
  beneficial ownership of shares 10.92
  class actions 6.71
  Committee on Foreign Investment in the United States 12.97
  Commodity Futures Trading Commission (CFTC) 2.23
  contingency fees 6.71
  disclosure
    continuous disclosure not required 5.14–5.15, 5.17
    disclosure-based regulation 3.11
    inside information 8.35
  Dodd-Frank Act 2.62, 2.75–2.76, 2.80
  Federal Reserve 2.61, 2.75
  financial centres 1.73

United States (*Cont.*)
  financial crisis 1.62, 2.62, 2.76
  Financial Services Oversight Council 2.75
  fraud-on-the-market theory 6.26
  insider trading 8.24, 8.35
    classical theory 8.35
    enforcement 8.62, 8.69
    equality-of-access theory 8.35
    front-running 8.41
    misappropriation theory 8.35
  institutional investors 1.52, 11.71
  insurance 1.44
  market manipulation 7.67–7.69
  misrepresentation 6.42
  mutual funds 9.08
  national security review of foreign investment 12.70, 12.97
  qualified investors for fund shares 9.89
  reforms 2.75–2.76, 2.80, 2.84
  regulatory staffing level 2.51
  'sectoral regulation' model 2.61, 2.73
  Securities and Exchange Commission (SEC) 2.23, 2.51, 2.61
    insider trading 8.62, 8.68
    role 2.64
  securities offerings 4.03
  takeovers
    compulsory buyouts 10.90
    court's role as arbiters of takeover defences 11.68, 11.72
    defences (Delaware Law) 11.57–11.60
    disclosure of substantial shareholdings 10.97
    disincentives to misuse of defences 11.70
    executive remuneration discouraging entrenchment defences 11.71
    fiduciary duties of target company directors 11.61, 11.72
    foreign M&A 12.70, 12.97
    hostile takeovers' low probability of success 11.74
    independent directors' role in use of takeover defences 11.71
    management discretion on defensive measures 11.68, 11.72
    modified business judgment rule 11.72–11.73
    no mandatory bid rule 10.68–10.69
    shareholder primacy 11.70
    shareholder protection 10.57–10.58, 11.72–11.74
    staggered board provision 11.54

World Trade Organization (WTO)
  China's accession 1.18, 1.23, 10.25